Praise for
Nourishing Broth

"Bone broth has long been prized by traditional cultures for its remarkable healing ability. In NOURISHING BROTH, Sally Fallon Morell and Kaayla Daniel bring us a fresh, modern perspective on this nutrient-dense food. They explore the science behind broth, how it works to support the structure of our bodies, and how it can be used to get relief from a variety of ailments, ranging from arthritis, to digestive problems, to cancer. And of course, they've included delicious recipes and tips on how to incorporate broth into your diet. This book is destined to become the authoritative primer on healing bone broth, and I look forward to recommending it to my patients and readers."

—Chris Kresser,
author of the *New York Times* bestseller *Your Personal Paleo Code*

"I have been a fan of Sally Fallon for many years. *Nourishing Traditions* was the best nutrition book of its time. This new book far exceeds the previous book as it covers cooking *and* consuming in a comprehensive way—a must for every chef's and homemaker's library of cooking."

—William Campbell Douglass II, MD

"Homemade bone broth has immense health benefits, from speeding healing and recuperation from illness to improving athletic performance. For best results, you really need to make up a fresh batch from scratch. Bone broth is loaded with beneficial nutrients like calcium, magnesium, phosphorus, silicon, sulfur, and trace minerals that your body can easily absorb. While the thought of making your own broth may seem intimidating at first, Sally Fallon Morell and Kaayla Daniel's wonderful new book, NOURISHING BROTH, removes all the guesswork and provides you with various broth-making techniques—from simple chicken broth to rich consommé, shrimp stock, and a variety of global stock-based recipes for breakfast, lunch, and dinner. Highly recommended."

—Dr. Joseph Mercola, founder of www.Mercola.com

"In our ultra-fast, modern society, we are suffering from a myriad of illnesses including cancer, fatigue, fibromyalgia, autoimmune disorders, and hormone imbalances. A healthy diet can provide the correct nutrients to not only prevent and overcome illness, but allow us to achieve our optimal health. NOURISHING BROTH provides the wisdom we need to eat a healthy diet. Sally Fallon Morell and Kaayla Daniel have written a wonderful book. I cannot recommend this book highly enough."

—David Brownstein, MD,
author of twelve books, DrBrownstein.com

"A fascinating read on one of mankind's most enduring and nutritious foods and why its revival in the modern diet holds much promise for resolution of the numerous and overwhelming health woes suffered by so many today. If every parent incorporated the traditional broth-making techniques and recipes described in NOURISHING BROTH, the health of the next generation and the viability of an overloaded healthcare system would profoundly benefit."

—Sarah Pope, The Healthy Home Economist,
author of *Get Your Fats Straight*, TheHealthyHomeEconomist.com

"Sally Fallon's first book, *Nourishing Traditions*, is a true treasure that has proven to be timeless, and will continue to be enjoyed for many generations. With NOURISHING BROTH, Sally and her co-author, Kaayla Daniel, have done it again. I have a book shelf with only my favorite, most well-researched, yet wonderfully practical books on nutrition. NOURISHING BROTH landed a spot on that shelf. The best word to describe this book is simply AWESOME!"

—Donna Gates,
bestselling author of *The Body Ecology Diet*

"NOURISHING BROTH proves our grandmothers were more than right about chicken soup: Not only does it cure what ails you, but it also contributes to our health in ways we never even imagined. In today's world we've lost the tradition of slow-cooked stock to quick boullion cubes, resulting in an empty hole in our nutrition. Sally and Kaayla show how broth is the missing ingredient in our present diet, then give complete instructions for making our own broth at home, as we should. This book is just as thorough and stellar as their previous works, and belongs close-at-hand in every healthy kitchen."

—Debra Lynn Dadd,
author of *Toxic Free* and blogger at ToxicFreeKitchen.com

Nourishing Broth

Other Books by Sally Fallon Morell

Nourishing Traditions: The Cookbook that Challenges Politically Correct Nutrition and the Diet Dictocrats (with Mary G. Enig, PhD)

The Nourishing Traditions Book of Baby & Child Care (with Thomas S. Cowan, MD)

Eat Fat Lose Fat (with Mary G. Enig, PhD)

Other Books by Kaayla T. Daniel, PhD, CCN

The Whole Soy Story: The Dark Side of America's Favorite Health Food

Practice Safe Soy

Nourishing Broth

An Old-Fashioned Remedy for the Modern World

SALLY FALLON MORELL

AND

KAAYLA T. DANIEL, PHD, CCN

Illustrations by Mary Woodin

GRAND CENTRAL
Life & Style
NEW YORK · BOSTON

Text copyright © 2014 by Sally Fallon Morell
Illustrations copyright © 2014 by Mary Woodin

Grand Central Life & Style
Hachette Book Group
1290 Avenue of the Americas
New York, NY 10104
GrandCentralLifeandStyle.com

Printed in the United States of America

RRD-H

Book design by Fearn Cutler de Vicq
First edition: September 2014
10 9 8 7 6 5

Grand Central Life & Style is an imprint of Grand Central Publishing.
The Grand Central Life & Style name and logo are trademarks of Hachette Book Group, Inc.

The Hachette Speakers Bureau provides a wide range of authors for speaking events. To find out more, go to www.HachetteSpeakersBureau.com or call (866) 376-6591.

The publisher is not responsible for websites (or their content) that are not owned by the publisher.

Library of Congress Cataloging-in-Publication Data

Fallon, Sally.
    Nourishing broth : an old-fashioned remedy for the modern world / Sally Fallon Morell and Kaayla T. Daniel, PhD, CCN ; illustrations by Mary Woodin.
        pages cm
    Includes bibliographical references and index.
    ISBN 978-1-4555-2922-3 (pb) — ISBN 978-1-4555-2923-0 (ebook) — ISBN 978-1-4789-5600-6 (audio download) 1. Soups—Therapeutic use. 2. Liquid diet. 3. Soups. 4. Cooking for the sick. I. Daniel, Kaayla T. II. Title.
    RM239.F35 2014
    641.81'3—dc23
                                    2014012998

To our grandmothers

Contents

Preface

In 1908, a Japanese researcher isolated a new taste substance from the seaweed kombu. He noted that the substance had a singular taste, different from sweet, salty, sour, and bitter. He called the taste *umami*. The chemical he discovered was free glutamic acid, which when combined with sodium gave the most pleasing umami taste. That substance is called monosodium glutamate, or MSG.

Within a year, a new company called Ajinomoto began manufacturing MSG for the food industry, and it was MSG that made possible the profound changes to the Western diet that occurred during the twentieth century, especially after World War II. That's because monosodium glutamate in its many guises—MSG, hydrolyzed protein, autolyzed protein, yeast extract, soy protein isolate—gave the food industry an inexpensive way to imitate the taste of broth.

As early as 1735, chefs had made dried bouillon in the form of tablets, cubes, and granules by dehydrating meat stock with vegetables, fat, salt, and seasonings. During the eighteenth and nineteenth centuries, chefs and cooks made frequent use of these home-made extracts.

MSG allowed the cheap and profitable industrial production of bouillon cubes starting in the early 1900s. Oxo cubes, popular since 1910 in Britain, contain very little extract of beef stock today; in fact they gain more flavor from the monosodium glutamate than the actual dried beef stock. The ingredients listed on the label are wheat flour, salt, yeast extract, cornflour, colouring, flavour enhancers (monosodium glutamate), beef fat, flavouring, dried beef bonestock, sugar, onion, pepper extract.

Wyler's Chicken Flavored Bouillon Cubes contain no dried bone stock at all; in fact, the ingredients list is a nightmarish collection of additives: Salt, Sugar, Mechanically Separated Cooked Ground Chicken Meat, Sodium Bicarbonate, Monosodium Glutamate, Hydrolyzed Corn Gluten, Corn Maltodextrin, Onion Powder, Chicken Fat, Hydrolyzed Corn Gluten Protein, Partially Hydrogenated Soybean Oil and Partially Hydrogenated Cottonseed Oil, Autolyzed Yeast Extract, Water, Garlic Powder, Disodium Inosinate and Disodium Guanylate, Dextrose, Cooked Chicken Powder, Natural Chicken Flavor, Hydrolyzed Soy Protein, Calcium Silicate, Gelatin, Soy Lecithin, Natural Flavor, Turmeric, Corn Syrup Solids,

Spice, Modified Cornstarch, Silicon Dioxide, Diacetyl (Flavor), Artificial Flavor, Tricalcium Phosphate, Alpha Tocopherols (Antioxidant), Corn Oil, BHA (Preservative), Propyl Gallate, Citric Acid, BHT (Preservative).

In addition to monosodium glutamate, at least three other ingredients in Wyler's cubes—hydrolyzed corn gluten protein, autolyzed yeast extract, and hydrolyzed soy protein—are sources of free glutamic acid or one of its salts. Even "natural flavor" can contain MSG.

MSG made possible the proliferation of new products that flooded the supermarket shelves after World War II. Manufacturers used it in canned bouillon, canned soups, and canned stews—allowing the food processing industry to imitate for pennies the natural flavor of carefully prepared broth. The earliest frozen TV dinners featured turkey with gravy—not gravy made with nourishing turkey stock but a gravylike substance comprised of water, thickeners, emulsifiers, artificial colorings, and artificial flavorings, mostly MSG. Canned spaghetti sauce was no longer an insipid imitation of the real thing but, thanks to MSG, something that had a seductive savory taste.

Whether MSG poses health problems is a matter of debate—the industry insists that MSG is a minor bother only for the rare sensitive individual and has no long-term consequences for the majority. But independent researchers are not so sure, citing neurological problems as the long-term consequence of this excitatory substance, especially in children and the elderly. Rarely mentioned is the fact that MSG is used to induce obesity in laboratory animals. Has the flood of MSG-laden foods contributed to today's epidemic of obesity? It is a question that needs to be explored.

Whatever the health hazards of MSG, one thing is certain: The use of MSG in our food has allowed the eclipse of nourishing broth, something that tradition tells us is good for us, something that science indicates should be in our diet on a daily basis. Before processed foods, cooks used broth to make soups, stews, sauces, and gravies; broth made these foods taste good, and everyone enjoyed the health benefits whether they were aware of them or not. MSG and its many cousins used in processed food have allowed cooks to forget valuable broth-making skills. One can of Campbell's Cream of Mushroom soup makes a casserole—skill in making cream sauce with chicken broth not required; a bouillon cube or two flavors the stew, so the stew gets eaten without the benefits of cartilage-rich broth. Gravy is produced by adding water to a packet of powder—which contains an overwhelming amount of MSG. Packets of flavoring put MSG into homemade meat loaf, chili, and spaghetti sauce. With instant broth taste in packets and cans, who needs to pull out the big broth pot and fill it with bones?

MSG quickly made its way into restaurants in the form of soup bases. When you see "homemade soup" on the menu, ask the server whether it is made in house from bones or from a base. Most likely the answer will be: "We make our soup in house from a base." That base is not nourishing broth but a canned powder, highly flavored with MSG. MSG is also in many of the sauces, salad dressings, gravies, and "au jus" garnishes that people relish when they have a restaurant meal, often waking up with a dry mouth and headache the next morning.

Fortunately, the Western world is re-embracing real food and traditional cooking—witness the explosion of interest in traditional, ethnic, and local foods. And nothing characterizes ancestral food as much as nourishing broth, the simmering stockpot, and broth-based soups, stews, gravies, and sauces.

And just in time! Today we are witnessing an epidemic of chronic disease that threatens to unhinge our modern world—cancer, arthritis, allergies, digestive problems, mental disorders, and even new types of life-threatening infectious illness. Bone broth, rich in the elements of cartilage, collagen, and healing amino acids, can provide protection from these ailments, can serve as an important element in recovery, and can nourish and enrich our lives in many ways.

This book provides many important reasons for putting the stockpot back on our stoves and, even more important, making broth-based soup the basis of meals in hospitals, nursing homes, military canteens, schools, and prisons. Unfortunately, soldiers, students, convalescents, and inmates today are fed the cheapest of industrial foods—imitation broth, soups based on artificial ingredients, fast foods loaded with industrial chemicals, Meals Ready-to-Eat (MREs), and "nutrition" concoctions in cans. Thus the nation gets sicker, academic standards decline, behavior degenerates, and recidivism soars.

Too many cooks may spoil the broth, but the many contributors to this book have greatly enriched its content with their testimonials and recipes. Dr. Kaayla Daniel is uniquely qualified to pull together all the science we have on broth. While studies on broth itself are lacking, we know a lot about broth's components. Modern science provides the explanation for the varied and worldwide traditions that extol broth's healing effects, and the many testimonials we have collected over the years indicate a wide range of conditions that broth can ameliorate or prevent.

"The most important piece of equipment in any kitchen," said Francis Pottenger Jr., MD, "is the stockpot." Dr. Pottenger was the author of a seminal article describing how gelatin-rich broth helps digestion. He recommended the stockpot as a gift for couples getting married.

I described Dr. Pottenger's 1938 article on gelatin (published in the *American Journal of Digestive Diseases*) and some of the traditions about broth in my cookbook *Nourishing Traditions*; the book, first published in 1996, piqued the public's interest in the health benefits of broth. I also made sure that information about broth was posted on the website of our nutrition information foundation, the Weston A. Price Foundation, founded in 1999.

During the ensuing years, interest in broth increased, and many homemakers and cooks discovered the satisfaction of making broth and employing it as the foundational ingredient in soups, stews, sauces, and gravies—or using broth therapeutically for colds, flu, digestive disorders, skin diseases, and joint problems. Many of these cooks have developed unique ways of making broth, not to mention many delicious broth-based recipes, and their discoveries form an important part of this book, allowing us to provide not only the scientific principles behind broth but also broth's practical applications. Those who have contributed recipes show us that it is easy to incorporate broth making into any lifestyle—from a simple slow cooker chicken broth prepared by the busy parent to a long-simmered consommé prepared by the gourmet chef.

We hope that this book will provide inspiration for making broth, because there's more than just love in that pot of chicken soup we prepare; there's much that will heal the ailments we suffer from. All this, and it tastes good too.

—Sally Fallon Morell, President,
The Weston A. Price Foundation

Nourishing Broth

Nourishing Broth: Folklore and History

For most people in the world, soup serves as a humble economy food crafted from leftover bones, shells, wilted vegetable scraps, and whatever else is available, according to the frugal principle of "waste not, want not." Wealthier households use whole chickens, fish, and hunks of lamb, beef, or pork to make the very best stock, while the poor often rely on carcasses and scraps from butchering.

Nourishing broth dates back to the Stone Age, a time when people didn't even have pots to cook in. The first soups were "stone soups," in which hot stones from nearby fires were added to the abdominal pouches of butchered animals in order to simmer up mixtures of meat, fat, bones, herbs, wild grains, and water. Shells of turtles or crustaceans may have supplied the first rigid pots. In Asia, bamboo tubes sealed at the ends with clay provided usable containers that could hold both food and water. Native Americans boiled bones in water by putting hot rocks into baskets lined with clay or pitch. It would take durable, heat-conducting containers, however, before soup could become a permanent fixture on the hearth.

The first earthenware pots were fired at low temperatures in pit fires or open bonfires. Crude, hand-formed, and undecorated, they date back to 22,000 years ago in China and about 12,000 years ago elsewhere. Metal pots forged of bronze appeared in the fourth millennium BCE, followed by pots made of iron and other metals. Among Europeans, Greeks used metal pots first, and soup apparently was popular there. In his satire *The Frogs*, playwright Aristophanes had Dionysus ask Heracles if he'd "ever felt a sudden urge for soup?" And our hero replied, "Soup? Ten thousand times so far." That idea has never failed to resonate, and soup advertisements still speak to our desire for deep nourishment, strength, power, and invincibility.

Until the modern era, most households kept a cauldron simmering over the fire or a stockpot on a stove's back burner. People regularly ate from it and continually added whatever ingredients became available, making long-cooked soups and stews the original "fast food." This practice has gone on just about forever, everywhere on the planet, and in every conceivable economic or political situation as long as people have had fuel for the hearth or stove. No food is as universally appreciated as soup.

While broth-making techniques and ingredients are similar everywhere, soup styles change with culinary fashion. What has remained constant is the use of soups and "meat teas" for health and healing. Chicken soup, of course, enjoys almost mystical status in Jewish culture and is known as "Jewish penicillin." The Jewish philosopher and physician Moses Maimonides gave it his stamp of approval in the twelfth century, having borrowed much from Galen, the second-century Greek philosopher, physician, and pathologist, and Hippocrates, who practiced even earlier, in the fourth century BC. While most people think the health claims for soup are the stuff of legend, we will show that these claims have a solid scientific basis. In short, chicken soup can do far more for us than moisten the gullet, steam out our sinuses, whet the appetite, and add the healing power of love.

Its reputation as Jewish penicillin notwithstanding, Asians actually consume the most chicken soup today. Inhabitants of Japan, Korea, China, and other Asian countries revere it for its preventive powers as well as its curative powers. According to Martin Yan, the Chinese-born, Hong Kong–American food writer and host of *Yan Can Cook*, this is "not a case of pure faith." Rather, Asians routinely enhance broth's healing power by adding "medicinal herbs and roots to...daily thirst-quenching soups to make them into elixirs at our dinner tables." Whenever Yan feels "worn down and haggard," he says, he remembers his "mother's words of wisdom at the dinner table, 'Drink your soup.'" Ever wonder why you can't purchase chicken feet in American supermarkets? It's because virtually all the feet from American industrial poultry production are shipped to China, where they go into the pot to make soup.

How much of soup's healing power should be credited to the love that goes into preparing homemade soups for family members? How much might be due to a nurturing lifestyle that includes sitting down for regular meals? These factors are too subjective to measure, but common sense suggests they have nothing but positive effects on health and longevity. In addition, anecdotal reports abound on the power of broth to relieve headaches, calm the mind, chase butterflies from the stomach, improve focus, and gain energy.

In her 1998 book *A Soothing Broth: Tonics, Custards, Soups and Other Cure-Alls for Colds, Coughs, Upset Tummies, and Out-of-Sorts Days*, Pat Willard notes old recipes for invalids almost always came with encouraging words like "This will cure for sure" or "In my experience, this has always proven beneficial." Invalid recipes in old cookbooks range from simple but strengthening beef teas to savory custards made with eggs, salt, pepper, and beef to choices of "restorative" or "stimulating" meat jellies. Many of the writers suggested adding unflavored gelatin to enhance whatever foods or drinks might otherwise appeal to the convalescent. In her 1859 book *Notes on Nursing*, Florence Nightingale emphasized the importance of "easy digestibility" and said, "Remember that sick cookery should do half the work of your poor patient's weak digestion." No food improves digestion better than broth.

Portable Soup

Broth would seem to be the least portable of foods, but "portable soup" dates back to the ninth and tenth centuries when Magyar warriors overran Europe. A fourteenth-century chronicle explains how they boiled beef until it fell apart, chopped it up, and dried it so it could be easily transported on horseback. To have broth for dinner, the men simply added hot water. In all probability, our ancestors developed portable soups all over the world in much the same way. Native Americans, for example, most likely made soup from powdered pemmican. Some portable soups, of course, were made of powdered peas, rye, and other grains, legumes, and vegetables, but the most nutritious included meat and/or gelatin.

In early seventeenth-century England, Sir Hugh Plat came up with instructions for a "drie gell…in pieces like mouth glew" in *Victuall for Warz*. It was made from "neat feete & legge of beeff…boiled to a great stiffness." In 1743 *Lady's Companion* described how "to make a veal glue or cake soup to be carried in the pocket." The recipe involved cooking a gelatinous broth, then boiling it down until it was so concentrated it could be laid out on pieces of fabric. It was then turned until hardened, dry, and stiff enough to be "carried in the Pocket without inconvenience." Many other cookbooks of the seventeenth and eighteenth centuries described how to prepare what was known as "veal glew," "cake soup," "cake gravey," "broth cakes," "solid soop," "portmanteau pottage," "pocket soup," "carry soup," and "soop always in readiness." Eliza Leslie, in her *Directions for Cookery* of 1837, advised, "If you have any friends going the overland journey to the Pacific, a box of portable soup may be the most useful present to them."

William Byrd II (1674–1744), founder of Richmond, Virginia, advised making portable soup with meat, bones, vegetables, and anchovies boiled down to a viscous mass and then dried in the sun: "Dissolve a piece of portable soup in water and a bason of good broth can be had in a few minutes." Scottish poet Robert Burns describes hunters carrying portable soup in their packs.

To successfully make portable soup, cookbook writers were clear: It was necessary to fill the stockpot with plenty of cartilage and connective tissue, which breaks down into gelatin. Without gelatin, there was no way the soup would harden.

Portable soups served travelers as well as the military. British ship captain and maritime fur trader Nathaniel Portlock described the use of portable soups on his expeditions in the 1780s. Captain Cook endorsed them because they "enable us to make several nourishing and wholesome messes and was the means of making the people eat a greater quantity of vegetables than they would otherwise have done." Apparently, the sailors didn't much like the soup, however, and Cook reportedly flogged men who refused to eat it.

Meriwether Lewis and William Clark took portable soup on the Corps of Discovery Expedition of 1804–1806, and considered it so essential they went over budget to pay $189.50 for 193 pounds of dried soup packed in thirty-two tin canisters—like ones used for storing gunpowder, not cans as we think of them today. Lewis and Clark spent more on soup than on instruments, arms, or ammunition. But as their journals made clear, no one much appreciated the dried soup, though it sustained them when there was "nothing else to eat."

Portable broth became commercially viable with Justus von Liebig (1803–1873), the German chemist known today as the "father

Campbell's Soup: "M'm! M'm! Good" to MSG

The military's need for portability and preservation not only led to "portable soups" and "extracts" but also to canning, which was invented in 1810 by Nicholas Appert (1749–1841) to help Napoleon Bonaparte keep his armies well fed. In 1870 Joseph Campbell joined many businessmen who'd decided to can food for the civilian market. One of his early products was white soup made from "large fat fowls." The recipe, adapted from Eliza Leslie's 1828 book *Directions for Cookery*, listed 250 to 300 pounds chicken, 100 pounds veal, 90 pounds rice, 12 ounces curry powder, 15 pounds butter, 1 quart Worcestershire sauce, 20 sticks celery, 25 bunches parsley, 50 pounds onions, 20 pounds salt, and other fresh, real ingredients.

Campbell's condensed soups began with John Thompson Dorrance (1873–1930), an MIT-trained chemist who joined the Campbell's company in 1897 at the grand salary of $7.50 a week, and who took over the company in 1914. Dorrance studied Carl von Voit's pioneering work on protein and gelatin in Europe and understood "the delicate flavorings of soups" from assisting the fine chefs at Le Café de Paris, Paillard, and the Waldorf. As a food connoisseur, he sought nothing less than to bring the taste, texture, aroma, and healing benefits of gourmet soups to the masses in a convenient ready-made form.

But Dorrance's ideas ultimately led to the disappearance of homemade broth from the average American diet. Campbell's ads planted the idea that "the boiling of joints and keeping up of soup stock" was "labor intensive," "beyond the reach of people of small means," "inconvenient to the rich," and "awkward in modern homes." Dorrance shrewdly promoted Campbell's products as help for the busy housewife, not as an improvement over her

of the fertilizer industry." In 1840 von Liebig developed a portable "beef extract" to feed the "craving multitudes" who desired but could not afford real meat. The only problem was the manufacturing process took thirty kilograms of meat to produce one kilogram of extract! Large-scale production became possible when he learned he could obtain cheap beef from the carcasses of cattle raised for their hides in Uruguay. At the time, the canning and freezing of meat was not yet the norm. Von Liebig's beef extract nourished Henry Morton Stanley on his adventure through Africa in search of Dr. David Livingstone; went along with the polar explorers Nansen, Amundsen, Shackleton, and Scott; and fed Allied soldiers during World War I. Marketed to housewives it became Oxo. Similarly, John Lawson Johnston developed "Johnston's Fluid Beef" in 1871, later marketed as Bovril. It, too, served soldiers, sailors, explorers, and adventurers in need of healthy but portable soups. Sadly, these and similar bouillon-type products have devolved from fairly "real foods" into meatlike products that rely on MSG, artificial flavorings, and other additives for their savoriness.

culinary talents, and catered to her mothering instincts with the promise that soup provided optimal nourishment for healthy and happy growing children.

By all accounts, Dorrance was completely in love with soup. He planted and tended tomatoes himself, always looking for the perfect tomatoes for the tomato soup. He specified frequent skimming, careful stirring of soups, and the precise measurements of all ingredients.

He insisted on using only "table quality" ingredients. Others, he said, could make soup "the old way with leftover pieces of meat and wilted vegetables." He wanted only the best, and offered product lineups that were varied, inventive, and even exotic, including gelatinous soups like printanier, a classic soup revered by Escoffier.

John Dorrance died in 1930, and standards seem to have remained high until the company went public in the 1950s.

Then stockholders demanded higher profits through product line expansion, the acquisition of Prego, Mrs. Paul's, Swanson, and dozens of other companies, and increasing penetration of global markets. Dorrance would never have guessed that a decision based on his singular good taste would be replaced by committee decisions from home economics departments and product development teams, or that real ingredients would give way to cheap imitation flavors from MSG, artificial flavors, and other dubious ingredients. He would be saddened to learn that Douglas Conant, President and CEO of the Campbell Soup Company from 2001 to 2011, took over when the company had lost half its market value in the prior year and "had cut costs to the point where they were literally taking the chicken out of chicken noodle soup."

◄○►

Soup and Gelatin

The development of "portable soups" and meat extracts coincided with the growth of the gelatin industry. Gelatin is the jiggly denatured collagen that shows up when properly made bone broths, soups, and stews are refrigerated. In 1679, Denis Papin (1657–1712), a physicist entranced with the potential of steam pressure and steam engines, invented a pressure cooker–like contraption called the Digester of Bones. His idea was to boil down bones into a gelatin that could be used to

thicken sauces or eaten directly as a jelly. He thought it would save money for poor people who needed to extract nutrition from bones but couldn't afford the fuel needed for long-term cooking. The contraption was too expensive, however, for all but the rich.

Papin served foods prepared in his digester for a number of learned men in London on April 12, 1682, greatly impressing a diarist named John Evelyn: "I went this afternoon with several of the Royal Society to a supper which was all dressed, both fish and flesh, in Monsieur Papin's digestors, by which the hardest bones of beef itself, and mutton, were made as soft as cheese, without water or other liquor, and with less than eight ounces of coals, producing an incredible quantity of gravy; and for close of all, a jelly made of the bones of beef, the best for clearness and good relish, and the most delicious that I had ever seen or tasted."

Although Papin's work with digesters never took off, the interest in gelatin continued, reaching its zenith in the late nineteenth and early twentieth centuries, when it was widely

---

Knox Gelatin

Charles Knox developed the world's first pregranulated gelatin in 1890 after watching his wife, Rose, suffer through the labor-intensive process of making gelatin at home. A flamboyant man known as the "Napoleon of Advertising," he promoted his gelatin products with a motorized balloon named "Gelatine," a racehorse renamed "Gelatine King," and other events that made headlines. After his death in 1908, Rose took over and dropped the stunts in favor of outreach campaigns that educated women on the health benefits of gelatin and showed them how to cook with it in the kitchen. Rose Knox ran the company for more than forty years until her death at age ninety-three in 1950, and was widely revered as a savvy businesswoman. Great Lakes Gelatin, formerly Grayslake Gelatin, also thrived during those years and today offers gelatin and collagen hydrolysate products from grass-fed beef, a qualitative difference over today's Knox products, which over the years came to be manufactured using commercial factory-farmed meats.

---

perceived as the ultimate solution to world hunger, malnutrition, war rations, and rescue and relief efforts. Though not a complete protein, researchers of the nineteenth and early twentieth centuries found that gelatin vastly improved the nutritional value of plant-based diets. It increases the protein availability of wheat, oats, and barley, though not of corn, and vastly improves the digestibility of meat and beans. This seemed a viable long-term solution for third-world people subsisting on grains and legumes and a short-term help for food banks and other rescue and relief efforts. Today it's still a useful dietary adjunct when genuine gelatin-rich broth is not available.

During the heyday of gelatin, researchers and clinicians also explored the myriad ways gelatin could improve health and reverse disease. Indeed, gelatin research caught the interest of many top scientists of the nineteenth and early twentieth centuries. We'll discuss their many findings in part 2.

The Scientific Validation of Traditional Wisdom

Folk wisdom throughout the world values broth for its healing powers, and we have found confirmation of these traditional beliefs in hundreds of nineteenth- and early twentieth–century studies on gelatin, and in thousands of modern investigations into glycine, cartilage, glucosamine, and other components found abundantly in broth. Even so, most people think of chicken soup as nothing more than a warm and fuzzy, soul-soothing comfort food and home remedy. Our ancestors may have sworn by it, but modern science tends to dismiss the healing stories as anecdotal evidence or old wives' tales.

While it would be great to have scores of studies proving the efficacy of bone broth itself, the truth is we don't have many. Science today follows the money, and unless something can be pilled, powdered, and patented, it's not likely to be investigated. Accordingly, much of our evidence focuses on the various fractional components of broth. We will then explore broth's role for the prevention—and possibly even the cure—of diseases like osteoarthritis and rheumatoid arthritis, scleroderma, psoriasis, cancer, colitis, and other digestive disorders and its use in antiaging and sports medicine. Finally, we'll present a range of recipes, from simple to complex, which allow you to incorporate homemade broth into your diet on a frequent basis.

Science and tradition tell us that bone broth is nourishing. Very nourishing. How nourishing will vary from batch to batch depending upon the diet and lifestyle of the animal, bird, or fish, its age and overall health, how it's processed, your cooking methods, and your choice of other vegetables, herbs, and other ingredients.

The nutritional profile will change depending on the types and proportions of bones, joints, tendons, ligaments, skin, and muscles. Veal bones from calves, for example, have more collagen and cartilage than bones from grown cows. Knucklebones, being joints, are higher in cartilage than shank bones from legs. Lamb and beef shanks contain rich treasure troves of bone marrow, while poultry bones, being lighter, thinner, and mostly hollow, have less. Fish heads and tiny dried whole fish offer the rich stores of iodine for healthy thyroid function.

The body's ability to repair connective tissue such as bone, tendon, ligament, cartilage, skin, hair, and nails diminishes with age and ill health. Bone broth, with its rich dissolves of collagen, cartilage, bone, and marrow, gives the body "the right stuff" to rebuild and rejuvenate. These components also include vitamins and minerals, the conditionally essential amino acids glycine, proline, and glutamine, and healing "essential" sugars known as proteoglycans.

According to the principle of "like feeds like," broth can give our bones strength and flexibility, our joints cushion and resilience, and our skin a youthful plumpness. What's more, the abundance of collagen in all types of bone broth supports heart health through strong and supple arteries, our vision with healthy corneas, digestion through gut healing, and overall disease prevention via immune system modulation. As we shall see, broth even contributes to emotional stability and a positive mental attitude.

Daily requirements for collagen and other components of broth vary from person to person; they increase with disease, physical activity, exercise, stress, and other factors. Brittle hair and nails, underdeveloped musculature, premature skin aging, osteoarthritis, osteoporosis, gut disorders, and autoimmune disease are sure signs of deficiencies in collagen and other nutrients, which can be remedied with the help of genuine old-fashioned bone broth. Although dietary supplements are always an option, there's a synergy in broth that simmers with a healing power far greater than the sum of its parts.

PART I

Basic Broth Science

CHAPTER 1

Collagen:
Holding the Body Together

Collagen is the glue that holds the body together. The word comes from *kolla*, the Greek word for glue, and our ancestors made glue by boiling down the skin and sinews of animals. When we make broth, we turn skin, cartilage, tendons, and ligaments into a gelatin-rich liquid glue instead.

Cooking breaks down collagenous protein into gelatin, which provides the amino acids the body needs to make the "glue" we call connective tissue. In the form of twisted cables, collagen strengthens the tendons that connect muscle to the bone and the ligaments that connect bones together. As vast, resilient sheets, collagen supports the skin and internal organs, helps skin retain its youthful firmness, suppleness, and elasticity, and builds a barrier that prevents the absorption and spread of pathogenic substances, environmental toxins, microorganisms, and cancerous cells. As found in cartilage, collagen is the secret to well-lubed and well-cushioned joints.

Types of Collagen

Indeed, collagen is needed just about everywhere in the body, and constitutes between 25 and 35 percent of the body's total protein. There are so many uses for collagen that as many as twenty-nine distinct types exist in animal tissues. Types I to V are the most common.

- Type I is found abundantly in skin, tendons, ligaments, internal organs, bones, and the vascular system. It constitutes 90 percent of the body's collagen and is found just about everywhere except in cartilage.
- Type II is the cartilage builder, and occurs in the cornea and vitreous humour of the eye.
- Type III collagen teams up with type I to keep the walls of our arteries and other hollow organs strong and supple.
- Type IV ensures the health of cell basement membranes and the filtration system of capillaries.
- Type V is needed for the surfaces of cells, healthy hair, and the placenta during pregnancy.

Whatever their type, collagenous proteins are gigantic molecules that each contain more than one thousand of the protein-building

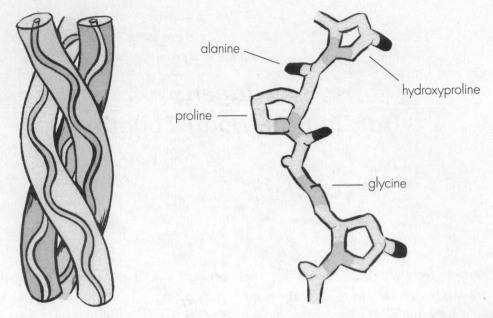

alanine

hydroxyproline

proline

glycine

Figure 1: Collagen is a major structural protein comprised of three chains wound together in a triple helix formation (shown at left). Shown here is a small part of the entire collagen molecule of about 1,400 amino acids. Every third amino acid is glycine.

blocks known as amino acids. The molecular structure is a triple helix. One-third of the amino acids are made up of glycine, a tiny amino whose small size is critical for structuring the very tightly packed molecular chains needed at the axis of the helix. Pointing outward, the team of proline and hydroxyproline twists into the tough, strong, and stable triple helix structure.

The structure of collagen varies somewhat among species, a fact that argues for our including bone broth from a variety of species in the diet. It also explains why taste and nutritional value can require different cooking times and preparation methods. For example, the amount of amino acids proline and hydroxyproline is lower in cold-water fish than in mammals. Accordingly, broth from fish is cooked short term, and gelatin obtained from fish is unsuited to many food processing and industrial applications.

Collagen and Aging

Collagen production in the body slows with age and ill health, causing skin, joints, and other body parts to become drier, less pliant, thinner, and weaker. The glue dries up and loses its stickiness, so to speak. This breakdown is most visible as sagging skin, but it can occur throughout the body. Tendons and ligaments lose elasticity, bones weaken, muscles atrophy, and cartilage cracks. Injuries are more likely to occur from repetitive motion, wear and tear, overexertion, or overuse at work, at the gym, or when playing sports. When the body is low in collagen and unable to produce enough of it, injuries are more likely to happen and are harder to heal. In addition, collagen plays a role in preventing and treating autoimmune disorders such as rheumatoid arthritis and Crohn's disease.

Satisfaction

When my body consumes broth, I can hear it sigh, *ahhhhhh!* My body loves broth!

–Angie Libert, Ogden, Utah

Mainstream science holds that breakdown is inevitable with age. The usual recommendation is to take NSAIDs and other nonsteroidal anti-inflammatory drugs to block pain. This approach is self-defeating, however. Inflammation is a painful but needed first stage in the body's healing process, one that sends nutrients to the site, leads to granular tissue formation, and ultimately the formation of collagen. Once the new collagen connects with threads to the damaged tissue, healing and strengthening can take place. Rather than take over-the-counter (OTC) or prescription drugs to block inflammation, the better solution is to give the body what it needs to produce optimum amounts of high-quality collagen.

Broth or Supplements?

The traditional way to accomplish this is by eating gelatin-rich homemade bone broth and plenty of collagen-rich foods such as chicken feet and pigs' hooves. Sadly, such foods have largely disappeared from the modern dinner table, partly for reasons of convenience and partly because so many "health experts" warn against the fat and cholesterol found in these animal products. The result is that most first-world people today subsist on collagen-poor diets, suffer chronic ill effects throughout the body, and embrace pharmaceutical or nutraceutical solutions.

Hair, Skin, Teeth, and Nails

I was a vegetarian for nearly thirteen years of my life but finally started appreciating the organic grass-fed animal protein the Lord has provided. Over the past several years I have had so much success with bone broth and credit it with growing enamel back into my front right incisor. I have also noticed that my skin tissue, hair, and nails are more vibrant and structurally sound. I feel so nourished and satisfied, and really that is what holistic nutrition is all about!

–Amber K.,
Greensboro, North Carolina

In terms of joint health, those who don't give up so easily may turn to the popular supplements glucosamine and chondroitin. Although both of these have well-proven benefits, they provide only two of the many raw ingredients the body needs for collagen production.

A more comprehensive solution is gelatin powders or supplements or whole cartilage products, preferably from pastured cows or chickens. In terms of gelatin powders, the best offer several versions of collagen: types I and II

What Is Gelatin?

Gelatin differs from meat concentrates in that it consists of only the denatured collagen component. It's intended to be added to other foods to improve digestibility or to be taken alone as a supplement to improve hair, nails, skin, or joints. It is a food as opposed to a food additive and consists of 84 to 90 percent protein, 1 to 2 percent mineral salts, and 8 to 15 percent water. In the food industry, gelatin is widely used to replace cream, egg yolks, and other ingredients in low-calorie, low-fat products that would otherwise lose acceptable texture and mouthfeel. Gelatin is a constituent of many commercial ice creams, yogurts, marshmallows, frostings, and most other processed, packaged products not targeted to the vegan market. Isinglass, a purified form of gelatin derived from fish bladders, is widely used in the wine and beer industries to accelerate the fining, or clarifying, of the products. A 2007 study in the *Journal of Food Science* suggests bovine gelatin sprays may soon be used to extend the shelf life of meat by blocking water loss and lipid oxidation. Gelatin also has a long history of commercial applications, most famously in the gelatin silver prints of black-and-white photography.

How Now Mad Cow

Despite the multiple health benefits of gelatin, some people avoid it because of fear of mad cow disease. In fact, most gelatin today is hide gelatin, not made from brains. Furthermore, processing procedures such as degreasing, acid demineralization, alkaline purification, washing, filtration, ion exchange, and sterilization reduce the chance of bovine spongiform encephalopathy to about zero. Back in 1992, the FDA took the mad cow fear seriously enough to forbid the import of any cow products including gelatin from countries where BSE had occurred, but the ban on gelatin was lifted in 1997. The main reason was that there have been no cases to date implicating either commercial or homemade gelatin in mad cow disease or any other neurological disorders.

to nourish skin, hair, and nails, and collagen type II to support connective tissue, joints, ligaments, and tendons. Most people benefit from both. Some trendy new products contain collagen from velvet deer antler, green-lipped mussels, sea cucumbers, or other exotic collagen sources. These products may even be pumped up with pomegranate or other additions to provide vitamin C and other collagen-building support for the body.

Interestingly, high-end supplements marketed for bone health are increasingly likely to contain collagen, as studies suggest it's even more important than calcium and other minerals for building strong flexible bones and preventing osteopenia and osteoporosis. Indeed, collagen is the likeliest reason bone broth supports bone health (and not its calcium content, which is surprisingly low. See chapter 3, pages 22–25).

Despite the booming supplement business, the most popular and heavily marketed products contain collagen and collagen enhancers for external use. These include creams, lotions, nail treatments, facial firming gels, and eye pads. In medicine, collagen and cartilage can be found in wound-dressing materials and skin substitutes for burn victims.

The FDA has also approved injectable collagens for cosmetic use. Purified to closely resemble human collagen, bovine collagens are injected to smooth out the fatigue and fret lines that furrow the aging face. Possible side effects are rashes, muscle pain, and headaches, and the results don't last. Sooner or later the body metabolizes injected collagen.

While many of the new collagen technologies look promising, common sense argues for ancestral wisdom. It's time to put gelatin-rich bone broth back on the daily menu and nourish the body from the inside out.

CHAPTER 2

Cartilage: Helping Us Move

Most people know cartilage as gristle. It's the blob on the bone of a T-bone steak, the globs on chicken drumsticks, and nearly the entire skeleton of man-eating sharks.

Human beings, too, are blessed with cartilage. Without cartilage, we couldn't wiggle our ears, scrunch up our noses, swallow with ease, or move our joints. Tough, elastic, spongy, and springy, cartilage has many vital roles: It acts as a framework, works as a shock absorber, and reduces the friction between moving parts.

The Many Roles of Cartilage

No bones about it, cartilage is a fascinating substance. There's nothing else quite like it in the body. Unlike its cousins connective tissue and bone, it contains no nerves, blood vessels, or lymph system. Nutrients needed to maintain it are not transported via blood or lymph fluid but by synovial fluid, which flows into every nook and cranny when pressure is applied to the joint and released.

Synovial fluid is a transparent, raw egg white–like substance that contains albumin, fat, mineral salts, and a large organic

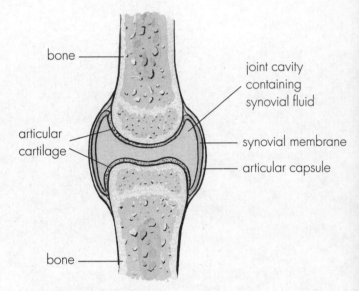

Figure 2: Shown here is a typical joint with the locations of bone, articular cartilage, a synovial membrane, and the joint cavity containing synovial fluid.

molecule called hyaluronic acid in addition to water. Indeed, water is the chief constituent of healthy cartilage—65 to 85 percent. Health experts like to say it is possible for us to starve our cartilage in two easy ways: by not drinking enough water and by not exercising. But water is not nearly as helpful as broth, a substance that includes not only water but the amino acids, collagen, and other components the body needs to manufacture healthy cartilage.

The remarkable resilience of cartilage comes from its gelatinous matrix. Jiggly but not amorphous, this matrix is highly structured with the complex combinations of proteins and sugars known as proteoglycans, whose principal job is to get and hold water. The most prominent proteoglycans in cartilage are the sulfur-containing molecules chondroitin sulfate and keratan sulfate. These molecules carry negative charges and repel each other, creating space for the water they need to attract and hold.

The most common type of cartilage in the human body is hyaline cartilage, a hard, gristly, bluish translucent material, which—when healthy—is also pliable. Its strength comes from a dense, crisscrossing ropey network of collagenous fibers. Its resilience derives from the gel-like matrix into which these fibers are embedded. The fibrils found on the outside of cartilage are so tough and densely packed that they are known as the "armor plate layer."

Chondrocytes Build Cartilage

Living within the matrix are the cartilage cells themselves. Known as chondrocytes, these cells reside in little isolation chambers known as lacunae, where they regulate cartilage metabolism, manufacture proteoglycan molecules and collagenous fibers, and build new cartilage as necessary. To do so, the chondrocytes need the right nutrients delivered in the right proportions to them by the water and synovial fluid. In addition, they require twenty to thirty different enzymes, without which the complex sugars cannot be properly synthesized and coupled to the core proteins.

During childhood and adolescence, chondrocytes regularly build new cartilage matrix, which can ossify into bone. In this way, nature designed our skeletons to grow to full size. In adulthood, the construction slows down and the chondrocytes lay new deposits of cartilage only on the surface of existing cartilage. Although for most adults the rate of cellular reproduction and repair is slow, individuals with healthy cartilage manage to maintain equilibrium between the creation of new cartilage and decomposition of the old.

◄○►

A Change in Proportion

If we compare the cartilage of young healthy mammals with old and sick ones, we see different proteoglycan formation. In young ones, the chondroitin sulfate chains are considerably longer than the keratan sulfate ones. Studies done on old folks and old cows, however, show shorter chondroitin sulfate chains and longer keratan sulfate chains. With aging, the two components of cartilage become about equal in length, which results in hunched-over little proteoglycans that are less able to hold and attract water. According to Arnold I. Caplan, PhD, of Case Western Reserve University, "This difference may be responsible, at least in part, for the development of some forms of osteoarthritis in older people. After all, if the proteoglycans made in cartilage by aging chondrocytes have a lessened capacity to structure water, the resilience of the cartilage must be compromised, and with it the cushioning of bones in the joints." This finding suggests the ideal broth for cartilage regeneration might come from young animals.

◄○►

Can We Regenerate Our Cartilage?

While common sense tells us "like can feed like," most people believe cartilage regeneration is improbable if not impossible. However, the late John F. Prudden, MD, DSci (1920–1998), known as the "father of cartilage therapy," liked to explain how cartilage regeneration could work by comparing it to "the mesenchyme in a growing fetus."

Mesenchyme is a tissue derived from the mesoderm, the layer of primordial tissue in the embryo from which muscles, bones, cartilage, tendons, ligaments, fat, and bone marrow develop. Mesoderm, endoderm, and ectoderm are the three primary germ layers from which all cells and tissues in the body derive.

Like cartilage itself, mesenchyme consists of a gelatinous matrix with fibers. Because its germ cells are the prototypes for healthy tissue, it comes rigged with maturation factors or biodirectors that tell the body not only how to create cartilage, bone marrow, the dermis of skin, the dentin of teeth, and other tissues, but also how to correct abnormalities.

Standard anatomy and physiology texts discuss mesenchyme primarily in terms of babies growing in the womb, but Dr. Prudden explained that we should consider what happens every time the human body mends a broken bone. First, the circulatory system cleans up the bony wreckage. Next,

undifferentiated (meaning unspecialized) cells that are remarkably similar to mesenchyme settle in, multiply, and develop into the specialized cartilage cells known as chondrocytes. These chondrocyte cells, in turn, produce the cartilage matrix that is needed to fill the gaps and bind the bone fragments together. As the cartilage calcifies, new bone forms.

This scenario suggests adults can rebuild cartilage, though it is rare indeed for it to happen spontaneously in the case of people with osteoarthritis and other rheumatoid diseases. Dr. Prudden, however, accomplished it with many of his patients using bovine tracheal cartilage supplements, and he published the results in major medical journals. The cartilage Dr. Prudden used was taken from the tracheas of young healthy calves and not from humans, but the match was close enough. He furthermore discovered that cartilage could reverse diseases such as psoriasis and cancer that would not seem to be cartilage-related at all. We'll discuss his pioneering work curing incurables with arthritis, autoimmune disorders, and cancer later in this book. For now, the commonsense principle of "you are what you eat" suggests the wisdom of consuming at least one cup of cartilage-rich broth daily for optimum health and longevity, more if you are dealing with degenerative disease.

Chondroitin sulfates play other important roles: They inhibit enzymes that like to chew up cartilage, and they interfere with enzymes that would hijack the transport of nutrients.

Both types of enzymes seem to be gluttonous in the cartilage of aging mammals.

Changes in chondroitin sulfate and keratan sulfate accompany other changes in aging or unhealthy joints as well. It seems that if one part of the cartilage system breaks down, another is sure to follow. If, for any reason, the collagen and elastic network loses its shape and its strength, the gelatinous matrix growing on and around it will suffer the loss of support as well. Once cartilage is unable to attract and hold water, the chondrocytes lose their source of nourishment and their much-needed ability to reproduce and repair. And so it goes. However the problems begin, the unhappy result is the decomposition of old cartilage at a faster pace than the creation of new cartilage.

Once this happens, it is only a matter of time before the cartilage that was once plump and resilient becomes painfully thin, dried out, worn down, stiff, cracked, and inflamed. Then the bones that the cartilage was designed to protect start rubbing each other the wrong way, causing bone spurs, bone hardening, inflammation, and pain (see the illustration comparing a normal joint to one with osteoarthritis on page 59).

Conventional medical opinion holds that joint problems are inevitable with aging and that damage is irreparable and irreversible. But it appears the human body can revert to the "young" type of cartilage and regenerate young healthy cartilage if provided with the right tools. And it's undoubtedly even easier to prevent the damage to begin with. That means providing the right constituents of cartilage—glycine, proline, glutamine, proteoglycans, and other nutrients found in cartilage-rich bone broth. The larger cartilage molecules may not be absorbed intact, but the components certainly are.

CHAPTER 3

Bone: The Body's Living Framework

Healthy bone is living tissue that supports, frames, and protects the body with flexibility and strength. Minerals in the matrix make bones hard, but collagen keeps them resilient. The last thing we want is brittle bones.

Bones serve us in many other ways as well: They allow our bodies to deposit and withdraw minerals; produce blood cells, stem cells, and growth factors; serve to buffer our blood against excessive pH changes; and even store energy. In Chinese medicine, deep "bone consciousness" is thought to ground and stabilize the life of the spirit. Poets favor the word *marrow* when writing of primal and mystical interior journeys.

Bones for Minerals

Made from bones, broth provides a variety of bioavailable minerals. The exact mineral content found in bones depends upon the overall health, age, diet, and environment of the animal as well as the species. About 50 percent of bone is minerals, 28 percent collagen, and 22 percent water. Of the minerals, the largest store by far is calcium phosphate, a combination of calcium and phosphorous arranged in a formation called hydroxyapatite. Bone also contains small amounts of magnesium, sodium, potassium, sulfur, and other trace minerals.

Given all the calcium in bone, it's reasonable to think broth would be an excellent source of this important mineral. Many people even claim its calcium content rivals that of dairy foods and recommend bone broth as a good substitute for people who cannot tolerate milk or other dairy products. In fact, the level of calcium in broth does not come even close. The most thorough study of this topic occurred in 1934 when researchers reported the calcium content of several types of bone broth at just 5.2 to 28.6 mg per 100 cc (12.30 to 67.7 mg per cup). The researchers compared this to 119 to 128 mg calcium per 100 cc (281 to 303 mg per cup) in cow's milk.

Recent testing confirms the low calcium levels found in 1934. Saffron Road and Flavor Chef broths, two excellent brands sold in health food stores, bear Nutrition Facts labels reporting 0 percent and 4 percent, respectively, per cup of the RDA for calcium. (As published by the National Academy of

Sciences, the basic RDA for calcium is 1000 mg per day, but up to 1300 mg per day for boys and girls between nine and eighteen, for pregnant and lactating women under the age of nineteen, and 1200 mg per day for women over the age of fifty-one and men over the age of seventy-one.) USDA figures for brand-name canned broths sold at supermarkets show calcium at 14 mg per cup (1.4% of the RDA) for beef and 9 mg (.9% of the RDA) per cup for chicken. By comparison, USDA reports 291 mg of calcium per cup for whole milk. Recent analyses of broth by Covance Laboratories of Madison, Wisconsin, also found low levels of calcium at 2.31 mg per cup for broth made by Kim Schuette, CN, of Biodynamic Wellness of Solana Beach, California (from a whole Mary's Free Range Chicken plus two chicken feet and no vegetables), and 6.14 mg per cup for Flavor Chef broth made with bones and vegetables.

The low calcium figures appear to be true even when long-term cooking softens and largely dissolves the bone. What's more, these figures are for broth made with the help of vinegar to help pull minerals from the bone. It appears the best way to increase the calcium content of broth is to include calcium-rich vegetables while making the broth and milk or cream in broth-based sauces.

Despite its low calcium content, broth apparently supports bone health. While levels of calcium and trace minerals may be low, they are nonetheless easily assimilated and present in appropriate ratios for bone building. In contrast, bone-building supplements are often formulated with high levels of calcium that are hard to absorb and missing full complements of bone-building trace minerals. Bone, after all, is not built on calcium alone.

Collagen for Strong Bones

The larger reason broth supports bone building is its high collagen content. Broth, of course, contains collagen dissolved not only from the bone itself but also from the attached skin and cartilage. The basic building blocks of bone are collagen fibrils that form a lattice-work for deposition of calcium phosphate and other minerals. The collagen cross-links are more important for whole bone strength and fracture resistance than mineral levels and patterns.

Broken Back

My son-in-law was in a horrific truck accident and broke his back in two places. He had to wear a brace, and the projected time for healing was at least three months. He went back for a check up and X-rays at two months and they were amazed. His back was almost totally healed. It really was amazing. My daughter was feeding him bone broth all day long! She made it all herself: chicken broth, beef broth, and venison broth. She made soups and stews, cooked grains in broth, and otherwise got broth into him as often as possible. The medical professionals were astounded with how quickly he healed. It was truly amazing. We attribute his strong healing to the broth.

–Candace Coffin,
Hillsville, Virginia

Indeed, some people have bones thick with calcium and other minerals that are weak and

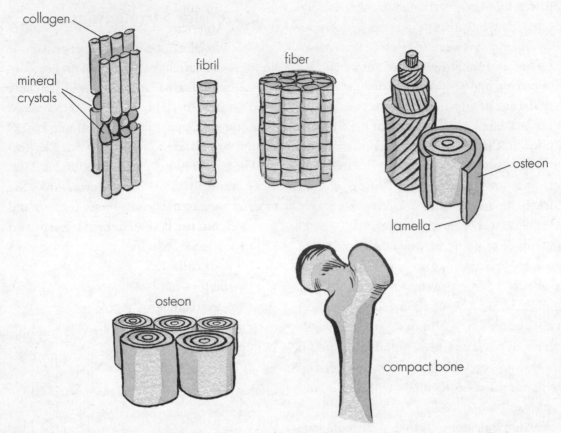

Figure 3: To build strong, flexible bone, the body lays down mineral crystals on a collagen structure as seen here.

crack under tension like unreinforced concrete. Diabetics, for example, may suffer from poor bones, not because of low mineral density but because their collagen is damaged by the advanced glycation end-products (AGEs) created when blood sugar levels are chronically high.

Although most published collagen studies have focused on osteoarthritis, Milan Adam, DSci of the Institute of Rheumatism Research in Prague (1928–2008), studied 120 osteoporosis patients over a period of three years. He treated half with calcium and half with collagen hydrolysate. The breakdown of substances indicating loss of collagen and bone mass were significantly lower in the collagen hydrolysate group than in the calcium group. Best of all, collagen hydrolysate reduced the likelihood of bone fractures significantly. A few years later, in 1996, he published a study on 108 post-menopausal women with osteoporosis and bone mineral density lower than 80 percent. He reported collagen hydrolysate enhanced and prolonged the beneficial effects of calcitonin and improved overall markers of bone metabolism. Calcitonin is a hormone secreted by the thyroid that has the effect of lowering blood calcium.

In 2000, Roland Moskowitz, MD, of Case Western Reserve University, reported success with collagen hydrolysate for both osteoarthritis and osteoporosis. He, too, found calcitonin plus collagen hydrolysate inhibited bone collagen breakdown better than calcitonin alone, making it "of interest as a therapeutic agent of potential utility in the treatment of osteoarthritis and osteoporosis. Its high level of safety makes it attractive as an agent for long-term use in these chronic disorders."

Bone Building

Today I saw a new gynecologist, a nurse practitioner who had just moved from New Jersey to Florida. She did a fine job with my annual exam and then asked me a few questions. One was "Are you taking a daily calcium supplement for your bones?" "No," I replied. "Oh," she said, "that's dangerous. You need 1200 to 1500 milligrams of calcium a day–" "But," I interrupted her, "I eat bone broth from grass-fed animals all the time. It's part of the Weston A. Price Foundation's recommended diet. That way I get all the bone-building minerals I need, not just one in isolation. Before I started I lost 12 percent of my total bone density in a year, but the next year with the bone broth I gained back 19 percent. I can hardly wait to see what my results will be this year." "You know," she replied, "you're the second person to tell me about bone broth. The other one was an elderly woman from Ecuador who said she put eggs in her broth and eats it on a regular basis."

–Kathy R.,
Winter Haven, Florida

With osteoporosis a threat for forty-four million American men and women over the age of fifty, these findings on collagen need to be taken seriously. For years, osteoporosis prevention relied on calcium alone. The focus then shifted to massive doses of vitamin D plus calcium, perhaps with a complement of trace minerals. But if we look back at the diets of traditional people who retained strong, flexible bones throughout long and productive lives, it's apparent the answer lies in nourishing food, not in pills. While it's fortunate that modern science supports bone building with food-based collagen hydrolysate and gelatin, the better—and tastier—solution is daily bowls of nourishing broth.

CHAPTER 4

Marrow: The Body's Blood Bank

Deep in the center of bones is marrow, a creamy substance valued by our ancestors for its life-giving, reproduction-enhancing, and brain-building fat and cholesterol. As the seedbed of blood and stem cells, it's prized as a sacred, energizing, and regenerative food in native cultures all over the world. When devouring a kill, animals instinctively go for it, first sucking out marrow, then consuming the organ meats, and eating muscle meat last of all. Hunter-gatherers knew just where to tap the femur bone of a large animal to break it open and extract the rope of nutrient-dense marrow.

The word *marrow* is familiar in language and literature as well. Henry David Thoreau famously wrote, "I wanted to live deep and suck out all the marrow of life."

Bone marrow has also played a major role in human evolution. As evolutionary anthropologist Professor Leslie Aiello of University College London puts it: "Bone marrow is highly nutritious, and contains many important elements for brain growth and development. It also takes much less energy to digest than plant food. Scientists have shown that brain size was beginning to increase in the

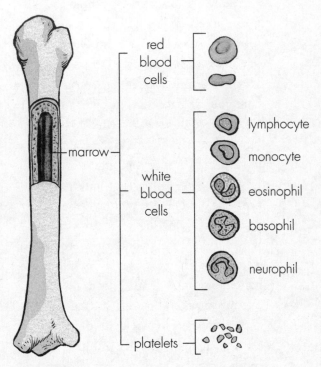

Figure 4: Bone marrow is a soft, spongy tissue found inside bones. Red blood cells, white blood cells, and platelets are produced in the bone marrow.

later australopithecines, and it could all be down to bone marrow as brain food."

With Professor Peter Wheeler of John Moores University in Liverpool, Aiello developed the expensive tissue hypothesis, which holds that humans were able to develop large "metabolically expensive" brains relative to body size because of an equivalent reduction in the size of the gastrointestinal tract. Without the adoption of a high-quality, animal-based diet, this transition would never have been possible.

Although marrowbones have largely disappeared from the modern table, they are just the thing for unapologetic carnivores who like to gnaw, lick, and suck their food and lustily

---

What's in Marrow?

The USDA doesn't provide data on lamb, beef, or big game marrow, much less on the minor amounts hiding in fish or poultry bones. Reports on the amount and type of fat in bone marrow vary considerably, and there are significant differences in marrow type and amount among African ruminants, caribou, grass-fed beef, and factory-farmed beef. Different types of marrow are also found within the same animal. Arctic explorer and ethnologist Vilhjalmur Stefansson (1879–1962) described two types of marrow in his book *The Fat of the Land*. The type from the lower leg was soft and "more like a particularly delicious cream in flavor," while the other from the humerus and femur was "hard and tallowy at room temperatures." The former suggests a marrow higher in monounsaturated fatty acids (MUFAs), the latter higher in saturated fat.

The percentage of fat in bone marrow also decreases with malnutrition and starvation. Indeed, a low level of bone marrow fat is considered a definitive diagnosis of starvation at animal autopsies. Researchers from Purdue found bone marrow averaged 91.54 percent fat in healthy cattle, but in malnourished cattle, the range went from 0.45 to 67.11 percent, with an average of just 18.82 percent.

In 1964, scientists analyzed the phospholipid content of human bone marrow. These make up only a small portion of bone marrow's total lipid content, but they are very important. The team identified many types of choline, of which 44 percent was lecithin and 22 percent a combination of phosphatidylethanolamine (PE) and phosphatidylserine (PS). PE and PS are vital to nervous system function and are found heavily in the white matter of the brain, nerves, neural tissue, and the spinal cord. PS is known to improve brain function and mental acuity and may possibly protect us from MSG toxicity.

As for vitamin and mineral content, the limited data suggest a little iron and phosphorous and almost no calcium in the marrow. Where there's fat, there should be fat-soluble vitamins, but reports of vitamin A in 100 grams of marrow run across the board at 240 IU, 67.2 IU, and 0.4 IU, which is just about zero. For some reason, vitamin D has not been analyzed, but one report has 0.3 mcg of vitamin K in 100 grams of roasted marrow. There's much more research to be done to understand this nourishing substance.

experience an animal's frothy, oily, and musky inner essence. Today marrow is often served in fine restaurants, usually roasted and presented upright to be eaten with little spoons that dig deep into the bone. Marrow may also appear as a rich garnish for filet mignon or as the high point of the Italian dish osso bucco. As an appetizer, it's often spread like butter on pointy pieces of toast. As Anthony Bourdain put it, "If God made butter, it would taste exactly like bone marrow."

Profound Benefits

However we eat it, straight up or dissolved in soup, the health benefits of marrow are profound. Wise tradition tells us so, yet precise and consistent nutritional data are not available.

Whatever's in it, marrow seems to have the right stuff for healing and rejuvenation. Because it hides deep in our bones, few people realize marrow is one of the largest organs in the human body—yes, bone marrow is considered a primary lymphatic organ. Babies start out life entirely with red bone marrow, the place where myeloid stem cells and lymphoid stem cells, precursors to red and white blood cells, are formed. By adulthood half of human bone marrow is yellow, serving primarily as a storage site for fat. Interestingly, with severe blood loss, the body can convert yellow marrow back to red to increase blood cell production. In cases of starvation, the body draws on the fat stores in yellow bone marrow in an attempt to survive.

Stem Cell Regeneration

The most rejuvenating part of bone marrow is its ability to perform hematopoiesis, the process by which stem cells generate the platelets, leukocytes, and erythrocytes needed for coagulation, immunity, and oxygen transport. Add in osteoblasts and osteoclasts for bone building and resorption, fibroblasts for connective tissue, and the hormone osteocalcin to help regulate blood sugar and fat deposition, and it's evident why marrow is revered in many cultures as the very source of life.

Bovine marrow and spleen also contain high levels of a class of lipids important in cell membranes known as alkylglycerols (AKGs). AKGs serve as powerful immune system boosters, helping us fight infectious diseases and even cancer. The AKG story began in Stockholm in 1952, when Dr. Astrid Brohult got the bright idea of serving bone marrow soup to children suffering from leukemia, a cancer that develops in or spreads to the bone marrow. Although the children improved dramatically, they strongly disliked the soup. Dr. Brohult and her husband, Dr. Sven Brohult, then determined to identify the active component found in bone marrow. A decade later, they identified it as AKG and shifted their research interest from bone marrow to shark liver oil, a concentrated source well suited to supplement manufacture.

Today research on bone marrow stem cells represents some of the most far-ranging work in modern science. Stem cells can be transformed into functional neural cells and have been used to treat irritable bowel syndrome, ischemic heart disease, and HIV; they are injected into patients seeking renewed vitality and eternal youth at anti-aging clinics. While Father Technology's high-tech stem cell treatments offer the excitement of promise, Mother Nature's low-tech bone broth is safe, effective, and available to all of us here and now.

Lupus and Rheumatoid Arthritis

I have lupus and rheumatoid arthritis. I was forty-two, the mother of four children, very healthy and into yoga and martial arts when my world came crashing down in 2002. I was then diagnosed with a pericardial effusion, which is a lot of fluid and inflammation around the heart. I had major surgery and was told to accept a "new normal" for my life. That was not easy because I was put on very bad meds—prednisone was the least of it. The chemotherapy drugs ruined my life. I lost everything I knew as normal. I lost my husband, my friends, my ability to parent properly...the ability to do much at all. The only thing I gained was sixty pounds from the prednisone, which kept me alive, and I use the term *alive* loosely because it was more like existing as a zombie. I landed in the hospital many times, sometimes every two weeks. I had a TIA (transient ischemic attack) and organ failures and felt every part of my body crashing in. I finally went off the steroids and chemo because of these side effects, but I was also nervous about developing leukemia or bone cancer down the road. I said to my doctors, "Kill me now."

The pericardial effusion was my first symptom of lupus. Rheumatoid arthritis followed. This all started with an outbreak at my daughter's school of something called fifth disease. It's normally a minor infection for children, but when it happens to adults, it can be severe. It has the effect of switching the immune system on, and then it's always on. I also got mycoplasma pneumonia, also called walking pneumonia. Mycoplasma are neither viruses nor bacteria. They mutate, they change. They are almost impossible to get rid of and are a probable cause of autoimmune disorders. I got help from a cutting-edge doctor who knew of Dr. Tom Brown's protocols and put me on the antibiotic doxycycline. I stayed on it for three years. It helped the lupus and RA a lot, but my digestive tract ended up overwhelmed.

In 2012, I started practicing yoga again in an amazing studio in Aventura, Florida, which I had founded myself years before. Out of the blue, I ran into my former student Diego Rutenberg. He took one look at me, pulled me aside—pulled me hard—and said, "You have to listen to me." He told me about broth and using its cartilage, which was something I could relate to because I'd loved to chew on bones as a child. He told me about functional medicine and how I had to go see Shantih Coro. I did. Shantih's program for me included custom probiotics, cod liver oil, fermented vegetables, and other things, but mostly a lot of broth. I had to commit, and I did everything without fail. For months and months I lived on broth with well-boiled vegetables like my grandmother used to make. I ate marrow and it was delicious. I loved the broth so much I got addicted. I lost weight. I could tell I was losing toxicity too. My color was better, stomach pains gone, and ability to do yoga returned. Today I am in remission, and that fact alone tells you everything.

—*Carla Berkowitz,*
Aventura, Florida

Dr. Weston A. Price learned marrow was highly prized by Native Americans of the North. "It is important that skeletons are rarely found where large game animals have been slaughtered by the Indians of the North. The skeletal remains are found as piles of finely broken bone chips or splinters that have been cracked up to obtain as much as possible of the marrow and nutritive qualities of the bones. These Indians obtain their fat-soluble vitamins and also most of their minerals from the organs of the animals. An important part of the nutrition of the children consisted in various preparations of bone marrow, both as a substitute for milk and as a special dietary ration."

When Price devised a nutrition plan for an orphanage, the meal included bone marrow. "About four ounces of tomato juice or orange juice and a teaspoonful of a mixture of equal parts of a very high vitamin natural cod liver oil and an especially high vitamin butter was given at the beginning of the meal. They then received a bowl containing approximately a pint of a very rich vegetable and meat stew, made largely from bone marrow and fine cuts of tender meat."

CHAPTER 5

Conditional Protein Power

When consumed as part of a rich and varied traditional diet, broth improves overall protein digestion and assimilation. It helps the body build collagen and cartilage, needed for the health of skin, joints, and bones. And it also serves as a "protein sparer," which means we can cut back on the complete proteins we would otherwise need to eat.

Despite these strengths, broth is often dismissed as a "poor protein" because it's not a complete protein. That's true, and that is the reason we should not attempt to survive on broth alone.

From the eighteenth to the early twentieth centuries, public health authorities enlisted top scientists to turn broth—or, more accurately, its chief constituent, gelatin—into a complete protein that could be cheaply manufactured and fed to the masses. They tried adding all sorts of substances, including tyrosine and other amino acids, whey or casein powders, and eventually even soy protein. The attempts proved inadequate, too expensive, or both, and efforts to turn gelatin into a cheap and portable superfood that could feed soldiers at war, disaster victims, and the poor were eventually scrapped.

Nearly all the cases in which gelatin caused health problems occurred when the subjects were fed excessive amounts of gelatin and little else. This happened quite frequently during the early to mid-nineteenth century when people running hospitals, soup kitchens, and poorhouses tried to economize by serving gelatin at every meal in the form of bouillon, gelatinous biscuits, and other gelatin-based edibles—or inedibles as the case may be. Gelatin bashers have long been fond of pointing out that dogs have died after a few weeks on a gelatin diet. But while it was true that the dogs died in one research study, Dr. Nathan R. Gotthoffer argued in his 1945 book *Gelatin in Nutrition and Medicine* that "no account was taken of the fact that the animals refused to eat the food after a few days."

Clearly science has proven we can't live on broth alone, but much research supports its health-giving role in a rich and varied diet. Gelatin increases the utilization of the protein in wheat, oats, and barley. It also improves the digestibility of beans, proving the traditional wisdom of cooking bean soups with hocks. Furthermore, gelatin improves the digestibility of meat protein in soups and stews or when served with gravy, as is the custom with many culinary traditions around the world.

The "sparing" effects of gelatin on protein were of particular interest to many early researchers. By sparing protein, they meant that the body is less likely to cannibalize the protein stored in its own muscles, a common occurrence during fasting or during rapid weight loss from illness. Because gelatin-rich broth diminishes the amount of complete protein needed by the body, it can reduce the strain on the digestive system. It is a healing food for convalescents and helps prevent unwanted weight loss and loss of muscle that occurs when the body goes out of nitrogen balance and cannibalizes the protein stored in its own muscles. In 1872, Carl von Voit, a German researcher who spent ten years studying gelatin, concluded gelatin prevented breakdown of protein in the body because it was itself decomposed. He found it could exert "remarkable sparing powers," but cautioned, however, that gelatin alone could not build up protein supplies in the body. For that, high-quality animal protein is required.

Our Need for Protein

We need high-quality protein in our diets for growth, repair, immune function, hormone formation, and all metabolic processes. Our bodies contain more than 50,000 types of proteins, all built from the building blocks known as amino acids. Nine of these amino acids are considered "essential" for humans because we cannot manufacture them on our own and must obtain them from the diet. They are histidine, isoleucine, leucine, lysine, methionine, phenylalanine, threonine, tryptophan, and valine. Arginine is considered essential for

babies and children. If these essential amino acids are present in sufficient quantities, we can build the "nonessential" amino acids, but if one or more are missing, the body will fail to synthesize many of the enzymes and antibodies and the other proteins it needs.

Protein synthesis breaks down not only when the essential amino acids are absent but also when supplies are low. We tend to lose the ability to produce sufficient amounts during periods of infection, chronic poor health, or physical or mental duress, or during the rapid growth expected of infants and children. Consequently, many scientists believe we need to obtain many more amino acids than the ones considered essential, and that at least eight other amino acids should be considered "conditionally essential." These include arginine, glycine, proline, glutamine, tyrosine, serine, cysteine, and taurine.

Traditionally animal products such as eggs, milk, fish, poultry, and meat have served as valued sources of the best proteins. These nutrient-dense foods contain a complete set of the essential amino acids in desirable proportions. In contrast, plant proteins are incomplete because they are low or missing some of the essential amino acids. It only takes a shortage of one of these to slow down or even shut down the body's protein manufacturing process. In soybeans and other legumes, the limiting amino acid is methionine. In grains, it is lysine.

Gelatin—as well as gelatin-rich bone broth—also has limiting amino acids, namely tryptophan, which goes missing, and histidine, tyrosine, and cysteine, which are low. Consequently, the ideal way to consume broth is in the form of soups and stews that also include high-quality animal products such as fish, meat, organ meats, poultry, eggs, or dairy, or in sauces and gravies on meat and fish.

Consumed alone, gelatin is obviously an incomplete protein. "An unquestionably poor protein," warn the writers of the popular textbook *Nutrition for Living*. Homemade broth is obviously better than a gelatin product, but even the best-quality broth cannot prevent malnutrition if people are starving from insufficient quantities of food or short of enough high-quality protein because of a high-carbohydrate diet. Such people need to consume broth along with more and better food.

Adding broth to the menu, however, can improve the health of people on South Beach, Zone, or other lean protein plans that promote the consumption of skinless, boneless chicken breasts, lean burgers, and chops and steaks trimmed of fat, skin, cartilage, and bones. Recommendations to eat only lean meat go against the ancestral wisdom of eating all parts of the animal, not just the muscle meat.

The Methionine Problem

What's wrong with muscle meats alone? Muscle meats are high in methionine, an essential amino acid that can contribute to excessive methylation in the body. Methylation refers to a complicated biochemical process involving transfers of methyl groups. It goes on in every cell of the body and when overdone can contribute to premature aging and other health problems.

The solution is not to avoid muscle meats entirely, but to balance them out by eating parts of the animal rich in proline and glycine, including the skin, cartilage, and bones. Eating liver and other organ meats provides rich stores of vitamin C and other vitamins and minerals needed for collagen and cartilage production. Proponents of plant-based diets correctly warn about the grave dangers of excess methionine but fail to recognize the fact that their recommendations lead to excess methylation as well because although their foods are low in methionine, they are also low in proline and glycine. Balance is key.

The healing power of broth is so dependent on proline, glycine, glutamine, and alanine that we'll discuss these four amino acids in depth in the next chapter. Their vital roles in gut health, immune system support, blood-sugar balancing, muscle building, healthy bones and joints, and smooth skin, as well as overall healing and rejuvenation, make them conditionally essential for life but absolutely essential for radiant good health.

CHAPTER 6

Four Key Amino Acids

Textbooks tell us that proline, glycine, glutamine, and alanine, the four main amino acids in broth, are nonessential amino acids. This means the body, theoretically at least, can manufacture them as needed. The ability to manufacture them easily and abundantly, however, is probably true only of people enjoying radiant good health.

Broth's collagen and cartilage-building strength comes from its rich content of proline and glycine. Proline and glycine are the keys to the tensile strength, resilience, and water-holding capacity of healthy collagen and cartilage, as discussed in chapters 1 and 2. Common sense suggests that the millions of people suffering from stiff joints, skin diseases, and many other disorders related to collagen, connective tissue, and cartilage are simply not healthy enough to manufacture sufficient proline and glycine.

Research on proline and glycine is far from a growth industry, but several studies clarify the essential nature of these supposedly nonessential aminos. Most of the research indicates that proline and glycine should at the very least be considered conditionally essential,

meaning that under most conditions, the body cannot make enough of these compounds and must get them from food. Let's look at proline first.

Proline for Healthy Collagen and Cartilage

When individuals in normal health are put on proline-free diets, their plasma levels fall by 20 to 30 percent. While this is obviously a highly artificial situation, it does suggest the body cannot produce proline in sufficient quantities without dietary assistance. Proline is found in virtually all animal and plant proteins except lactalbumin, so deficiency should be rare when people obtain enough to eat. However, individuals will show low proline levels if they consume too little protein, a possibility among people on high-carbohydrate, low-protein, low-fat, or vegan diets. For most of these individuals, the way to bring proline consumption up to par is obvious—add good-quality animal protein to the diet. Curiously, some people on high-protein diets also suffer a proline shortfall, not because proline doesn't exist in their foods, but because there's too little compared to the excess methionine in their diets, a problem discussed in chapter 5.

People can also become proline deficient if their bodies are unable to metabolize proline into the active form of hydroxyproline because of vitamin C deficiency. Iron is another needed cofactor, and vitamin C is well known to improve iron assimilation. We need hydroxyproline along with lysine to make collagen and cartilage.

Glycine for Healthy Blood, Fat Digestion, Detoxification... and More

Glycine is the other important conditionally essential amino acid found abundantly in broth. It is the simplest of all the amino acids, and serves as the basic module for the manufacture of other amino acids. Researchers consider it to be conditionally essential because of its vital role in the synthesis of hemoglobin (for healthy blood); creatine (for supplying energy to our cells); porphyrin (also for healthy blood); bile salts (for digesting fat); glutathione (for detoxification); and DNA and RNA. Glycine is also involved in glucose manufacture, and low levels contribute to hypoglycemia. It furthermore reduces inflammation throughout the body and has shown potential for treating a wide variety of diseases currently treated with anti-inflammatory drugs.

Adequately nourished people should not be deficient in glycine, but compromised status is common when the body has increased needs, such as during pregnancy, infection, or illness. Because the glycine needs of the growing fetus are very high—both in absolute terms and relative to the other amino acids—glycine status is considered an important marker of a normal pregnancy. Glycine is the go-to amino acid that must be obtained through food or supplements if children are to recover from malnutrition. For people suffering from sickle cell disease, the ongoing disintegration of red blood cells creates a high demand for glycine, far beyond what the body can produce internally.

In terms of digestion, glycine contributes to gastric acid secretion, a fact that has led doctors to recommend it for patients with acid reflux and other gastrointestinal disorders. Aging, genetics, use of certain medications, and a variety of other factors decrease digestive ability and increase the need for glycine.

Glycine also plays a vital role in wound healing, which is a time when the body has increased needs, is under extreme stress, and cannot make all it needs. When researchers at Rutgers University fed rats supplements of glycine plus arginine or glycine plus ornithine, they found the glycine-plus-arginine combination significantly improved nitrogen retention in both traumatized and nontraumatized rats. The researchers theorized the glycine-arginine combo was the most helpful because both "occur in particularly high concentrations in skin and connective tissue and might, therefore, be required in greater amounts for tissue repair." They further speculated that the beneficial effect of arginine-plus-glycine is "related to the creatine synthesis needed for wound healing." These findings support the idea that broth could be helpful as well; broth not only is high in glycine but also contains more than adequate arginine.

The human body requires copious amounts of glycine for detoxification of mercury, lead, cadmium, and other toxic metals, pesticides, and industrial chemicals. Glycine is a precursor amino acid needed for glutathione, a powerful cancer-curbing, age-slowing antioxidant, needed among many other things for liver detoxification.

Scientists have also shown supplemental glycine can improve methylation, reducing high homocysteine levels, which, in turn, could reduce our risk of heart disease, cancer, premature aging, and other health problems.

To meet so many and diverse metabolic demands, glycine must be readily available. The body can make it, obviously, but there are plenty of reasons to think that even healthy people might not be able to make enough, especially during periods of stress such as pregnancy, injury, and exposure to toxins. It serves many metabolic functions in the body, and unless people enjoy a diet rich in broth, it's not likely to be present in sufficient quantity.

Glutamine: Gut Health, Immunity, and More

The third most common amino acid in broth is glutamine. This, too, is a nonessential amino acid with well-recognized, health-giving potential. Ideally it's produced abundantly in our muscles and released to all parts of our bodies that need it. In reality, most people are so stressed out mentally and physically that they benefit from increasing their dietary sources of glutamine.

Glutamine becomes a conditionally essential amino acid whenever cell proliferation is desirable. It's vital to gut health because gut cells turn over rapidly and prefer feeding on glutamine over any other amino acid. Glutamine helps the villi of the small intestine to heal and grow, an important consideration for people suffering from malabsorption from the flattened villi caused by celiac or other gut diseases. Glutamine's gut-healing capacity has helped heal ulcers, irritable bowel syndrome, colitis, and Crohn's disease.

> ## Multiple Sclerosis
>
> I am a retired RN and have had multiple sclerosis for twenty-three years. Recently my friend told me about bone broth, but I pooh-poohed it, as it sounded like too much work. I only have so much energy with this illness. Then I visited her and was surprised at how beautiful and youthful she appeared. She had had chronic health issues but was no longer using a walker or cane. I wanted to know what medications she was on. She told me it was just the bone broth! I was quite surprised, to be honest, but have always believed in the power and possibilities of healthy food. I had always had a love for big salads and had consumed minimal amounts of meat but came to realize this wasn't helping me. I have a small frame and also live in Wisconsin, where it's cold for many months. I was in a rough place, so I finally decided to get serious about incorporating the soup into my diet. I left salads behind and now eat steamed vegetables with fish or meat and drink one cup of the soup two to three times daily before meals. It is warming and good. I am very respectful of the soup and visualize daily that it is helping me become healthier and stronger. And it is.
>
> *—Ellen B. Drury,*
> *Milwaukee, Wisconsin*

Glutamine stimulates immune cells, causing the proliferation of lymphocytes (a type of white blood cell); the production of cytokines (involved in cell signaling); the killing of bacteria by neutrophils (another type of white blood cells); and phagocytic and secretory activities by macrophages (white blood cells that ingest foreign material). Along with proline and glycine, it enhances recovery from injuries, wounds, burns, stress, post-surgery trauma, and most major illnesses. Patients whose diets have been supplemented with glutamine show quicker recoveries and earlier hospital releases.

Glutamine also supports liver health and detoxification. Along with cysteine and glycine, we need glutamine to produce glutathione, the master antioxidant so important for liver detoxification.

Soup is frequently prescribed for weight loss. Although most of the popular diet books talk about filling up with soup to eat less, the more complete and scientific explanation is that glutamine not only boosts metabolism but cuts cravings for sugar and carbohydrates. In fact, the research shows that glutamine is helpful for anyone with addiction problems, whether to sugar, alcohol, or drugs. We also have evidence that the glutamine in broth is the main protein-sparing factor, allowing us to stay healthy while eating smaller amounts of muscle-meat protein.

Glutamine helps people who need to lose weight, but it is even better at helping convalescents and others who have become too thin to put weight on or keep it on. Because much of the glutamine in the body is made and stored in muscles, extra glutamine prevents the muscle wasting and atrophy associated with illness. Glutamine can even counter some of the severe side effects of chemotherapy, bone marrow transplants, traumatic wounds, and surgery. In terms of side effects from chemotherapy, glutamine supplements have soothed swelling inside the mouth, alleviated nerve pain, and stopped diarrhea, muscle wasting, and unwanted weight loss.

For fitness buffs, glutamine stimulates muscle building and repair. It's a popular supplement for overtraining syndrome, in which an overworked body cannot produce enough glutamine on its own. Declining stores of glutamine are also associated with an increase in the rate of infection among athletes, further suggesting our need for this "nonessential" amino acid.

Finally, glutamine is a "brain food" that crosses the blood-brain barrier. Its presence in broth is one explanation why broth can help people turn around depression, irritability, anxiety, mood swings, and even conditions like ADD and ADHD. It has helped neurological diseases such as epilepsy and Parkinson's disease as well. What's more, it helps people calm down and sleep well. Given that broth is devoid of tryptophan, the essential amino acid most associated with sleep, a cream soup offers the best of both worlds—glycine and glutamine from the broth and tryptophan from the milk or cream.

Sadly, more and more people today, including many autistic children, react poorly to glutamine in the diet, even as found in traditional foods such as bone broth. This is such an important topic that we discuss it in depth in the boxed text on pages 40–41.

Long-Cooked Versus Short-Cooked Broth

The top four amino acids found in bone broth are glycine, glutamic acid (glutamine), proline, and alanine. The amino acid levels are about three times higher in the long-cooked broth than in the short-cooked broth. The samples tested here came from broth prepared from pastured chickens. Similar amino acid patterns have been found in all bone broths and in gelatin products. The results suggest that those sensitive to glutamine should consume only short-cooked broth until the condition clears.

Amino Acids in 24 Fluid Ounces of Chicken Bone Broths

Amino Acids	Long-Cooked Broth (mg)	Short-Cooked Broth (mg)
Aspartic acid	1660	483
Threonine	642	211
Serine	728	257
Glutamic acid	3040	1100
Proline	2960	727
Glycine	5320	1350
Alanine	2320	643
Valine	543	191
Isoleucine	395	129
Leucine	829	277
Tyrosine	229	102
Phenylalanine	577	170
Lysine	909	383
Histidine	281	296
Arginine	2090	512
Cystine	<72.1	<71.3
Methionine	289	78.4

Both the long- and short-term broths were prepared by Kim Schuette of Biodynamic Wellness, Solana Beach, California. Certificate of Analyses from Covance Laboratories, August 12, 2013, report numbers 852397-0 and 352398-0.

Alanine: For Athletes and Anti-Aging

The fourth most prevalent amino acid in broth is alanine, a nonessential amino acid that has roles in liver function, glycolysis, gluconeogenesis (production of glucose), and the citric acid cycle. Although easily made by a healthy body, many athletes and body-builders take extra for endurance and the building of muscle mass. Extra can also be useful to improve physical functioning in the elderly. Alanine has been proposed as an anti-aging compound, though more research is needed.

The Takeaway

The exact levels and ratios of amino acids found in broth depend on the type of broth, the recipe, the source of the ingredients, its concentration, and other factors, However it is made, broth always comes up high in proline, glycine, glutamine, and alanine, low in cysteine, tyrosine, and histidine, and missing the essential amino acid tryptophan. This leads some people to worry about the best way to compensate. No problem. We can easily get all the amino acids we need simply by adding meat, poultry, fish, dairy, and vegetables and grains to our soups and stews. Or turn it into sauce or gravy to accompany meat with other foods in a rich and varied omnivorous diet.

Bones to Pick with the Lead in Bone Broth Study

Early in 2013, a study out of the UK about lead in chicken broth ruffled a lot of feathers, and unfortunately is still scaring people away from broth. The study, which appeared in the journal *Medical Hypotheses*, reported that broth made from organic chickens was contaminated with lead, one of the deadliest toxic metals known.

That was scary news, and if the study were valid, there would be plenty of reason for concern. Lead, after all, is a neurotoxin that can cross the placenta and blood-brain barrier. It is associated with abnormal fetal development as well as a very long list of neurobehavioral disorders and diseases in children and adults, including ADHD, violence, social withdrawal, depression, substance abuse, and Parkinson's disease.

The study left a flock of unanswered questions, starting with the type of cookware and the broth ingredients and ending with a need for more details about the source of those "organic chickens," the feed they were fed, the water they drank, whether they were free range or confined, where they were raised, and what their living conditions were. All the article reported was they were "organic birds." Soon after the article's publication, we discussed all of these issues in depth in an article at the Weston A. Price Foundation's website. Then, six months after the study was published, the researchers discovered the chickens were not organic after all, thus proving a whole lot of people had been alarmed unnecessarily. In the meantime, we tested chicken and beef broth made from pastured chickens and cows raised at several locations in California and found undetectable levels of lead, even at five parts per billion.

The takeaway? The lead/broth flap was a lot of clucked-up nonsense. But take care with the source of your broth.

The Downside of Glutamine: The MSG Connection

Despite its many virtues, glutamine has risks. High supplemental doses as taken by some bodybuilders have caused dizziness, headaches, and neurological problems. But it's not just people going overboard with supplements who are reacting poorly to glutamine. Many people today are having problems metabolizing it properly, a problem caused by multiple factors, ranging from vitamin B_6 deficiency to lead toxicity to the widespread use of MSG in our food supply.

The problem develops when glutamine gets past the blood-brain barrier and is metabolized to glutamate. In healthy individuals this does not happen willy-nilly but is tightly controlled by the body. Glutamine converts as needed to either glutamate, which can excite neurons, or to GABA, which has a calming effect. Both are needed by the body and brain. The glutamine found naturally in healthy foods such as homemade bone broth should not be a problem, but all bets are off if MSG in the diet has led to glutamate buildup and excitotoxicity.

MSG (monosodium glutamate) differs from glutamate by a single sodium atom (monosodium) attached to the molecule. Although many people think of MSG solely as a flavor enhancer added to Chinese foods, it is widely added to processed, packaged, and fast foods (including soy protein and other plant-based meat substitutes) to "wake up" flavors. It hides on ingredient lists under aliases such as autolyzed yeast extract, natural and artificial flavorings, hydrolyzed protein, protein isolates, and spices. Some of the MSG is added, but much is a residue of hydrolyzing and other modern processing methods. Commercial broths and bouillons almost always contain MSG.

MSG, of course, differs from the naturally occurring glutamine produced in the body and found in real foods. If we didn't need glutamine, we wouldn't make it ourselves, and if we didn't need glutamate we wouldn't have

Health Restored

In October 2011, my husband was deathly ill. He was down to 115 pounds with chronic pneumonia, thyroid problems, several types of anemia, and other problems, and had been sliding downhill for six years. We had seen many doctors including specialists and naturopaths, and spent tens of thousands of dollars on tests without finding any answers. The lack of any diagnosis resulted in lots of drugs to treat the separate symptoms, but nothing helped. After I was given the book *Nourishing Traditions* by a WAPF member in our church, we began drinking lots and lots of broth. My husband has now gained thirty pounds and is back to work as a self-employed contractor out working in the weather. He is not 100 percent well, but he has a new normal. We have glutamate receptors throughout the body and brain. MSG, on the other hand, is a potentially dangerous excitotoxin that builds up in the body and brain.

Sadly, some people sensitive to MSG react poorly to broth. Autistic children and others with sensitive and damaged guts often react to it even though they desperately need the gut healing that glutamine could assist. Some of these people are so sensitive they react not only to broth but to any good dietary source of glutamine, including beef, chicken, fish, eggs, and dairy products.

What to do? The GAPS (Gut and Psychology Syndrome) diet relies heavily on broth for its healing benefit for children with autism and other disorders, but Natasha Campbell-McBride, MD, author of *Gut and Psychology Syndrome*, starts many patients out with a lightly cooked bone broth, progressing over time to long-cooked bone broth. The glutamine content of broth increases with cooking time. And as we show in the table on page 38, the levels of all other amino acids also increase, making long-cooked bone broth preferable for all who can tolerate it.

Appropriate supplementation and detoxification may help sensitive people handle glutamine. People with severe MSG sensitivity are often low in vitamin B_6 and too sick to convert it to the active form of pyridoxal-5-phosphate (p5p). Becoming replete in B_6 and the other B vitamins may help. So might glycine supplementation. Glutamine sensitivity can also come from lead toxicity, widespread today due to lead contamination in much of our food supply. Working with a health practitioner on eliminating lead and other toxic metals from the body might be in order. Reducing exposure from lead in food and the environment is also critical. Lead is also a problem with chickens grown on lead-contaminated soil, a problem that can result in high lead content in eggs, meat, and bone broth (see "Bones to Pick with the Lead in Bone Broth Study" on page 39).

—◦—

six children between two and ten years old. At first we had dismissed a lot of his "tiredness" to having small children. I am seriously motivated to keep him around. His recovery has been 100 percent from diet!

–Deanne Yoder,
Molalla, Oregon

CHAPTER 7

Proteoglycans: Sweet on Collagen, Cartilage, and Bones

In the 1930s, Dr. Francis Pottenger concluded that the healing power of broth came from its hydrophilic, water-loving nature. Every pot of properly made broth is full of huge, water-trapping molecules known as proteoglycans, a word that derives from *proteo*, meaning "of protein," and *glykos*, meaning "sweet." Proteoglycans wind over, under, and around the collagenous fiber networks that appear in skin, cartilage, and bones. Their principal job is to get and hold water. They are very, very thirsty.

The Goo Molecule for Lubrication and Shock Absorption

Hyaluronic acid (HA) is a type of proteoglycan known as the "goo molecule." It's comprised of thousands of the protein sugars known as GAGs and found just about everywhere in the human body. HA goo is the key to broth that gels.

HA lubricates and cushions joints, muscles, bones, and other movable parts, and is a major component of synovial fluid. Elbows, knees, and other joints are surrounded by

---◦---

Structured Like a Christmas Tree

Jiggly yet structured, proteoglycan molecules are a primary component of the matrix or filler substance that exists between cells. Proteoglycans resemble freshly cut Christmas trees with a central trunk and bushy branches. Hyaluronic acid forms the trunk, and the sulfur-containing molecules chondroitin sulfate and keratan sulfate make up the branches. All are a type of mucosaccharide known as glycosaminoglycans (GAGs). Mucopolysaccharides are long chains of sugar molecules tricked out with some amino acids. In electrical terms, the chondroitin sulfate and keratan sulfate molecules carry negative charges and repel each other. By keeping their distance from one another, they keep cartilage plump and create space for the water they need to attract and hold.

---◦---

a capsule that secretes synovial fluid. A key function of this viscous fluid is shock absorption to prevent wear and tear on the joint. Because healthy cartilage has no blood vessels, synovial fluid carries nutrients to the cartilage and removes waste from the joint capsule.

HA abounds in the gristle known as hyaline cartilage. Indeed, hyaline is short for hyaluronic acid. Hyaline cartilage covers the ends of the long bones where articulation occurs and provides a cushioning effect for the bones. Hyaline cartilage also supports the tip of the nose, connects the ribs to the sternum, and forms most of the larynx and supporting cartilage of the trachea and bronchial tubes in the lungs.

Every cell in the body contains some HA, but it's concentrated in skin tissue. It is found in the deep underlying dermal areas as well as the visible epidermal top layers. That means it is also concentrated in the "skin" tissue that lines the intestinal tract. The HA provides continuous moisture by binding up to a thousand times its weight in water. With age and ill health, the ability of the skin to produce HA decreases. The general public knows HA best for its use in cosmetics, particularly in creams for "intense hydration" and "lip plumping."

Because HA lives three days or less in most of the body and less than a day in the skin, the body needs to make a lot of it—and often. Giving the body the raw materials it needs to make HA by including a lot of broth in the diet is clearly a good policy and a recipe for radiant skin.

For use in medicine, HA was once extracted from rooster combs but now tends to be manufactured in labs using a strain of *Bacillus subtilis* genetically modified to yield maximum hyaluronan content. It's often incorporated into skin lotions for eczema, psoriasis, and other itchy, dry skin conditions; incorporated into scaffolding applied to wounds postoperatively to speed healing; and injected right into the joints of arthritis patients. Without HA, there would be fewer successful cataract operations, corneal transplants, detached retina repairs, and other eye surgeries.

Astonishingly, modern medicine may soon promote HA to improve our sex lives. In the May 2013 issue of the *International Journal of Impotence Research*, we learn that 110 "Italian stallions" underwent injections of HA into the penis to increase volume and circumference, prevent premature ejaculation, and improve overall sexual satisfaction. According to their doctors at the Centro di Medicina Sessuale in Milan, both the men and their partners concluded the procedure was worth it and that size really does matter.

Glucosamine Creates and Renews Cartilage

Glucosamine is a natural constituent of GAGs, made up from glucose (the principal sugar the body uses for fuel) and glutamine (a conditionally essential amino acid found abundantly in broth). The body uses up glucosamine when it creates and renews cartilage, intervertebral discs, and synovial fluid. Glucosamine is best known as a supplement that helps repair cartilage, decrease inflammation, alleviate joint pain, and increase range of motion, but it has many other uses as well.

In the gut, glucosamine helps repair the defensive barrier in the mucosa called the glycosaminoglycan layer, or GAG layer. Defects in the GAG layer of the intestines contribute to autism, Crohn's disease, rheumatoid arthritis, and other autoimmune disorders. In the bladder, defects in the GAG layer contribute to interstitial cystitis. All of these conditions seem to improve with the help of GAG-rich bone broth.

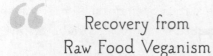

Recovery from Raw Food Veganism

I am from Romania, and am currently studying in the United States to become a health coach and spread the word about traditional food. For me, bone broth has played a big part in my full recovery from a year on a high raw vegan diet. I realized what a big mistake the raw food diet was when I saw my twenty-two-month-old baby daughter start to get brown stains on her front teeth. Shortly after introducing the broth and other traditional foods, her tooth decay stopped. She still has the stains, but the rest of her teeth are perfect.

I am convinced that the bone broth keeps us away from colds, even when all the children around are on antibiotics and coughing. While we were on the raw foods diet, my daughter would get colds easily. She also now prefers to be very lightly dressed, even during winter. For me there is no more pain in the joints of my toes, which surely occurred from the lack of bones and cartilage in my raw foods diet. I have also gotten rid of a very upsetting eczema on both my palms, which had also developed under the raw foods diet.

Best of all, I am seven months pregnant with my second child, who was conceived on our very first try. My daughter, who is now three years old, was conceived with difficulty after several years of trying. At that time I was eating pretty much a traditional diet, though always careful not to eat much fat. My pregnancy is going really well and my body is stronger than ever. Bone broth is one of the foods that we have on our table every single day, especially as a soup made with vegetables, meat, and eggs, and soured with borscht (a fermented liquid made mainly from grains). We make chicken, pork, duck, and veal bone broth on a regular basis. We also enjoy chicken and pork meat jelly.

–Simona D.,
Bucharest, Romania

Galactosamine for Immunity

Galactosamine, the other sugar found in GAGs, is less well known but promoted as able to slow down tumor growth and enhance cellular communication. Changes in glycosylation involving galactosamine are associated with the immune complex formation found in autoimmune disorders such as rheumatoid arthritis. Low levels of it have been associated with heart disease.

Glucosamine and galactosamine together would appear to help the immune system to normalize, whether it needs calming because it is overactive or needs boosting because it is underactive. Amply present in collagen, cartilage, and broth itself, these saccharides offer help to people suffering from osteoarthritis, autoimmune disorders, infectious diseases, and even cancer.

Chondroitin Sulfate Cushions and Protects Cartilage

Chondroitin is a large, gel-forming molecule that cushions cartilage and protects it from compression. It is a key proteoglycan found in cartilage and widely sold along with glucosamine as an osteoarthritis remedy. Critics contend that chondroitin is too large to

The Body's Many Sugars

Glucosamine and galactosamine are metabolic derivatives of N-acetylglucosamine and N-acetylgalactosamine, two of eight sugars that a few scientists and many multilevel marketers consider essential. The others are glucose, mannose, galactose, xylose, fucose, and N-acetylneuraminic acid. The body needs these sugars to form glycoproteins (sugars with protein, including proteoglycans, a glycoprotein with extra sugars) and glycolipids (sugars with fats).

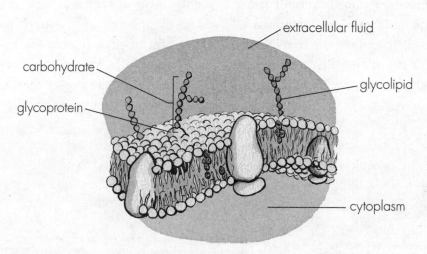

Figure 5: Glyconutrients: Glycoproteins (sugars with protein) and glycolipids (sugars with fat) are little antennae that stick out from the surface of every one of fifty trillion or so cells in the body. They perform many functions including the sending, receiving, and coding of information.

Hunter-gatherers ate plenty of the insects, leaves, roots, mushrooms, and seaweeds that contain these essential sugars, but such foods tend to be scarce in the modern diet. In theory the body can produce needed saccharides from glucose, but in practice production can slow down or even fail if the body is inadequately nourished, sick, or stressed.

In their search for good health, many people today have chosen to supplement with beta glucans, maitake D-fraction, mannose, larch bark extract, aloe vera, inulin, and other saccharide-rich products. Foodwise, good sources are reishi, maitake, shiitake, and cordyceps mushrooms, garlic and onions, coconut meat, oatmeal, the pectins in fruits such as apples and grapefruit, chitin from the shells of insects and crustaceans, and breast milk. Glucosamine and galactosamine are present in good old-fashioned bone broth.

be absorbed, yet it seems to be absorbed sufficiently to make a difference for those seeking arthritis cures. As a supplement, chondroitin derives from the cartilage of cows, pigs, poultry, or fish, although some manufacturers are pulling it from algae. In the diet, we get chondroitin sulfate every time we chew the gristle on a drumstick or partake of cartilage-rich bone broth.

Proteoglycans are valued for their mucopolysaccharide content, but sulfur—as in glucosamine sulfate and chondroitin sulfate—deserves credit as well. People suffering from osteoarthritis and other chronic diseases rapidly turn over sulfur supplies in the body.

Sulfur deficiency then inhibits GAG production, and a vicious cycle begins. Sulfur deficiency is widespread today because of foods grown on depleted soil and plant-based diet fads.

Clearly, science supports glucosamine, GAGs, and goo for health, healing, and anti-aging. But why settle for fractions that have been pilled, patented, and packaged for profit when nourishing bone broth offers proteoglycans and much, much more? "Just a spoonful of sugar makes the medicine go down" sang Julie Andrews in *Mary Poppins*. In broth, the complex sugars known as proteoglycans are part of the medicine.

PART II

The Healing Power of Broth

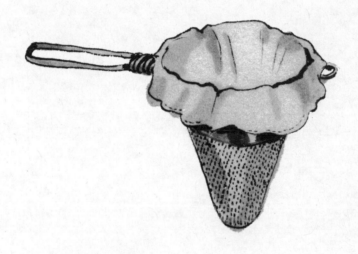

CHAPTER 8

Research Pioneers

Now that we have looked at the individual components of broth, it's time to turn our attention to broth's healing powers—how it can help prevent and control arthritis, bone loss, digestive disorders, skin problems, and even cancer and mental illness. We owe much of our knowledge to two pioneers, Nathan R. Gotthoffer, PhD, and John F. Prudden, MD. As we will discuss, the work of these mostly forgotten researchers may be old but should never be forgotten. Indeed, their findings could help millions of people whose health challenges have not resolved with pharmaceuticals and who could benefit from a return to a real foods diet rich in old-fashioned broth or its descendant gelatin.

Gotthoffer and Gelatin Research

Nathan R. Gotthoffer, PhD, spent eighteen years digging up nineteenth- and early twentieth–century studies from the heyday of gelatin. He analyzed these studies for his book *Gelatin in Nutrition and Medicine*, published in 1945. Dr. Gotthoffer concluded that the research was inconsistent and contradictory but that gelatin nonetheless seemed to offer undeniable health benefits. This valuable research is discussed in chapters 9 to 19.

The big question is why so many early studies showing the healing power of gelatin have languished in obscurity. The easy explanation is that after the 1930s, pharmaceutical drugs were widely prescribed for ills that were once healed with gelatin. To be fair, many early study results could not be replicated. One scientist would find that gelatin helps prevent, say, muscular fatigue; the next would find some benefit; and a third would see no benefit at all. And so on with anemia, jaundice, ulcers, and other ailments. Unable to repeat and verify results, scientists moved on to other substances and apparently never found the key to why gelatin sometimes worked well and sometimes did not.

Why were the studies so variable in their results? The most probable explanation is that the substance described as gelatin was not consistent from study to study. Most commercial gelatins today are brewed exclusively from pigskins or cowhide and so include no cartilage or bones. Years ago, however, many commercial gelatins came from mystery blends of cartilage, bones, skin, and other junked animal parts. All these combinations differed in terms of their physical and chemical characteristics and in their physiologic actions. Even glue sometimes was sold as gelatin. Complicating matters further, some of the so-called gelatin studies were done with the isolated amino acid glycine. Given the inconsistencies and hazards of gelatin manufacture, it is no wonder that study results were inconsistent.

Magic

Broth fills a deep need in my body and feels like a magical elixir.
–*Hilary Giovale,*
Flagstaff, Arizona

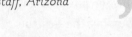

Dr. Prudden and Cartilage Research

Also in support of broth we have the life's work of Dr. John F. Prudden (1920–1998), who found that cartilage had a powerful and consistently positive effect on wound healing, arthritis, cancer, and other diseases. Because cartilage is an essential part of homemade bone broth, his findings are highly relevant. In 1995, Dr. Prudden won the Linus Pauling Scientist of the Year Award for "altruistic efforts in forwarding the knowledge base in the field of nutrition and cancer; an uncommon persistence and brilliance in overcoming obstacles to his work; and his vision of a world without cancer." In more than forty years, he was rarely proven wrong, one-upped, or scorned. His credentials were impeccable. He worked with the best and brightest, published in respected journals, kept his distance from alternative

medicine, and mostly played by establishment rules. Yet his findings aroused comparatively little interest in his lifetime and have been almost completely ignored since his death.

Cartilage as Medicine Versus Cartilage as Food

Dr. Prudden's studies involved cartilage extracts taken either orally or by injection. These products are obviously different from the cartilage found in homemade bone broth. Given that he never tested broth, Dr. Prudden's findings might seem irrelevant. In truth, we would not be discussing Dr. Prudden's work in such depth if well-designed scientific studies on the healing benefits of bone broth itself existed. In the absence of those needed studies, the best we can do is look at evidence of healing from cartilage and the other components found in broth.

Clearly, Dr. Prudden's research using pills is more relevant than the injections. Both food and pills, after all, are processed through the digestive system. We also think patients treated with injectable cartilage could have benefited from components that are destroyed during the digestive process such as anti-angiogenesis factors (which block the growth of new blood vessels and can stem the runaway skin proliferation of psoriasis or the growth of tumors in cancer) and growth factors (which could help arthritis patients grow new cartilage). But because these useful factors have both pros and cons, Dr. Prudden ultimately recommended cartilage pills. He believed the key healing components survived the digestive process and were assimilated well even in individuals with compromised digestive systems.

As was his wont, Dr. Prudden had some things to say about this lack of interest: "At the start I was just absolutely transported by these findings and was dumbfounded when their announcement produced nothing but silence. There seemed to be not one bit of curiosity. Distinguished oncologists have seen that their terminally ill patients were indubitably cured, but not once did any one of them make an inquiry of me. Is it the herd mentality? Fear of turf invasion? Whatever. It is an intellectual desert out there. It's not a new problem, this group condemnation of anything off the standard. It is absolutely typical of human nature to just believe the given of the day. The Galileo story is typical of the human mind-set. He was far ahead of his time, persecuted, and excommunicated. Four hundred years later, he was unexcommunicated. He must now be feeling a deep sense of relief! I hope he was smart enough at the time to realize it was all balderdash."

Dr. Prudden thought the problem was compounded by the nature of medical school training. "There is so much to siphon up that students learn the standard procedures like a catechism, and then carry the rote learning approach unquestioningly on into their practices. Standard practitioners don't even believe they can discover things for themselves anymore. They believe what they're told. We old clinicians are fading into the sunset."

How Much Broth Would Dr. Prudden Recommend?

How much broth would Dr. Prudden recommend? We hear that question all the time from people who would like to replicate Dr. Prudden's successes on their own at home. Sorry to say, but Dr. Prudden never tested broth. This was not because he didn't appreciate its potential healing power but because it would have been impossible to test the efficacy of a product that varies so much from batch to batch. As discussed on page 9, the nutritional profile of broth depends on both the quality and the quantity of the ingredients. Levels of cartilage will be obviously higher in broth cooked from joints, but broths from bones and skin will also produce many of the same healing components.

Although we have received numerous testimonies as to the healing power of broth, its most established benefits are for disease prevention and overall health maintenance.

As a general rule, we recommend 1 cup of broth per day in soups, stews, sauces, gravies, or just in a mug for prevention and long-term health; if dealing with a medical condition, we recommend 3 cups per day, taken morning, noon, and evening.

We strongly advise that those who would like to treat illness enlist the help of an alternative medical doctor or other health practitioner. Doctors who recommend a protocol based on Dr. Prudden's research will most likely recommend 9 grams a day of a therapeutic-quality bovine cartilage product. (For appropriate brands of therapeutic-quality bovine cartilage products, visit the Resource page at our website, www.nourishingbroth.com.) We look forward to the day when doctors routinely recommend nourishing broth as a key part of the dietary foundation and as a useful adjunct to any healing protocol.

Graves' Disease

My story begins in November 2005, when I was diagnosed with Graves' disease, an autoimmune hyperactive thyroid. My journey into traditional foods had begun just a few months before when my daughter suggested that I read *Nourishing Traditions*. Since 1989, I had been the fat-free queen. I had also been taking a soy protein shake product and isoflavone supplements for menopause. While I was not vegetarian, I would only eat meat, milk, or cheese if it was nearly fat-free. Reading Sally's book taught me about the dangers of soy, and then Kaayla's book *The Whole Soy Story* told me more. I started to eat butter, but it was a very big hurdle for me to get over.

Then Graves' disease reared its ugly head. My endocrinologist told me I had two options to treat it. One, take radioactive iodine, kill my thyroid, and be on replacement for the rest of my life. An ex-president and his wife had both had this done, and he said if it was good enough for the president then it should be good enough for me. I asked about option two. It was drugs. There are only two that treat Graves' disease. I asked about a door number three, if there was any other way to treat this. He told me to go buy lottery tickets, as I would have better odds.

I decided to try the drugs, but two months later my liver enzymes were sky-high and I was in terrible pain and in a total panic. He put me on the second drug and told me if this one didn't work, I would have no option but to do the radioactive iodine.

I was in a pretty dark place by then. I decided to go look for some "lottery tickets" and made an appointment with Dr. Tom Cowan. The first thing he told me was that there was nothing wrong with my thyroid and we needed to work on my immune system. He said I had to make broth. He said that my thyroid needed the protein in the gelatin and it also needed the minerals to function. I was willing to try anything at that point. I had lost a lot of my muscle mass, my heart was under attack, and I was very weak. I could not walk across the room without becoming breathless. My heart beat so fast that sleep was difficult. I was also struggling with my liver. Dr. Cowan prescribed at least one cup of broth with each meal plus more throughout the day.

I went home and made that first pot of broth. I never tasted anything so good. Dr. Cowan also put me on many supplements and some iodine. Long story short, in June 2006, I was able to go off the drugs, and by March of 2008, I was off all supplements and had no symptoms. Later I came off the iodine too. In the summer of 2011, Dr. Cowan tested my antibodies and they were quite low. He declared me in remission. While I can't say that broth was the only thing that helped me, I can say it was a major part of it.

As for the endocrinologist, I sent him a lottery ticket!

—Joy Eriksen,
Novato, California

Classically, it was the clinicians who made the significant discoveries. Dr. Prudden explained, "We developed them in the university hospitals, tried them out and if they worked, interested a drug company in producing them. Wondrous things were discovered. Now it is completely turned around. Everything starts with a twenty-five-million-dollar project at Lilly or Merck. Sloan Kettering and nearly all the big research centers are in the business of testing agents for pharmaceutical companies. As if it is high science to do randomized, double-blind studies! A seventh grader could do that! The real science is in discovering biological efficacy. From their indoctrination in medical school to the seminars they later attend courtesy of pharmaceutical companies, they learn to look for high-tech stealth bomber–style medications that can successfully attack and destroy."

Scorn for Simple Solutions

Doctors today are trained to think it unlikely that a simple, relatively inexpensive natural substance such as bovine tracheal cartilage could have a powerful effect on diseases as deadly as glioblastoma, pancreatic cancers, or metastatic adenocarcinomas of the lung. Or as intractable as scleroderma, psoriasis, rheumatoid arthritis, and ulcerative colitis. No matter how many reports come in from patients who've felt benefits or from clinicians who've observed them, simple, traditional remedies remain suspect. For a long time, doctors were even taught food has little or no effect on disease.

Equally ingrained is the idea that no single substance could possibly be effective against a wide variety of diseases. Indeed, medical watchdogs routinely warn consumers that doctors who claim that one agent can cure many diseases are quacks. The AMA's and FDA's long-standing reluctance to sanction natural products has also led many doctors to wait for isolated, purified, patentable extracts, available only by prescription. In terms of cartilage, Dr. Prudden valued the whole food product. Though intrigued by research on its fractions, he was not convinced they worked better, faster, or more reliably. "Mother Nature put cartilage together over eons of time," he said. "We should never underestimate Mother Nature. Yet mainline medicine is sold on the necessity of waiting for fractionalization. That is stupid, for if it works, it works. Use it now."

Homemade broth, of course, is a whole food product. It's a slow food, whole food, and real food that has been nourishing and healing people for tens of thousands of years. People around the world know this is true, and they still know it today. Soup stories from history, however, find it hard to compete against spanking-new drugs announced, as Dr. Prudden put it, "with ruffles, flourishes, color brochures, pictures of fantasized molecular sequences, and prose draped in academic gowns." Compared to the glittering promise of genetic engineering and recombinant DNA technology, old-fashioned broth and gelatin look both quaint and dull. The idea that "like feeds like" and that broth's bones, cartilage, and collagen can nourish our bones, joints, and skin even sounds a little tidy, rather along the lines of "you are what you eat."

The Boredom of Broth

That boredom of broth, however, has advantages, including a long history of safe usage with a complete absence of unwanted side effects. Even the fractionated components of broth such as glucosamine have proven to be extremely safe substances, with only occasional minor side effects and no serious safety concerns. FDA trials on Dr. Prudden's bovine tracheal cartilage supplement, for example, proved it so safe that there was no dosage at which it produced adverse effects. While many alternative doctors and nutritionists advocate these products for the prevention of the diseases they often cure, why not follow the example of our ancestors and just enjoy a daily diet rich in broth?

Nathan R. Gotthoffer, PhD

Little is known today about Nathan Ralph Gotthoffer (1901–1983). His primary claim to fame is that between 1927 and 1945 he dug up every bit of research ever published on the topic of gelatin and seems to have met many of the researchers as well. He would undoubtedly be surprised to learn that his book *Gelatin in Nutrition and Medicine* has sold more copies in the past couple of years as a Kindle book on Amazon than were sold in all the years since it was first published in 1945.

Bob Busscher, President of Great Lakes Gelatin (formerly Grayslake), says employees at Grayslake always referred to him as Dr. Gotthoffer and thought he obtained his degree in biochemistry after the war. At Grayslake, Dr. Gotthoffer served as Director of Research. In addition to *Gelatin in Nutrition and Medicine*, he coauthored *The Ice Cream Production Guide* with N. E. Olson.

In the late 1940s, Dr. Gotthoffer joined the Drackett Company in Cincinnati, Ohio, as Research Administrator. His projects included investigating soy for cardboard packaging and

❝ Back from Nearly Dead

My mother is in her late seventies. Last winter when she came to my house for the holidays, she was weak and looked nearly dead. It took her over ten minutes to walk, assisted, from the car to the house. She had no appetite and would not eat for anybody for several weeks. She was not even complaining, which was a huge sign that something was seriously wrong.

I had just made a pot of rich chicken stock and decided to add a tiny amount of broken vermicelli pasta and finely chopped parsley. When I lived in Yugoslavia in 1986, my host family would make this for the midday meal. I had a feeling it would stimulate her appetite. When she asked for a cup of tea, I told her that I was out, but she could sip some broth. She did. In fact, she asked for a second cup. A few hours later for dinner, I made a Japanese soup rich in vegetables, fresh bacon, and buckwheat noodles with a dollop of miso. She

ate a small bowl, then asked for more food. For the next day and a half, I continued to feed her broth and a few other foods to stimulate her appetite. By dinner, she was eating almost as much as anyone else at the table. She began to engage in conversation again—rational conversation to boot! She was walking very confidently and unassisted.

The transformation in less than forty-eight hours was unbelievable. The next time she came to visit about eleven months later, she was trying to find ways of helping with cooking and cleaning up around the house. Broth brought her back from the dead.

–Adrienne Hew,
Kailua-Kona, Hawaii

The World Health Organization's Action Programme on Essential Drugs defines a drug as essential if it is "as relevant today as it was twenty years ago." Four criteria must be met:

other industrial applications. Though Drackett was active in soy research during the 1930s and 1940s, the company is best known for inventing Drano, Vanish, Windex, Renuzit, and other household products.

In 1950, Dr. Gotthoffer opened his own offices in Cincinnati as a chemical consultant specializing in gelatin, glue, soy, and other vegetable proteins and their industrial applications. He also marketed his expertise in the treatment of water and industrial wastes. He held several patents, including a 1955 patent on soy protein manufacture. In 1971, *Cornell University Alumni News* reported that he was still active as a chemical consultant and had visited the Caribbean, South America, Central America, Ireland, and the southern United States. In the summer of 1977, he and his wife, Hope, celebrated their fiftieth anniversary and enjoyed a trip to Tahiti, Bora Bora, and other places in the South Pacific. By 1980, he was reportedly "taking life easy" in Cincinnati, and he died there at age eighty-two on March 2, 1983.

◄○►

A drug must be evidence-based, efficient, flexible, and forward-looking. While it's hardly a drug, broth not only complies with these requirements but is as relevant today as it was thousands of years ago.

How many lives could daily broth save right now? Maybe millions. How much human suffering could it stop? Impossible to calculate. How much money could it save? Perhaps half a trillion dollars per year. The next eleven chapters present the science and tell why it's time to round up grass-roots support for broth.

John F. Prudden, MD, DSci

John Fletcher Prudden, MD, DSci, was born February 4, 1920, in Fostoria, Ohio, the only son of a schoolteacher and a country doctor. His father graduated from Kirksville, the original osteopathic school in the United States, and settled in Fostoria in 1913 at the invitation of Richard Sheppard, a well-known osteopath of the time and the father of Dr. Sam Sheppard, the Cleveland physician who in 1954 was falsely accused and convicted of beating his wife to death. The case inspired the television show *The Fugitive*. "Sam was about my age. We played together growing up. For all of us, that was a great tragedy," John told me.

John majored in biochemistry at Harvard, graduated cum laude in 1942, and then headed to Harvard Medical School because of pressure from his father, who badly wanted a medical doctor in the family. Like many osteopaths, Dr. Meryl Prudden had been harassed by the local medical academy, called a "quack," and forced off the staff of the local hospital. His son—who years later admitted having had "all the arrogance of having spent two years at Harvard"—wrote a flaming letter to the local newspaper claiming that the very taxpayers who funded the hospital and had been healed for years by his father—who was "often paid only in tomatoes, potatoes, corn and rutabagas"—were denied their rights. His father was promptly reinstated.

Originally scheduled to go to Korea to head the MASH unit, Dr. Prudden missed his chance to inspire the Hawkeye Pierce character of movie and TV fame, and instead spent 1952 to 1954 as Chief of the Laboratory Division and Physiology Section of the Surgical Research Unit at Fort Sam, Texas. The job was no sinecure. "We worked our bottoms off around the clock," he remembered, and several researchers with doctoral degrees he'd hoped to induct into his laboratory at Fort Sam volunteered instead to "agitate the gravel in Korea." Though patching up so many severely injured soldiers was a profound learning experience, the job pressure kept him away from his wife, Shirley, and their three children and contributed to the end of his first marriage.

In 1954, Dr. Prudden returned to Manhattan, where he'd accepted a position as an instructor (later associate professor) of surgery at Columbia-Presbyterian Medical Center. Within a few days of arrival, he both discovered the potential of cartilage for wound healing (as detailed in chapter 13) and met his future wife, Carla, a Swedish-born nurse, in the hospital cafeteria. With Carla, he had another three children.

Dr. Prudden first tested cartilage's mettle with wound healing, then went on to explore its anti-inflammatory and immune system–enhancing effects. These discoveries led, in turn, to studies on arthritis, psoriasis, cancer, and other incurable and intractable conditions. Without making sensational claims, Dr. Prudden authored or coauthored sixty-five papers, many of which were published in major peer-reviewed scientific and medical journals.

Most important, he treated thousands of patients whose battles with wounds, arthritis, cancer, psoriasis, and other diseases inspired his research. His long resume also included positions as a consultant in surgery at Harlem, Delafield, Nyack, Doctors, Roosevelt, and Helen Hayes hospitals. At the time of his death, he maintained an active practice in Waccabuc, New York, treating new patients and following up earlier cases. He was also hard at work on an article documenting his success with 140 "incurable" cancer patients. He died at age seventy-eight of acute leukemia, which he ruefully admitted was one of the few types of cancer that never respond to bovine tracheal cartilage. As a nonbeliever in most forms of alternative medicine, he chose radiation and other forms of conventional medicine and died at Northern Westchester Hospital in Mt. Kisco, New York, on September 12, 1998.

◄○►

CHAPTER 9

Osteoarthritis

More than 52.5 million Americans have firsthand experience with osteoarthritis. Count in the bum knees, "tennis elbows," and other crippling cartilage injuries sustained by professional athletes, weekend wannabes, and accident victims, and we have as many as eighty million sufferers in the United States alone. Just about everyone knows something about arthritis. Except what causes it and how to get rid of it.

Osteoarthritis Myths

It's a myth, for instance, that osteoarthritis (OA) is caused by the "wear and tear" of old age and that everyone who lives long enough will be affected sooner or later. Although roughly 80 percent of Americans over the age of fifty suffer from some degree of osteoarthritis, 20 percent remain unscathed, a fact that raises serious questions about inevitability. If "everyone" sooner or later will—to quote a popular advertisement—"eventually feel the effects of a lifetime of use"—every senior citizen would be hobbled by arthritis. This is obviously not the case. Nor does the "wear and tear" hypothesis fit the fact that women are

more prone to arthritis than men. Yes, women live longer than men, but osteoarthritis strikes them in larger numbers at every age.

The "lifetime-of-use" theory makes sense when cartilage cushions large weight-bearing joints such as the knee and hip joints and especially when people are overweight or obese. But it fails to explain why another popular spot for the disease is the fingers, which, though they may experience strain, are not called upon to bear weight at all.

Finally, if long-term wear and tear is the culprit, then why are increasing numbers of thirty- and forty-year-olds experiencing crippling pain? Surely, they are not moving their joints fast and furiously in double time. If anything, most of them work sedentary desk jobs.

The wear-and-tear theory does fit the manifestations of secondary osteoarthritis, the type caused by athletic injury, trauma, accident, or repetitive motion. The pitcher who throws a baseball over and over again is susceptible, as is a jackhammer operator whose shoulders take a beating from the rattling, vibrating device day in and day out. Primary osteoarthritis, in contrast, does not have such a clear-cut effect.

Skeletal evidence proves that arthritic degeneration has plagued humankind since the Stone Age. Egyptian mummies, Anasazi remains, and Roman baths all testify to ancient pain and suffering. Whales, birds, amphibians, and reptiles also come down with arthritis, and the dinosaurs had it two hundred million years ago. Though many researchers think this evidence suggests the disease is an inevitable part of aging, it only proves that arthritis has been around for ages.

However, we need only look at the bones of healthy primitive people to see that strong, flexible, straight bodies are our birthright. In the 1930s, Dr. Weston A. Price, DDS, traveled to isolated parts of the globe to study the health of populations untouched by Western civilization. The groups he visited included sequestered villages in Switzerland, Gaelic communities in the Outer Hebrides, indigenous peoples of North and South America, Melanesian and Polynesian South Sea Islanders, African tribes, Australian Aborigines, and New Zealand Maori. Wherever he went, he found people of all ages who were remarkably free of dental cavities, osteoarthritis, and other degenerative diseases.

Dr. Price's findings make it clear that it is time to put to rest the wear-and-tear theory of arthritis. The problem is not old age but the fact that cartilage is breaking down faster than it is built up. The question is why, and the answer requires a revolution in our thinking about arthritis and an open mind to the ancestral wisdom of eating plenty of broth and other cartilage-rich foods.

What Is Osteoarthritis?

The name *osteoarthritis*—from the Greek words *osteo* for bone, *arthro* for joint, and *itis* for inflammation—suggests osteoarthritis is inflammation of the bones and joints. More accurately, the disease is marked by the quantitative and qualitative destruction of the articular cartilage in the joints within the hands and knees. Because inflammation is not always present, many doctors prefer to call OA degenerative joint disease.

Articular cartilage—a term referring to the cartilage that wraps and protects the ends of bones—is crucial at movable joints such as the knee, elbow, or knuckles because it absorbs shock and reduces friction. When

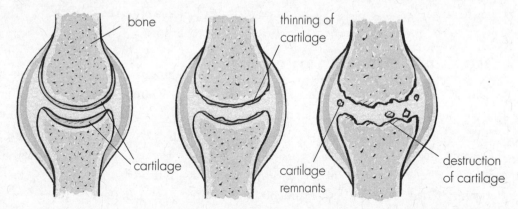

Figure 6: This illustration shows the progression of osteoarthritis from a normal, healthy joint (left) to the thinning of cartilage (middle) to its destruction (right).

healthy articular cartilage is present, it continuously releases lubricating fluid to ensure that the joints glide slickly and smoothly against each other.

"Imagine rubbing together two perfectly flat, smooth, slightly wet ice cubes," explains Jason Theodosakis, MD, of the Arizona College of Medicine in Tucson, in his bestseller *The Arthritis Cure*. "They glide across each other quickly and easily, never catching or slowing. Now imagine a surface that's five to eight times more slippery than ice. That's your cartilage, the material that makes it possible for the ends of your bones to slide smoothly and easily across each other. No manmade substance can compare to the low friction and shock absorbing properties of healthy cartilage."

When the cartilage dries, thins, and cracks, we get the painful scraping of osteoarthritis with loss of joint motion, stiffness, swelling, and pain. Given that this unhappy chain of events occurs to people who do not subject their joints to excessive wear and tear or other trauma, as well as to only some of those who do, it is reasonable to conclude that a fundamental difference in the biochemistry of the cartilage exists that would account for the difference.

What Causes Osteoarthritis?

No one knows what initial event triggers the biochemical change that leads to osteoarthritis, but once articular cartilage begins to degenerate, the bones below harden and form unwanted bony spurs at the margins of the joints where tendons and ligaments are attached. Though pure cartilage has no blood vessels, blood vessels will invade cartilage once it starts to calcify into bone, contributing to the inflammation and pain of arthritis.

So where might the problem start? Most likely in the gelatinous matrix. People afflicted with osteoarthritis either do not produce enough of the protein sugars known as proteoglycans that are the building blocks of springy, plump, healthy cartilage or they do not produce them fast enough. People with OA are also prone to producing hunched-over little proteoglycans that hold water poorly because age or ill health have tipped the balance in favor of keratan sulfates instead of chondroitin sulfates (see the discussion on page 19). Finally, the body's cartilage-chewing enzymes elastase and hyaluronase may develop an eating disorder that leads them to prematurely destroy cartilage.

What to Do?

The solution is as commonsensical as it is simple: Furnish the body with a food that contains the key biochemical components of healthy young cartilage. That food is old-fashioned bone broth. Soups and stews are staples in traditional cuisines all over the world and were regularly eaten by the healthy primitive people observed by Dr. Price. These people notably engaged in "nose to tail" eating, which meant no part of the animal went to waste. Cartilaginous cuts either were eaten directly or went into the stockpot. Today health experts are so out of touch that many believe there are few or even no dietary sources of cartilage. The University of Maryland Medical Center's health information website flat-out states, "You can't get cartilage from food. It's available only in supplements."

Consumed every day, bone broth supplies

the components our bodies need to repair and rebuild cartilage and keep those gluttonous cartilage-eating enzymes under control. The twelfth-century Benedictine abbess Hildegard von Bingen recommended "frequent and adequate" portions of a broth made from ox feet for joint pain—and this remains good advice today.

Broth also helps us recover from the athletic injuries, trauma, or accidents that can lead to "trick knees" and other cases of secondary osteoarthritis. Standard therapies are hot packs, ultrasound, and manipulation by physical therapists, intended to increase the blood supply and speed the healing of the injured joint. But the bottom line is, if you flood a joint with blood lacking the nutrients needed to heal the injured tissues, the therapies will be mostly in vain. Because broth provides the necessary nutrients, it should form an essential part of any diet for athletes and for active people who want to remain vigorous into old age.

The Science

Broth is a staple in the diets of healthy people around the world and a probable reason they are free of osteoarthritis. Unfortunately, scientists have not studied the healing power of broth for arthritis prevention and reversal. Yet indirect evidence shows significant joint benefits from taking gelatin, cartilage, and collagen supplements and the building blocks glucosamine and chondroitin sulfate.

Surprisingly, Nathan R. Gotthoffer made only a single mention of "gouty arthritis" and wrote nothing at all about osteoarthritis, although his 1945 book *Gelatin in Nutrition and Medicine* exhaustively reports the science backing the use of gelatin for infectious and hemorrhagic diseases, muscular dystrophy, diabetes, and other diseases and disorders. Given the passion and thoroughness with which he researched this subject between 1927 and 1945, it's likely no early studies exist.

According to the 2007 textbook *Gelatine Handbook*, German researchers took up the study of collagen hydrolysate for osteoarthritis in the 1970s. Collagen hydrolysate—a form of gelatin that's been "conditioned" through a process known as enzymatic hydrolysis—is readily soluble in water. It is thus easy to stir into hot or cold food or beverages at home or mixed smoothly into products during food manufacture. Unlike the other widely available commercial proteins of casein, whey and soy, collagen hydrolysate does not become bitter from hydrolysis. This made it a useful and potentially very profitable product, and by the 1980s there were studies showing its efficacy.

In 1982, a report by B. Goetz appeared in the German medical journal *Aerztliche Praxis*. Sixty patients ages eight to thirty-three afflicted with youthful chondropathia patellae (arthritic knees) were tested after using collagen hydrolysate for one month, two months, and three months. At the end of three months, 75 percent were free of pain and cartilage regeneration had occurred in 80 percent of these cases.

In 1989, Drs. Klaus Seeligmuller and H. K. Happel of Bonn, Germany, reported on 356 patients suffering from arthritis of the knees, hips, and spine over a period of three to twelve months in the journal *Therapiewoche*. They measured "good" or "very good" results after using collagen hydrolysate with an astonishing 99.2 percent of the patients, with the strongest effect on knee and finger joints.

Knee Injury

By 1994 my knee problems had increased to where the discomfort kept me from riding a bike even a few feet. Looking at both knees through an arthroscope, you could see the usual cartilage covering was gone and the bare bone exposed. My orthopedic surgeon did some "housecleaning," by which I mean he trimmed the unstable articular cartilage that was about to fall off around the edges of the exposed bone. The hope was the body's healing response would result in a layer of scar tissue. While that's a poor substitute for cartilage, it is better than nothing. My symptoms improved, but I always had fluid in the knee joints, indicating they were not as well as I could have hoped. Then about two years ago my knee symptoms started improving further and instead of always having fluid I now seldom have it.

When I asked the surgeon if I should thank him for this unexpected recent improvement, he said not at all. He said what he did could at best temporarily lessen symptoms and delay the need for artificial knee joints by months or a few years. What, then, might have caused the change? One of my farm activities is raising chickens on pasture, processing, and direct-marketing them. For years we gave away the chicken feet for free, but two years ago we began making very thick chicken foot broth for ourselves and adding this to all our soups and stews. Our broth consumption also greatly increased when we began marketing some of our pastured cows as ground beef, thus keeping most of the skeleton for ourselves.

I am physically active most all day every day caring for 470 acres with cattle herd, sheep flock, laying hens, and the few broilers for our extended family by myself. I heat two homes and one large farm building entirely with the wood I cut and haul. I have essentially no knee symptoms. I do such things as jump over the side of a three-quarter-ton truck to the ground below without bother but then lecture myself to be thankful for how well the knees are doing and not flaunt it by such abuse.

–Charles Henkel,
Norfolk, Nebraska

In 1991, Milan Adam, DSci, of Prague's Institute of Rheumatism Research, also published positive results in *Therapiewoche*. His randomized double-blind study on eighty-one patients suffering from OA showed a 50 percent reduction in pain for patients treated with collagen hydrolysate. The study led to patents for collagen hydrolysate in both Europe and the United States.

Since then, there have been at least nine clinical trials with more than two thousand patients afflicted with age- and activity-related OA. Most of the researchers reported that improvement of OA occurs gradually over a period of months of faithfully taking a daily dose of 10 grams of collagen hydrolysate. Given the propensity of arthritis sufferers to drop out before results could reasonably be expected to occur, the researchers counseled patients to be patient. Generally patients noted benefits to hair, nails, and skin ahead of experiencing improvement to their OA. Anecdotally, people report much the same from consuming two or three mugs of bone broth per day.

Over the years, sports physiologists have

performed most of the collagen hydrolysate studies, including Dr. Friedhelm Beuker of the Institute for Sports Sciences at the University of Dusseldorf in Germany; Dr. Klaus Seeligmuller, a specialist in orthopedics, sports medicine, and physical therapy in Bonn, Germany; and James M. Rippe, MD, of the Rippe Lifestyle Institute in Shrewsbury, Massachusetts. In 2008, Kristine L. Clark, PhD, RD, a specialist in sports nutrition at Penn State, investigated the use of collagen hydrolysate to treat joint pain in athletes with no evidence of joint disease. She, too, announced significant improvement.

Collagen hydrolysate received its biggest boost in 2000 when Roland Moskowitz, MD, of Case Western Reserve University, studied the healing power of collagen hydrolysate at twenty medical centers in the United States, Great Britain, and Germany. Best known for his research linking OA to a defective collagen gene, Dr. Moskowitz's six-month study showed a decrease in pain, increase in physical function, and increase in overall patient satisfaction. The best response came from those who'd been suffering the most severe symptoms. Interestingly, the greatest success occurred with Germans, not Brits or Americans, who dropped out of the study at the rates of 37 percent and 42 percent, respectively.

Even so, bad news has come in for collagen hydrolysate supporters. In 2012, J. P. Van Vijven and colleagues at the Erasmus University Medical Center Rotterdam, the Netherlands, examined eight studies on OA using gelatin, undenatured collagen, and collagen hydrolysate and reported that "the overall quality of evidence was moderate to very low," and concluded there was insufficient evidence to recommend them in daily practice.

The biggest beneficiary of the studies from the 1980s and 1990s was probably Knox Gelatin, which introduced its NutraJoint product with great fanfare. Not long after, in 1997, the editors of the *Tufts University Health and Nutrition Letter* advised consumers not to buy NutraJoint or similar supplements because the idea that gelatin can contribute to the building of strong cartilage and bones "is a theory that has yet to be investigated." As for the theory itself, they sniffed that it "sounds tidy—rather along the lines of 'you are what you eat.'" In fact, collagen does seem to build collagen and cartilage, but cartilage may do it even better. Bone broth, which contains both, may do it best of all.

Cartilage Therapy

Dr. John F. Prudden, MD, DSci (1920–1998), is known as the "father of cartilage therapy." Although his first studies involved cartilage injections, he subsequently worked with oral doses of 9 grams a day of a whole food–based bovine tracheal cartilage supplement first known as Catrix and later as VitaCarte. (For an up-to-date list of products that would have met Dr. Prudden's quality standards, visit our website, www.nourishingbroth.com.)

In a major article published in the summer 1974 issue of *Seminars in Arthritis and Rheumatism*, Dr. Prudden detailed the cases of twenty-eight people suffering from pain and disability caused by OA. They'd tried nearly every drug in the anti-arthritis pharmacopoeia, but nothing had helped much or for long. The patients were, in Dr. Prudden's words, "desperate over their pain and disability, and because of this, willing to subject themselves to experimental therapy."

Over a period of three to eight weeks, Dr. Prudden and his team administered subcutaneous injections of 50 cc of bovine cartilage daily to each of the participants. By the end of the study, nineteen of the twenty-eight were in "excellent" condition with a complete elimination of pain and discomfort. Six were in "good" condition with a marked decrease in pain and an increase in mobility. Two experienced only minor benefits and one showed no discernible effect. No toxicity was reported, and no toxicity was shown through the batteries of laboratory tests. These included complete blood count (CBC), urine analyses, and scores of other standard predictive and assessment indices. Most remarkably, the relief lasted from a minimum of six weeks to more than a year due to ongoing absorption of the injected cartilage under the skin. Cartilage injections obviously differ from consuming cartilage-rich broth, although key components survive the digestive process.

Thrilled by this success, Dr. Prudden tested the effectiveness of cartilage pills on seven hundred people, reporting 49 percent with "excellent" results and 26 percent "good," for a total improvement rate of 85 percent. When the patients stopped taking the pills, the average length of remission was six to eight weeks. While this was a much shorter time than the results achieved by injection, it was easily remedied with an ongoing maintenance dose of pills.

Dr. Prudden considered the injectable form more effective for severe arthritis because it bypassed the gut, where digestive enzymes dismantle and destroy growth factor proteins. That problem, of course, also occurs with the digestion of cartilage-rich bone broth. Injected, the growth factors in cartilage are absorbed into the bloodstream and used. "Growth factors are ideal for someone who needs to grow more tissue, such as someone with osteoarthritis," explained Dr. Prudden, "but they're not for someone with a malignancy, which is why we prefer the pills for people with cancer."

Since Dr. Prudden published his findings in 1974, other researchers have confirmed his findings in long-term studies. A ten-year study conducted in the 1970s and 1980s in Eastern Europe was published in *Seminars in Arthritis and Rheumatism* in 1987. Dr. Václav Rejholec of Charles University in Prague collected data on arthritis sufferers and reported that patients who took bovine tracheal cartilage supplements took an average of twenty sick days per year. Those who did not take cartilage saw their disease progress and pain increase as they stayed home from work more and more, culminating in a loss of 180 out of 250 working days by the tenth year. These patients used the standard NSAID drugs or placebos to fight pain and inflammation.

Dr. Rejholec concluded, "It is clear that any form of medication that is well tolerated and shown to be capable of influencing the natural history of OA either by slowing progression or by bringing about actual regression must be regarded as a major advance in the therapy for this condition. The implications in terms of relief of suffering, health care resources and socio-economic costs to the community are similarly far reaching."

An earlier study of great interest to Dr. Prudden was published by Alfred Jay Bollet, MD, in the journal *Arthritis and Rheumatism* in 1968. It proved that cartilage extracts stimulate chondroitin sulfate synthesis.

This component of cartilage matrix not only attracts the water needed for plump, healthy cartilage but also reduces excessive numbers of cartilage-chewing enzymes.

Cartilage Therapy in the Limelight

Dr. Prudden stayed out of the limelight while testing bovine tracheal cartilage in well-designed long-term studies. In contrast, during the same period, I. William Lane, PhD (1922–2011), began heavily promoting shark cartilage as a cure for osteoarthritis as well as cancer in his bestselling book *Sharks Don't Get Cancer.*

Lane claimed the key curative agents in shark cartilage were proteins known as anti-angiogenesis factors, a term that refers to the inhibition of new blood vessel formation. Because normal, healthy cartilage has no blood vessels, all cartilage comes equipped with this protein factor. Shark skeletons have it and so do bovine tracheas, chicken sternums, kangaroo tails, and human joints.

Anti-angiogenesis factors would be helpful to people suffering from osteoarthritis because the initial degeneration and thinning of articular cartilage is followed by the invasion of blood vessels. Because healthy cartilage is avascular, blood vessels bring on further breakdown and pain. The problem with the theory is that anti-angiogenesis factors in oral supplements break down in the gut, just as they do in broth. That was the view not only of Dr. Prudden, but also of Judah Folkman, MD, of Children's Hospital and Harvard Medical School, the discoverer of the anti-angiogenesis factor. Robert Langer, ScD, of the Massachusetts Institute of Technology, another expert in anti-angiogenesis, concurred. Despite the efforts of Prudden, Folkman, and Langer to put a stop to the claims, Lane persisted, and numerous websites today still sell products marketed with this untruth.

Furthermore, Lane built much of his case for shark cartilage as a cure for arthritis and cancer using studies that were actually done on bovine cartilage, including the work of Drs. Prudden and Rejholec. Research by Serge Orloff, MD, of Brugmann University Hospital in Brussels and the Executive General Secretary of the International League Against Rheumatism, did show dramatic results, but the study was on a single patient. A study by Jose A. Orcasita, MD, of the University of Miami School of Medicine, was on just six elderly patients and lasted only three weeks. A third, by Dr. Carlos Luis Alpizar, a gerontologist in Costa Rica, was on ten patients and also lasted three weeks.

Clearly Lane's marketing was ahead of the science. This is not to say that shark cartilage couldn't be useful. It has been valued for its medicinal properties ever since the ancient Chinese began singing the praises of shark fin soup. Dr. Prudden himself found that the cartilage of calves, sharks, teju lizards, and crocodiles all possessed similar healing properties. That said, shark cartilage has some distinct drawbacks, including the necessity of doses so high they cause nausea and lack of appetite, as well as a cost that can top one thousand dollars a month. There are also safety concerns about high calcium content. Shark cartilage is 20 to 22 percent calcium, whereas bovine cartilage is only 1 percent calcium. Taken at the full therapeutic dose of 70 grams a day, shark cartilage provides 14 grams of calcium, which is a whopping 14 times the RDA. The therapeutic dose of Dr. Prudden's bovine cartilage was only 9 grams per day.

Hip Trouble

I have had very few health issues and take no medications, but around age fifty, I began having a lot of trouble with my hips. I experienced pain, difficulty walking, sciatica, etc. I tried many approaches, including muscle therapy and physical therapy, but nothing really helped until I committed to drinking a cup of bone broth every day. I started doing this and within a week, the pain was greatly reduced. My joints are also more flexible and I can now walk normally. I love to hike, so you can imagine how important this is to me! To say I'm thrilled is an understatement!

Interestingly enough, I already had known about the benefits of bone broth for arthritic pain, but didn't commit until I met an older carpenter at one of our chapter meetings who told me that WAPF had saved his life. He was going to have to quit working because of the pain in his knee, but two months of drinking two cups of bone broth a day eliminated the pain. His story motivated me to finally get serious about bone broth.

–Nancy Eason,
Fort Collins, Colorado

Other Cartilage Fractions

Studies on chicken sternal cartilage and chicken sternal collagen type II are sparse, but include a 2012 study published in the *Journal of Agriculture and Food Chemistry* by Alexander

Schauss, PhD, and colleagues at AIBMR Life Sciences in Puyallup, Washington. This randomized, double-blind, placebo-controlled trial looked at eighty patients and reported their patented product BioCell to be well tolerated, well absorbed, and effective in managing OA-associated symptoms.

Despite success with whole food collagen and cartilage supplements over the past forty years, most researchers have chosen to focus on fractions of cartilage, particularly glucosamine sulfate and chondroitin sulfate. As discussed in chapter 7, glucosamine is a naturally occurring amino sugar that is a major constituent of proteoglycans and glycosaminoglycans (GAGs), the water-loving molecules in cartilage. Most supplements on the market come from crab, lobster, and shrimp cells.

Chondroitin sulfate is a large, gel-forming molecule that helps keep cartilage cushy and able to cope with compression. Supplements come from extracts taken from cow, pig, fish, or bird cartilage.

Glucosamine and chondroitin supplements are some of the most popular supplements ever sold at health food stores and drugstores. Although the initial fad was set off by the bestselling book *The Arthritis Cure*, first published in 1997, consumers would not continue to purchase these products if they obtained no benefits.

Side Effect Dangers

Even so, glucosamine and chondroitin sulfate have not lived up to the initial promise of a miracle pill capable of curing incurable osteoarthritis. To date, the studies have been inconsistent, inconclusive, and controversial, with the most reliable outcome being mild relief from pain. Although this would seem to be a rather unremarkable benefit, it makes it possible for patients to reduce their consumption of NSAIDs and other drugs, most of which come with a long list of unwanted side effects including stomach irritation, bleeding, and ulceration. High blood pressure, kidney problems, and liver damage are other possibilities. The longer the use, the higher the dose, the greater the risks.

The dangers of these over-the-counter drugs are far greater than most people imagine, and these "minor" arthritis drugs directly or indirectly kill between seven and ten thousand Americans each year and result in more than one hundred thousand hospitalizations.

Clearly glucosamine and chondroitin are worthwhile, even if all they can do is alleviate some of the pain of osteoarthritis and cut down on NSAID usage.

Other Studies and Trials

Findings that glucosamine and chondroitin can stop or even reverse disease progression are less consistent. The supplements appear to work better on mild osteoarthritis than severe forms, though well-documented cases of success with both exist. Overall the thousands of studies on glucosamine and chondroitin sulfate alone and in combination are inconsistent, contradictory, and confusing. The problems are many, and pertain to study design, data gathering, data analysis, too short duration, insufficient dosing, poor patient compliance, and uncontrolled co-medication and over-the-counter and prescription drugs. Industry-sponsored trials have also shown more pronounced differences between supplements and placebos than industry-independent trials. As a result, glucosamine and chondroi-

tin products remain controversial. The usual conclusion to the studies is some variation of "Further investigations in larger cohorts of patients for longer time periods are needed to prove its usefulness as a symptom modifying drug in OA."

The Glucosamine/Chondroitin Arthritis Intervention Trial (GAIT) cost the American taxpayers fourteen million dollars and was supposed to put the questions to bed once and for all. Sponsored by the National Institutes of Health (NIH), this double-blind placebo-controlled study was conducted over a four-year period at sixteen sites across the United States and enrolled nearly sixteen hundred patients. The long and confusing results were rolled out in the *New England Journal of Medicine* in 2006. In brief, the researchers concluded the combo of glucosamine and chondroitin showed no significant difference compared to placebo, though a subset of patients with moderate to severe pain did see good results. In 2008, a twenty-four-month follow-up to GAIT again found patients on glucosamine and chondroitin who fared no better than those on a placebo. This follow-up study, however, was seriously flawed for many reasons, including patient dropout, a recurring pattern with glucosamine and chondroitin studies.

Although patient dropout complicates study outcomes, it reflects the real world, where patient adherence to arthritis medication and supplement protocols is notoriously low. As Tracey-Lea Laba, PhD, and colleagues from the University of Australia in Sydney explain, "The negative relative likelihood of NSAID continuation was mostly driven by the side effect profile. The predicted probability of continuing with glucosamine decreased with increasing out-of-pocket costs."

Fraction Versus Whole

Why else might glucosamine not work as well as might be hoped? The deeper problem might be the inadequacy of fractionated supplements. In short, there's more to cartilage than glucosamine alone.

Asked about *The Arthritis Cure* a year before his death, Dr. Prudden said glucosamine was an inferior remedy compared to whole cartilage extracts because the molecule was too small and too soluble to end up in the joints. "It doesn't work as well because it gets gobbled up by the capillaries, goes into the blood stream and quickly out of the body via the kidney," he explained. "In contrast, the whole cartilage molecule is large and breaks down slowly. The body's lysozyme cleaves the large molecule. Nothing works as well."

Dr. Prudden furthermore said he tested glucosamine, chondroitin, and collagen in his wound-healing experiments during the 1950s and 1960s and only whole cartilage—which of course we find in cartilage-rich broth—did the trick. "I would say that the restoration of broken down cartilage would require wound healing capacity," he said, though he conceded that a diminishing inflammation and other symptoms through glucosamine or other supplements might, in some cases, improve conditions enough for the body to begin restoration on its own. In contrast to Father Technology's laboratory-extracted fractions, he saw cartilage as "Mother Nature's mixture, arrived at over an immense span of time."

The question is, would cartilage-rich bone broth soup work even better, at least for disease prevention and overall health maintenance? Although interest in soup as a source of healing has languished since the advent of "quick fix" drugs and supplements, traditional wisdom holds it should be served at least daily and as the foundation of a real foods diet. Over the past fifteen years countless numbers of people have told us "broth is beautiful" and thanked us for encouraging them to get the stockpot out and the soup simmering. Those with severe symptoms might need to work with an alternative medical doctor or other health practitioner and give supplements a try as well. Any way we look at it, there's plenty of evidence that contradicts the notion that the only way to heal osteoarthritis is, well, not at all.

CHAPTER 10

Rheumatoid Arthritis

A five-thousand-year-old mummy found in Egypt has been identified as the remains of a Syrian immigrant who had suffered greatly from the swollen fingers, knees, and feet typical of rheumatoid arthritis (RA). If he was seeking pain relief, he should have headed up to Greece, where the herb willow bark (an herbal predecessor of aspirin) was in favor long before Hippocrates recommended it, around 400 BC.

What's curious—besides the fact that the ancient remedies have not been improved on all that much today—is that the father of medicine identified rheumatoid arthritis as a disease of men. Around AD 2, his follower Soranus of Ephesus noted that it occasionally occurred in women but never in eunuchs. Given the shortage of eunuchs today, statisticians can collect little data on RA incidence among them. However, they report that RA is now three times more common in women than men.

This fact, plus a paucity of rheumatoid arthritis references in the Bible, art, or literature up to the early twentieth century, leads many experts to conclude that the disease has not only increased but changed with modern civilization. The rare early evidence of rheumatoid arthritis may, in fact, represent special cases of gout combined with osteoarthritis. Although references to swollen, deformed joints make people think of RA, sure diagnostic techniques were not available until the advent of the X-ray machine in 1900 and the identification of the so-called rheumatoid factor in blood in 1948.

Today the disease is commonplace enough to affect between 1.3 and three million people in the United States alone. The numbers depend on who is counting and who is being counted. The statistical difficulty is considerable given the fact that the course of this disease is both variable and erratic. Indeed, there are so many variations of rheumatoid arthritis that some scientists wonder whether it is a single disease or a collection of discrete symptoms with features in common. The one group counted without fail are those who fall prey to a vicious form of the disease that progresses until the joints become painfully deformed and possibly dislocated and body organs harmed. The result can be complete invalidism.

Members of the public sometimes confuse osteoarthritis and rheumatoid arthritis, but there are substantial differences. RA is primarily a disease of the soft tissue, one reason the only proof of it in early humankind is found in mummified as opposed to skeletal remains. Unlike osteoarthritis, RA generally affects both sides of the body symmetrically—both hands, both knees, are affected. Also unlike OA, it tends to come on suddenly and appear as a waxing and waning condition. Although people with OA also have their ups and downs, their disease generally progresses steadily over time. Yet another difference is that RA usually first attacks between the ages of twenty and forty, although older persons and children are occasionally afflicted.

What brings on rheumatoid arthritis? Theories abound, but no one knows for sure. Some people believe the disease originates with bacteria or is triggered by bacteria or viruses. Whatever the cause, the initial infection is followed by an immunologic overreaction that perpetuates the disease. That makes it an autoimmune disease in which the body's own immune system mistakes its very own tissues for foreign invaders and attacks them.

Synovitis—an inflamed joint lining—is the classic sign of RA. It is caused by armies of white blood cells that overreact to the triggering inflammation. They then multiply prolifically, stick around too long, and cause the normally thin, smooth inner membrane known as the synovium to become abnormally thick and swollen. The synovial fluid, which is usually transparent like raw egg whites, thickens into pus and eventually dries out. Adding injury to the insult, the renegade white blood cells also release enzymes and growth factors that cause runaway growth of the synovial membrane. Once it is built up it becomes known as a pannus and may start to invade and destroy the cartilage, bones, tendons, and ligaments. No wonder there is so much pain, swelling, and burning!

Seeking a Cure

Can broth help rheumatoid arthritis? Anecdotal evidence and clinician reports suggest it can, although we do not have much hard science. Gelatin researcher Nathan R. Gotthoffer apparently found nothing on RA, though gelatin's effect on infectious diseases suggests the potential for prevention if RA is precipitated by either a bacterial or a viral attack as many researchers believe; or, as we'll discuss later in this chapter, if RA is actually caused and perpetuated by pleomorphic bacteria in the cartilage as per the controversial theory of the late Thomas McPherson Brown, MD (1906–1989).

Whatever its cause, over the past fifty years, bovine tracheal cartilage, chicken sternal cartilage, and collagen hydrolysate have all been successfully employed in RA treatment. Unfortunately, the studies have been limited, and the most rigorous of them showed success through injection and at therapeutic doses far in excess of what is ever found in broth. That doesn't mean that broth can't help with RA—we've heard from many people that it does, and it's something that every sufferer should try.

An indication that broth might work came from John F. Prudden, MD, DSci, in 1970 when he decided to test bovine tracheal cartilage on rheumatoid arthritis patients. At the time, he simply hoped its anti-inflammatory powers would stave off pain and possibly halt the self-perpetuating progression of the disease. To his complete surprise, his first case proved the soundness of his theory—and more. Injected cartilage actually healed the diseased joints of his first nine rheumatoid arthritis patients.

In a major article published in *Seminars in Arthritis and Rheumatism* in 1974, Dr. Prudden reported the cases of nine rheumatoid arthritis patients ages forty-three to sixty-nine. Each had been injected with 500 cc of bovine cartilage for ten to thirty-five days, followed up by booster shots at three- to four-week intervals. As most doctors will attest, RA patients respond very slowly to medications. This was the case with Dr. Prudden's patients as well. Indeed, most became temporarily worse, perhaps experiencing what natural healers often call a "healing crisis." This generally turns the tide of the illness, and those who manage to grin and bear it tend to eventually see dramatic improvements. Of Dr. Prudden's nine cases, three improved from severe to excellent and the remaining six improved from severe to good.

What's most striking about this success is that many of the patients had already experienced either the destruction or the partial destruction of some of their major joints. Several had undergone artificial joint replacements, fusions, and other serious surgical procedures. Even so, Dr. Prudden was able to report that "there was no patient who did not show what was considered by us and the patient as either an excellent or good response." And there were no unfavorable side effects.

Because Dr. Prudden used injections, the anti-angiogenic factors in cartilage can be credited with some of the good effect. *Anti-angiogenic* means the inhibition of blood vessel formation and growth. Abnormal capillary growth into cartilage, after all, begins the destruction of joint cartilage. Oral cartilage supplements—bovine, chicken, shark—would not be expected to work as well or even at all because the anti-angiogenic factors are destroyed in the gut by digestive enzymes. The same, of course, would be true of broth or gelatin. This does not make Dr. Prudden's findings irrelevant, however; rather, it suggests added benefit from the injections, especially for people with advanced cases of RA or other autoimmune diseases. In fact, oral therapies using bovine tracheal cartilage, shark cartilage, type II collagen, collagen hydrolysate, and glucosamine have all shown benefits to patients with RA.

During his lifetime, I. William Lane, PhD, of *Sharks Don't Get Cancer* fame, marketed shark cartilage for RA as well as for cancer and other diseases. Although Lane's trumped-up claims for anti-angiogenesis from oral use were roundly dismissed by Judah Folkman, MD, the scientist who founded the field of angiogenesis research, useful mucopolysaccharides and other active components are found in all cartilages. Studies on shark cartilage for RA are scant, but a 2012 study from the Institute of Pharmacy, Shandong Traffic Hospital in Jinan, China, showed benefits for rats in terms of improved joint alignment and smooth articular surface.

Not surprisingly, glucosamine has been tried on RA, not only because it can repair cartilage—as discussed in chapter 9 on osteoarthritis—but because of its track record of lowering circulating levels of TNF-α and C-reactive protein, two biomarkers used to measure the progression of RA and other inflammatory disorders. In a study published in *ISRN Pharmacology* in 2013, rats treated with glucosamine showed not only reduced levels of those biomarkers but also reduced histopathological changes in the joints. The researchers concluded that glucosamine suppressed the chronic inflammatory phase of RA and obtained a "rapid and significant beneficial effect."

Overall, the studies on glucosamine are inconsistent, whether researchers are trying it on osteoarthritis, rheumatoid arthritis, or other diseases. That fact has led researchers to try all manner of doses as well as combinations with other remedies. In 2012, a team from the Juntendo University Graduate School of Medicine in Tokyo tested glucosamine, methionine, and a combination of glucosamine plus methionine on rats. They determined glucosamine and methionine each worked in minor fashion alone, but much better in combination, a result that suggests to us the need for a traditional diet balanced in methionine-rich muscle meats as well as collagen-rich skin and bones. Rat chows based on soy protein would be low in methionine unless extra has been added.

Given that glucosamine cannot be patented, it is not surprising that researchers have tried to improve on it. Accordingly, the Pharmacology Unit at the International Center for Chemical and Biological Sciences at the University of Karachi, Pakistan, "took an interest in the synthetic manipulation of amino sugars to develop some efficient pharmacophores." Because good old glucosamine had not proved good "enough to combat severe inflammatory RA," they came up with a "novel synthetic analogue" and tested it on rats. In Inflammation Research, they announced β-D-glucosamine had both anti-arthritis and anti-inflammatory properties and could be useful in the treatment of rheumatoid arthritis.

Oral Tolerance Therapy

In a very different approach to RA, collagen type II is used for a therapy called oral tolerance or oral tolerization. Basically patients are fed the "hair of the dog"—small amounts of collagen II. The idea is to help them tolerate their own collagen and shut down the body's overreactive autoimmune rejection system. Study results suggest that a daily dose of broth might be just the thing for overcoming the immune reactions that occur in RA.

Oral tolerance therapy came about when researchers realized healthy people rarely mount an immune response to food. As explained by medical writer Thomas H. Maugh II in the Los Angeles Times, "If a calf's liver is transplanted into a human, it is quickly and violently rejected because the body recognizes proteins in the liver as foreign and attacks them. But if the organ is fried and eaten, those same proteins are easily absorbed. That's because the stomach and intestines have their own branch of the immune system, an unusual mechanism that suppresses, rather than triggers, immune responses to foreign material. Without it, we would not be able to eat meat and many other foods."

In 1993, in the journal Science, David E. Trentham, MD, of Harvard Medical School and Beth Israel Hospital in Boston, published the results of a randomized, double-blind trial. He and his colleagues treated sixty patients with severe active rheumatoid arthritis with small doses of chicken sternal cartilage for a month and then an increased dose for the next two months. Both the treatment group and the placebo group had similar demographics and clinical and laboratory measures. Dr. Trentham measured objective improvements in the number of swollen and tender joints, morning stiffness, walking time, grip strength, Westergren erythrocyte sedimentation rate, and subjective physician and patient assessments. All these patients had been on serious immunosuppressive and anti-inflammatory drugs such as methotrexate and mercaptopurine, yet the ones in the treatment group experienced a 25 to 30 percent reduction in symptoms such as swelling. The placebo group, which had also been taken off the drugs, deteriorated. Four of the treated patients had complete remissions, an effect that Dr. Howard L. Weiner, one of the researchers from Beth Israel, said, "rarely happens on its own."

Dr. Trentham and eleven other researchers followed up with 274 patients who were randomized to receive either a placebo or one of four doses of collagen II. The oral doses given were 20, 100, 500, or 2500 mcg per day. As reported in *Arthritis and Rheumatism* in 1998, only eighty-three patients completed the full twenty-four weeks of treatment, but the best results came from the low-dose, 20-mcg-per-day treatment group, suggesting that less can be more.

In 1996, Trentham and two colleagues did a pilot trial of oral type II collagen for juvenile RA and reported it, too, to be a safe and effective therapy worthy of further investigation.

Can a daily dose of collagen in the form of broth help treat RA and other autoimmune collagen diseases? Common sense and the evidence of oral tolerance therapy suggests it can. In contrast, the typical medical treatments for RA are notoriously ineffective, often with horrendous side effects. The first line of assault is typically aspirin or nonsteroidal anti-inflammatory drugs (NSAIDs) to stop the pain and reduce the inflammation, followed by steroids, methotrexate, and other highly toxic drugs with downsides such as kidney damage, lung inflammation, bone marrow suppression, and severe liver damage.

Mycobacteria Theory

In the more distant past, surgeons removed the gallbladders and other organs of rheumatoid arthritics thinking they "seeded" the diseased joints, an approach that was notoriously unsuccessful. Though it is easy to mock that approach today, what will future physicians say about the millions of prescriptions written today for high-priced drugs that rarely work well, that at best only address symptoms, and almost always carry ghastly side effects?

Fifty years ago, Dr. Prudden published research showing incontestable success with the nontoxic natural substance of cartilage. His work has never been disproven. Yet with none of the profit-minded pharmaceutical companies pushing it, few people are even aware of it today, the injections are not available, and it's challenging to even find whole bovine cartilage products.

Likewise, there has been a marked lack of interest in the work of Thomas McPherson Brown, MD (1906–1989), a renowned rheumatologist who published more than a hundred papers in major medical journals and was former chairman of the Department of Medicine at George Washington University School of Medicine in Washington, DC. While working as a young man at the Rockefeller Institute in New York City, Dr. Brown first isolated mycobacteria from the joint fluid of a woman with rheumatoid arthritis. Albert Sabin, MD, searching for the answer to infantile paralysis, was working nearby.

" Arthritis and Colitis

Several years ago, food poisoning triggered a violent case of reactive rheumatoid arthritis and ulcerated colitis. My inflammation levels were higher than my naturopath had ever seen or heard of, and I was in a wheelchair for three months. Eventually I was able to get the inflammation down, but was left with acute arthritis where the least bit of stress or cold caused the inflammation to flare up again. I also continued to battle colitis. Then I learned about the Weston A. Price Foundation and bone broth. I make a lot of soups and stews and cook my eggs, rice, and vegetable dishes with bone broth, and it adds flavor and richness to these dishes. I find that if I eat about two cups a day for at least six days a week I have *no* inflammation in my joints, *no* colitis or gut problems, and a greatly improved immune system. I can really tell the difference if I go off of the bone broth for over a week. Bone broth is my healer.

–*Marilyn Skousen,*
Orem, Utah "

Dr. Brown suspected the mycobacteria settled into connective tissue and provoked severe allergic and inflammatory reactions, and he published an important paper in 1939. Although his theory was favorably received for a time, World War II intervened, and establishment medicine moved on to cortisone therapies. Soon after, the very arthritis foundations and groups Dr. Brown had helped found turned on his ideas, calling them "disproven and dangerous." In 1988, Joan Lunden on *Good Morning America* introduced him as a doctor with a bestselling book *The Road Back*, which was "turning the American medical establishment upside down." Dr. Brown, who had once been at the pinnacle of his profession, joked that he was trying to "turn it right side up!"

Dr. Brown's theory of RA has earned the respect of many health experts over the years, including Harold E. Paulus, MD, of the University of California at Los Angeles, who observed, "A well-protected infection may be at least partially responsible for rheumatoid arthritis manifestations and the treatment may suppress the infection."

More recently scientists have come up with a theory of "molecular mimicry" that helps explain this phenomenon. The idea is that some viruses and bacteria have evolved to successfully "hide out" from immune cells by camouflaging themselves with amino acid sequences similar to those found in cellular proteins. While this initially fools the immune cells, they eventually do attack, but appear to be attacking the body itself as in an autoimmune disorder.

Many alternative practitioners, including David Brownstein, MD, and Joseph Mercola, DO, have modified Dr. Brown's protocol to include diet and have used it to treat RA as well as other rheumatic diseases such as scleroderma, lupus, psoriatic arthritis, polymyositis, and dermatomyositis.

Thomas Cowan, MD, author of *The Fourfold Path to Healing*, and a founding board member of the Weston A. Price Foundation, believes Dr. Brown's treatment can be helpful, though he qualifies that "the holistic view sees the mycoplasma merely as a symptom of a more basic cause." In his medical practice, Dr. Cowan has successfully used small doses of tetracycline along with omega-3 oils, evening primrose oil, willow bark extract, boswellia complex, liver-strengthening formulas, and oral tolerance therapy.

Dr. Trentham's work may have made news headlines in the early 1990s, but Royal Lee, DDS (1895–1967), actually discovered it sixty years before. Discussing Dr. Lee and oral tolerance therapy, Dr. Cowan explains, "When the body has an excessive immune or antibody reaction against a particular tissue, such as cartilage, we can 'trick' the body by giving it oral doses of the same tissue from an animal. For rheumatoid arthritis, Dr. Lee formulated oral Ostrophin or cartilage tissue from a bull. According to Dr. Lee, Ostrophin stimulates destructive antibodies, many of which are located in the intestines, to direct their attack against the medicine instead of the body's own tissue. This theory may explain why chicken soup, containing an abundance of dissolved cartilage, is such a time-honored method for treating rheumatism. The use of cartilage-rich broths, along with Ostrophin from Standard Process, often provides enough relief from inflammation to permit the patient to address the more fundamental causes of his disorder."

Though Dr. Brown recommended the antibiotic minocycline, Dr. Prudden found bovine tracheal cartilage alone could do the job. As discussed in chapter 13 on wound healing, it has pronounced antibacterial effects but without the side effects of antibiotics, and without the risk of breeding stronger, antibiotic-resistant bacteria. Cartilage supplements nourish the body's own immune system, equipping it to dispatch all harmful microbes, bacteria included. At the same time, its built-in "watchdogs" curb any tendency of the immune system to overreact and perpetuate an autoimmune disorder. In that bovine tracheal cartilage also has distinguished itself in treating nearly every possible disorder affecting connective tissue, it seems a reasonable weapon against mycoplasma bacteria lurking in connective tissue.

Whether broth can do much the same is a theory unproven but instinctively understood. Anecdotal evidence suggests it can, and oral tolerance therapy suggests a mechanism. At the very least, ancestral wisdom supports the value of broth for nourishing good overall health, which includes joint health and a high-functioning, finely tuned immune system.

CHAPTER 11

Scleroderma

Orthodox medicine considers scleroderma incurable. Over the years, much has been tried, but nothing has put so much as a dent in its tough hide.

Scleroderma comes from the Greek words *skleros*, for hardening, and *derma*, for skin. Also known as "hidebound" disease, it makes victims want to hide, though "hidebound" refers to a leathery thickness that can bind so tightly that victims feel like prisoners in their own skin. About 300,000 people in the United States have been diagnosed with scleroderma.

Scleroderma results from a runaway growth process created when the body produces too much collagen and connective tissue. The thick overgrowth tightens over the fascia of the muscles, causing rigidity. Typically scleroderma begins with taut, shiny, discolored skin on the face and fingers and sometimes stops there. If it progresses, it takes over the arms and legs, then advances toward the middle of the body until the entire body surface is involved.

In severe cases, the connective tissues of the colon, lungs, kidneys, and heart are affected and scleroderma lives up to its other medical name, progressive systemic sclerosis. When

the lungs are involved, breathing becomes difficult, because inhaling and exhaling depend on flexibility. If the GI tract becomes stiff, peristalsis stops and the victim becomes chronically constipated. Cardiac disturbances, kidney malfunction, and cirrhosis of the liver and other organ breakdowns may occur in the course of what can be an agonizing, unpredictable disease.

Scleroderma is an autoimmune disease related to rheumatoid arthritis, and blood tests on scleroderma patients usually show a positive latex fixation test, a test used to detect antigens. Hemolytic anemia, an autoimmune disorder characterized by chronic premature destruction of red blood cells, is also often part of the scleroderma clinical picture. As of yet, no drug has significantly influenced the outcome, though all manner of pharmaceutical formulas have been enlisted to attack the symptoms.

During the early 1970s, Dr. John F. Prudden successfully treated a number of severe cases of scleroderma with injections of bovine tracheal cartilage and reported them in *Seminars in Arthritis and Rheumatism*. "It was a phenomenal thing," he remembered. "Very dramatic. We'd give it a depot injection and see a wide area totally turn soft, within about five minutes." This skin change occurred so rapidly "that it must necessarily have been due to quick depolymerization of the excess collagen deposition." The skin would then stay soft for about two days before beginning to harden again. In severe cases, the injections had to be repeated weekly in order to achieve and maintain the improvement.

Almost forty years later, in 2013, an interesting treatment for the first stage of scleroderma turned up in the *Journal of Wound Care*. A woman with a painful calcinosis cutis lesion on her buttocks was surgically treated with excision followed by the application of a regeneration template made of bovine collagen types I, II, and V coated with elastin. The patient's wound healed quickly without complication, without needing a skin graft, and with no recurrence as of the ten-month follow-up. Calcinosis cutis is the first stage in the clinical pattern of scleroderma known as CREST, an acronym for calcinosis cutis, Raynaud's phenomenon, esophageal dysmotility, sclerodactyly, and telangiectasia. Dr. Prudden would have been pleased though hardly surprised. As we discuss in chapter 13, he was applying cartilage to wounds with good effect back in the 1950s.

Over the years, Dr. Prudden also proved that bovine tracheal cartilage has strong antimicrobial powers. This fact is relevant if we believe scleroderma—like rheumatoid arthritis and other autoimmune diseases—is caused by infection from pleomorphic bacteria. This controversial theory holds that elusive bacteria hide in connective tissue, inciting the body's immune system to attack it over and over. Because these bacteria are extremely good at eluding their attackers, the body ends up destroying its own collagen and cartilage-rich tissues.

In 1946, Virginia Wuerthele-Caspe, MD (1906–1990), found teeming crowds of pleomorphic bacteria in the skin of a nurse afflicted with severe scleroderma. The bacteria were acid-fast, indicating that they stained in a way similar to the mycobacteria that cause tuberculosis and leprosy. In laboratory culture, the scleroderma microbe was highly pleomorphic, meaning it appeared in multiple forms. When she injected these bugs into guinea pigs, the guinea pigs promptly developed scleroderma. The doctor then named the microbe *Sclerobacillus Wuerthele-Caspe* after herself, published a paper naming them as the probable cause of scleroderma, and proposed treatment with antibacterials.

Dr. Wuerthele-Caspe then noticed that some of the sclerodermic guinea pigs developed cancer, a rare occurrence among guinea pigs. That revelation led, in turn, to her identification of a microbial cause and a possible cure for cancer. In 1977, Dr. Wuerthele-Caspe—later known as Dr. Livingston-Wheeler and finally simply Dr. Livingston—wrote that "the disease entities of tuberculosis, leprosy, generalized sclerosis and cancer have certain features in common. All four are characterized by a simultaneous process of production and destruction of tissue and by a progressive systemic involvement of the host." Her discovery was then confirmed in 1953 by researchers at the Pasteur Institute of Brussels, who found the bacteria in nine additional cases.

Thomas McPherson Brown, MD (1906–1989), also staked his career on mycobacteria. As a young man at the Rockefeller Institute in New York City, Brown identified them as the probable cause of rheumatoid arthritis and for more than fifty years successfully used antibiotics to treat patients with RA, scleroderma, lupus, juvenile rheumatoid arthritis, fibromyalgia, and other rheumatic diseases. A respected "doctor's doctor" in the field of rheumatology prior to World War II, he fell out of favor afterward when cortisone became all the rage. Although neither cortisone nor subsequent drugs have softened scleroderma's thick hide, Dr. Brown's treatment is dismissed by mainstream arthritis organizations as "disproven and dangerous." The popular book *Scleroderma: The Proven Therapy that Can Save Your Life* by Henry Scammell, coauthor of Dr. Brown's book *The Road Back*, has kept the idea in the public eye.

Similarly, Alan R. Cantwell Jr., MD, born in 1934, was a respected dermatologist at Kaiser-Permanente in Hollywood, California, who wrote or coauthored more than thirty articles published in major, peer-reviewed medical journals. At least thirteen of these, published between 1966 and 1984, reported the presence of acid-fast pleomorphic bacteria (the type of bacteria that causes TB) in cases of scleroderma, pseudoscleroderma, diabetic sclerodermatitis, lupus erythematosus, and related diseases.

Dr. Cantwell writes, "I naturally thought all these reports in the medical journals would be recognized by other dermatologists and scientists, and that scleroderma would be recognized as an infectious disease caused by acid-fast bacteria. But after more than a half-century, I'm sad to say that scleroderma is still considered a disease 'of unknown etiology' and the bacteria we found are simply ignored...As a result, physicians cling to the belief that the body is attacking itself through 'autoimmune' mechanisms; and doctors persist in advocating conventional therapies for systemic scleroderma, which are widely regarded as ineffective. We believe the body is not attacking itself, but is desperately trying to rid itself of disease-producing microbes that are not recognized by the scientific community." Now that theories of "molecular mimicry" are capturing the interest of scientists, Dr. Cantwell may yet live to see a wider acceptance of his infectious cause of scleroderma and other auto-immune disorders.

" Warts

About ten years ago I started to learn about the health benefits of broth, so I decided to create a batch. Being a novice in the kitchen, I had no idea what to do with it once it was made, so it sat in the fridge for a while. Then I decided to drink a cup a day. Within one week the wart I had on my finger was gone. Gone. I'm a chiropractor and have been able to convince only three other people to try this, but it worked for them, too, and one of them had dozens of warts all over.

—*Jon Peterson, DC,*
Hilbert, Wisconsin

In recent years, Dr. Cantwell has stepped up to full-blown medical heretic status. His work with Kaposi's sarcoma, an AIDS-related skin cancer, led him to investigate the origin of HIV, and publish his findings in the books *AIDS and the Doctors of Death* (1992) and *Queer Blood: Secret AIDS Genocide Plot* (1993). His writings also include "Virginia Livingston, MD: Cancer Quack or Medical Genius?" and he has called the controversial

Dr. Livingston "the greatest physician of the twentieth century."

So what do mutating bacteria, medical heretics, and conspiracy theories have to do with broth? Nathan R. Gotthoffer, in *Gelatin in Nutrition and Medicine*, reported cases from the late nineteenth and early twentieth centuries in which gelatin helped heal tuberculosis, a disease caused by the acid-fast pleomorphic bacterium *Mycobacterium tuberculosis*. Earlier, Avicenna, a tenth-century philosopher and scientist during Islam's Golden Age, claimed the very best cure for leprosy (caused by the same type of bacterium) was the broth made from a "young fat hen." Moses Maimonides, the twelfth-century codifier of Jewish law, also recommended it for leprosy. In the twentieth century, TB and leprosy were researched by Dr. Livingston early in her career and more recently by Dr. Cantwell, who was exploring the possible role of *Mycobacterium tuberculosis* as a primary agent in HIV.

Gotthoffer also reported gelatin to be effective with many other infectious diseases and helpful for the prevention of infections during wound healing. Although the gelatin studies are inconsistent, benefits from gelatin go well beyond providing nourishment during convalescence. Of course, that's not surprising given chicken soup's long-standing reputation as "Jewish penicillin." Furthermore, from the early 1950s to his death in 1998, Dr. Prudden found bovine cartilage surprisingly capable of killing dangerous microbes.

Obviously, Dr. Prudden's doses were higher than would be expected from daily broth drinking or gelatin supplementation, but as discussed in chapter 10, sometimes "less is more." As research on oral tolerance therapy has established, autoimmune disorders can sometimes be turned around with tiny doses of collagen—comparable to what could be consumed in broth.

Clearly, collagen, cartilage, and broth itself deserve further research as treatments for any and all rheumatic diseases. And broth should also be widely recommended as part of a nourishing diet that could prevent scleroderma to begin with. Instead, mainstream doctors continue to attack scleroderma with pharmaceuticals that suppress the immune system and inhibit cell proliferation, drugs that show limited benefits at best and horrendous side effects at worst.

In the early 1970s, Dr. Prudden visited a colleague who was a renowned scleroderma expert at Columbia-Presbyterian Hospital to share his findings. Although the specialist was "staggered" to see the hardened areas on a chronically ill scleroderma patient turn soft, he politely declined to test cartilage injections on his own patients. As Dr. Prudden put it, "I thought for sure he would want to start a project, but he did not. I was moving on to cancer research and hoped he would take over, but he apparently wanted to continue what he was doing already, though that was ineffectual at best and of no value at all at worst. I expect that the skin of his patients still looks like corpses prepared by the embalmer."

CHAPTER 12

Psoriasis

Nearly 7.5 million Americans know the heartbreak of psoriasis. Neither the heavily advertised standard over-the-counter remedies nor prescription drugs help much.

The word *psoriasis* comes from the Greek word *psora*, which means "to itch."

The problem begins when the epidermis—the outer layer of the skin—experiences a growth spurt. Though a lively turnover of cells in young people contributes to smooth, radiant skin, the right balance must be struck between the arrival of the new and the sloughing off of the old. Psoriasis sufferers know no such balance, for the epidermal turnover turns over and over and over again, frightfully out of control. Soon excess skin cells crowd together, pile up, and die, forming the thick, flat, red patches and silvery scales of psoriasis.

The most common sites are the elbows, knees, arms, legs, lower back, ears, and scalp. When the disease is at its worst, these areas reach out to others until psoriasis covers much of the body. The skin may crack, bleed, ooze, and itch. Fingernails and toenails develop ridges and pits.

Fueling this horror—and perhaps causing it—is an abnormally rich network of capillaries under the skin. These tiny blood vessels are the points of exchange where nutrients are delivered from the little arteries known as arterioles and where wastes are picked up from the little veins known as venules. Without the support of this capillary bed, the wildly growing skin of psoriasis sufferers would slow down and return to normal. Without the wildly proliferating skin of psoriasis, the extra capillaries would be underemployed. It's a "which came first, the chicken or the egg?" situation.

Though medical scientists have yet to agree on a cause of psoriasis, there is abundant data on aggravating factors: stress, viral or bacterial infections, sunburn, poison ivy, cuts, surgery, and over-the-counter and pharmaceutical drugs. For most people, the problem comes and goes and is usually better in the summer. Though this last observation has led to prescriptions of fun in the sun, treatments with ultraviolet light, and high doses of vitamin D, the healing results have been partial at best.

Psoriasis is one more example of collagen disease—often categorized as an autoimmune disease—that seems to respond well not only to the dietary improvement of consuming broth but to supplements with collagen, cartilage, glucosamine, and other broth components.

In midcareer Dr. John Prudden was called in to treat a man cursed with an ulcerating wound that would not heal and discovered that bovine tracheal cartilage heals psoriasis. Located on the inside of the leg above his ankle, the ulcer was but one horror among many, for the poor man's leg was also covered with patches of psoriasis.

With the intention of healing only the wound—psoriasis, after all, was "known" to be incurable—Dr. Prudden applied cartilage powder to it, dressed it, and wrapped it with an elastic bandage. Within three days it had improved greatly. And so had the nearby psoriasis.

It was no surprise to Dr. Prudden that the wound had improved quickly and eventually healed completely. The wonder was that the psoriasis had also responded. Though never treated directly, the flaking patches received the benefit of cartilage powder that had seeped out from under the bandage along with pus and other fluids escaping from the ulcer.

Of all the remarkable cases of his long career, none made a more striking impression on the doctor than this one. It led, in turn, to his studies of the anti-inflammatory effect of cartilage on osteoporosis, as well as on a host of autoimmune diseases such as rheumatoid arthritis, lupus erythematosus, and scleroderma. Indeed, Dr. Prudden thought psoriasis itself should be classified as an autoimmune disease, the red patches and silvery scales the result of the victim's own overzealous immune system attacking the skin and connective tissues. Dr. Prudden pointed out that it is well known that a persistent injurious stimulus—either physical or chemical—can cause antibodies and antigens to pile up at the site. This, in turn, causes chronic inflammation, capillary growth, and a proliferation of macrophages, which are white blood cells that—as their name *macro* (meaning "big") and *phage* (meaning "eat") suggests—are "big eaters." They are able and willing to devour several times their weight in foreign invaders. Or, as is the case in autoimmune disorders, what appear to be foreign invaders. Dr. Prudden also pointed to the so-called Koebner phenomenon, named after a nineteenth-century Polish dermatologist. In explaining why psoriasis appears most commonly and tenaciously at the elbows and knees, Koebner theorized that it develops at points of chronic trauma, even minor trauma.

Having seen the dramatic improvement of one case of psoriasis and having often witnessed bovine tracheal cartilage's power to heal wounds and relieve chronic inflammation, Dr. Prudden decided to find out whether bovine tracheal cartilage would relieve the suffering of other psoriasis sufferers. To that end, he gave bovine cartilage injections to thirty-nine cases of severe psoriasis in which lesions were on all parts of the body and covered up to 70 percent of the body surface. These patients had undergone every known form of medical treatment for years without results.

The result was that nineteen people experienced the miracle of total remission, with a complete disappearance of all lesions for six weeks to more than a year. The average period of remission was five months. In each case, the bovine tracheal cartilage injections prompted a descaling of the skin, which soon became smooth. As treatment continued, the capillary network supporting the disease shut down and the dermis and epidermis layers of the skin returned to normal.

" Wasting Away and Horrible Eczema

Our son, Joseph, was basically dying by wasting away. He was nine years old, absorbing no nutrients, had horrible eczema, had lost twenty pounds, and was fading fast.

We had been using elements of the *Nourishing Traditions* book for a few months at that point, but prior to that had been mostly organic vegetarians (not strict). Our chiropractor, Dr. Mark Stern, used a number of different Standard Process products and some manipulations and recommended a grain-free, sugar-free, mostly dairy-free diet to heal Joseph's gut. I fed him *stock* every day! I had read all the articles on the Weston A. Price website about the healing properties of stock and how it was used in wasting diseases. So I put stock in rice and beans (although for the first several months we ate very little of those two) and in soup of every imaginable kind. All kinds of different vegetable soups—with whole vegetables or "creaming" them with a stick blender, cream of broccoli, cream of cauliflower, cream of kale, cream of tomato…But basically any vegetable or combination of vegetables with stock, Celtic sea salt, sautéed onions, and celery.

I just figured, at that stage, where he had lost so much weight every bite had to count and be as full of nutrients as I could get it. The stock made every nutrient more digestible.

–*Lauri Tauscher, Tigard, Oregon* "

Of the sixteen psoriasis patients who did not go into complete remission, twelve did so after receiving additional booster injections in three-week intervals and from applying an ointment called Psoriasin T two or three times a day after bathing. The ointment combined cartilage with coal tar (a remedy long prescribed for psoriasis) and led to more rapid descaling. Once the skin smoothed out, Dr. Prudden prescribed continued treatment with a coal tar–free Psoriasin.

Dr. Prudden found in most cases it was generally possible to stop the booster shots of cartilage as soon as steady improvement was under way. Where relapses occurred, they could be reversed with cream or ointment alone.

Not all was a total success. Many of the patients had severe forms of the malady and were highly pessimistic after years of trying therapies without success. That pessimism proved a problem when it came to compliance. As Dr. Prudden put it, "They cling doggedly to an almost mystical hope that they will one day be cured of their affliction by the development of a new drug that will work like magic. Since their attitude virtually always consists of this strange combination of mystic faith and profound skepticism, it is exceedingly difficult to 'keep a foot on 'em' and thereby ensure a consistent and careful follow-up with fair evaluation of the therapy employed."

A big reason for patient discouragement was the fact that treatment of psoriasis often begins with a bang followed by a crash. Patients who are ecstatic to see the fading of long-term lesions become glum when newborn lesions pop up all over the body. This phenomenon—which Dr. Prudden called churning but today is often known as a detox reaction—often goes on for three to six weeks, leading many patients to conclude they are getting worse.

Eczema

I have noticed my eczema has cleared up entirely since incorporating broth and higher-fat foods into my diet. My skin had never been worse than when I was a vegetarian for seven years. Both of my children eat broth and I give them "Japanese"-style soupspoons that are deep to slurp up their broth. For whatever it is worth, both my children now have an amazing ability to focus in school, rarely get ill, and have nice healthy teeth.

–Emily Marenghi,
Portola Valley, California

What causes this churning? Apparently the existing lesions in their death throes release substances capable of spreading the psoriasis known as psoriagens. But once these are either excreted or metabolized by the liver, widespread improvement is the rule. Indeed, we have every reason to presume that the chemical source of the original lesions is being ousted once and for all.

Of the five patients in the study who were not completely healed, three improved a great deal but did not clear completely. Despite their improvement, they did not return for follow-up treatments because they had pessimistically concluded nothing more could be done to help them. Dr. Prudden classified the fifth case as a failure. This was a fifty-eight-year-old man who had one of the worst cases of psoriasis imaginable, with what appeared to be feathers in place of skin. From the get-go, this man was resigned to his fate and had to be persuaded over and over not to expect rapid results and to keep up the therapy. He quit right at the point Dr. Prudden noted a "good descaling had begun."

For those with minor patches of psoriasis, Dr. Prudden recommended just cartilage cream applied two or three times per day, after bathing. Though he and his associates did not investigate the use of the cream as completely or follow it up as thoroughly as the injections, most of his patients reported they did well with it. Those who did not clear their lesions entirely with the cream did so with the help of a few injections. The results in many cases seemed miraculous, but Dr. Prudden cautioned patients to understand the importance of consistent and prolonged therapy. As the doctor put it, "Extensive psoriasis is, in all probability, a profound civil war within the patient. Cartilage therapy yields slow but steady progress, and unlike pharmaceutical drugs, addresses the very cause of the disease."

Dr. Prudden's success with bovine cartilage was not lost on I. William Lane, PhD. The author of *Sharks Don't Get Cancer* touted shark cartilage as a natural cure for cancer, rheumatoid arthritis, psoriasis, and other diseases because it inhibits angiogenesis (the growth of new blood vessels). Healthy cartilage, after all, is an avascular tissue. Given the birth and proliferation of blood vessels in advanced psoriasis, anti-angiogenic factors would obviously be desirable. Not surprisingly, researchers in 1998 reported success with psoriasis topically treated with extracts of shark cartilage rich in the anti-angiogenesis factor. As reported in the *Journal of Cutaneous Medicine and Surgery*, the extract was successfully applied to the forearms of a patient with psoriasis and has a great future treating "cutaneous and systemic diseases associated with altered vascularity."

Lane, however, staked his reputation and marketing of shark cartilage on his belief that any form of cartilage—injected, topical, or pill—worked because of anti-angiogenesis. Unfortunately for Lane's credibility, Judah Folkman, MD, the medical scientist who founded the field of anti-angiogenesis research, insisted that the anti-angiogenic factors could not survive digestion in the gut. Dr. Prudden agreed, and always pointed out his psoriasis treatments involved injections and topicals. Yet some clinicians think at least some of the anti-angiogenic factors do get through, and we have many clinical cases as well as anecdotes from people who have cleared psoriasis with cartilage pills or with cartilage-rich broth.

In 2002, an article in the *Journal of the American Academy of Dermatology* confirmed the fact that anti-angiogenic factors survive the digestive process, although in a heavily dose-related way. Patients taking the highest doses of an extract from shark cartilage of the anti-angiogenic factors showed significant improvements in their Psoriasis Area and Severity Index score. However, they were also more likely to experience nausea, diarrhea, vomiting, flatulence, and constipation. Some even developed acne or a rash. These findings accord with the most frequent side effects reported by clinicians who've prescribed high doses of whole shark cartilage products. Notably, the recommended doses of bovine and chicken cartilage are far lower than those for shark cartilage. And there appear to be no risks at all from enjoying cartilage-rich broth, soups, and stews.

Studies on glucosamine and chondroitin sulfate for psoriasis are scant. In 1997, in *Medical Hypotheses*, nutritionist M. F. McCarty of Nutrition 21 in San Diego, California, proposed ways in which glucosamine could inhibit a variety of growth factors that can lead to skin proliferation and psoriasis. A literature review of chondroitin sulfate (CS), published in *Osteoarthritis and Cartilage* in 2010, concluded there was "preliminary evidence in humans that CS improves moderate to severe psoriasis," and further suggested it may prove "a useful therapeutic agent" in a host of other autoimmune diseases, including irritable bowel syndrome, atherosclerosis, Parkinson's disease, Alzheimer's disease, multiple sclerosis, amyotrophic lateral sclerosis, rheumatoid arthritis, and lupus.

The voluminous scientific literature on gelatin from the nineteenth and twentieth centuries says nothing about psoriasis, although it has a great deal to say about eczema, including the types known as infantile and varicose eczemas. Gelatin served well, whether taken orally, by injection, or applied topically using special masks and "boots."

Those early scientists also found ample evidence that gelatin protects us from infection. This is relevant to psoriasis because bacteria or viruses appear to play important roles in the onset of psoriasis. Mainstream medicine then thinks the body's immune system goes amuck, attacking its own cells. An alternative possibility is that the body in its wisdom engages in an ongoing attack on an elusive adversary known as pleomorphic bacteria. Indeed, the type known as *Mycoplasma fermentans* is associated with not only psoriasis, but also arthritis, lupus, chronic fatigue syndrome, Crohn's disease, irritable bowel syndrome, multiple sclerosis, AIDS, and cancer. Either way, gelatin and, of course, broth can help fight deep, systemic infection.

Clearly, the arguments over the cause and cure of psoriasis are not going to be resolved anytime soon. What to do? Accept the fact that we don't need all the answers. Embrace traditional wisdom instead. Prevent—and even reverse—the heartbreak of psoriasis with heartwarming, nourishing broth.

Turning Back MS

I was vegan for a decade and thought I was on the world's most perfect diet. Then after periodic problems with unexplained numbness, spasticity, and memory blackouts, I was diagnosed with RRMS (relapsing-remitting multiple sclerosis). I was terrified it would progress and searched the Internet for answers. I discovered the work of Dr. Terry Wahls through her TEDx talk and, a few months later, found her book *The Wahls Protocol*. The thought of eating meat felt wrong to me, but she had healed her own MS with her version of a paleo diet and, at that point, I was desperate enough to try anything—even liver and broth made from the carcasses of dead animals. This was frankly repugnant to me, but I did what I had to do. What I never would have guessed was how much stronger the liver would make me feel and how immensely comforting the warm soups became for me. I could feel my starved body just suck in the nourishment and start to heal. I've had some ups and downs but overall my inflammation is down, my energy up, and my mood much improved. I felt hopeless last year, but I now know I've turned the corner.

–Patricia W.,
Hartford, Connecticut

CHAPTER 13

Wound Healing

For many years, doctors thought there was no way to speed up the healing of a wound. Nature set the pace and nothing researchers came up with seemed to help her along.

In the 1940s, however, some possibilities came up in the booming new field of vitamin and mineral research. Researchers revealed how malnutrition could slow wound healing and confirmed the body's need for a full complement of vitamins and minerals to synthesize connective tissue. They showed that the adrenal glands need vitamins B_2 and B_5 to generate hormones and learned that patients' adrenals are typically exhausted by the second or third day following surgery. They found that rectifying folate deficiencies alone could help many patients whose wounds failed to heal. Finally, at least eight studies proved wound healing depends on adequate vitamin C status because connective tissue cannot be synthesized without it.

Because the body doesn't store vitamin C or the B complex for long, researchers recommended supplements for surgery patients to compensate for the fact that people in hospitals rarely eat well. While appropriate supplements can favorably influence healing from surgery, there's another obvious take-away: Hospital food needs a checkup—and needs to include old-fashioned bone broth as well as other nutrient-rich foods. In their wisdom, our ancestors served plenty of easy-to-digest broth and gelatin-rich foods to patients recovering from illness or injury. Modern hospitals keep up the tradition, but with industrially processed soups made from hydrolyzed vegetable protein, not bones, and gelatin in the form of sugary, brightly colored Jell-O. What patients need is nourishing broth, rich in cartilage, collagen, glycine, glutamine, and other healing components.

Gelatin was first heavily investigated as a dietary staple and wound healer during the Napoleonic Wars. Nineteenth-century researchers explored its use as a hemostatic agent to stop the loss of blood and then to build new blood. Because sterile gelatin is hypoallergenic, it even served as a plasma substitute in the treatment of severe hemorrhage or shock. During World War I, gelatin saline solutions were routinely used as emergency substitutes for whole blood transfusions, though hospital technicians were none too fond of its habit of setting like Jell-O in the tubes and cannulae if rooms were too cold. Investigators found no evidence of liver damage or impairment of kidney function from IV gelatin. Plant-based pectins and other substitutes were also tried but proved riskier and less effective than gelatin.

Though most of this gelatin research was driven by the need to help the war wounded, the scientists also found that gelatin could help bleeding from hemorrhoids, ulcers, hemophilia, dysentery, anemia, excessive menstrual flow, and childbirth. Indeed, history records its therapeutic usage as a hemostatic agent back to the first century AD. Similarly, Chinese medicine has long recommended donkey gelatin for bleeding disorders.

Gelatin biscuits, bonbons, and cubes were also heavily used as war rations through World War I. Florence Nightingale, who came to prominence as a nurse during the Crimean War, wrote in *Notes on Nursing* that many patients were actually starving to death because of overreliance on the nutritional benefits of "meat tea."

By the 1930s and 1940s, interest shifted from gelatin—which had been oversold as a "wonder food" and had failed to live up to grandiose claims—to the emerging research in vitamins and minerals. The subject was new and controversial, but even open-minded surgeons who checked out the research on vitamins, minerals, and wound healing could not fail to note that the research showed they would help only patients who were seriously deficient in those substances to begin with. People who tested as clinically normal except for their wounds did not seem to benefit from supplements.

In the meantime, the research on wound healing went on, with persistent researchers testing one topical substance after another, including products as curious as colchicine, detergents, cod liver oil, and even aluminum foil. But nothing worked well or worked consistently. During the Korean War, surgeons called out in desperation for a wound-healing agent that could counteract the notoriously bad effects of cortisone. Cortisone had burst on the scene in 1949 as a wonder drug capable of stopping inflammation, fever, and pain. This it did, but with a significant downside. Inflammation is the first step in wound healing for a reason. It's the phase in which the body dispatches microbes, foreign material, and dying tissue in preparation for repair. Take it away with cortisone and the regeneration of connective tissue is retarded—the last thing needed for the healing of a wound.

Worse, cortisone had an unseemly tendency to reopen wounds, spilling guts and gore. Young Dr. John F. Prudden, tending to severely injured Korean War soldiers as head of the wound-healing unit at Fort Sam, Houston, Texas, saw it all. "Anastomoses in the bowel fell apart, producing peritonitis. Bronchial stump closures split open. Abdominal and chest wounds fell apart. All producing fatalities." The drug furthermore was linked to leaking blood vessels, infections, metabolic disturbances, and the creation of non-healing ulcers. Not surprisingly, surgeons considered finding a remedy a high priority. Speeding normal wound healing was highly desirable; reversing the deleterious side effects of cortisone was a necessity.

The answer to both prayers was cartilage.

Dr. Prudden didn't discover the wound-healing properties of cartilage, but his name will be linked with it forever. In 1954, he returned to New York City from service in the Army Medical Corps to read a draft of a research paper by his old professor Raffaele Lattes, MD, MSD. It recounted a surprising discovery: Cartilage could counteract the harmful effects of cortisone on wound healing.

Dr. Lattes, a professor of surgical pathology at Columbia University, along with two other colleagues from Columbia, Karl Meyer, a biochemist, and Charles Regan, a professor of surgery, had completed a wound-healing experiment involving laboratory rats. Each rat had been equipped with tiny chambers inserted under an area of skin that was wounded with an incision. The chamber was then filled with cortisone plus a substance that the researchers hoped would counteract the drug's unwanted side effects.

An Upstart's Advice

Although many substances were tried, nothing worked, and the rats rallied poorly, if at all. Watching the attempts every Tuesday was J. R. Martin, a young doctor from the Royal Victoria Hospital in Montreal, who had come to Columbia-Presbyterian to study with Dr. Arthur Purdy Stout, the world-famous director of surgical pathology. As the respected older scientists tried and failed every week, the upstart started offering unasked-for advice, including the tip that cartilage chips might be just the thing to try.

"This suggestion was astonishing to the three professors for different reasons but universally rejected," said Dr. Prudden. "But this young man was made of stern Canadian stuff and did not cease from harassing them, saying that was what they should do. Finally he drove them into a state of distraction with his constant suggestion, so they decided to humor him. They attained some cartilage chips from the knee joint of a recently amputated human leg, made it into micro chips, and placed it in the wounds in rats. Their hope was he would see it did not work, leave with his tail between his legs and stop bothering them." Instead, the fast and positive result astonished everyone. Everyone, apparently, but the Canadian, who mysteriously disappeared before the results even came in.

> ## Knee Surgery
>
> I can't praise bone broth enough for its therapeutic value. I suffered for eight years after knee surgery with almost constant pain and swelling. When I started drinking bone broth twice daily, the pain and swelling went down after about three weeks. It's been several months now and my knee has been great. I'm still amazed!
>
> —Stuart Haas,
> Glen Rock, New Jersey

Though this was a remarkable discovery, Dr. Lattes and the other eminent researchers decided they were too busy to pursue further studies. "They all sang the same song: 'I haven't got enough money, haven't got enough time, too many students. I'm not going to follow up on it in the foreseeable future,'" said Dr. Prudden. "So I sang the song I already had sung, that I felt it was glittering with promise, that they were making a very bad mistake, and said 'If you aren't going to do it, then I am.'"

Thus Dr. Prudden began the research on

cartilage that would lead from the break-throughs in wound healing to the discoveries that oral cartilage could turn around incurable diseases such as osteoarthritis, Crohn's disease, scleroderma, and stage four cancers.

His first step was to try to round up Dr. Martin. As he told the story, "At Columbia-Presbyterian, I heard he had gone back to the Royal Vic, but no one there had seen him, and there was no record on file of immediate family. I called the Canadian Medical Association in case he'd gone off to treat the Eskimos. I got the AMA looking for him in case he'd stayed here. Finally, I became suspicious of foul play and asked the New York Police Department if any unidentified bodies had turned up. Nothing. It's a complete mystery. Who was this messenger from on high who came in to show me the way and then disappeared into the void?"

Unable to find Dr. Martin, Dr. Prudden got to work. For a tightly controlled experimental model, he chose to wound rats with precisely placed, carefully cut and measured incisions. To determine the speed and extent of wound healing, he decided to measure tensile strength, which is the amount of stress a wound can accept without splitting open. The key issues under investigation were why some wounds fail to attain adequate structural strength and whether it is possible to achieve this strength earlier than usual.

Most of these wound-healing experiments involved pairs of laboratory rats who were purposely wounded with incisions. In each case, one of the rats was treated with cartilage powder, which was applied as a thin "frost" on the edges of the wound, and the other received none. After a given period (usually seven days), the researchers removed the sutures and evaluated the wound strength by inflating a balloon in the peritoneal cavity until the wound broke open. This proved the cartilage-treated wounds gained tensile strength more quickly and helped Dr. Prudden ascertain the rate of gain.

Further investigation involved testing cartilage in the form of pellets implanted under the rats' skin. Even when implanted far from the wound, they had a good effect. Studies by other researchers followed, including one by Dr. John C. Houck of the Biochemical Research Laboratory at the Children's Hospital in Washington, DC, who proved that cartilage aided the healing of the chronically inflamed, tumor-like lesions known as granulomas. Treated by cartilage, they healed in a mere fifteen days compared to twenty-eight days in the control group.

Most of the rats in the early experiments were hale and hardy, a fact that raised an obvious question about how well cartilage would do on sicker specimens. After all, hospitalized people in need of wound-healing acceleration are far from prime specimens. Normally very sick rats afflicted with Alloxan diabetes (a laboratory-induced diabetes) or Cushing's syndrome (hyperadrenocorticism) heal their wounds very slowly if at all. The question Dr. Prudden asked was, would they heal more quickly and strongly with cartilage therapy? Experiments proved that the answer was an unequivocal yes.

Wound Treatment in Humans

By the early 1960s, it was time to let rats retire and put human volunteers to work. Dr. Prudden then set up two sets of experiments. The first involved the treatment of sixty long-suffering patients troubled by chronic, non-granulating wounds that had failed to fill in with the grainy, pink, capillary-rich newborn connective tissue that customarily forms during the wound-healing process. The wounds were truly chronic, never less than two months in age, and up to seven years in duration. The question was, would cartilage initiate this long-delayed granulation? It did.

The second was a better-controlled study in which two incisions were made in the skin of each of fifteen human volunteers. Some of the subjects were private patients of Dr. Prudden; others were inmates at Sing Sing Prison. Of the paired incisions on each body, one was treated with powdered cartilage, the other was not. When the wounds were later tested for tensile strength, twelve of the fifteen people showed cartilage-treated wounds stronger than the controls. The net increase in mean strength was an impressive 41.8 percent.

Dr. Prudden then decided it was time to quantify Dr. Lattes's finding that cartilage could counteract the effects of cortisone. His study, published in *Surgery, Gynecology and Obstetrics* in 1967, reported the wound-healing progress of rats in the light of different dosages of cartilage and cortisone. As expected, cartilage reversed the drug's inhibition of wound healing consistently and considerably, even at excessively high doses of cortisone. Surprisingly, the study also showed that cartilage potentiated cortisone—allowing it to fulfill its wonder drug potential.

All in all, Dr. Prudden published nineteen studies in major medical journals, proving cartilage had the right stuff to speed wound healing. Equally remarkable, though less often reported, is the finding that cartilage could also put on the brakes. Otherwise, cartilage-treated wounds would grow and grow into the massive, raised overgrowths of scar tissue known as keloids. What happens is quite the reverse. Cartilage-treated wounds look better cosmetically—smoother, flatter, altogether more natural—than wounds treated without it. At the same time, cartilage-treated wounds are stronger, more flexible, and less likely to rupture.

Aneurism and Brain Surgery

When I was recovering from a brain aneurysm and brain surgery, I was in ICU for several weeks. My brother-in-law made his Lebanese mother's beef bone broth recipe, which is virtually identical to the one in the *Nourishing Traditions*, and brought it to me repeatedly in the hospital. I was in bad shape, had nearly died, was racked with pain, and was recovering tethered to machines. The bone broth felt like liquid gold and seemed to bring me exactly what I needed. I had excellent medical care, and was surrounded by many loving family members and friends who brought much to my recovery, but that bone broth was life-sustaining medicine, a healing substance like none other. The doctors reported that I had one of those mysterious miraculous recoveries, with no deficits nor difficulties past the initial recovery from the surgery. It is almost as if the aneurysm never actually happened.

–Stacey J.,
Sacramento, California

Dr. Prudden most often used cartilage from the tracheas of calves. The obvious question was whether this was the best type for rats, and the evidence came in that rat cartilage worked as well as the calf cartilage but not better. The cartilage of sharks, tegu lizards, crocodiles, and cow fetuses possessed similar healing properties, provided proper processing had taken place. The cartilage from older animals, however, was less potent. Whatever the type of cartilage chosen, it seemed to work on all animals, including rats, mice, guinea pigs, dogs, and humans.

How cartilage induced and accelerated healing was a mystery that intrigued Dr. Prudden for the rest of his life. "We always believed that one of our most important tasks was the isolation of the specific chemical agent responsible for this striking biologic phenomenon," he said. Over the years he explored multiple possibilities, ultimately deciding credit needed to go to the multiple synergistic factors found naturally in whole cartilage products. Research on the many individual components of cartilage—as well as the additional ones found in broth prepared from skin, cartilage, and bones—continues apace today, as scientists test fractionated "active factors."

Still Not in Use

Dr. Prudden's findings should have set the standard for wound healing. He not only published multiple articles on this topic in major medical journals throughout the 1950s and 1960s but saw his work lauded in *Sabiston's Textbook of Surgery*, where Dr. J. Madden wrote, "After decades of experimentation, only one substance has been shown to affect healing unequivocally." Yet fifty years later cartilage is still not in general use in hospitals, a fact that frustrated Dr. Prudden during his lifetime.

By the 1990s, genetic engineering had emerged as Big Pharma's great white hope for wound healing. Compared to low-cost, low-tech, all-natural cartilage, recombinant DNA technology offered an artificially made molecule that could be replicated and sold at great profit. It involves using enzymes to break isolated DNA molecules into fragments, then rearranging them in a more desirable sequence. Dr. Prudden's comments in 1997 remain relevant today. "There has been considerable premature publicity regarding the capability of these entities to accelerate wound healing," he said. "Yes, in laboratory tissue cultures they can speed the growth of fibroblasts, but that doesn't prove a thing. There's a bottom to the laboratory pot so the growth factors have nothing to do but stick around. It never seems to occur to them that in human beings they're not going to be there anymore! The molecular weight of growth factors is so low that they are sucked into the wound capillaries and excreted through the kidney."

Back in 1965, an editorial in the *Journal of the American Medical Association (JAMA)* recognized Dr. Prudden for the high quality of his wound-healing work and concluded with the words, "The value of these observations is appreciated if we remember that most of the correctable morbidity and mortality of surgery is due to failures of wound healing."

Almost sixty years later, "correctable morbidity and mortality" goes on with attendant pain, suffering—and profit.

CHAPTER 14

Infectious Disease

Broth has served as a traditional folk remedy for the common cold, flu, pneumonia, and other infectious diseases around the world for thousands of years, and chicken soup carries the nickname "Jewish penicillin." Everyone seems to know it works. How it works is the unanswered question.

Studies on Chicken Soup

Over the years, people have come up with various explanations for chicken soup's healing effect. Although some people dismiss its healing reputation as an old wives' tale, most concede that broth at least increases hydration and helps convalescents feel warm and loved. That became official in 1978 when researchers at Mount Sinai Medical Center in Miami Beach, Florida, proved chicken soup offers more than water and a warm and nourishing placebo effect. They investigated the effect of chicken soup on the air flow and mucus in the noses of fifteen volunteers and found hot fluids helped increase the movement of nasal mucus; chicken soup did it even better, and cold water had no effect at all.

The study cited most often to establish chicken soup's healing power comes from Stephen Rennard, MD, a pulmonary care expert at the University of Nebraska Medical Center. For years, Dr. Rennard had watched his wife, Barbara, cook up her Lithuanian grandmother's chicken soup recipe whenever someone in their family felt a cold coming on. In 1993, he decided to find out why chicken soup seemed to have an anti-inflammatory effect. He published his results in *CHEST: The Journal of the American College of Chest Physicians*. His in vitro study came out in 2000 in the same journal, and concludes that some component of chicken soup inhibits neutrophil mobility.

The question is, is this desirable? Neutrophils are the most common white blood cell in the human body, and the body's first line of defense. In the case of colds, they contribute to mucus production and the unpleasant symptoms of cough, runny nose, and sore throat. Although most people seek to stop the surface respiratory symptoms, that can send the infection deeper, ultimately making things worse. If we accept the fact that the body in its wisdom has given us neutrophils, it doesn't make sense that the healing power of broth would lie in inhibiting them or killing them off.

Dr. Rennard also tested thirteen supermarket soup products and found five with an even greater neutrophil-inhibiting effect than the homemade soup. They were Knorr Chicken Flavor, Campbell's Home Cookin' Chicken Vegetable, Campbell's Healthy Request Chicken Noodle, Lipton Cup-a-Soup Chicken Noodle, and Progresso Chicken Noodle. Even Campbell's Vegetarian Vegetable had some neutrophil-inhibiting effect. Omaha tap water, the control, had no effect on them. Strikingly, the neutrophils seem to have actually become more active in Campbell's Chicken Flavor Ramen Noodles, perhaps from the excitatory effect of the product's MSG.

Given that commercial soups loaded with MSG and other dubious additives had both greater and weaker effects on the neutrophils, we have to ask whether neutrophils like swimming about in lab bowls of soup. Normally neutrophils in the body wouldn't even be exposed to chicken broth, as it would be digested before entering the bloodstream. As Tara Parker-Pope in the *New York Times* concluded, "It's not known whether the changes measured in the laboratory really have a meaningful effect on people."

Magic Bullets?

Most of the other studies done on broth over the years have not shown white blood cell inhibition. Rather, the various components appear to boost, balance, and essentially modulate the immune system as needed. The latest magic bullet reported is carnosine, an amino-acid derivative from the amino acids alanine and histidine, which may strengthen the body's immune system so it can fight off the viruses that cause colds and flu in the early stages. As reported in the *American Journal of Therapeutics* in 2012, carnosine's effect on immunity is short term. In other words, people need to consume soup every day during an illness. While that's a good plan, we think broth every day in sickness and in health is the ticket to maintaining a high-functioning immune system.

Glutamine, the third most common amino acid found in broth, also nourishes the immune system. In the 1950s, Harry Eagle, MD (1905–1992), of the National Institutes of Health, found glutamine essential for the growth of all cells, including immune cells. More recently, John Alverdy, MD, of the University of Chicago Medical Center, reports glutamine as critical for gut integrity and for a high-functioning secretory IgA immune system. Biochemist Eric Newsholme, DSc, PhD (1935–2011), linked glutamine depletion to immunosuppression in a series of studies, many on athletes. His work has led to widespread glutamine supplementation for people who are prone to infection because of extreme physical and mental stress.

Cartilage for the Immune System

The most heavily researched component of broth has been cartilage. Although Dr. John F. Prudden never tested the effect of cartilage on cold and flu viruses, he treated people for herpes, shingles, mononucleosis, Epstein-Barr virus, and other viral infections. In the case of these diseases, he found bovine tracheal cartilage stimulated the immune system into action, whether injected or taken orally. He also saw remarkable cures of autoimmune disorders such as rheumatoid arthritis, scleroderma, Crohn's disease, and psoriasis, in which the immune system needed calming down.

"I like to call it a 'potent normalizer,'" said Dr. Prudden. "That is the extraordinary thing about it. It responds to any aberrancy from normal." How so? "Undoubtedly, it is because cartilage comes from the fetal mesenchyme," he explained. "Mother Nature gave the mesenchyme bio-directors to help the fetus develop. If something in your muscles, skin, cartilage, or bone marrow needs to be directed or corrected, one of those macromolecular entities steps in. Obviously, there's very complex chemistry involved, but that's the key to the paradoxical activity of bovine cartilage."

Cartilage doesn't kill viruses directly, however. "With herpes, it was initially assumed that these remarkable effects were due to the direct effect of cartilage on the herpes virus itself," he said. "Yet when they were directly exposed in viral cultures absolutely no effect was observed. This necessarily means that the unique clinical effects observed are due to stimulation of the immune system."

Arthur G. Johnson, PhD, Professor Emeritus, Department of Anatomy, Microbiology, and Pathology at the School of Medicine of the University of Minnesota in Duluth, has studied bovine cartilage intensively. He reported that it is "a true biological response modifier," meaning it increases the ability of white blood cells to destroy bacteria and viruses.

Dr. Johnson found that cartilage particularly activates the white blood cells known as macrophages. As the name implies—*macro* means "big" and *phage* means "eater"—macrophages pig out on bacteria, viruses, fungi, and other foreign microbes and their toxins. In addition, macrophages secrete the tumor necrosis factor alpha, which brings about the necrosis or death of tumors.

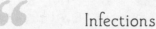

Infections

Bone broth saved me. After the birth of my third child, I got a uterine staph infection at five weeks postpartum. I went to the hospital and spent five days on IV antibiotics; consequently, two weeks later, I contracted *Clostridium difficile*. Again, they put me on antibiotics...I soon grew tired of the antibiotic merry-go-round, and found the Gut and Psychology Syndrome (GAPS) diet of Dr. Natasha Campbell-McBride. A major tenet of that diet is healing bone broth. I have not looked back since. Whenever I get a flare-up with digestive pain, loose bowels, and low energy, I go right to the bone broth. It eases the pain and is gentle on my digestive system. One of my favorite concoctions morning, noon, and night is bone broth with two heaping and healing tablespoons of sauerkraut.

–Sheila Walsh Dunton,
Santa Cruz, California

Macrophages aren't the only white blood cells so activated. Dr. Prudden reported bovine cartilage ignites cytotoxic T-cells, also known as killer T-cells. These kill bacteria, viruses, fungi, transplanted cells, and cancer cells directly and also recruit other lymphocytes and macrophages. Bovine cartilage is particularly effective at encouraging certain T-cells to order B-cells to differentiate into plasma cells. Plasma cells are little antibody factories that produce specific antibodies, which travel via the lymph and blood to the site of the battle.

Finally, Dr. Prudden found that bovine

cartilage usually—though not always—increases the numbers of natural killer (NK) cells. NK cells produce interferons that inhibit viral replication and provide the first line of defense against cancer cells and against cells infected by agents other than viruses. The number of NK cells is down in cancer patients and the rate of decrease is directly related to the severity of the disease.

Additional research carried out at New York University studied bovine cartilage in the test tube and with mice. The team found that bovine cartilage rouses the B-lymphocytes of the spleen. Working with Brian G. M. Durie, MD, and other researchers, Dr. Prudden found that bovine cartilage not only achieved a consistent clinical rise in IgG and IgM but also in immunoglobulin A (IgA). IgA—the main type of antibody in saliva, nasal mucus, gastric juice, and breast milk—helps control respiratory and digestive viruses.

Bovine cartilage itself does not directly produce antibodies. It does so indirectly by stimulating the B-lymphocytes to respond to foreign antigens (such as bacteria and viruses) by manufacturing the right antibodies. Because it works indirectly, allergic reactions to bovine cartilage are virtually nonexistent. The same has been found of gelatin by many researchers over the years.

Yet another way cartilage affects the immune system is by inciting cells to release colony stimulating factor (CSF) and causing an increase in serum CSF. This factor is known to stimulate the growth of granulocytes and monocytes, activate macrophages, and increase eosinophil leukotriene production.

Leukotrienes are compounds closely related to prostaglandins, which are a family of fatty acid molecules that regulate functions throughout the body. Because leukotrienes play a role in the development of allergic and auto-allergic diseases such as asthma and rheumatoid arthritis, it would seem that upping leukotriene production would be undesirable for people with autoimmune disorders. In fact, the ingestion of bovine cartilage is not contraindicated at all. Somehow the bio-directors in bovine cartilage know when to turn the leukotriene switch off or on.

In brief, cartilage seems capable of stimulating just about every type of white blood cell the body needs to mount a strong defense against unwanted microbes. It seems able to eradicate microbial disease without the use of antibiotics, antiviral drugs, and other pharmaceuticals, providing a more natural option for treating ear infections, urinary tract infections, bronchitis, and other infectious diseases. And that's good news given that antibiotics reverse short-term symptoms at the expense of long-term health by stripping the digestive tract of beneficial bacteria along with the disease-causing ones. Good bacteria keep our digestive tracts functioning efficiently, producing natural antibiotics, anticarcinogens, and other beneficial substances. We attack them at our peril.

Gelatin for Infectious Disease

Many of the modern findings dovetail with research on gelatin from the eighteenth to the early twentieth centuries. In those days, gelatin prepared from a powder was not only prescribed for the common cold and flu, but for acute infections such as typhus, scarlet fever, measles, cholera, dysentery, appendicitis, and pleuritis. Gelatin was also used to treat agues, a term referring to fevers marked by paroxysms of chills, fever, and sweating. Although clinicians reported gelatin to be helpful, disease and death rates did not go down until public sanitation was greatly improved.

66 Urinary Tract Infection

I accidentally discovered that oxtail soup was particularly beneficial in eliminating a chronic health problem that I, like many menopausal women, had developed in midlife: frequent urinary tract infections (UTIs).

I had been plagued with urethral discomfort and frequent urination for over six years. One day I made a large pot of oxtail soup for dinner on a cold winter night and consumed a large bowl of the soup for three to four consecutive days. After that, I noticed that I was symptom-free for the next couple of weeks. However, the symptoms reappeared. So I made the oxtail soup again and found the same beneficial effect. I then prepared a large pot of oxtail soup every three weeks and ate the soup several days in a row to see what would happen long term. Since doing this, I have been almost entirely symptom-free. Other broths also are helpful to me, but I have not found the same preventive effect from UTIs as with oxtail soup.

–Beverly Rubik, PhD,
Oakland, California 99

People afflicted with urinary tract and other chronic infections also benefited from gelatin. It was especially valued for slowing the progression of wasting diseases like tuberculosis. Its benefits were many, including increased strength, better digestion, and restful sleep.

In 1803, an Italian scientist named G. Gautieri counted two ways in which gelatin is useful for infection: promoting perspiration through the skin and providing nutrition. In 1932, researchers showed that gelatin stimulates phagocytosis, the process by which a cell surrounds, engulfs, and eats microorganisms and cellular debris.

Inconsistent and Contradictory Results

Overall, however, the early studies on gelatin show inconsistent and often contradictory results. As discussed in chapter 8, there are many reasons for this, including qualitative issues with gelatin manufacture. The findings can also be confusing because oral as well as topical and intravenous forms of gelatins were used. What we know for sure is that these long-dead scientists and their mostly forgotten research consistently reported gelatin to be easy to digest and ideally suited to help recovery from acute infections and chronic illness. During their lifetimes, their recommendations were taken to heart in popular books on the subject of "invalid cooking," which recommended "meat teas" and consommés to help weak appetites, queasy stomachs, and poor digestion. As Florence Nightingale wrote in her 1859 book, *Notes on Nursing*, "Remember that sick cookery should do half the work of your poor patient's weak digestion."

With the modern science on cartilage, it's clear that cartilage-rich broth has the capacity to support the immune system. Looking to traditional wisdom, anecdotal evidence, and clinical reports, it's evident that broth can bring health, balance, and integrity to the body as a whole. If, as Royal Lee, DDS, observed, we don't have an immune system, we are an immune system, then broth honors our immunity and ourselves as the ideal healing food.

Scarlet Fever and Diphtheria

I grew up in Germany during World War II. In the winter of 1943, I became sick with scarlet fever and diphtheria. I had to be quarantined on the third floor of our house in Hamburg. My mother's bone broth was the only food I could tolerate. A local butcher saved the bones for her, and my mother used her beef stock as a basis for many soups. Broth saved my life.

–*Elly von Scharnberg Morrison, PhD,*
Bellingham, Washington

Flu

My twelve- and sixteen-year-olds fought a bad case of the flu with fevers never dropping below 101 and rising as high as 102.6. On the third day of this, I started giving them bone broth. That evening their fevers finally dropped below 100 and for the duration of the flu it never again went above 102. They both were completely better within a few days. The bone broth helped them to turn a corner, and I believe was the catalyst to their healing. If there is a next time, I will be giving it to them on the first day of an illness.

–*Charlotte Corbitt,*
Queen Creek, Arizona

Colds and Flu

My mom and grandmother always cured colds and flu with chicken noodle soup. The bones were a big part of the soup. Between the benefits from the bones and the heat of the soup, it always worked. The hot soup would keep the throat open. Eating the chicken was a bonus.

–*Rosalee Dodson,*
Lewistown, Pennsylvania

Body Couldn't Get Enough

We just had two severe immune deficiency/digestive emergency cases here with two friends and once again chicken broth/soup turned them around. Both had the same exact quote: "It's like my body couldn't get enough of it." Just sending you some more of what we all know. So interesting to be in the room when the GI doc came in!

–*Tara Rayburn,*
Henderson, Nevada

CHAPTER 15

Digestive Disorders

Tens of millions of Americans suffer from digestive disorders, at a cost of ninety-eight billion dollars per year in direct payments for doctors, meds, and surgeries and indirect costs of forty-four billion dollars more in lost productivity. The cost in pain and suffering is incalculable. Furthermore, digestive difficulties never exist in isolation. When digestion suffers, the whole body suffers. As Hippocrates put it, "All disease begins in the gut."

Many alternative MDs and popular health experts recommend the healing of digestive disorders with food, exercise, stress management, and lifestyle changes. While there is much wisdom in the body-mind-spirit approach, much of the nutritional advice dispensed involves low-fat, high-fiber, plant-based diet plans, an approach that is more likely to become part of the problem than the solution. Only rarely do today's doctors see a significant role for nourishing broth in gut healing. Yet broth's reputation as a digestive aid and remedy for digestive difficulties goes back thousands of years, and broth is a staple of folk medicine around the world.

Widely Prescribed

In the nineteenth century, broth and gelatin were widely prescribed for convalescents who lacked the strength to digest and assimilate food properly. Florence Nightingale and others recommended it not only as the basis for soups and stews but in the forms of meat teas and aspics. In that era broth was thought to "increase appetite" and "finely distribute the nutrients in food," meaning increase their digestion, assimilation, and utilization in the body. Broth offered nourishment for people with few or no teeth, not only because it could be swallowed without the risk of choking but because it could begin the digestive process itself with or without the release of amylase and other digestive enzymes from chewing.

Broth and gelatin were also widely prescribed for acid reflux and peptic ulcers because they were thought to either "stop excess gastric secretion" or "fix a good deal of hydrochloric acid" in the process of digestion. Broth was also seen as useful for people with kidney disease who were required to restrict protein consumption.

In *Gelatin in Nutrition and Medicine*, Nathan Gotthoffer reported on nineteenth-century German studies showing gelatin to be helpful for infant nutrition. Gelatin improved the digestibility of baby formula, was an effective remedy for catarrh (a buildup of mucus in the nose and throat), a soother and even healer of acid reflux and "spit up" tendencies, and an efficient way to restore nourishment and fluids following bouts of vomiting or diarrhea.

Nutrition textbooks of the 1920s and 1930s recommended mixing gelatin into infant formulas to help bring cow's milk closer to human milk. That recommendation drew on more than thirty years of research studies showing gelatin could improve the digestion of milk and milk products. As Dr. Gotthoffer explained it, "The curd obtained from the coagulation of woman's milk was softer and more easily digested than that of cow's milk. However, when gelatin was added to cow's milk, a curd of equally desirable characteristics was formed. In addition, gelatin exerted a very important influence on the milk fat. It served not only to emulsify the fat but also, by stabilizing the casein, improved the digestibility and absorption of the fat, which otherwise would be carried down with casein in a lumpy mass." As a result, infants fed gelatin-enriched formulas showed reduced allergic symptoms, vomiting, colic, diarrhea, constipation, and respiratory ailments compared to those fed straight cow's milk. These clinical observations—along with the modern science that supports them—are reasons why Mary G. Enig, PhD, added gelatin to the homemade baby formula recipes recommended by the Weston A. Price Foundation for mothers who are unable to breast-feed.

Nineteenth- and early twentieth-century writers also noted that convalescing adults who had lost weight and strength because of operations, dysentery, cancer, or other reasons fared better if gelatin was added to their diets. "It is said to be retained by the most sensitive stomach and will nourish when almost nothing else will be tolerated," wrote Dr. L. E. Hogan in 1909. Gelatin was valued not only because it improved digestion but because it reduced the amount of complete protein needed by the body.

Gut Damage from Radiation

Thirty years ago I had three thousand rads of full-torso radiation and for many years was dysfunctional due to frequent bouts of rolling-on-the-floor gut pain. After about a year of making and eating homemade broth, homemade sauerkraut, and homemade kombucha, my gut is starting to heal. After so many years of pain, this is amazing. Today broth helps me to survive, and to calm down when under stress and warm up when cold.

–Carol S.,
Olympia, Washington

Gelatin was also widely recognized in both the popular and medical literature as the best possible food for cases of cholera, typhoid fever, and other infectious diseases marked by severe diarrhea. The scientists proposed various theories for this: Some thought it "neutralized" intestinal poisons; others theorized it provided protection by coating the mucous membrane; still others thought gelatin's low tyrosine and absent tryptophan prevented buildups of toxins found in troubled GI tracts (such as indole, skatol, indolacetic acid, and indolepropionic acid).

Doctors also valued gelatin for celiac and sprue patients wasting away from diarrhea and malnutrition. In his 1908 textbook *On Infantilism from Chronic Intestinal Infection*, Christian Archibald Herter, MD (1865–1910), called celiac disease "intestinal infantilism" and noted fat was better tolerated than carbohydrates by celiacs. Most important, he reported the efficacy of gelatin not only in the treatment of celiac disease but for any GI tract infection.

Herter explained, "The use of gelatin as a foodstuff in bacterial infections of the intestinal tract has never received the attention it deserves. The physician is not infrequently confronted with a dietetic problem which consists in endeavoring to maintain nutrition under conditions where no combination of the ordinary proteins with fats and carbohydrates suffices to maintain a fair state of nutrition. The difficulty which most frequently arises is that every attempt to use carbohydrate food is followed by fermentative disturbances of an acute or subacute nature which delay recovery or even favor an existing infection to the point of threatening life. The attempt to replace the carbohydrates in large degree by proteins is blocked by the serious difficulty that all the ordinary proteins, which when given in amounts distinctly in excess of the habitual quantities, afford material for putrefactive decompositions which it is necessary to restrict. A great desideratum, therefore, is a food which, while readily undergoing absorption, shall furnish a supply of caloric energy and which at the same time shall be exempt from ordinary fermentative decomposition. Such a food exists in gelatin."

Although Dr. Herter thought gelatin had not gotten the attention it deserved, he was hardly alone in his opinion that it could improve digestion. Typical dietary advice of the era was: Creams and blancmanges thickened with gelatin could be better digested by patients than those made with flour. Fruits would be more digestible when served in gelatin desserts. Eggs could be "more easily taken" by patients if thickened with gelatin. Milk swallowed with gelatin did bodies good. Gallbladder patients who were challenged by fat digestion could enjoy creamy desserts without ill consequences if gelatin filled in for some of the eggs and cream.

Not surprisingly, broth was a staple in the stomach-soothing "bland diets." These were widely prescribed by doctors from the mid-nineteenth to the mid-twentieth centuries for patients who had undergone stomach or intestinal surgery, been poisoned, or suffered from heartburn, ulcers, nausea (including morning sickness), bloating, or flatulence. Doctors lauded broth's power to "behave like a solid liquid" and give patients a palatable alternative to the soft, pasty, mushy, low-fiber, and unspicy "bland" food staples.

Dr. Francis Pottenger

Perhaps the most significant article ever written on the value of gelatin and health came in 1937, when Francis Pottenger Jr., MD (1901–1967), announced his theories and research at the Annual Meeting of the American Therapeutic Society in Atlantic City.

"Gelatin may be used in conjunction with almost any diet that the clinician feels is indicated," he said. "Its colloidal properties aid the digestion of any foods which cause the patient to suffer from 'sour stomach.' Even foods to which individuals may be definitely sensitive, as proven by the leucopenic index and elimination diets, frequently may be tolerated with slight discomfort or none at all if gelatin is made part of the diet."

Dr. Pottenger thought gelatin had such a "favorable effect on digestion" that pureeing might not be necessary. He found that after even a short trial of gelatin therapy, "raw vegetables, green salads and fruits which are usually taboo may often be given to those patients with impunity." Dr. Pottenger recited a long list of conditions that could be relieved by gelatin, including slow digestion, nervous digestion, vomiting, diarrhea, gas formation, and heartburn. He found it especially helpful for children with allergies and failure to thrive. Having thoroughly reviewed the literature published up to that time, Dr. Pottenger concluded, "An interesting aspect . . . is the universal agreement, so rarely encountered in gelatin researches, of all the investigators. Research workers and clinicians, from widely separated points and over an extended period of time, have without exception found gelatin to be of great value in the treatment of these diseases of the digestive system."

In his experiments Dr. Pottenger analyzed the contents of stomachs after various meals. He found that with gelatin in the mix, the "gluey mass" was "not sour" like the control, showed no acidity until the colloid was broken down, and "under these conditions, digestion is generally distributed throughout the mass rather than layered."

Dr. Pottenger thought gelatin could compensate for the lack of hydrophilic colloids in most cooked foods and "combat" any digestive disturbances caused by cooking. To condense his main points:

- Gelatin brings about conditions in the stomach during digestion that approach those resulting from the consumption of foods in their natural (that is, raw) state.
- Gelatin can lessen gastric irritation by absorbing the digestive secretions of the stomach so that digestion takes place within a mass of food.
- Gelatin is an "admirable" hydrophilic colloid because of its availability, digestibility, affordability, non-toxicity, and versatility in recipes.
- The amount of gelatin needed will vary from person to person, but it must be of good quality and sufficient quantity.
- Gelatin has proven effective for a variety of gastrointestinal ailments ranging from the atonia of the chronic invalid to the irritation present in patients with gastric ulcer.

Gelatin, broth, and bland diets went out of fashion as "unnecessary" once antacids, anticholinergics, gastrin antagonists, and other pharmaceuticals became widely available. As people adopted modern diets high in bran and other fibers, raw or undercooked vegetables, canned soups, and quick-cooked steaks and muscle meats, traditional bone broth soups, stews, and "meat teas" largely disappeared from diets. Soymilk, tofu, and other soy foods, as well as many processed food products containing soy protein ingredients, also contribute to digestive distress. Although soy is heavily marketed as a complete protein, all soybeans contain protease inhibitors that block the digestive enzymes needed to break down that protein. Over time, the stress on the overworked pancreas can lead to pancreatitis. These dietary changes have driven the market for over-the-counter and prescription drugs. As more and more people recognize the dark side of these drugs, the time is ripe to restore broth to its traditional role of digestive aid and remedy.

Many components in broth contribute to its digestive power. Properly prepared broths, made from bones, cartilage, and skin, are rich in glycosaminoglycans (GAGs), the best known of which are glucosamine and chondroitin sulfate. These provide the raw ingredients needed for the body to produce the healing mucus required throughout the digestive system. While the raw food community spouts the myth that mucus is merely unwanted gunky buildup caused by meat, dairy, and cooked foods, the truth is we need plenty of healthy mucus for optimum digestion, a high-functioning immune system, and the soothing of any GI tract inflammation.

How does mucus help? Let us count the ways. In the stomach, a thick layer of mucus coated with a bicarbonate solution keeps acid from burning the stomach lining. In the small intestines, mucus lubricates the passage of food, nourishes good bacteria, blocks bad bacteria, and plays key roles in immune response. Indeed, the mucous layer—along with the underlying gut-associated lymphoid tissue (GALT)—is our front line of defense against physical and chemical injury from ingested foods, microbes, microbial products, heavy metals, and other toxins.

During acute intestinal infections, mucus is secreted promptly and prolifically throughout the emergency to encase bacteria and otherwise protect the body from invasion. Chronic infections, however, result in the depletion of mucus-secreting cells, alterations in mucous layers, disruption of bacterial colonies, defective immune responses, and overall upset of the intestinal homeostasis. The result is "leaky gut," a condition that leads to inflammation, injury, and other adverse effects throughout the brain and body.

Food Poisoning

I recently suffered from intense food poisoning, possibly brought on by contaminated eggs. Bedridden for three days, I drank only beef bone broth fortified with lacto-fermented vegetable juice and fermented raw milk whey. This cured the diarrhea without any medication. My gut flora seems to be well and happy again, and so am I. Our bone broth slow cooker is working full time.

–René Archner,
Warkworth, New Zealand

Gut ecology also depends on mucus. Science now recognizes the fact that the microbiome, with its wealth of different microorganisms and their collective genetic material, is metabolically active and plays myriad roles in the body, including the absorption and transport of nutrients across the gut barrier. These bacteria are nourished directly by sugars and protein sugars, including GAGs, and indirectly by the vitamins and minerals concentrated within the mucous matrix. The bacteria hang out in mucus to avoid expulsion from the body, and their presence stimulates the production of additional mucus. This symbiotic relationship builds and maintains a healthy gut for the host while allowing further colonization by the bacteria.

As scientists learn more and more about the complexity of the gut, they talk of developing novel—meaning patentable—therapeutic approaches to the prevention and management of intestinal disease. These include methods to promote or strengthen the intestinal mucous layer or nourish bioactive protective molecules. While these possibilities are intriguing, alternative medical doctors are already healing the gut with protocols that depend on a foundation of good old-fashioned broth.

Broth is a staple in Dr. Natasha Campbell-McBride's GAPS (Gut and Psychology Syndrome) diet, Dr. Joseph Brasco and Jordan Rubin's Guts and Glory program, Donna Gates's Body Ecology diet, and other gut-healing diets. These programs are intended to heal allergies, autism, and immune system breakdown as well as treat obvious gut problems such as candida, parasites, bloating, flatulence, gastrointestinal reflux disease (GERD), constipation, diarrhea, celiac disease, irritable bowel syndrome (IBS), ulcerative colitis, and Crohn's disease. Essential to this goal is the healing of the condition colloquially known as leaky gut syndrome. Furthermore, glycine and glutamine in broth contribute to the liver's production of the glutathione needed to detoxify mercury and other heavy metals commonly stored in the gut lining, contributing to gut, brain, and immune system dysfunction.

Why does broth heal the gut? Primarily by feeding its cells the protein sugars known as glycosaminoglycans, or GAGs. Given that

leaky gut syndrome is sometimes called the GAG defect, common sense suggests the glucosamine, chondroitin sulfate, and other GAGs found in broth could help the body rebuild the GAG layer. Most of the research to date has shown success with a polysaccharide known as heparin, which is primarily sold as a prescription blood thinner. Patients diagnosed with ulcerative colitis and Crohn's disease, however, have tested as deficient in the essential sugar N-acetylglucosamine. Glucosamine supplementation might help, but the study results are mixed. As for feeding gut bacteria, Robert Koch, the discoverer of the tuberculosis bacterium, succeeded in growing bacterial colonies in petri dishes when he added gelatin to the mix.

Glycine

The high glycine content of broth and gelatin aids digestion by enhancing gastric acid secretion. While scientists have known for more than thirty years that only proteins stimulate gastric acid secretion, not all amino acids do so. Glycine is one of those that do, a fact first shown in 1925. Researchers in the *American Journal of Physiology* have already proposed that "glycine may have application in the design of chemically defined diets for patients with gastrointestinal disorders."

Glycine is the single most important amino acid that must be supplied to children recovering from malnutrition, many of whom suffer from digestive problems, and it is indispensable for rapid growth. Glycine status also serves as an important marker of a healthy pregnancy. Because the glycine needs of mothers-to-be increase throughout pregnancy, endogenous production of glycine may be insufficient. It is thus a good policy for pregnant women to drink plenty of broth. Infants also seem to need glycine. Infant feeding studies have shown that total free amino acids found in plasma increase after feeding, but the ratio of glycine to valine falls.

Glutamine

Broth's high glutamine content is also critical for gut health. It's the primary nutrient for enterocytes, the cells that absorb digested food from the lumen and transport the nutrients into the bloodstream. Enterocytes contain glutaminase, the enzyme that breaks glutamine up into glutamic acid and ammonia. Glutamic acid is broken down into adenosine triphosphate (ATP), a key compound in cellular reactions throughout the body, while the ammonia must be detoxed by the liver.

In the 1970s, Herbert G. Windmueller, a pharmacologist at the National Institute of Arthritis, Metabolism and Digestive Diseases of the National Institutes of Health in Bethesda, Maryland, discovered a surprising function for glutamine. In a laboratory experiment that involved keeping a large segment of rat intestine alive, Dr. Windmueller tested the high-glucose solutions used in feeding tubes at hospitals and concluded they were not up to the job. To many people's surprise, he found glutamine was far more important than glucose, a finding later confirmed in human and animal studies. Without glutamine, the primary fuel of enterocytes, villous atrophy and death occurred. And it's not just the digestive system that atrophies. Intestinal health is so important to the body that muscles will give up great stores of glutamine to help the intestines handle the stress of illness or accident. Indeed, the body's continual need for glutamine to turn over mucosal lining cells probably plays a bigger role in muscle wasting than inactivity due to bed rest.

Glutamine also nourishes the GALT (gut-associated lymphoid tissue) layer underlying the mucosa. Insufficient glutamine there contributes to leaky gut, a key factor in allergies, autism, behavioral disorders, and most other physical and mental health problems. Any form of severe stress on the body, whether caused by injury, infection, vaccination, or other trauma, will deplete glutamine, increasing the likelihood of gut weakness, permeability, and other damage.

Glutamine furthermore stems the loss of electrolytes and water from the intestines during either acute or chronic diarrhea, and has greatly benefited patients with IBS, ulcerative colitis, Crohn's disease, and other severe bowel diseases. Patients who have experienced surgical removal of parts of their small intestines are less likely to suffer malnutrition from short bowel syndrome if tube-fed glutamine along with their other nutrients. Colon cancer patients with colostomy bags have experienced less infection and inflammation thanks to glutamine supplementation. Although most patients who've undergone chemotherapy experience side effects of nausea, vomiting, and diarrhea caused by the death of the rapidly growing cells in the intestine, patients taking high doses of glutamine suffer fewer of these side effects.

Digestion

I went through a time of extreme stress in my life, which resulted in indigestion, heartburn, and bloating. After incorporating bone broth and fermented foods into my diet, I haven't had any digestive problems since. I'm a naturopathic doctor, and bone broth and fermented foods are now a regular part of what I recommend to my patients with digestive disturbances.

–Todd Ferguson, ND,
Moorhead, Minnesota

How else does glutamine serve the digestive system? It may be good for people suffering from peptic ulcers, but one study suggests it could worsen acid reflux. Finally, it feeds the pancreas, particularly the exocrine part that produces enzymes required for digestive and metabolic functions.

Cartilage

John F. Prudden, MD, DSci, the "father of cartilage therapy," successfully treated severe cases of ulcerative colitis and Crohn's disease with bovine tracheal cartilage. Because these diseases are autoimmune disorders, he thought cartilage might help. Buttressing his conviction was the fact that two other diseases with an autoimmune component—arthritis and psoriasis—had been dramatically helped by cartilage. Either or both often accompany Crohn's disease and ulcerative colitis. Later Dr. Prudden would show that cartilage could cure cancer as well, a major consideration for colitis victims, who have a greatly increased risk of developing cancer of the colon. For victims of ulcerative colitis who have lived with their disease for forty years, the odds are about 70 percent.

As per his usual policy, Dr. Prudden worked exclusively with people with severe, supposedly incurable cases. All had suffered from Crohn's disease or ulcerative colitis for many years and had responded poorly if at all to standard treatments. As reported in *Seminars in Arthritis and Rheumatism*, Dr. Prudden's results were good but not perfect. The problem for many patients was that the cartilage itself produced some osmotic diarrhea. Because diarrhea—or rather the lack of it—is how colitis patients judge their progress, the increased diarrhea alarmed them. Even so, their colons were on the mend, as evidenced by sigmoidoscope.

So much so, in fact, that six of the nine ulcerative colitis patients in Dr. Prudden's study were able to forgo proctocolectomy. Even the so-called failures experienced some gain. For example, a patient whose condition had only improved to "fair" with the cartilage advanced a notch once he began taking prednisone along with the cartilage. Drugs alone had had no positive effect on his condition, but with cartilage, there was a positive synergistic effect.

Recovery from Parasites and Antibiotics

My mother-in-law emigrated from Ireland as a young woman and raised eleven healthy children by avoiding the standard American diet. Now in her early seventies, she walks five miles a day, keeps a garden, and takes no prescription medications. Right before Thanksgiving, she came down with gastrointestinal symptoms that sent her to the emergency room for dehydration. The doctors told her it was probably something viral and her symptoms would soon resolve on their own. However, after the holiday, her symptoms worsened and she also realized that no one else around her had developed "something viral." Her doctor finally did a culture, and we were all surprised to learn she had picked up a waterborne parasite from China! Since she rarely dines out, she was able to name the restaurant where she picked this up in her food.

A round of Cipro antibiotic gave her a clean culture but left her weak. Her doctor told her it could take up to six months for her to fully recover. I decided to print out the benefits of bone broth and bring her two pints from the freezer. She was hesitant, almost resistant, to trying the broth, so we got her to start with a few sips a day. By Christmas several major symptoms had disappeared and she wanted to know the recipe! That night I printed out the directions and sent her three more pints. I'm relieved to report that she is on the mend.

–Roxanne McDaniel,
Park Ridge, Illinois

Likewise, four severe cases of Crohn's disease improved. All the patients had been taking prednisone or ACTH in high doses for years. Many had segments of their ileum or colon removed surgically. All had been going downhill steadily with weight loss and malnutrition. Yet with bovine tracheal cartilage they all were able to reduce their drug dosage or eliminate it entirely. None of the patients were restored to complete health, but all gained weight, strength, and optimism. Although there was no control group, Dr. Prudden said that "the course of the disease is clearly an adequate control in these severe and chronic cases."

Digestive Problems

I am sixty-five years old and have suffered from digestive issues for most of my life. About six months ago I started making stock, mostly with elk bones because they are accessible to me, but also beef and chicken bones. Just lately I have started adding about six chicken feet to any kind of stock I make. I drink the stock three times a day and also eat soup made with stock usually twice a day. I love it! My digestive system is healing quickly, and tests show I have very high levels of minerals in my system. Stock is definitely very healing.

–Monica Beauchane,
Northwood, North Dakota

Why might cartilage work? Dr. Prudden thought the healing component might be the glycosaminoglycans, or GAGs. Proline, glycine, glutamine, and other components probably play a part as well. Cartilage, after all, is a whole food supplement, rich in many bioactive substances. It's also a key component of any broth cooked from a mixture of bones, cartilage, and skin. That said, Dr. Prudden prescribed 9 grams a day of bovine tracheal cartilage, an amount unlikely to be consumed as food even by the most avid broth drinker. Even so, we have numerous testimonies on how daily broth consumption reversed chronic cases of irritable bowel syndrome, ulcerative colitis, and Crohn's disease.

Where broth clearly excels is at prevention. When digestive diseases and disorders are already advanced, supplements may speed the healing, but broth should still stand as the dietary foundation. Those who don't favor diets rich in soups and stews may achieve some of the benefits by adding gelatin powder to foods.

In conclusion, it's time to trust our guts and know in our hearts that nourishing broth can heal body and soul.

CHAPTER 16

Cancer

More than fifteen hundred Americans will die of cancer in the next twenty-four hours—more than one death every minute. One out of two American men and one out of three American women will contract cancer. No wonder Susan Sontag called it "an evil, invincible predator," and most people consider a diagnosis predictive of disability and death.

Surprisingly, old-fashioned broth can play a role in preventing and even curing this disease. And that's not just because broth keeps people well-nourished and in optimal health. Broth contains components with known anticarcinogenic activities, the most notable of which is cartilage.

Cartilage for Cancer

Dr. John F. Prudden discovered the power of bovine tracheal cartilage on cancer back in 1972. Treating a woman with a malignant, bleeding, pustulating ulceration that infested her entire chest, he not only healed the wound but shrank the tumor. This led him to wonder what it was in cartilage that could cause such a potent effect.

A study conducted by Brian G. M. Durie, MD, published in 1985 in the *Journal of Biological Response Modifiers*, provided some of his answer. Dr. Durie, then with the Department of Internal Medicine at the University of Arizona Health Sciences Center in Tucson and now world renowned for his work with myeloma, performed in vitro laboratory experiments that showed the direct antimitotic effect of bovine tracheal cartilage on human ovarian, testicular, pancreatic, and colon cancers. *Antimitotic* means it inhibits cell division. Cell division, of course, is the key to the spread of cancer, which is a catchall name for a number of diseases that are marked by a wild, unruly, runaway growth of cells. In contrast, normal cell growth takes place in an orderly fashion with no population explosions. Because cancer cells divide at high rates but also die at high rates, a cancer will die off on its own if the reproduction rate can be slowed.

Stopping Cell Division

What is it in cartilage that stops cell division? Dr. Prudden thought it was the large

How Cartilage Fights Cancer

Arthur G. Johnson, PhD, Professor Emeritus, Department of Anatomy, Microbiology and Pathology at the University of Minnesota School of Medicine in Duluth, discovered that cartilage can activate and increase the numbers of macrophages, the "big eater" white blood cells whose mission in life is to hungrily devour foreign cells. The macrophages also secrete a substance called necrosis factor alpha, which, as its name implies, causes the necrosis (death) of solid tumors.

Dr. Johnson also found that cartilage activates cytotoxic (killer) T-cells and stimulates B-cells. The increase in the number of B-cells, in turn, produces a rise in the number of antibodies known as immunoglobulins A, G, and M (IgA, IgG, and IgM). IgA combines with a protein in the mucosa to defend body surfaces against invading microorganisms and triggers antigen-antibody reaction. IgG is a specialized protein synthesized by the body in response to invasions by bacteria, fungi, and viruses. And IgM, which is found in all circulating fluids, is the first immunoglobulin the body produces when challenged by antigens.

Dr. Johnson found as well that the numbers of natural killer (NK) cells usually—but not always—increase thanks to cartilage. NK cells are part of the body's first line of defense. Unlike the killer T-cells, they can destroy tumor cells nonspecifically, that is, without having had prior exposure to the tumor antigens. Clearly, all these players have key roles in cancer prevention and cures.

sugar and protein molecules known as glycosaminoglycans (GAGs). These adhere to the cell membrane of cancerous cells and interfere with cell division but don't harm normal cells.

In contrast, chemotherapy interferes with the multiplication of cancer cells but poisons normal tissues as well, particularly the rapidly dividing cells of the bone marrow, intestinal wall, and hair follicles. The result is a depressed immune system, profound digestive disturbances, and hair loss.

Dr. Durie's studies on cartilage were done in a laboratory, not in a human host. But because the lab dish obviously had no immune system to contribute to the cancer cells' demise, Dr. Durie's studies established the fact that cartilage can prevent tumor growth without any assistance from the host's immune system. That is good news indeed for cancer patients, who might not have cancer at all if they had immune systems able to recognize cancer cells as foreign and dispatch them before they divide, conquer, and multiply to point of a cancer diagnosis.

For the tens of thousands of cancer patients whose immune systems have been wasted by radiation and chemotherapy, their best hope lies in finding a therapy that does not depend for its effectiveness on enlisting the immune response. That is one reason that almost all cancer research is done on "nude" mice, which have been genetically stripped of their natural immune capabilities. The power of bovine cartilage lies in the fact that it not only slows cell division and normalizes the aberrant and malignant cells but simultaneously nourishes the immune system.

Some Possible Causes of Cancer

For decades, scientists have theorized that cancer is caused by a "somatic mutation," in which a gene unaccountably develops a flaw that disorganizes cellular function. Known causes of such flaws are X-rays, nuclear radiation, industrial chemicals, pesticides, pollution, and other environmental toxins, many of which are prevalent in our air, water, and food supply. Bruce Ames, PhD, of the University of California at Berkeley, has estimated that each of the sixty trillion cells in our body undergoes from one thousand to ten thousand "hits" each day. Normally DNA repair mechanisms and immune system surveillance keep the genetic damage under control. A nourishing diet, including broth, can help maintain that control, allowing genes to express their full, intended potential.

Another possible cause of cancer is viruses capable of invading cells, corrupting the DNA and causing the cells' progeny to become outlaws. This theory dates back to 1910 when Peyton Rous, MD (1879–1970), a medical researcher at the Rockefeller Institute, found a cancer-causing agent in fowl. His claim that this mysterious infectious agent could pass through the smallest filter known to science made him the laughingstock of his colleagues. However, the discovery of viruses and the unraveling of the genetic code led to new respect for Rous's iconoclastic theory, and in 1966 he won the Nobel Prize. Though proponents of the virus theory of cancer have high hopes of finding a cancer vaccine, they have so far failed to do so. After more than fifty years and hundreds of millions of dollars spent on research, the role of viruses is known in only a few human cancers, namely Burkitt's lymphoma and nasopharyngeal carcinoma.

Theories of pleomorphic bacteria also exist despite dismissal by cancer experts for more than sixty years. These particular bacteria are capable of shifting shape, form, and size as they pass through various stages. Indeed, the Rous "virus" itself may be just such a bacterium. Though their existence is not accepted by orthodox microbiologists, pleomorphic bacteria have been spied in live blood samples viewed under dark field microscopes by some of the most controversial and persecuted men and women ever to work at curing cancer. Royal R. Rife; Gaston Naessens (who named the pleomorphic bacteria *somatids*); Gunther Enderlein (who called them *endobionts*); and others all followed Antoine Beauchamp, the nineteenth-century bacteriologist and rival of Louis Pasteur who contended that bacteria could not only change forms but could also devolve into smaller, unseen forms, which he called *microzymia*.

From 1946 until her death in 1990, Virginia Livingston, MD, was a forceful exponent of that theory. "Instead of a bacillus being a bacillus ad infinitum," she wrote, "it can and does change into numerous other forms dictated by its need to survive or stimulated to greater productivity by an unusually favorable environment."

Dr. Livingston—who also used the last names Wuerthele-Caspe and Livingston-Wheeler at various points in her career—named the cancer-causing bacillus *Progenitor cryptocides* (PC), and claimed that it was closely related to the bacteria known to cause tuberculosis and leprosy. In 1972, she found these bacteria were capable of producing human choriogonadotropin (hCG), a hormone once thought to be exclusively human. The presence of hCG establishes the existence of choriocarcinoma (a rare form of cancer associated with an ill-fated pregnancy) and is a marker for other types of cancer as well.

Cartilage as an Anticancer Agent

Any of these possible cancer causes—alone or in combination—would suggest why cartilage has proven such a successful anticancer agent. Because cartilage stimulates the immune system, it prompts surveillance against aberrant cells. If cancer itself is caused by microbial infection, then cartilage's antibacterial and antiviral powers come into play.

Instead, the medical establishment attempts to induce, enhance, or suppress the immune system with stratospherically priced chemicals that are developed and announced with great fanfare. These agents have included alpha and gamma interferon; monoclonal antibodies; interleukin-2 and interleukin-7; tumor necrosis factor (TNF); and genetically engineered T-cells, among others. Although chemical immunotherapy is an acceptable established treatment blessed by the American Cancer Society, the National Cancer Institute, Memorial Sloan Kettering, and other major cancer centers, even its proponents acknowledge that the results have been disappointing. The problem is that rather than help the cancer patient's already beleaguered immune system kick in, these artificially isolated immunostimulants unbalance and further disrupt it. The results are so toxic that some patients have died as a direct result of such therapy.

Because cancer cells are generally larger-than-normal cells, the impact of any therapy on them shows up with the help of a scanning electron microscope. Biopsies taken from patients treated with bovine cartilage show a progressive decrease in size of the malignant cells until they achieve the dimensions of healthy cells. Dr. Prudden repeatedly demonstrated "a progressive normalization in the appearance of the cancer cells in sequential biopsies obtained during treatment."

Colon Health

My grandfather died of colon cancer, my mom has an enlarged colon, my brother has colitis, and my problems started in childhood. After going to university, I started having bloody diarrhea. It became a very aggressive form of colitis, and I had as many as fifty bowel movements a day. If I had to go somewhere, I had to make sure there was always a bathroom nearby. My life was about that. At five feet eight inches I was below one hundred pounds and dropping.

None of the medicines helped, so the doctors said I was a candidate for surgery. My dad, a retired doctor, then took me home to his farm and put me on a diet similar to the Gut and Psychology Syndrome (GAPS) diet. I drank at least a quart of broth a day. The diarrhea stopped. After a year, I had a colonoscopy and there were no more signs of Crohn's. I had also had severe polyps, and they were gone too. It's now been twelve years. I no longer take medications, have lots of energy, and weigh a healthy 165 pounds. I'm still careful to have plenty of broth. Other than that, I eat heartily and have no digestive problems. I've become a dietitian and now help many people with the same problems.

—*Shantih Coro,*
Miami, Florida

Given that the cancer cells also start acting like normal cells, we might say that cartilage therapy declines to kill the aberrant cells in favor of rehabilitating them. In contrast, chemotherapy and radiation kill cancer cells directly. Though the death penalty might seem to be in order, the price is steep: death or damage to many of the noncancerous cells in the body as well as destruction of the immune system. Why not, as Dr. Prudden suggested, choose a therapy that is totally benign, with no untoward side effects and that "burns no immunological or hematological bridges"?

The therapy Dr. Prudden proposed was bovine tracheal cartilage, a component of beef broth, but chicken, shark, and other cartilages have similar effect. Proof of its efficacy came out in 1985 when Dr. Prudden published "The Treatment of Human Cancer with Agents Prepared from Bovine Cartilage" in the December 1985 issue of the *Journal of Biological Response Modifiers*. The article documents an eleven-year study begun in 1972, in which Dr. Prudden tracked the progress of thirty-one patients treated with cartilage who had suffered from a wide variety of cancers.

Every one of his thirty-one patients was considered morbidly ill and "beyond hope." The standard slash, poison, and burn techniques had proved worthless—or had been refused by the patients—and the patients had been sent home to die. "With few exceptions, only those for whom standard therapy had failed or was conceded to be of no value were accepted for the studies," said Dr. Prudden. Prior to starting the therapy with his patients, Dr. Prudden ordered extensive laboratory blood work, the details of which can be found in his article in the *Journal of Biological Response Modifiers*.

Each treatment began with a "loading phase" in which patients were injected with bovine tracheal cartilage in their thighs, flanks, abdomen, back, and chest, and occasionally in other locations (such as the nose for a patient afflicted with nasal cancer). Treatments varied somewhat depending on the patient's condition, but the typical dose was 100 ml per session for a total of 2000 ml over a period of several weeks. A few patients got more. These amounts are much more than we would find in broth or soup, of course, but do suggest that these delicious foods have the potential for prevention.

Recovery from Cancer Treatments

While recovering from chemotherapy and radiation treatment for throat cancer last year, I took all of my nourishment from a feeding tube in my stomach. The first homemade formula we used was a vegetable broth with ground salmon. Then a friend made me aware of how beef bone broth could be of great benefit during recovery from an illness such as mine. I was fortunate to find a supply of the broth available from a local source. The addition of the bone broth nutrients to my diet contributed greatly to my successful recovery. I now take all my nourishment by mouth and still use the bone broth as part of my diet.

−Edward C.,
Lancaster, Pennsylvania

Dr. Prudden found no limit to the amount of cartilage that could be given safely, whether orally, topically, or by injection. On one occasion he gave a whopping 900 ml injection to an anesthetized patient without "discernible problems of any kind." A few other patients received 6000 ml over a number of weeks. Though these are obviously very large amounts, laboratory tests run on the patients turned up no new abnormalities, and there was no other indication of toxicity. Only one negative side effect was ever observed—local redness, swelling, and itching at the injection sites. And that was soon remedied.

Once the initial "loading phase" was complete, Dr. Prudden advised most of the patients to swallow 3 grams of bovine cartilage, three times a day, for a total of 9 grams per day.

During the course of the study, Dr. Prudden also completed toxicity testing as mandated by the Food and Drug Administration (FDA). A two-year carcinogenesis study—designed to determine whether cartilage was capable of causing cancer—and a sixteen-month teratogenicity study—to judge whether or not cartilage could cause birth defects—both proved negative. Cartilage was found to be totally benign. "This is a most important feature of this therapy," said Dr. Prudden, "because of the extraordinary contrast with the debility regularly induced by chemotherapy."

Dr. Prudden emphasized the fact that cartilage is not an instant miracle cure. A definite response might not be observed for four months, and users should be prepared to see the cancer worsen for a time before the action of the cartilage kicks in. Once remission is achieved, he said, it is important to continue the cartilage therapy. Though many stayed well after quitting the capsules, others saw their cancer return. In general, Dr. Prudden recommended that his patients take the pills in

a maintenance dose for life. Strictly speaking, this makes the therapy not a cure but a control.

Summing up his results in his forty-four-page paper, Dr. Prudden reported that bovine tracheal cartilage had a "major inhibitory effect upon a wide-spectrum of cancers." Of the thirty-one patients, eleven had a "complete response" with a probable cure. Eight cases had a complete response with a relapse. Of those who had a partial response (meaning a 50 percent decrease in the size of the lesions or of another measure of the cancer), six had a partial response and three had a partial response and relapse. One person had an improved response, one showed no change, and one saw the cancer progress.

If this sounds like a considerably less-than-perfect score, remember that all thirty-one of these patients had been evaluated as "hopeless" by doctors and oncologists other than Dr. Prudden. Medical opinion held that 100 percent would be pushing up daisies within a year. Many of the patients were already extremely debilitated by orthodox treatments. Some had persisted in bad habits including smoking and drinking, and one actually died of pentobarbital abuse. In those cases where the treatment was successful but the patient died, the deaths most often came from heart attacks, strokes, pneumonia, or urinary tract infections. Not one can be attributed—either directly or indirectly—to a side effect of cartilage therapy. (All thirty-one cases, warts and all, including details from the 1985 article and updates on the patients up to 1997 are posted at our website for this book, www.nourishingbroth.com.) Many of the failures can be laid at the feet of patients who got overconfident and chose to quit taking their maintenance dose of cartilage, against Dr.

Prudden's advice. That turned out to be a big mistake, for their cancer generally returned.

At the time of his death in 1998, Dr. Prudden had carried out long-term follow-up on all of the 31 pilot cases and accumulated extensive data on 140 other cases. The latter group contained more cancers of the brain, lung, pharynx, and ovary—cases that are generally considered incurable. As of 1997, Dr. Prudden reported the patients were "doing considerably better than anyone else would have anticipated and the results are even more impressive than the original thirty-one." The only real change in treatment was that Dr. Prudden stopped the "loading phase" with injectable cartilage to work with the cartilage pills alone. Sadly, this paper has yet to be published, and Dr. Prudden's dream of seeing bovine cartilage accepted in the orthodox medical community has failed to materialize.

During his lifetime, many people in the scientific community asked Dr. Prudden why he did not do blind randomized studies. He cited ethical reasons: "It is not necessary when one is dealing with malignancies whose deadly outcome is inexorable. Double-blind studies are important for osteoarthritics because there can be much day-to-day variation in the course of the illness. With pancreatic cancer, renal cell carcinoma, brain cancer, there is no such variation. They are never cured or very seldom cured by standard therapies. To insist on double-blind studies in these cases guarantees the patients will be blind—blind because they are dead! It's nonsense to say anything other than double-blind study is an anecdotal report. Death, of course, can be reported."

Dr. Prudden also used rigorous statistical analysis to compare his results with standard cancer therapies. This was to ensure that what appears to be an outstanding advantage was not due to a fortuitous selection of cases. When statistician Jack Silverston compared the thirty-one cases to those reported to the cancer epidemiological section of the Connecticut Health Department during the same period of time and subjected them to a Wilcoxon Rank Analysis, he claimed that the difference was "highly significant," with a "p" value of less than .002. Such a remarkable series of successes could not have been assembled through the use of any other mode of cancer treatment. The analysis was accepted after careful review by the U.S. Patent Office.

In the mid-1980s, Dr. Prudden switched from the injectable form of cartilage to pills. As he perceived it, the injectable form had both pluses and minuses. On the plus side, the shots bypassed the digestive system—often a weak point in morbidly ill patients—so the cartilage could be absorbed directly into the blood. This means more of the cartilage could be absorbed and used. But quantity is not the only criterion here. "More" also refers to more of the components of the cartilage itself. Taken orally, the protein components of cartilage are denatured, dismantled, and digested in the human gut.

Although this would seem to be a major strike against cartilage pills—and against cartilage-rich broth as well—Dr. Prudden saw it differently. Though he demonstrated outstanding results on the cancer patients who were injected with cartilage, he was concerned about the fact that whole cartilage contains "growth factors"—hormones that stimulate cell growth and cell division.

While growth factors would seem to be the last thing cancer patients need, the scenario is not quite so simple. Cartilage contains "bio-directors" that know instinctively when to turn cell division off and turn it on. This would explain why Dr. Durie discovered an antimitotic effect on cancer cells in the laboratory and why Dr. Prudden had succeeded in annihilating cancer when working with patients clinically. Even so, he thought it wise to be cautious about giving cancer patients growth factors in any form. Accordingly, his future plans had included testing an injectable form of cartilage from which the growth factors had been removed.

Anti-Angiogenesis

On the plus side, the injectable form of cartilage contains an anti-angiogenesis protein that Dr. Prudden considered highly valuable for cancer treatment. *Angio-genesis* comes from the Greek words *angio*, meaning "blood," and *genesis*, meaning "formation of." The term was coined back in 1935 to describe the new blood vessels forming in the placenta during pregnancy. It now commonly refers to the formation of new blood vessels during any bodily growth spurt, from the replacement of blood vessels after an injury to the ability of malignant tissues to rapidly form the network of blood vessels that they need for runaway growth.

Normal cartilage has no blood vessels and so contains an anti-angiogenesis factor that specifically inhibits the incursion of blood vessels. When blood vessels do enter cartilage, it is a preliminary to bone formation.

Dr. Prudden's interest in anti-angiogenesis followed the pioneering work of Judah Folkman, MD (1933–2008), of Children's Hospital and Harvard Medical School. Beginning in 1971, Dr. Folkman hypothesized in the *New England Journal of Medicine (NEJM)* and other medical journals that tumor growth could be stopped if angiogenesis was first stopped.

Without a network of blood vessels to supply nutrients and remove waste, a tumor has no choice but to shrivel up and die. Later, Robert Langer, ScD, at the Massachusetts Institute of Technology, discovered that cartilage taken from the shoulders of calves could inhibit the vascularization of solid tumors.

Both Drs. Folkman and Langer asserted, however, that the large and fragile protein molecules that give cartilage its anti-angiogenic properties could not survive the digestive processes of the human gut. If the oral forms of cartilage cure cancer, they said, it must be from factors other than anti-angiogenesis. "If you give large molecules orally, you find they get destroyed," said Dr. Langer. "Insulin is a classic example of this." Injected, however, the proteins would enter the bloodstream intact, a fact that potentiates the cancer-curing powers of cartilage. One of Dr. Prudden's dreams was to obtain the funds to perfect an injectable form of cartilage in which growth factors were removed but the anti-angiogenesis factors retained.

Neither the Harvard nor the MIT researchers were happy about I. William Lane's book *Sharks Don't Get Cancer* and his trumped-up claim that shark cartilage pills possessed the magic bullet of anti-angiogenesis factors. Drs. Folkman, Langer, and Prudden all tried to dissuade Lane from making his claims, to no avail. Dr. Langer also spoke out against Lane's totally unwarranted claim that shark cartilage was "one thousand times more potent" than bovine cartilage based on the ratio of raw material needed to produce a product of a known dose. What is relevant is the amount of each type of cartilage that must be taken each day to have a therapeutic effect. Here bovine cartilage shines, for the recommended daily dose is 9 grams a day, versus 70 grams a day for shark cartilage. On average that means about eight times more shark cartilage to be swallowed. This is not a minor point because, as Dr. Lane himself acknowledged, the huge amounts of shark cartilage prescribed frequently led to nausea and noncompliance.

As found in the human diet, we could all conceivably eat 9 grams (less than 2 teaspoons) a day of bovine or chicken cartilage through broth, soups, and stews and by chewing on chicken wings and drumsticks. But even the most avid eater of shark fin soup could never down 70 grams' worth of cartilage a day.

Why is so much less bovine cartilage needed? Dr. Prudden pointed to the fact that cows are mammals and so are more similar to human beings than sharks. "The potency of shark cartilage is from ten to twenty times less than bovine, depending on the test system employed," he said. "This is not surprising when one considers that sharks separated from our hominoid ancestors on the Tree of Life more than twenty-five million years ago."

Dr. Prudden was intrigued by anti-angiogenesis but believed the active cancer-curing agents in cartilage might not be proteins at all, but the sugars, known variously as mucopolysaccharides, proteoglycans, and glycosaminoglycans (GAGs). "The fact is, all studies show that a positive 'cartilage effect' in any pathological situation is not due to one specific agent, but to an interaction of a complex array of molecular entities capable of stimulating immunological resistance to cancer," he said. He added that Dr. Lane's entrancement with anti-angiogenesis also missed the point that both angiogenesis and anti-angiogenesis are needed if the body is to stay in balance. Dr. Prudden found that all types of cartilage contain biological directors that prevent

angiogenesis in cases of cancer and arthritis but promote angiogenesis in wound healing.

The fall of Lane's anti-angiogenesis theory does not make shark cartilage useless, and some clinicians have reported good results from using it for cancer therapy. The late Robert Atkins, MD, of the Atkins Center in New York City, incorporated both shark and bovine cartilages into comprehensive programs, making it hard to tease out the results of either form of cartilage alone. Alan Gaby, MD, past president of the American Holistic Medical Association, wrote in the April 1994 issue of the *Townsend Letter for Doctors*, "As far as clinical results are concerned, I have not met any physicians who are excited about their results with shark cartilage." Lane, however, cites scores of studies in his book *Sharks Don't Get Cancer* and its sequel, *Sharks Still Don't Get Cancer*, including much early research that was actually performed with bovine cartilage. As for the studies done with shark cartilage in Mexico, Cuba, Panama, Chile, and Belgium, good results have been reported, but without long-term follow-up. None was strict enough in its protocol to warrant publication in major medical or scientific journals. Particularly bad news for shark cartilage came from a study by the Cancer Treatment Research Foundation in Arlington Heights, Illinois, and published in the November 1998 issue of the *Journal of Clinical Oncology*. As tested on sixty terminally ill cancer patients, shark cartilage did nothing to slow their disease or improve their quality of life. However, the problem may not have been the shark cartilage but the short duration of the study, which lasted only three months. Dr. Prudden insisted it took a minimum of four months to see results with bovine cartilage, and, despite Lane's claims, there's no reason to think shark cartilage would be speedier.

Preparing for a Colonoscopy

I am almost sixty years old, and for the last five years, my doctor had been telling me I needed to have a colonoscopy. The problem is when I miss even one meal, I get awful headaches, which bring on migraines, usually with nausea and vomiting. I could only imagine the shape I would be in after not eating anything substantial for a whole day to prepare for a colonoscopy. However, three months previously, my mother died of colon cancer, and that was the impetus I needed to get myself in gear.

So I called the endoscopy center and bravely scheduled my appointment. I made sure I had plenty of migraine meds and anti-nausea meds for extra insurance and peace of mind. I made bone broth from vegetables and chickens, including the heads and the feet so I would have plenty of gel and good nutrition. I made sure to strain it extra well through a towel, so there would be no large particles. I even removed the layer of fat off the top (which I usually drink) because I wasn't sure whether that fat would remain in the colon. On the day before the procedure, I drank lots of water as directed. For breakfast, lunch, and dinner, I drank a large mug of hot chicken broth. In the midafternoon slump, I drank some kombucha. And guess what?

Yep. No headache. I could not believe what was happening. Sure, I was hungry, but I did not feel weak and I never got a headache. Even the next morning, before the procedure, I felt amazingly well. And I know it was due in large part to the bone broth. It gave my body what it needed (pretty much all by itself) to make it through the preparation day with flying colors. I had three benign growths that were removed, and I don't have to fret the next colonoscopy because I know how to make it through. And now you do too!

–Kathy Mellin,
Littleton, Colorado

Non-Cartilage Components of Broth for Cancer

As of yet, very little cancer research exists on the non-cartilage components of broth. In 2009, the Health Research Center of Aichi-Gakuin University in Aichi, Japan, reported in *Experimental Oncology* that injections of porcine skin gelatin prolonged the survival of mice morbidly ill from liver or colon cancers. A year earlier the same Japanese team had reported in *Experimental Oncology* on antitumor activity in vitro from porcine skin gelatin. In 2009, the *Journal of Dermatological Science* reported success with bovine collagen hydrolysate against melanoma cell proliferation, also in vitro.

Three recent studies on glucosamine and cancer are of interest. In 2013, *Molecular Medicine Reports* published results from China Medical University in Shenyang, Liaoning, China, on glucosamine inhibition of lung cell proliferation in vitro.

In 2013, a team from the Public Health Sciences Division of the Fred Hutchinson Cancer Research Center in Seattle published the results of an "exploratory analysis conducted within the VITamins And Lifestyle (VITAL) study." The team wanted to know whether the use of glucosamine and chondroitin sulfate could be associated with reduced risk of colorectal cancer. The study involved over 75,000 western Washington State residents, ages fifty to seventy-six, who completed a mailed VITAL questionnaire between 2000 and 2002. The conclusion, published in *Cancer Causes and Control*, was that glucosamine and chondroitin supplements "merit further attention as a potential chemopreventive agent."

While these studies are of interest, they mostly suggest fertile areas for further research, highlight the stellar quality of Dr. Prudden's work, and remind us of the fact that this work has languished since his death in 1998. Sadly, the reputation of bovine tracheal cartilage has been smudged by investigators who were less than strict with protocol. A good example is a company that developed a bovine cartilage product and received an Investigational New Drug (IND) grant from the Food and Drug Administration (FDA) in the mid-1980s. It began trials with twenty-five patients in Hershey, Pennsylvania, and Newark, New Jersey. Of the twenty-five patients, only one survived.

The failure, said Dr. Prudden, should not have been blamed on cartilage, but on the selection of patients, who, without exception, had only a few days left to live at the start of the study. "Look," he said. "I have never promised resurrection. Those patients were essentially dead and did not fail to perish, except for one brilliant triumph. That triumph was a person with renal cell carcinoma, who was still alive nine years later. A presumptive cure. That itself is a blazing star in the sky."

Dr. Prudden, of course, worked exclusively with terminally ill patients in his own pilot studies. The difference, he said, was that the Hershey and Newark patients were "already breathing their last and died, on average, thirty days from the start of treatment."

Glutamine and Cancer

Broth and gelatin have helped people recover from cancer and other illnesses for many years, yet recent research has cast doubt on the value of their glutamine component. Broth and gelatin, as we discussed in chapter 6, are naturally high in glutamine, a conditionally essential amino acid that improves strength, muscle mass, gut healing, immunity, and liver detoxification. Numerous studies show that glutamine enhances recovery from stress, trauma, injury, and illness, as well as damage to the body from radiation and chemotherapy.

The dark side of glutamine is the fact that it plays an important role in cancer cell adaptation, survival, and progression, and has even been called "ambrosia for cancer cells." Accordingly, some doctors are warning cancer patients to steer clear of glutamine. By extension, that warning would include broth.

What to think? Consider this: Cancer cells are wily survivors that can get all the glutamine they need from the glutamine produced naturally in the body. If we cut back on broth, meats, and other good sources of glutamine, it is our healthy cells that lose out. And with low glutamine, we get low glutathione, lower immune function, loss of muscle mass, and other unwanted conditions caused by glutamine depletion.

What to do? Eat plenty of nourishing traditional foods that are naturally rich in glutamine, but avoid artificially high supplemental doses.

As Dr. Prudden found, it normally takes four months to see whether cartilage is working. "I'm a clinician, and I know when the jig is up," he said. "There can be a large load of cancer and it can have spread, but it must not have shut down body systems that are needed to survive." Sloan Kettering, Columbia-Presbyterian, and other cancer centers have protocols by which they test the bio-efficacy of new drugs only on people who still have some life in them. They also routinely eliminate from their studies anyone who is seriously ill from another disease.

Though the *Journal of Biological Response Modifiers* is one of the world's leading medical journals, little attention was paid to Dr. Prudden's 1985 article, even at the time. "I'd thought I'd go to my apotheosis trailing clouds of glory, but there was nothing but silence. It produced nothing. That was, I must confess, a great astonishment to me." Though discouraged, Dr. Prudden felt it may have been beneficial in the long run. Had he attained celebrity status as a cancer curer, he said, it would have been more difficult to achieve "responsible development of the findings."

Dr. Prudden's article concluded with a plea that the scientific and medical communities examine the work thoroughly and speed it on its way, but this has not happened. Although Dr. Prudden felt massive research was needed to reveal cartilage's full potential, he thought oncologists should use cartilage in the meantime. "There is absolutely no reason to delay except the dead weight of habit and its handmaiden, the regulatory apparatus," he said. "I find it interesting but very sad that sub-lethal amounts of toxic drugs are approved for use with a minimum quantity of preliminary evidence, but nutritional therapies such as cartilage are expected to wait for some sort of 'final proof of effectiveness' before they can join the mainstream of modern medicine."

That attitude has led to the deaths of more than twenty million Americans from cancer since Dr. Prudden published his groundbreaking cancer article in 1985. Many of these people might have benefited from taking cartilage or even consuming cartilage-rich broth, but neither they nor their doctors had ever heard of it.

CHAPTER 17

Mental Health

What's good for the body is good for the brain. With an ongoing mental illness epidemic in the Western world, bone broth could help. The numbers are sobering. One in four American adults now suffers from a diagnosable mental disorder. That's nearly fifty-eight million people altogether, with twenty-one million adults suffering from depression and other mood disorders, forty million afflicted with anxiety disorders, fifteen million with social phobia, six million with panic disorders, more than two million with obsessive-compulsive disorders (OCD), and almost eight million with post-traumatic stress disorder (PTSD). Add in the millions of adults and children with ADD/ADHD, anger issues, and other behavioral problems who have not been diagnosed, and it's clear we have a problem of disastrous proportions.

Our ancestors instinctively understood the importance of making broth from bones, cartilage, and skin and not eating muscle meats alone. Muscle meats are high in methionine, a sulfur-based amino acid needed for just about every process in the body and brain. But as discussed in chapter 5, too much of this essential amino acid can lead to excessive methylation in the body, contributing to mental distress and other health problems. The solution is eating muscle meats rich in methionine along with skin, cartilage, and bones rich in proline, glycine, and glutamine. Eating the skin and gnawing on bones will do the trick, and so will sipping old-fashioned broth.

Not enough methylation leads to brittle mental states in which change does not occur easily. Such people may get stuck in their ways until the frustration erupts in sudden bursts of anger or violence. Too much methylation, on the other hand, can lead to the excessive flexibility and malleability found in persons who bend and sway with others' agendas and fail to effectively shape their own lives. As Chris Masterjohn, PhD, wrote in his article "Meat, Organs, Bones and Skin: Nutrition for Mental Illness," "Our goal is not to increase methylation or decrease methylation, but to provide our brains with the raw materials they need to regulate the process properly."

In some mentally ill people, the extremes of rigidity versus flightiness and spaciness may both be present, varying from day to day or even moment to moment. What's wanted is the right balance of stability and flexibility. While genetics certainly creates predispositions to mental illness, right diet, including broth, can help.

" Nerve Pain and Depression

My husband has virtually cured his sciatic nerve pain with bone broth. That's true for him unless he severely abuses his body. I've been diagnosed with copper toxicity, candida, and leaky gut. Fermented food has helped, but when I consistently add more bone broth, my energy level and depression improve too. Pills don't fix the problem, only cover the symptoms. I've gone through a lot of stress in my life, and I'm thrilled to say what a difference three to four cups of broth a day have meant for both of us.

–Ann Parker, St. Jacob, Illinois "

Physicians have recognized the value of broth for mental illness since at least the twelfth century, when Moses Maimonides prescribed it. Although the Egyptian Jewish physician and philosopher is best known for recommending chicken soup for respiratory infections, he also touted it for mental disorders, most notably "melancholy." In his book *On the Causes of Symptoms*, Maimonides recommended the meat and broth of hens and roosters to "rectify corrupted humors, especially the black humor" (that is, black bile), an excess of which was thought to cause melancholy. He thought soup from turtledoves was the best for improving memory and intelligence, though the soup from any form of fowl would turn around feeble-mindedness or senility. To treat anxiety and frustration, Maimonides was a big fan of schmaltz (rendered animal fat), especially chicken fat.

In traditional Chinese medicine, broth is a key component of many brain therapies. Because it's thought to nourish the kidneys, it is valued as the building block of bones, cartilage, tendons, ligaments, and also the brain. From the Chinese medical perspective, broth is a yin tonic that both fuels and lubes the body. As explained by Rebecca Schwartz, ND, LAc, "When our yin is replete, we feel like we are a well oiled machine. We also feel like we have plenty of calm energy to draw upon. When yin is low, we feel 'burned out,' or running on empty. When we feel like this, we need to replenish ourselves and rest. Winter is a perfect time to nourish our yin."

To date, most of the scientific research has focused on the amino acids and other fractionated components of broth. One exception is a 2003 study entitled "Effect of taking chicken essence on stress and cognition of human volunteers." Malaysian researchers from the Hospital Kuala Lumpur tested a condensed broth that contained higher levels of amino acids and other components than would be found in a bowl of homemade chicken soup. The team concluded that this concentrated broth quelled test anxiety because students who consumed it fared "significantly better" than those taking either a placebo or carrageenan. Given that carrageenan is a toxic ingredient that causes gut inflammation and other health risks, it would be good to know how "chicken essence" would fare against a more appropriate control.

Mental Health and Clarity

Around 2007, I realized that many traditional people who didn't use dairy products did bone broth daily, and decided to be more regular in my use of bone broth. I started a weekly ritual of making a large amount of bone broth-based soup each weekend and having it at work five days a week and also on the weekends. There were days in the summer I felt silly, sweating after having my bone broth soup for lunch. Regardless, I kept going with it.

After three months of daily broth, I started noticing a profound sense of strength—mentally and emotionally. What was unusual was that this wasn't coming from better brain function. It was very clearly a feeling in my abdomen. This continued for about a week, and then over the course of a day I realized that what was becoming clear in my gut was that the relationship I'd been in for almost twenty years wasn't working and I finally had the courage—the intestinal fortitude? the guts?—to realize it. My partner and I decided to separate, and we are both happier for it. I mentioned this to friends who'd been struggling in their relationships, and they had exactly the same experience after three months. The difference was they found the intestinal fortitude to finally commit to their relationship and save their marriages, which were now happier than they had been for years.

My take on this is that our brains can rationalize all sorts of delusions, but our gut generally speaks the truth. At the very least, a strong gut seems to be necessary for the big choices, the hard decisions with which every life is presented. Without a strong sense of strength in our gut, we're at risk for poor decisions when courage and clarity are challenged.

–Kevin F., Chicago, Illinois

Gelatin and Mental Health

Nathan Gotthoffer, PhD, turned up surprisingly few studies on gelatin and mental health during the eighteen years he spent researching *Gelatin in Nutrition and Medicine*. The few he found were carried out by his contemporaries in the mid-1930s. They wanted to know whether gelatin could help with the malnutrition, weight loss, and weakness typically found in schizophrenics and other mentally ill patients, not with healing the mental illness itself. In 1935, Isidore Finkelman, MD, announced in the *American Journal of Psychiatry* that he'd found gelatin helpful for the weight loss that accompanied manic-depressive psychosis and dementia praecox. Dr. W. F. Dutton in *Clinical Medicine and Surgery* observed gelatin solutions were helpful not only for patients with severe psychoses but run-of-the mill hysterias, hypochondriasis, and neurasthenias. Archie D. Carr, MD, writing for *Archives of Neurology and Psychiatry*, reported attempts "made to feed a solution with large quantities of gelatin" to patients with a variety of mental and physical symptoms, including headache, visual disturbance, convulsions, weakness, fatigue, memory loss, and undesirable mental changes. At the end of the experiments, the "entire picture was so striking" that Dr. Carr decided to continue feeding the gelatin.

Return to Health

From about the age of fifteen, I had constantly and consistently experienced deteriorating health. My health history included immune dysfunction, eczema, asthma, and stress, and was exclusively treated with allopathic medicine. This finally resulted in a nervous breakdown and eight to ten years of chronic fatigue syndrome, depression, and post-traumatic stress disorder. In addition, at eighteen months, my son had developmental and behavioral issues and extreme eczema. It was because of him that I discovered the Weston A. Price Foundation and then the Gut and Psychology Syndrome (GAPS) diet. I began making bone broths and eating good-quality lard. Our butcher is fantastic, and our beef comes from the pristine pastures of Tasmania (it is not certified organic, but that is quite unnecessary in this part of the world). My health and my son's health are now pretty much fantastic!

—Sarah N.,
Melbourne, Australia

In the 1930s, Francis Pottenger Jr., MD, found gelatin had a very positive effect on digestion (see chapter 15). Although he didn't say much about gelatin and mental health, he instinctively understood what is now known as the gut-brain connection and speculated that "better digestion in the presence of gelatin" could "relieve nerve irritation."

Most of the recent science involves studies of the conditionally essential amino acids glycine and glutamine, two supplements known to relieve stress. Both have been linked to improved alertness, concentration, and energy as well as overall emotional stability and increased feelings of well-being.

Because of glycine's role in glucose manufacture, people with low levels are more likely to suffer from hypoglycemia, metabolic syndrome, and other blood sugar issues marked by mood swings. Glycine may also help diabetics control blood sugar, bolster immunity, delay the onset and the progression of cataracts, and reduce the severity of other diabetic complications.

Glycine also improves sleep quality by assisting the body in the production and utilization of melatonin. One study even showed that subjects were better rested on 25 percent less sleep over three consecutive nights if dosed with 3 grams of glycine. Subjectively and objectively, people have also attained better sleep quality with the help of glycine than from sleeping pills.

Glutamine and Mood Disorders

Both glycine and glutamine are critical for gut healing. The gut—sometimes called our "second brain"—has more nerve endings than the spine and manufactures more neurotransmitters than the brain. Indeed, 95 percent of our serotonin is manufactured in the gut. With insufficient serotonin, we are more likely to experience insomnia, depression, and other mood disorders, and are targets for serotonin reuptake inhibitor drugs like Prozac.

Most inhibitory neurons in the brain and spinal cord use either GABA (gamma amino butyric acid) or glycine as a neurotransmitter. Glutamine plays a key role in the glutamate-GABA-glutamine cycle involving either the release of GABA or glutamate from neurons and the uptake into the star-shaped brain cells known as astrocytes. GABA is an inhibitory neurotransmitter that has tranquilizing effects on both the physical and emotional body. The gifts of GABA include calming anxiety, lifting depression, improving overall mood, quieting a chattering mind, and improving sleep quality. It has shown promise for attention deficit hyperactivity disorder (ADHD), high blood pressure reduction, pain relief, premenstrual syndrome (PMS), and seizures.

In 1976, Renato Cocchi, MD, PhD, a neurologist and psychologist, reported "clear anti-depressive properties" for glutamine and clear patient improvement from the "slowed-down motor activity" of endogenous depression up to what he called a "vital level." Whether glutamine alone or its role in GABA caused this beneficial effect is not known, but Dr. Cocchi has since included glutamine in numerous protocols along with antidepressants and other pharmaceutical drugs.

Not everyone has found glutamine so beneficial. Once glutamine from the diet or supplements gets past the blood-brain barrier, it is converted to either GABA, which has a calming effect, or to glutamate, which is excitatory. Both have important roles in brain function, but glutamate toxicity has become a major problem today because of the widespread use of MSG in processed, packaged, and fast foods. Manufacturers of commercial broths, soups, gelatins, and bouillons almost always ramp up the flavor with added MSG. On top of that, hydrolyzing and many other modern processing methods create MSG-like residues. Sadly, even the glutamine found naturally in homemade broth can cause problems for extremely sensitive individuals. For this reason, Natasha Campbell-McBride, MD, starts autistic children and other sensitive patients on the GAPS (Gut and Psychology Syndrome) diet with a lightly cooked meat stock that is low in glutamine (see chapter 6).

Glutamine supplements are widely recommended by alternative medical doctors to help cancer patients heal mouth sores, gut damage, and other adverse effects from chemotherapy and radiation. Far less known is the fact that glutamine can boost the mood of patients. In a study at Brigham and Women's Hospital in Boston, patients given bone marrow transplants were tube-fed either the standard total parenteral nutrition (TPN) or the TPN plus 4 grams of glutamine. The ones on glutamine reported greater well-being and less fatigue and manifested far less anger. The researchers stated, "This is one of the first studies to illustrate an improvement in patients' psychosocial status associated with a nutrition intervention." Typically glutamine studies have focused on objective outcomes, such as nitrogen balance, wound healing, or muscle strength rather than patients' more subjective impressions of their quality of life.

Synergistic Effects

Few people will drink enough broth to get anywhere close to 4 grams in a day. But broth is not built of glutamine alone, and the synergistic effect of glycine, glutamine, collagen, and other components in broth should not be discounted. The bottom line is that broth has been helping convalescents feel mentally and physically nourished for thousands of years. With rates of depression, anxiety, paranoia, memory loss, attention deficit and hyperactivity, low self-esteem, and other mental health disorders at an all-time high, it's time to put old-fashioned broth back on the daily menu.

CHAPTER 18

Sports and Fitness

Eating lots of lean protein to build muscle, look sexy, and stay trim?

Everyone's heard that's the way to go, but what if almost everything we've ever been taught about sports nutrition is wrong? What if all that lean protein brings short-term benefits but long-term harm? What if the simple step of drinking broth every day could optimize the health and longevity of bodybuilders, strength trainers, athletes, joggers, jocks, spinners, skaters, and weekend warriors?

Athletes have known for years that lean meat builds rippling muscles, but those muscles can come at a cost. High-protein diets can lead to deficiencies of fat-soluble vitamins as well as significant imbalances of vitamins, minerals, amino acids, and fatty acids. Those who choose lean proteins in the form of shake powders based on soy, pea, rice, whey, and other protein isolates can compound the risks by consuming MSG, nitrosamines, and other toxins and carcinogens created by modern, industrial processing techniques.

In contrast to these modern experiments, our healthy ancestors honored animals by eating all parts of them. They sucked out the marrow, favored the organ meats, chewed on the gristle, dipped deeply into the fat, and rejected lean cuts whenever possible. With the wisdom of instinct and experience, they knew their guts-and-grease diets conferred strength, endurance, and supreme good health.

Lean protein at its worst comes in the protein powders that first took off in the 1940s and 1950s. Portable and shelf stable, they seemed a practical solution for disaster relief and world hunger efforts and a profitable path for food manufacturers. For the vegetable oil industry, soy protein powders presented a way to profit from the protein left over from the manufacture of soy oil, margarine, and shortening.

Not surprisingly, bodybuilders in the pre–anabolic steroid era started adding powdered proteins to diets already high in protein. As Randy Roach explained in *Muscle, Smoke and Mirrors*, there was great economic incentive to promote soy as a perfect protein. Roach noted, however, that Vince Gironda, Armand Tanny, and other top competitors warned followers off the soy. Gironda pulled no punches when he called it "that s***!"

Prior to the 1990s, when soy was successfully marketed as a "miracle" food, most bodybuilders hedged their bets by taking mixes of soy, whey, and other protein powders along with raw eggs, milk, and other high-quality real foods. Many also took gelatin, a concentrate that bodybuilders had favored since the early twentieth century. Every morning, Steve Reeves, Mr. Universe 1947 and the star of *Hercules* and *Hercules Unchained*, stirred Knox gelatin faithfully into a breakfast shake of fresh orange juice, honey, banana, raw eggs, skim milk, egg white, and soy protein.

Gelatin and Strength

The gelatin prescription dates back to the era of Eugen Sandow, a Florenz Ziegfeld vaudeville star renowned for charisma, strength, and a finely chiseled physique. In his lifelong attempt to hack the secrets to bodybuilding, Sandow looked to science, and undoubtedly found the nineteenth- and early twentieth-century studies that suggested gelatin was the answer to world hunger, recovery from injury, and prevention of illness, and the cure-all of just about anything, including indigestion. Given that Sandow strongly believed in facilitating good digestion, adding gelatin to meals surely seemed a good insurance policy.

Some of Sandow's colleagues recommended using "beef extract" for rapid muscle recovery, and strongman Arthur Saxon endorsed a beef gelatin product known as Bovril. Bovril ads ranged from illustrations of lively bulls with the words *powerful and invigorating* to a view of the pope blessing the meat tea and smiling at the caption "The Two Infallible Powers—the Pope and Bovril." Whether Leo XIII had a beef with the ad is unknown, but the unmistakable message to the public was that Bovril conferred strength, virility, invincibility, and infallibility. Although a product of that name is still sold, its formula has devolved over the years from beef to beef-like, changes that can only have diminished the product's alleged former superpowers.

Nineteenth- and early twentieth-century scientists looked to gelatin as a solution for malnutrition and the muscle wasting of convalescence. In the 1930s, they turned to questions of strength and endurance. Leading the pack was Walter Meredith Boothby, MD (1880–1953), hired by the Mayo Clinic in 1917 to establish a laboratory of basal metabolism. He originally focused on the metabolism of patients with hypothyroidism and hyperthyroidism, but by 1934 he had turned his attention to muscle strength and endurance. Dr. Boothby found that 15 grams of glycine—a conditionally essential amino acid found abundantly in broth and gelatin—increased muscular strength and skill, delayed the onset of fatigue, and even restored the wasted muscle tissues in myasthenia gravis and related diseases.

Dr. Boothby's finding was confirmed by Doctors G. B. Ray, J. R. Johnson, and M. M. Taylor at the Long Island College of Medicine—though none of them quite knew what to make of their finding that glycine seemed to increase the work output of men but not of women. The Long Island team also learned that patients who were unable to take high doses of glycine without discomfort did well on a commercial gelatin product containing about 25 percent glycine. A generous 30 grams of gelatin could be given in a single dose if mixed well into chilled orange juice.

A few years earlier, in 1932, Professor Lazar Remen at the University of Münster had also reported on glycine's good effects on muscle. So did Regidius M. Kaczmarek, Professor of Physiology at the University of Notre Dame, who noted the "superior influence" of gelatin on athletes and nonathletes who pedaled bikes until they dropped from exhaustion. In Dr. Kaczmarek's experiments, the gelatin-using athletes increased their average daily work output by 216 percent, but nonathletes by just 52 percent. Contrary to the findings of the Long Island Medical Center researchers, he reported gelatin exerted a "favorable influence" on "the girl subjects," though this may have been due to their age (under seventeen and still growing) rather than gender. Dr. Kaczmarek reported that none of his subjects "manifested any gustatory dislike for or physiological intolerance of gelatin."

Why gelatin increased endurance and "work output" was the burning question. The scientists jockeyed for power with various explanations. Given that Banting and Best had discovered insulin in 1921, theories on blood sugar and metabolism abounded. Gelatin fit perfectly into such discussions because its abundant glycine, glutamine, and alanine stores are glucogenic (that is, promote the release of glucose into the bloodstream), while its adequate arginine, cystine, proline, and serine are glycogenic (promote the storage of glucose). The Long Island College of Medicine Team rooted for glycine, because of its role as a creatine precursor, a theory that proved popular for a time but never quite held up.

Glycine and Endurance

Russell Morse Wilder, MD (1885–1959), of the Mayo Clinic, is remembered today for his pioneering diabetes research, metabolic studies, and creation of a ketogenic diet that stopped epileptic seizures. Dr. Wilder also weighed in on the glycine-endurance controversy: "I am satisfied that I have been capable of more sustained effort since taking glycine and other healthy subjects will tell the same story, but testimonial evidence such as this will not satisfy the critical mind. An ideal experiment would require two full companies of soldiers with an equally robust and equally well-trained personnel. If one company could then be fed glycine for from four to six weeks but the other not, and then if both companies could be subjected to a grueling march, the number of stragglers in each company would supply the objective evidence we need so badly. It is possible that such an experiment can be conducted by the medical officers at some army post."

That soldier experiment never took place, and the confusion continued as researchers analyzed a large variety of studies, many of dubious design and value. One such effort compared the performance of a group of cyclists imbibing glycine-spiked wine with a control group on wine alone. (While glycine improved the performance, there is no evidence the subjects were any less drunk or might have benefited from the resveratrol content.) Not surprisingly, some researchers scratched their heads, threw up their hands, and resorted to talk about "psychological effects" or "training factors." Nathan Gotthoffer, PhD, who probably found and meticulously reviewed every piece of gelatin research ever published for *Gelatin in Nutrition and Medicine*, didn't buy that. The limits of exercise alone ought to have been readily apparent to anyone who reviewed the results of taking gelatin compared to sham feedings, he said.

Even so, he was unable to draw any conclusions about the cause, and settled for noting that gelatin's "positive effect" on strength and endurance "has been observed and is no doubt real."

Given the confusion, it's not surprising that gelatin never quite took off in the bodybuilding world. Many trainers and champions still recommended adding it to breakfast shakes, consuming bouillon to whet the appetite for weight-gaining meals, and eating soup to curb hunger on weight-loss diets, but it constituted only a minor part of the diet. The level was probably typical of that consumed by the general public. Knox Gelatin, after all, was successfully marketing its product as a helpmate in the kitchen and maker of strong, healthy nails.

He-Man Diets

Clearly, the results of bodybuilders cannot be extrapolated to the general population—or even to people who like to stay healthy, active, and fit. Bodybuilders, after all, represent a subset of the population, one that eats massive amounts of food, works out obsessively, and aspires to attain what many people consider freakish ideals of physical perfection. Even so, it's interesting to ponder why all the emphasis on protein in the 1940s and 1950s did not lead to the deficiencies, imbalances, and health problems we see so widely today. The main reason was that the earlier "he-man" diets talked protein but included raw eggs, raw milk, liver, and plenty of other real foods. Although some bodybuilders supplemented with soy, whey, and wheat protein powders during those decades, the dietary foundation remained high-quality animal food, not

fractionated processed and packaged products. Today's obsession with shakes, smoothies, and energy bars is a new development.

Notably, raw milk was in the bodybuilding mix from the get-go. Sandow, Saxon, and other early greats recommended it, as did Bernarr MacFadden (1868–1955), the father of physical culture. MacFadden is often thought to have been a vegetarian because of all the beet juice, raw carrots, fruits, dates, raisins, grains, and nuts he grazed on. He ate small amounts of meat, however, and also drank copious amounts of raw milk, sometimes topping off at more than a gallon a day. He also recommended regular raw milk fasts, then a mainstream rejuvenation remedy endorsed by the Mayo Clinic. Less well known is the fact that he experimented with veganism, but found himself too weak to work out, and gave it up entirely after his wife first gave birth to an underweight baby and later suffered a miscarriage. MacFadden's preaching about meat polluting the body with "impurities" then came to a stop, and he conceded we all need some red meat, at least once in a while.

Although most of the early superstar bodybuilders and trainers ate more meat than MacFadden, they all agreed on the importance of raw milk and cream. So did Vince Gironda, (1917–1997), the "Iron Guru" who came to prominence in the late 1940s as a bodybuilder and trainer to the stars. Gironda raised the nutritional bar by recommending dozens of eggs, gallons of raw milk, sticks of raw butter, blood-building liver, and bloody red meat.

Most of these men knew and respected the work of Robert McCarrison (1879–1962) and Vilhjalmur Stefansson (1878–1960). McCarrison investigated the food and lifestyle of the Hunza, a group who thrived on a mostly lacto-vegetarian diet that also included some meat and broth. Stefansson found good health among Arctic carnivores who ate all parts of the animal, complete with sucking on bone marrow and chewing on gristle. Their findings were widely publicized in the 1930s, the decade in which Weston A. Price, DDS, visited primitive cultures around the world and established clear relationships between diet and degeneration.

Somehow the bodybuilders missed the parts about primal diets valuing bones, gristle, marrow, and broth. But with so much raw milk in their diets, their emphasis on muscle meat did not lead to dietary failure. Milk contains glutamine, glycine, and proline, three conditionally essential amino acids found abundantly in broth and gelatin. Although these amino acids are present in gelatin powder at ten to twenty times the concentration found in other proteins, the bodybuilders consumed enormous quantities of milk, eggs, and meat. For people whose primary goal is to look trim and toned, such quantities would lead to overweight. Yet, without these choices, lean meat–oriented dietary regimens inevitably lead to deficiencies in glycine, glutamine, and other nutrients. Although a daily bowl of broth could easily solve the problem, most trainers don't know that and instead recommend supplements.

Supplements for Bodybuilders

A particularly useful supplement is glycine, recommended for help with protein digestion, detoxification, wound healing, and a host of other metabolic needs. Because it's a conditionally essential amino acid, the body can obviously make it, but there are many reasons to think that even normal healthy people might not be able to make enough. In 1985, researchers concluded that prolonged restriction of dietary protein or too little glycine and other amino acids could limit the capacity of tissues to form creatine, porphyrins, purines, and glutathione. Creatine, of course, has a huge impact on muscles, strength, and endurance. While this study might seem irrelevant in that few restrict their protein, diets that revolve around lean muscle meat provide a surplus of methionine, a deficiency of glycine, and an overall protein imbalance.

Another popular supplement among athletes is glutamine, the most abundant amino acid in the body and the third-highest amino acid found in broth and gelatin. Scientists looked hard at glutamine from the late 1970s through the 1980s and discovered that muscle cells contain high amounts of free glutamine. When glutamine is needed anywhere in the body to help address physical or emotional stress, the muscles give some up. As a result, glutamine stores are rapidly depleted when bodies are stressed from accident, injury, burns, illness, or overtraining. If glutamine is not quickly repleted by the consumption of meat, broth, gelatin, or other glutamine-rich foods, muscle wasting begins.

These findings have led many alternative physicians and other health practitioners to recommend glutamine supplements whenever the body is under stress, including stress from intense, exhausting exercise. For example, the glutamine levels in a runner's blood will be reduced by around 20 percent after he or she completes a marathon. If the runner takes glutamine en route, however, this occurrence can be reduced or even prevented altogether. Bodies on glutamine recover from extreme exertion more quickly. Stressed-out athletes whose bodies go into acidosis can also benefit greatly from glutamine.

Furthermore, glutamine supports the immune system, helping physically stressed athletes resist colds, flu, and other infections. In terms of recovering from illness or injury, glutamine can help athletes and non-athletes alike. Added to IV feeding tubes in hospitals, glutamine promotes speedier healing and reduces muscle atrophy. As an oral supplement it can aid gut healing, reduce oxidative stress, speed postsurgical healing, and help patients rebound from debilitating cancer treatments.

Even so, some researchers have reported little beneficial effect from glutamine supplementation. How can that be? The most likely reason is that extra glutamine is not necessary, at least not in healthy, well-nourished individuals. As a conditionally essential amino acid, the body can make it, after all. But while optimally healthy people can make plenty of it and easily meet any increased needs, few of us today are healthy enough to rise to that challenge day after day. Under conditions of chronic physical and emotional stress, extra glutamine seems to make sense. Day to day, glutamine-rich broth can prevent such stress.

Glutamine can also prove useful as a precursor to the neurotransmitter GABA. When glutamine gets past the blood-brain barrier, it is metabolized either to glutamate (which is excitatory) or to GABA (which has a calming effect). Both are needed by the body and brain. GABA not only keeps people calm but helps them lose fat, gain muscle, increase energy, prevent muscle spasms, increase cardiac output, increase bone mass, increase exercise endurance, enhance sexual performance, and even produce human growth hormone (hGH).

The hGH claim might seem a bit of a stretcher, but has actually interested researchers for decades. It comes from the fact that GABA plays a significant role in hypothalamic-pituitary function. The pituitary gland is the master endocrine gland affecting all hormonal functions of the body including growth hormone.

As discussed in chapter 9, numerous components found in broth can help with osteo-arthritis, particularly the type known as secondary osteoarthritis, which is caused by athletic injury, trauma, accident, or repetitive motion.

Few sports nutritionists today tout gelatin, much less broth. Instead, collagen hydrolysate, a gelatin derivative that dissolves easily in both hot and cold water, has been in the news. Dr. Friedhelm Beuker of the Institute for Sports Sciences at the University of Dusseldorf in Germany; Dr. Klaus Seeligmuller, a specialist in orthopedics, sports medicine, and physical therapy in Bonn, Germany; James M. Rippe, MD, of the Rippe Lifestyle Institute in Shrewsbury, Massachusetts; and Kristine L. Clark, PhD, RD, a specialist in sports nutrition at Penn State, have all shown significant improvements for athletes suffering from joint pain after taking collagen hydrolysate.

Recovery from Injury

Training for any endurance, speed, or strength sport involves purposeful micro-tearing of tissue and inflammation. When all is well, repair takes place and the body comes back stronger. An exercise program that is too intense or does not allow sufficient recovery time, however, can lead to sprains, strains, stress fractures, and serious sidelining injuries.

Sports

I train in Brazilian jiu-jitsu, a ground-fighting art that demands high flexibility and joint health. Since incorporating bone broths into my diet, I have had fewer injuries, and no serious ones, to my joints. I do not take supplements, so the bone broths are my way to get materials into my body that are beneficial for joints. Our bone broths are frequently made with wild animals, including ruffed grouse, wild turkey, and white-tailed deer, though we use pastured chickens and free-range sheep as well. We focus on the joints of larger animals so plenty of cartilage and connective tissue are simmered.

–Arthur Haines,
Canton, Maine

The usual treatment for strains and sprains is NSAIDs and other anti-inflammatories. These can control the pain but come with a long list of side effects. Taking them regularly can lead to gastrointestinal tract upset, including stomach irritation, bleeding, and ulceration. Less common side effects include high blood pressure, kidney problems, and liver damage. Furthermore, their usage can defeat the very purpose of exercise in that NSAIDs accelerate the process of joint destruction by lowering the level of cartilage-healing prostaglandins, GAGs (glycosaminoglycans), and hyaluronic acid.

What to do instead? First of all, remember that injuries are most likely to happen to people who fail to warm up adequately, train too long or too often, lift overly heavy weights using poor form, or fail to take sufficient time off between workouts for healing and recovery. Next, prioritize proper nutrition. A nutrient-dense diet rich in broth not only helps build strong flexible bones, joints, tendons, and ligaments but helps us recover quickly from overuse or injury. With proper nutrition, appropriate exercise promotes health. Without it, exercise stress saps us of energy, accelerates the degenerative process, and can even cause crippling injury. As the inimitable William Campbell Douglass II, MD, puts it, "The next thing you know, you're using whatever's left of your strength to put tennis balls on your walker so it doesn't scratch the floor."

Although Dr. Douglass thinks it's a lie that we need to "sweat, sweat, sweat in a gym," the researchers at Tufts have proven that strong people stay young. While that's partially about building biceps, abs, and quads, it applies to the muscles we can't see as well, including those that power the heart. As with any lifestyle choice, we must balance possible benefits against proven risks.

Dr. Weston A. Price reported no aerobics classes or Nautilus machines in cultures where people lived long healthy lives without slack muscles, thin bones, and creaky joints. Yet exercise was a natural and consistent way of life. People hunted, gathered, fished, worked the fields, stretched, lifted, walked, and sprinted as part of their daily routine. Old and young alike found it impossible to avoid daily physical activity, a fact that impacted their impressive longevity, high levels of energy, and vibrant good health. We also know none of them dined on lean protein, shake powders, or pills. Clearly it's time to up our nutritional game with a traditional diet rich in old-fashioned broth.

CHAPTER 19

Anti-Aging

Can broth prevent the very diseases that it may help cure? Can it lead to optimum health, high energy, maximum longevity, and ageless aging? Those who demand hard scientific evidence will not find much. Prevention trials take years and years to complete plus millions of dollars in funding. Given that no one stands to profit much from genuine bone broth—or even cartilage, collagen, or gelatin supplement products—we don't expect to see any studies in the foreseeable future. Still, ancestral wisdom and common sense alike argue for putting broth front and center in any anti-aging plan.

Linus Pauling, PhD, winner of the Nobel Prize for Chemistry in 1954 and the Nobel Peace Prize in 1964, suggested that a long line of "minor" infections will wear out the body, making it more susceptible to other diseases, shortening life expectancy and accelerating the aging process. Given broth's long-standing reputation for preventing infections and speeding recovery from illnesses or wounds, it clearly makes sense to drink up.

If Hippocrates was right that all disease begins in the gut, then broth also belongs in every disease-prevention program. Besides healing the gut and supporting the proliferation of good microflora, broth provides vital nutrients and improves the digestion, assimilation, utilization, and elimination of food.

It's important to remember that health problems rarely emerge as full-blown diseases overnight. Typically people report feeling "out of sorts" with a variety of digestive complaints, fatigue, and other symptoms for months or even years. Though conventional medicine tends to think of people as being either "sick" or "well," most of us lie somewhere in between. Ideally, we will each take stock of our health—and make stock in our kitchens—before disease can make serious progress.

Broth's proven power to modulate the immune system and soothe inflammation could be the ticket to preventing or even reversing colitis, Crohn's disease, and other digestive disorders, not to mention autoimmune diseases such as rheumatoid arthritis, lupus erythematosus, psoriasis, and scleroderma. Its ability to nourish the joints could stop osteoarthritis early on before creakiness even gets noticed. Because cartilage has no nerves, pain is not experienced until it has degenerated to the point where it thins, cracks, and impacts on other tissues. With broth on the menu, many diseases and disorders just don't happen.

Likewise, the best time to cure cancer is in the earliest stages when it is still undiagnosable by conventional medical doctors. For those who have a family history of cancer or other risk factors, adopting a nutrient-dense traditional diet that includes broth offers a viable alternative to worrying, waiting, and relying on early detection. Fear, after all, can itself contribute to stress and immune system breakdown, and even attract the very condition that is feared. In any case, orthodox medicine's reliance on early detection of cancer is not a form of prevention, does not guarantee a cure, and is usually anything but early. Worse, early detection can mean a longer course of painful, disabling, expensive, and often ineffective treatments. Indeed, many people who have survived cancer for five years after early detection attain the dubious distinction of being counted among the American Cancer Society's "cures," even if they die soon after.

Broth for Weight Control

Currently 65 percent of Americans are overweight, with 35 percent obese. Despite massive public health initiatives, booming sales of weight-loss products, and a glut of diet books, rates of obesity continue to increase, and we all know that overweight has been linked to diabetes, cardiovascular disease, infertility, cancer, and nearly every other health problem.

Over the years, numerous diet books have stressed the importance of soup in weight-loss programs. However, the authors' reasoning rarely transcends the idea that filling up on broth means less room for dinner and dessert. That may well be the case, and at least one study has shown a lower calorie intake with soup on the menu, but there are sound scientific reasons for this recommendation as well.

Broth improves the digestibility and assimilation of food, giving the body the critical message that it is deeply nourished, happy, and full. Individuals who feel physical and emotional satisfaction from their food also experience fewer cravings for sugar and starchy carbohydrates. That not only influences the attainment and maintenance of a healthy weight but minimizes the likelihood of developing diabetes or other blood sugar issues that contribute to the condition popularized by Mark Hyman, MD, as *diabesity*. With gut healing we also are able to house more beneficial microflora, which, in turn, bring reduced storage of carbohydrates as body fat. In contrast, poor gut bacteria increase insulin production, leading to insulin resistance and increased storage of body fat.

Although broth can contribute to the normalization of weight, it should not be seen as a magically quick weight-loss solution. That may well be for the best. A recent study in the journal *Obesity* suggests a little plumpness—or what used to be considered "normal" weight—confers longevity. Those who are rail thin (what the media promote as fashionably thin) or super fit (rippling muscles with virtually no body fat) do as poorly in terms of longevity as those who are obese. This surprising finding has been dubbed the "obesity paradox" because some earlier studies have suggested "undernutrition without malnutrition" is the ticket to maximum life span. In fact, those studies showed that skinny rats lived longer but were perpetually hungry and cranky.

Bone Building, Weight Loss, and More

The doctor I see most regularly is an American-born hormone specialist of Chinese descent. He is triple-board-certified in internal medicine, endocrinology, and anti-aging medicine. Besides being an avid learner, he is an athletic runner and biker. He ran the first bone density scan on me in late 2009, and it showed I had osteopenia in my lower spine, hips, and thighbones. A year later, when matters had gotten even worse, he prescribed weight-bearing exercise and bioidentical estrogen.

In September 2011, I started to incorporate Weston A. Price Foundation principles into my diet. Chief among them was making bone broth. When the results from my latest bone scan came back in the summer of 2012, the doctor was amazed to see that I had gained back almost 20 percent of my total bone density. His X-ray technician told me such results were unheard of in one year, so the doctor wanted to know what else I had been doing to make such gains.

When I told him about making myself two or three pots full of bone broth each week, he smiled and said, "My wife is Korean, and she makes a couple pots of traditional Asian chicken feet soup each week for our family. My boys love it." I then said, "But how is it you give all your patients advice on how to eat and have even written a cookbook, but nowhere have you mentioned bone broth?" "Well," he replied, "it's unusual for most Americans. I figure it's enough if I can get them to eat whole foods and stay away from the processed stuff." I answered, "You really need to incorporate bone broth into your recommendations, Doctor. After all, I've lost twenty-one pounds, improved my digestion, my mood, my

bone density, and my skin texture, and healed several inflamed lymph glands just by adding bone broth to a diet that already consisted of whole foods." So now I'm sharing my secret to being smart, thin, and happy—eat bone broth on a regular basis!

–Kathleen R.,
Winter Haven, Florida

Far better to enjoy your life and food, concluded David Weeks, MD, a neuropsychologist who in the late 1970s began an eighteen-year study investigating the traits of "superyoung" people who look, act, think, and feel years—and sometimes decades—younger than their chronological ages. In *Secrets of the Superyoung*, Dr. Weeks reported these fortunate individuals enjoyed a variety of foods, did not fuss over their weight, and did not adopt dietary fads. And unlike the cranky rats, they tended to be outgoing, social, and accepting of others. This accords so well with common sense that it's reasonable to conclude that some of the healing power of broth comes from its being a "slow food" that appears on the tables of families who cook, eat, and stay together, and friends who like to get together. The act of making broth alone represents a significant lifestyle choice, a slowing down that can slow the aging process. In short, broth can help us get a grip on the stress that reduces the quality and quantity of modern lives.

Broth can also have a positive effect on longevity by detoxification. The glycine abundant in broth contributes to the liver's manufacture of glutathione, the master antioxidant needed by the liver to detoxify mercury, aluminum, and other toxic metals, as well as formaldehyde and other chemicals, environmental estrogens, and pharmaceutical drug residues that are prevalent in our modern world. Unless eliminated, these toxins will perturb every metabolic pathway in the body, contributing to premature aging and disease.

Anti-Aging Effect of Broth on Skin

The anti-aging effect of broth reported most often is the improvement in skin, nails, and hair. Although media attention focuses on collagen products used cosmetically as topicals and injectables, beautiful skin is never just "skin deep." Broth feeds the epidermis, dermis, and underlying connective tissue layers of the skin from the inside out with the collagen, elastin, and other nutrients it needs to plump out. Broth not only smooths little fret lines that furrow the face but also soothes the wounded skin of acne, eczema, psoriasis, and other skin diseases. As discussed in chapters 11 and 12, Dr. John F. Prudden found that cartilage had a remarkable effect on the healing of scleroderma and psoriasis. As part of the GAPS (Gut and Psychology Syndrome) diet, it has helped heal many cases of childhood eczema.

Some of Dr. Prudden's least known research involved the topical use of cartilage cream on the dry, flaky skin of stewardesses, the cystic acne of teenagers, itchy rashes from poison ivy, and the raw, irritated hides that come from harsh wrinkle-obliterating peels and "resurfacing" techniques used by skin doctors. Dermatologists typically treat "peel sensitivity" with topical corticosteroids, but the *Journal of Dermatological Treatment* reported cartilage cream to be "the first topical anti-inflammatory agent of a nonsteroidal nature that is both safe and effective."

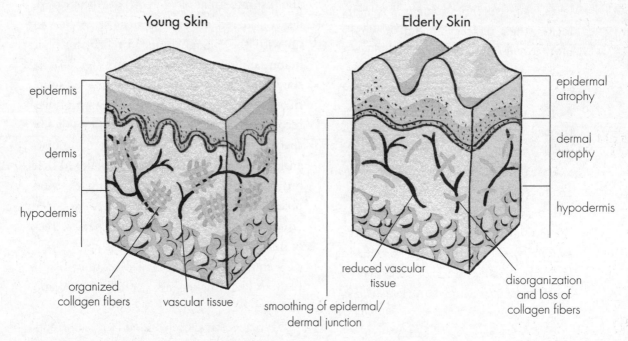

Figure 7: Young, healthy skin is blessed with an abundance of collagen fibers and vascular tissue. Older or unhealthy skin shows reduced quantities of fiber and tissue as well as a more disorganized structure.

Beauty

I swear by bone broth because I have found such success in healing my dysbiosis and intestinal permeability. A clean diet rich in grass-fed animal proteins and fats, minimal grains, and plenty of organic vegetables and fruits proved helpful, but it wasn't until I incorporated bone broths on a daily basis that I saw exponential success in healing my intestinal walls. As a positive side effect, my creaky knees no longer hurt after long hikes and my skin looks radiant. I have been asked several times, "What are you using on your skin? You are absolutely glowing!"

Since my own personal success, I have recommended this broth to all of my clients, including endurance athletes, post-surgery patients, seniors losing their strength, and a young mother-to-be. All have reported dramatic improvements in energy, hormonal balance, strength, skin and hair beauty, and most notably arthritis pain relief. Upon introducing bone broth to clients, they were initially skeptical because of the word *bone*, so I renamed the bone broth Liquid Beauty in a Jar and Rejuvenating Broth. One ingredient that I encourage everyone to try adding is homemade fermented sauerkraut to each cup of broth at each meal for a little saltiness and texture.

—*Megan R. Ulrichs,*
Bozeman, Montana

Cartilage cream and suppositories have also healed areas where the sun doesn't shine. Dr. Prudden found cartilage cleared pruritis ani (a chronic condition in which the skin around the anus itches); anal fissure (a laceration of the skin of the anus); and internal and external hemorrhoids (varicose veins of the rectum and anus). Unfortunately, Dr. Prudden performed no studies with bovine tracheal cartilage pills, although he noted "striking improvements" in skin while curing patients with cancer, arthritis, autoimmune, and other diseases. No studies prove that broth will help painful skin conditions, but limited anecdotal evidence suggests it can.

Broth for Libido

Last but not least, broth is a libido booster that can help men and women maintain love and lust into great old age. All over the world, it's considered an aphrodisiac when cooked up with the "naughty bits" of fish, fowl, or mammals in recipes such as rooster testicle soup, cod sperm soup, and cow uterus soup. In the twelfth century, Moses Maimonides recommended dining often on testicles of any species because of their "warming and moistening" libidinous effect. He also believed that ordinary chicken soup could increase sexual potential. In 1692, *Lo Scalco alla Moderna*, a famous cookbook published in Naples, recommended that lovers and others enjoy a rich stew comprised of pieces of pigeon, breast of veal, stuffed chicken neck, and cock's comb and testicles.

Testicle festivals celebrated by the ancients as fertility festivals are today a bit of a joke, events attended by rowdy good ol' boys. The more upscale aphrodisiac is velvet deer antler, a cartilage-rich product recommended by Chinese doctors for thousands of years to treat sexual impotence and infertility and to help men keep their harems happy. Traditionally valued as a special soup, velvet deer antler today is carefully harvested, cold processed, and sold as an expensive anti-aging, energizing, libido-enhancing elixir. It's also sold to Olympic athletes and aspiring immortalists as an all-natural source of youth-enhancing, muscle-building growth hormone. What does the trick is the antlers of deer, elk, caribou, reindeer, or moose, not the horns of cattle, water buffalo, mountain goats, bighorn sheep, bison, and antelope. Antlers are mostly young moist cartilage, while horns are old decrepit keratin. Unlike rhino horn, tiger penis, and many other traditional aphrodisiacs, velvet antler grows and is shed annually and can apparently be harvested humanely.

While anti-aging, cure-all supplements are always tempting, the myths and marketing tend to be more alluring than reality. In any event, we need not depend upon expensive products to stay juicy for life. Science certainly supports some life-enhancing effects, but ancestral wisdom suggests we can age gracefully and extend our life spans with the lifestyle choice of a "slow foods" diet rich in broth.

Broth for Cellulite

No one knows for sure how many women have cellulite, but best guesstimates are from 85 to 98 percent. It's a problem of fat deposition, and not just found on overweight women. Indeed, lean women often have it, including Hollywood stars who are regularly shamed for their dimpled thighs with unflattering close-ups in the pages of supermarket tabloids. Clearly, the cellulite problem is not solved by being young, lean, and fit. Being male does help, however, as only about 10 percent of men have cellulite.

Many people assume that cellulite comes with fatness. But studies show cellulite sufferers do not have larger fat lobes or even more of them. The problem only arises when those cottage cheese–like lobes poke through. What prevents that is healthy connective tissue that is strong, flexible, and able to hold things in. Men have an advantage in cellulite-prone parts of the body because their connective tissue has a crisscrossing structure unlike women's, which is more linear. Think a cross-linked fence compared to a picket fence and its greater ability to tightly contain things in your yard. That said, women without cellulite have stronger and more resilient "picket fences" with some crosslinking.

Women are also more prone to cellulite than men because they have three subcutaneous fat layers, not just one, and because they have nine times more alpha estrogen receptors (which produce fat) than beta receptors (which break down fat).

Although some health experts blame pesticides, preservatives, fluoride, and other environmental toxins stored in the fat tissue of our bodies, old photographs and paintings show that the dimpling and lumpiness of cellulite is not a modern phenomenon.

Most attempts to reduce cellulite naturally focus on reducing fat and attaining lean body mass through diet and exercise. Exercise definitely helps, because it increases blood flow to the connective tissue and strengthens the muscles that support our skin. But exercise alone won't do the trick unless the diet also includes plenty of foods that nourish our collagen and cartilage. American women currently spend $62 million a year on cellulite treatments ranging from creams to massage to liposuction that offer partial and temporary solutions at best, leading *Scientific American* to conclude that a "'miracle cellulite assassin' has yet to be uncovered." We disagree. That miracle is bone broth.

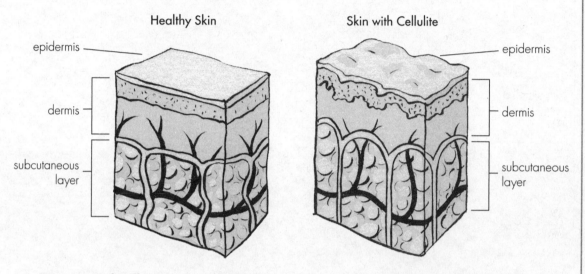

Figure 8: In the illustration at left, healthy connective tissue contains the fat cells. In the illustration at right, weaker connective tissue allows the fat cells to poke through, producing the dimpled appearance of cellulite.

PART III
Recipes

CHAPTER 20

Basic Techniques

Now that we have learned about the proven health benefits of bone broth, it's time to get into the kitchen and cook. The wonderful thing about preparing bone broth or stock is that it leads to so many delicious dishes; indeed, stock is the basis of soups, stews, sauces, gravies, and many other comfort foods. "Without stock," said the master chef Escoffier, "nothing else can be done."

The happy exercise of making broth inevitably leads the neophyte chef to devising other dishes and gaining a reputation as a wonderful cook.

Stock Versus Broth

Is there a difference? Purists insist there is; unfortunately, the explanations for the difference between stock and broth vary considerably.

The word *stock* derives from an old Germanic root meaning "tree trunk." The word has more than sixty related meanings tied to the idea of basic materials, sources, and supplies. The word *broth* derives from another Germanic root meaning "to prepare by boiling." It is related to the words *bouillon* and *brew*.

Today the word *stock* has come to mean, for most people, the thin liquid produced by simmering raw ingredients (vegetables and bones), after which all the solid ingredients are removed—thus it serves as a basic material or source for sauces and soups. In contrast, broth is a basic soup in which the solid pieces of meat or fish, along with some vegetables, remain. It is often made more substantial by adding starches such as rice, barley, or pulses. According to this definition, then, chicken broth and chicken soup have the same meaning.

In the culinary world, both stock and broth start with the same basic foundation: water, onions, celery, carrots, black peppercorns, and herbs. Broth is then enriched with the meat of a chicken—usually a whole chicken. The mixture is simmered and strained; it is light, with a clean flavor. Stock, on the other hand, starts with the same foundational ingredients, but rather than simmering it with the meat of the chicken, stock is made with bones. In this definition, stock ends up with more gelatin than broth.

Compounding the confusion between the generally accepted notion of hearty stock and lighter broth, practitioners of the GAPS (Gut and Psychology Syndrome) diet, a therapeutic diet designed to heal the intestinal tract, refer to "meat stock" as stock cooked using plenty of meat and few bones and cooked for only a short period of time, in contrast to broth, which is made with plenty of bones and cooked much longer. Thus, this diet distinguishes between "light stock" and "rich broth."

Among some chefs, stock is technically what is made when you simmer vegetables, meat scraps, bones, and aromatics in order to extract their flavor. Stock isn't meant to be eaten on its own; rather, stock serves as the basis for soups, sauces, and stews, and therefore should not be salted or highly seasoned. Broth is defined as "seasoned stock," which can be eaten on its own, as a soup.

Slight differences in definition—but all very confusing! Since the experts disagree, in this book we can be forgiven for using the terms interchangeably throughout this book. Both stock and broth are a clear or semiclear liquid; soup is made by adding ingredients to stock or broth.

When Stock Won't Gel

The goal is gelatinous stock, stock that sets up as a solid gel if you put it in the fridge, so solid that you can turn the container over and the gel will stay in place. Second best is stock or broth that has visibly thickened but may not be solid. And if your broth hardly thickens at all, it is still worth consuming, as there will always be some gelatin in it, not to mention minerals and many other nutrients.

The gel in well-made stock or broth comes from the unique qualities of collagen fibers. Most proteins from animals and plants unfold from their normal compact shape when heated;

the strands "become entangled and form strong bonds with each other so that they coagulate permanently and irreversibly into a firm solid. Thus, liquid eggs solidify, pliable muscle tissue becomes tough meat, and milk curdles," according to Harold McGee. Collagen fibers behave in the opposite way. With heat, collagen molecules unwind from their ropelike structure and disperse in the cooking water like spaghetti strands—the unwound, separate chains are what we call gelatin. When the liquid is cooled, the strands rebond to each other, forming a gel structure; reheat and the strands disperse again.

"Won't gel" is the most common complaint we get from neophyte broth makers. Here are the main reasons that your stock won't gel:

1. Not the right kind of bones. You want bones that have lots of cartilage. Meat contains only about 1 percent by weight of collagen; bones contain about 20 percent; skin, such as chicken skin and pig skin, contains up to 30 percent; and veal knuckles contain up to 40 percent. This means for chicken stock you'll want to include the backs, wings, and necks; for beef and veal stock, use cartilaginous knuckles or tailbones (usually sold as oxtail) along with more cartilage-rich meaty bones like short ribs or shanks; fish stock usually gels easily from the copious amounts of cartilage in the fish carcass.

One way to ensure plenty of gelatin is to include feet—chicken feet (and heads also!) for chicken broth and beef or calves' feet for beef and veal stock. Since these are difficult to obtain—especially from a conventional supermarket—pigs' feet can be used in any stock to ensure an adequate gel. Most supermarkets carry split pigs' feet (although you may need to ask your market to get them). One or two pieces of split pig's foot (fresh, not smoked) in any kind of stock will guarantee a gel.

If you are cooking a whole chicken for broth (and to have meat left over), remember that the skin contains a lot of cartilage along with other good things; still, it's wise to add chicken feet or a split pig's foot to the pot if you can.

As a general rule, to get the right mix of bones that yield gelatin and other types of bones that add flavor and color, make sure you use one of the following ingredient combinations:

- 1 whole free-range chicken with neck and wings, preferably also with feet and head
- 3 to 4 pounds bony chicken parts such as necks, backs, and wings, with the skin on, plus feet and head or a split pig's foot
- Picked carcasses of 2 meat chickens plus feet and heads or split pig's foot
- 7 pounds total beef or veal bones (4 pounds cartilage-rich bones, such as tail and knuckles, and 3 pounds meaty bones, such as short ribs or shank)

Many cooks report that they get a better gel using pasture-raised chickens than conventional or simply organic chicken. Such poultry will also be more nutritious for your family and much less likely to contain toxins like lead or arsenic.

2. Not enough bones and too much water. When you make stock, the water should just cover the bones. For chicken, the correct proportion is 3 to 4 pounds bones per about 4 quarts filtered water, or just enough water to cover the bones. For beef stock, the correct proportion is 7 pounds bones per about 4 quarts of water or enough water to cover the bones.

3. The stock was heated to too high a temperature. If stock is brought to a rolling boil, the heat will break down the collagen fibers into shorter strands. These do not coagulate as well when the stock is cooled—and hence a less than satisfactory gel may result. (Nevertheless, the cartilage strands are still there, and if the stock is reduced by boiling to make a sauce, the strands will concentrate enough to thicken the sauce.)

This means you need to watch the pot as you get your stock going. It should be heated over medium heat until the liquid starts to "roll," and then turned down to low heat so that the stock barely simmers. You will need to learn to know your stove and stockpot. You may need a burner separator to lift the pan higher from the flame or coils of your stove; if your stockpot cooks too hot, you can leave the top slightly askew to prevent boiling.

French culinary tradition always cooks stock with the lid off. This helps prevent boiling and also allows the gradual reduction of the stock and concentration of gelatin.

4. The stock did not cook long enough—or it cooked too long! You need to cook the stock long enough to extract the collagen, but not so long that the gelatin fibers break into short pieces. Optimum extraction times depend on the size of the bones and the age of the animal; "the more cross-linked collagen of a steer takes longer to free than the collagen from a veal calf." As a general rule, cook chicken or veal stocks for 4 to 6 hours and beef stock for a full day or overnight.

The collagen in fish is less cross-linked than that of mammals and birds, so it melts and dissolves at much lower temperatures and in a relatively short time. Fish collagen will dissolve into the water at temperatures well below the boil and in as little as a half hour.

Raw Bones or Cooked?

Most recipes call for raw bones, but you can also use bones that have been cooked—most commonly bones from cooked or baked chicken, but any leftover bones from a roast or a bird can go into the stockpot or slow cooker for broth. There should be no difference in flavor or nutritional properties.

Mixing Species in the Stockpot

In many recipes we add a split pig's foot to chicken stock, and some people save up all

Preparing Chicken Feet for the Stockpot

In many cases, the chicken feet will arrive already prepared. However, if you get them directly from a farm, you may need to dress the chicken feet yourself; that is, if the feet are covered with a yellow membrane, this will have to be removed. Rub the feet with salt and scald them briefly in boiling water followed by an icy bath. When blanching the chicken feet, take great care not to blanch the feet too long or you will overcook the feet, which will cause the yellow membrane to fuse to the foot and activate the gelling process. Moreover, overcooking will also cause the tendons in the feet to contract, making peeling pretty much impossible. Blanching for just the right length of time—usually less than a minute—enables you to more easily peel the yellow membrane off the foot. After removing the yellow membrane, some cooks like to chop the talons off at the first knuckle, but this is not really necessary. To see photos of chicken feet in the three stages of preparation, visit http://nourishedkitchen.com/chicken-feet-stock/.

their bones and make stock of several species mixed together. While this practice might not appeal to culinary purists, there is no reason to stick to one species only. Adding a split or whole pig's foot to any kind of broth increases gelatin content, and a stock made with several species of bones will not be less nutritious or less flavorful, especially if you are using the stock in a highly flavored soup or stew. However, for gourmet sauces, where you want to enhance the flavor of your meat, use a stock made with the same meat—chicken stock for chicken, beef stock for beef, and so on.

Where to Buy Bones

The sad truth is that it can be hard to find good bones for stock, especially the cartilaginous bones of feet and knuckles.

If your only choice is a supermarket, you can still find oxtail and probably pigs' feet, but you may need to make a special request for them. Beef shank and beef short ribs are your best choices for meaty bones, as they contain a lot of cartilage.

Many of the best cuts, including chicken feet, veal knuckles and feet, and beef feet, can be found in kosher markets and Middle Eastern, Asian, Latin American, and other ethnic markets.

The ideal is to purchase your bones and meat directly from a farmer engaged in non-toxic pasture feeding. A growing number of farmers can supply you with naturally raised chicken, including heads and feet, and bones and meat from pigs, calves, and steers (but obtaining calves' or beef feet from these farmers may be problematic because most small butchers do not possess the special equipment required for processing the feet). To find a farm near you, contact your nearest local chapter of the Weston A. Price Foundation (westonaprice.org). You will find that the bones of pastured animals release their cartilage more quickly than the bones of conventionally raised animals, and the smell of the stock they produce is absolutely delicious.

Finally, you can obtain good bones and even ready-made broth from a number of suppliers by mail (see Sources, page 295); and the Shopping Guide of the Weston A. Price Foundation provides a list of sources that is updated yearly. The Shopping Guide is now available as an iPhone app.

The Stockpot

The ideal stockpot is made of good-quality enamel on steel, cast iron, or aluminum. Uncoated stainless steel can give a metallic taste to the stock from leaching undesirable metals like nickel. Uncoated aluminum pots should never be used.

Three good sources of enameled stockpots are Le Creuset, Cuisinart, and Martha Stewart (check the Internet for best buys of these brands). Speckled enamelware, purchased in hardware stores, also works well and is easy on the budget. You should have a range of sizes, from eight to twenty quarts.

Stock can also be made in a slow cooker and even in a pressure cooker (see page 296).

Flavor

Flavor in basic stock comes from the meat, not the bones. If you are using your stock to make soup or aspic, you may not want much flavor in your stock. In that case, you can use stock made mostly with bones and very little meat. The Simple Slow Cooker Pig's Foot Broth (page 157) has a neutral flavor, gels beautifully, and can be used wherever you are looking for gelatin without a strong taste.

Quality Counts

I have found that the quality of chicken determines how a broth performs. I have done tests with organic, free-range, pastured, and "in-between" (non-GMO soy-fed and corn-fed "outdoor" summer chickens in Minnesota) to see what gives the most medicinal stock for those who are ailing. I find that even an organic chicken produces a muddy taste. (Organic chickens may be labeled "free-range" or "cage free" but they are still mostly raised in barns and never see sunlight or green grass.) The best taste comes from pastured and "in-between" chicken. Broth made from these pastured birds does not get muddy, even with a long simmer at 200°F. I first bring the stock to a hint of a boil and then reduce to a simmer and skim as it cooks. In my research I have found that making a stock from a conventional chicken using the same technique results in a taste extremely different and sometimes downright nasty.

—Lydia Rose Sifferien,
Oakland, California

For a very flavorful (and also more nutritious) broth, you can make what is called a double stock by straining the bones and vegetables out of your stock and then cooking more bones and vegetables in the original stock. This highly prized double stock is especially delicious—great for consommé or French onion soup.

Clear or Cloudy?

Most stock ends up slightly cloudy, which is just fine for gravies, blended soups, and thickened stews. But for clear soups, clear reduction sauces, and aspics, you will want your stock to be clear.

Cloudiness can be reduced by careful cooking techniques. Start by washing the bones and meat thoroughly before adding to the pot (if you are browning the bones, wash and wipe them dry before browning in the oven). Set the bones in a pot and cover with cold filtered water plus a little vinegar, let soak for 30 to 60 minutes, and then slowly bring the water to a gentle simmer. McGee explains, "The cold start and slow heating allow the soluble proteins to escape the solids and coagulate slowly, forming large aggregates that either rise to the surface

For a stock with lots of flavor—flavor that will concentrate when you boil down the stock to make a reduction sauce—you'll need to include lots of meaty bones, such as short ribs and shank. For best flavor, first brown the meaty bones in a hot oven (set at 400°F to 450°F) for about 30 minutes. This will create Maillard reactions with lots of complex flavor molecules—and also impart a beautiful brown color to the broth.

and are easily skimmed off or settle onto the sides and bottom. A hot start produces many separate and tiny protein particles that remain suspended and cloud the stock."

An important technique for avoiding cloudiness in the stock is to skim the scum that rises to the top as the stock starts to cook. Skim as thoroughly as possible at the beginning of the process, and then occasionally throughout cooking. An interesting observation: Bones from pastured animals produce very little scum, while those from conventional sources can produce lots of it. The scum carries impurities and may give a bitter flavor to the stock, so take care to remove as much as you can—certainly at the beginning of the cooking process and occasionally throughout the long simmer. This is all the more important when you are using bones from conventionally raised animals, as that scum will be carrying a lot of the junk that cooking dislodges.

The key to producing a clear broth is to never let it come to a boil. Instead, simmer it with the lid off or slightly askew.

When stock is chilled, the particles that cause impurities settle to the bottom. An easy way to get a fairly clear stock is simply to let the stock come to room temperature then pour all but the bottom half inch or so into a pan, discarding the cloudy stock at the bottom of the container.

You may want to invest in a chinois, a cone-shaped straining tool. It can be lined with cheesecloth or a thin towel to produce the clearest of broths. Even better is a jelly strainer bag, available online. Another great tip is to pour your stock through a disposable coffee filter—this easy technique works beautifully for small amounts of stock. For about 1 cup of stock, use a coffee filter placed in a 4-inch strainer set above a bowl.

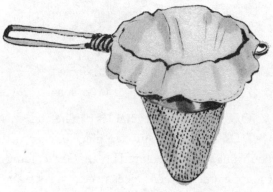

Finally, the traditional method for clarifying a cloudy stock is to add beaten egg whites to the strained stock. Bring to a slow boil, allow the egg whites to rise to the surface, and boil gently for 30 minutes or so. The whites will coagulate, carrying any impurities with them. After cooling, you can lift them off to discover the clearest of stocks underneath. Strain through a fine-mesh strainer to remove any remaining egg white.

Vegetables and Herbs

Classic stock calls for the addition of vegetables and herbs, often referred to as aromatics.

Ideally these are added after the initial skimming process, as vegetables rising to the surface make the broth hard to skim. Vegetables and herbs add not only flavor and color to the broth but also lots of important minerals.

The classic vegetable combination is onions, celery, and carrots, called a *mirepoix* in French cuisine. Many leave the skins on the onions to add flavor and color to the broth, but the carrots should be peeled, as the peelings can be bitter. Onions and carrots add sweetness to the broth and celery adds a distinctive flavor.

Of course other vegetables can be added as well. Use peeled parsnips in place of carrots if you want a lighter-colored broth. Garlic, tomatoes, peppers, greens, leeks, celery root and leaves, and parsley can all be added. In fact, making broth provides a good opportunity to clean out the vegetable drawer in your refrigerator. Vegetables that are limp and oldish can still go into the pot. (Cruciferous vegetables like cabbage, broccoli, and Brussels sprouts might give too strong a flavor to the broth, so use with caution.)

As for herbs, the classic addition is a *bouquet garni*, sprigs of parsley and thyme plus a bay leaf or two tied together with string; any number of other herbs can be tied with the *bouquet garni* as well. Peppercorns provide great flavor to broth. Ideally use the softer green or white peppercorns, which you can crush in your hands or in a mortar and pestle

before adding, but the harder black peppercorns will soften up in the broth and also add flavor. It's best to add the peppercorns after the initial skimming.

Salt

The one seasoning that should never be added to stock is salt. Meat releases some salt, but the main reason for leaving it out is that if you boil down or concentrate the stock, you may end up with liquid that is too salty. Add salt to your soup, stew, sauce, or gravy at the end of the cooking process, when the desired thickness is obtained.

The Water

You will want to use clean, filtered water for your stock—definitely not city tap water containing fluoride, chloramine, and other chemicals. Remember that your stock will likely be reduced and concentrated, thus concentrating whatever is in the water you use. (Unlike chlorine, used in years past, chloramine, widely used for water treatment today, does not evaporate or boil off.)

Home-filtered water, bottled spring water, and clean well water are all good choices for making stock.

Vinegar

Most of our recipes for stock call for the addition of small amounts of vinegar. This helps extract minerals from the bones and vegetables, even when diluted with the water. Small amounts of vinegar do not change the flavor of the broth. The vinegar need not be raw, as it will be heated during cooking anyway, and apple cider vinegar, wine vinegar, or another type of vinegar can be used in the recipes.

Finishing and Straining Your Stock

When the stock is finished cooking, use tongs and a slotted spoon to remove the bones and meat pieces, then pour the liquid through a fine-mesh strainer set over a bowl to remove the vegetables and herbs. Two-quart Pyrex measuring containers make the ideal receptacle for strained stock (you'll need more than one of them for many of our stock recipes). Just set your strainer over the measuring containers and ladle or pour your stock through. Then your stock is in containers from which it can easily be poured. The stock is now ready to use.

If, however, you want a defatted stock for gourmet sauces or clear soups, set your Pyrex measuring containers of strained stock in the refrigerator until completely cooled. The fat will rise to the top and can be easily skimmed

off the jellied stock (you may use this fat, especially beef and veal fat, for cooking if you wish). After removing the fat, transfer your stock to glass jars or plastic containers for storage. The stock can then be reheated and clarified if needed (see pages 148–49). (You can also chill and freeze the stock without defatting.)

Storage

The ideal storage container for broth is freezer-safe, wide-mouth, quart-size mason jars. You can also use jars that close with a clamp and rubber gasket, such as those made by Weck or Libby. The possibility of breakage can be minimized by taking two important steps:

1. Fill the jars only three-quarters full.

2. Let cool, and then chill the jars in the refrigerator, allowing the temperature to drop gradually, before transferring to the freezer.

In fact, you can cool your finished stock in the pot, then ladle it directly from the pot through a cone-shaped strainer into your jars. Refrigerate and then remove the congealed fat if desired, then transfer the jars to the freezer.

The jars are easy to clean in the dishwasher and of course can be reused an infinite number of times. When the tops of mason jars become rusted or unsightly, they can be replaced, as can the rubber gaskets for jars that close with clamps. Plastic lids that avoid the rust problem are also available for mason jars.

For plastic, use plastic containers with a rating of 1, 2, 4, or 5. Plastic containing BPA is rated 3, 6, or 7. Make sure your stock is thoroughly cooled before transferring to plastic containers.

Those with limited freezer space can reduce the stock by boiling to make *fumet*, or concentrated stock. It can then be cooled somewhat and poured into ice cube trays or put into zip-top bags (but not zipper bags because they have a weaker grip). When you need stock for broth or soup, you simply remove a cube or two from the ice cube tray or remove the contents from one zip-top bag and melt it in a pan with water. Water is the magic ingredient that restores concentrated stock to thinner broth for soups and stews.

What to Do with Those Bones

What to do with those bones after making stock? Soft bones from chicken stock can be given to your dog or cat…or even to your backyard chickens. Larger bones from beef or veal can be simmered a second and even third time. They can then be discarded or even put in a compost pile (although they will take a long time to soften and decompose). See "A Farmer's Tips for Making Broth" on page 153 for an ingenious method of recycling the bones and vegetables from making stock.

By the way, the meat still on the meaty bones or chicken bones will be tender and delicious. Don't throw it away; instead, pick it off and reserve it for soups, meat or chicken salads, or stews. It can be stored for a few days in the refrigerator or several months in the freezer.

Some cooks like to place softened bones in the blender and make a thick bone paste, which can then be thinned with a little stock. While not exactly a gourmet dish, "bone soup" is obviously nutritious and much higher in calcium than regular bone broth.

MSG Sensitivity

Some people are very sensitive to monosodium glutamate (MSG), even to its more natural form, free glutamic acid. Glutamine, or glutamic acid, is an essential amino acid abundant in meat and cartilage, and the process of making stock brings it out into the liquid. Indeed, it is glutamic acid that gives broth its savory, meatlike flavor.

Those with extreme sensitivities to MSG will also react to the free glutamic acid in broth. The solution is to make a meat stock with lots of meat and very few bones and simmer it for a short time, about an hour. One reader reports to us that she can't tolerate bone broth cooked more than six hours. These individuals will need to use their broth in soups and not as reduced, concentrated sauces.

Recipes That Make Their Own Stock

You can make gelatin-rich soups and stews without making stock beforehand! For soups,

A Farmer's Tips for Making Broth

Here are some tips and tricks I have developed for making broth, as well as something to do with the leftover bones once you're done (that is, if you live on a farm or have chickens).

Save your veggie scraps in the freezer for use in making stock later. I save all my onion skins and tops, celery tops and ends, and any other scraps that would be good in a stock. I also save bones and fat any time we eat meat. This cuts down on our garbage and compost waste and also enables me to make large batches of stock at one time instead of a little at a time.

You can make several batches of stock from one pot of bones! Once you make the first batch, add more water to the pot and simmer for another day. The second and even third batch of stock is just as flavorful as the first and often gels just as well too.

After making stock at our farm, we use the spent bones and veggie scraps to create protein treats for our chickens. We have a wire basket lined with straw on their coop that we put all the waste in. We put a bit more straw on top, wait a few days, and watch as fat little maggots come dropping out of the basket to be joyfully gobbled up by our chickens! They love these protein-rich little grubs, and we love the fact that our stock waste isn't waste at all, but is getting used yet another time to create two more nutritious foods (grub for the chickens and eggs and meat for us!). This also helps control the fly population over time, because every maggot that is eaten by a chicken is another maggot not turning into a fly later. Once the maggot numbers have dropped off, we take the straw and what's left of the stock waste (not much!) and add it to our compost. This is best for a farm, but it can be done on a very small scale for a few backyard chickens. There is a little smell for a day or two, but that goes away pretty quickly. The straw also helps absorb the smell quite well.

—Rachel Armistead, Woodsboro, Maryland

---

simply add a split pig's foot, a couple of chicken feet, or a cartilage-rich ham hock or two to the soup while it is cooking. Oxtail soup will be naturally rich in gelatin.

For stews, use the cuts that have the most cartilage, such as short ribs or shanks, and add some cartilage-rich bones such as a pig's foot, veal or beef knuckle, or beef or veal foot.

Portable Stock

Stock boiled down into a thick gel makes a great portable soup for camping trips. It can be poured into shallow trays and dehydrated in a dehydrator to the point where it becomes brittle. Place these pieces of stock in individual plastic bags along with dried vegetables, pieces of beef jerky, and a little salt. Rehydrate in water over a campfire for instant soup!

Purchased Broth

What to do if you really don't have time to make stock? Fortunately, we have many sources of genuine stock made from bones, usually provided frozen. Many of these sources will provide stock by mail order—at a price, of course.

Some sources are listed in our Sources section (pages 295–96); for updated information, you can purchase the Shopping Guide from the Weston A. Price Foundation or the Foundation's Find Real Food App. Local chapters of the Weston A. Price Foundation may know of individuals making stock for the local market (find your nearest local chapter at www.westonaprice.org/local-chapters).

What about broth in cans and asceptic containers? Here's a test that anyone can do. Put the contents of the can or container in a bowl and place in the refrigerator. Does it gel? Usually the answer is no, not at all. Most of these products are made with water and flavorings, with very little in the way of bones and virtually no gelatin or cartilage material.

An additional problem with the asceptic packaging is that the boxes are flash-heated to way above the boiling point, an unnatural process that almost certainly warps and distorts any amino acids that may be in the broth.

We also have the question of what the cans and packaging are lined with—plastics in the case of cans and aluminum in the case of aseptic containers. These products are not worth the money and may actually be harmful.

Let's Get Cooking!

If you have never made broth, you are in for a surprise. It's fun to do and sets you on the path to being a good cook. So let's roll up our sleeves and get started!

CHAPTER 21

Stock and Broth Recipes

Now that we have learned about the health benefits of stock and broth, it's time to get into the kitchen and make it for ourselves. If you have never made broth before, start with the simple recipes made in a slow cooker. You will find this a fun and rewarding experience; then, after you have gained confidence, you can graduate to the classic stock recipes, double-cooked broth, and consommé.

Simple Slow Cooker Stock

This stock is as simple as can be to make and reliably turns out well. The onion floats to the top and caramelizes with the long cooking, adding delicious flavor. You should use enough bones to completely fill the slow cooker.

Makes about 2 quarts

A bunch of chicken bones, about 6 cups
2 chicken feet or 1 piece split pig's foot
1 onion, coarsely chopped
2 tablespoons vinegar
Cold filtered water

Place the chicken bones in a large stockpot. Add the feet and onion to the pot, then add the vinegar and enough cold filtered water to cover the bones. Let stand for 30 to 60 minutes. Cover and cook on low for 6 to 12 hours, checking occasionally to ensure that the bones remain covered with water and adding more water as needed.

Remove the bones with tongs and a slotted spoon. Strain the stock through a fine-mesh strainer into 2-quart Pyrex measuring containers or a large heatproof bowl (see tips for straining on page 149) and it's ready to use in your recipes. If not using right away, cool to room temperature, then refrigerate uncovered for several hours, until the fat rises to the top and congeals. If desired, skim off this fat (you can use it in your cooking) and transfer the stock to containers (see tips on choosing and filling your containers on pages 151–52), cover, and store in the refrigerator for up to 5 days or in the freezer for many months.

Mixed Bones Slow Cooker Stock

Use any bones that you have purchased or saved up—not necessarily from the same species—and include chicken feet and heads and also a split pig's foot or piece of calf's foot if you can. This is a good way to clear out any wilted vegetables in your refrigerator drawers and can get you into a routine of making stock once a week or so, broth you can use right away and won't need to freeze.

Makes about 4 quarts

About 8 cups bones
¼ cup vinegar
About 4 cups chopped vegetables, such as onion, leek, peeled carrots, celery, peeled turnip,
    and parsley
About 4 quarts cold filtered water

Place the bones in a slow cooker and pour the vinegar over them. Toss and then press them down into the slow cooker. Strew the vegetables on top and add enough cold filtered water to cover. Cover and cook on low for 12 to 24 hours, checking occasionally to ensure that the ingredients remain covered with water and adding more water as needed. If your slow cooker won't maintain a simmer, leave the lid slightly ajar to prevent boiling.

Remove the bones and vegetables with tongs and a slotted spoon, then strain the stock through a fine-mesh strainer into 2-quart measuring containers or a large heatproof bowl (see tips for straining on page 149), and it's ready to use in your recipes. If not using right away, cool to room temperature, then refrigerate uncovered for several hours, until the fat rises to the top and congeals. If desired, skim off this fat (you can use it in your cooking) and transfer the stock to containers (see tips on choosing and filling your containers on pages 151–52), cover, and store in the refrigerator for up to 5 days or in the freezer for many months.

Alternatively, place the slow cooker insert with the broth in the refrigerator until well chilled. Skim off the fat, then scoop out the stock as needed using a measuring cup or ladle.

Simple Slow Cooker Pig's Foot Broth

This easy broth has a neutral flavor and can be used in any dish calling for gelatinous stock. It works very well with the aspic recipes (pages 225–34) and generally gels beautifully.

Makes about 2 quarts

2 whole pig's feet
2 tablespoons vinegar
About 2 quarts cold filtered water

Place the pig's feet in a slow cooker, add the vinegar, then add enough cold filtered water to cover the bones. Let stand for 30 to 60 minutes. Cover and cook on low for about 12 hours, checking occasionally to ensure that the feet remain covered with water and adding more water as needed.

Remove the feet with tongs (you can use the feet to make jellied pig's feet; page 228), then strain the broth through a fine-mesh strainer into 2-quart measuring containers or a large heatproof bowl (see tips for straining on page 149), and it's ready to use in your recipes. If not using right away, cool to room temperature, then refrigerate uncovered for several hours, until the fat rises to the top and congeals. If desired, skim off this fat (you can use it in your cooking) and transfer the broth to containers (see tips on choosing and filling your containers on pages 151–52), cover, and store in the refrigerator for up to 5 days or in the freezer for many months.

Classic Chicken Stock

Makes about 3 quarts

1 whole chicken (preferably pasture-raised), or 3 to 4 pounds of bony chicken parts, such as
    necks, backs, breastbones, and wings
2 chicken feet plus 1 chicken head, or 1 split pig's foot (optional)
2 tablespoons vinegar

About 4 quarts cold filtered water

2 large onions, ends cut off and coarsely chopped (skin may be left on)

2 carrots, peeled and coarsely chopped

2 celery sticks, coarsely chopped

1 *bouquet garni* made with parsley sprigs, thyme sprigs, and a bay leaf, tied together with kitchen string

1 tablespoon whole black peppercorns, or green or white peppercorns, crushed

If you are using a whole chicken, remove the neck, fat glands, and innards from the cavity (you'll be using the neck; reserve the fat and innards for other uses such as making pâté or feeding to your pet).

Place the chicken with its neck or the chicken parts in a large stockpot. Add the chicken feet and head or the split pig's foot to the pot, then add the vinegar and enough cold filtered water to cover the bones. Let stand for 30 to 60 minutes. Place over medium heat, uncovered, bring to a bare simmer, and carefully spoon off any scum that rises to the top. Add the onions, carrots, celery, *bouquet garni*, and peppercorns, return to a simmer, then lower the heat to low. Cook at a bare simmer with the lid off or slightly askew for 4 to 6 hours, occasionally skimming scum from the top as needed, checking to ensure that the bones remain covered with water and adding more water as needed.

Remove the whole chicken and bones with tongs and a slotted spoon. If you are using a whole chicken, let cool and remove the meat from the carcass (the best way to do this is using your hands). Reserve the meat for other dishes, such as chicken salad, enchiladas, sandwiches, or curries.

Strain the stock through a fine-mesh strainer into 2-quart Pyrex measuring containers or a large heatproof bowl (see tips for straining on page 149), and it's ready to use in your recipes. If not using right away, cool to room temperature, then refrigerate uncovered for several hours, until the fat rises to the top and congeals. If desired, skim off this fat (you can use it in your cooking) and transfer the stock to containers (see tips on choosing and filling your containers on pages 151–52), cover, and store in the refrigerator for up to 5 days or in the freezer for many months.

Double-Cooked Mexican Caldo

Liz Escobar-Ausman, San Jose, California

This yummy soup brings back memories of the Mexican *caldo* of my childhood. My family wasn't a fan of the flavor of once-cooked broth, so I came up with this, and it has converted them—they love broth now! As a bonus, the chicken is delicious enjoyed in the soup, pulled the next day for cold chicken salad, or shredded and sautéed in coconut oil with diced onion, cumin, coriander, salt, and pepper for tacos. The *caldo* is also the basis for Tortilla Soup (page 195).

Makes about 1½ quarts

3 cups homemade chicken broth

1 quart cold filtered water

2 pieces bone in, skin-on chicken (such as the thigh and leg)

½ large onion, ends cut off and coarsely chopped (skin may be left on)

2 celery sticks, chopped

2 medium carrots, peeled and chopped

½ cup chopped fresh cilantro

2 tablespoons chopped fresh mint leaves

Sea salt

Lemon wedges

Tortillas

Combine the broth, filtered water, and chicken in a stockpot. Place over medium heat, uncovered, bring to a bare simmer, and carefully spoon off any scum that rises to the top. Add the onion, celery, and carrots, then lower the heat to low. Cover and cook at a bare simmer for 40 to 50 minutes, occasionally skimming scum from the top. Uncover, add the cilantro and mint, and simmer for 10 minutes. Season generously with salt. Remove the chicken pieces with a slotted spoon, strain, and serve the clear broth with lemon wedges and tortillas alongside.

Quick Great Gel Chicken Stock

Guy Furno, Holbrook, New York

This ingenious stock, developed by chiropractor Guy Furno, can be made in less than an hour, and it gels beautifully. It does require cutting up a chicken with a cleaver, so it needs someone with a strong arm.

Makes 2 quarts

1 medium chicken
2 tablespoons butter, lard, olive oil, or other fat
2 onions, peeled and chopped
2 quarts boiling filtered water
Sea salt and freshly ground black pepper

With a cleaver, cut the chicken including the bones into 1-inch pieces. Heat the butter or other fat in a large, heavy-bottomed saucepan over medium heat. Add the onions and sauté until softened but not browned, about 5 minutes. Remove the onions to a bowl using a slotted spoon, then add the chicken in two batches and sauté, stirring, for about 5 minutes per batch, until lightly colored. Return all the chicken and onions to the pan, reduce the heat to very low, cover, and sweat the ingredients for about 20 minutes. Add the boiling filtered water to the pan, bring to a simmer, and simmer for 20 to 25 minutes. Season with salt and pepper.

Remove from the heat, cool, and strain into a bowl or 2-quart Pyrex measuring container or a large heatproof bowl (see tips for straining on page 149), and it's ready to use in your recipes. (You can pick the chicken off the bones and use it in dishes such as stir-fries, curries, soups, chicken salad, or tacos.) If not using the stock right away, cool to room temperature, then refrigerate uncovered until the fat rises to the top and congeals. If desired, skim off this fat and transfer the stock to containers (see tips on choosing and filling your containers on pages 151–52), cover, and store in the refrigerator for up to 5 days or in the freezer for many months.

Rich Chicken Broth

Karen McFarland, Mansfield, Texas

I make a chicken broth from chicken soup bones provided at the Dallas farmers market by a local rancher who raises the chickens on organic pastures and only uses organic feed. I feel so blessed to have access to these bones. I use the bones raw for the soup and supplement with any leftover cooked chicken bones I've saved up.

Makes 3 to 4 quarts

3 to 4 raw chicken carcasses

Any bones you have left over from cooked chicken

8 to 9 pair chicken feet

½ cup apple cider vinegar

About 4 quarts cold filtered water

2 large carrots, peeled and chopped

1 large celery stick, chopped

1 large yellow onion, ends cut off and coarsely chopped (skin may be left on)

1 head unpeeled garlic, cut in half

Place the chicken carcasses, bones, and feet in a large stockpot and toss with the vinegar. Let stand for 30 to 60 minutes. Add cold filtered water to cover, place over medium heat, uncovered, bring to a bare simmer, and carefully spoon off any scum that rises to the top. Add the carrots, celery, onion, and garlic, return to a simmer, then lower the heat to low. Cook at a bare simmer with the lid off or slightly askew for about 6 hours, occasionally skimming scum from the top as needed and checking to ensure that the bones remain covered with water and adding more water as needed.

Remove the bones and feet with tongs and a slotted spoon. Strain the broth through a fine-mesh strainer into 2-quart Pyrex measuring containers or a large heatproof bowl (see tips for straining on page 149), and it's ready to use in your recipes. If not using right away, cool to room temperature, then refrigerate uncovered for several hours, until the fat rises to the top and congeals. Skim off this fat (you can use it in your cooking) and transfer the broth to containers (see tips on choosing and filling your containers on pages 151–52), cover, and store in the refrigerator for up to 5 days or in the freezer for many months.

Chinese Chicken Stock

Good Chinese restaurants make their own stock, which is a light, clear, delicate yellow.

Makes about 2 quarts

Carcass of 1 whole chicken
About 2 quarts cold filtered water

Place the chicken carcass in a stockpot and add cold filtered water to cover. Place over medium heat and bring just to a boil (the water will become foamy). Strain the bones into a colander set in the sink (pouring away the liquid and saving the bones).

Rinse out the pot and return the bones to the pot. Add cold filtered water to cover, place over medium heat, bring to a bare simmer, then lower the heat to low. Cook at a bare simmer with the lid off or slightly askew for 5 to 6 hours, occasionally skimming scum from the top as needed and checking occasionally to ensure that the bones remain covered with water and adding more water as needed.

Remove the bones with tongs and a slotted spoon. Strain the stock through a fine-mesh strainer into 2-quart Pyrex measuring containers or a large heatproof bowl (see tips for straining on page 149), and it's ready to use in your recipes. If not using right away, cool to room temperature, then refrigerate uncovered until the fat rises to the top and congeals. Skim off this fat and transfer the stock to containers (see tips on choosing and filling your containers on pages 151–52), cover, and store in the refrigerator for up to 5 days or in the freezer for many months.

Turkey Stock

Makes about 2 quarts

2 turkey drumsticks
1 turkey neck (optional)
2 tablespoons vinegar
2 to 3 quarts cold filtered water
1 large onion, ends cut off and coarsely chopped (skin may be left on)
3 celery sticks, coarsely chopped

1 *bouquet garni* made with parsley sprigs, thyme sprigs, and a bay leaf, tied together with
    kitchen string

1 tablespoon whole black peppercorns, or green or white peppercorns, crushed

Place the turkey pieces in a small stockpot. Add the vinegar and enough cold water to cover the bones. Let stand for 30 to 60 minutes. Place over medium heat, uncovered, bring to a bare simmer, and carefully spoon off any scum that rises to the top. Add the onion, celery, *bouquet garni*, and peppercorns, return to a simmer, then lower the heat. Cook at a bare simmer with the lid off or slightly askew for 4 to 6 hours, occasionally skimming scum from the top as needed and checking to ensure that the bones remain covered with water and adding more water as needed.

Remove the turkey pieces with tongs and a slotted spoon. Strain the stock through a fine-mesh strainer into 2-quart Pyrex measuring containers or a large heatproof bowl (see tips for straining on page 149), and it's ready to use in your recipes. If not using right away, cool to room temperature, then refrigerate uncovered for several hours, until the fat rises to the top and congeals. If desired, skim off this fat (you can use it in your cooking) and transfer the stock to containers (see tips on choosing and filling your containers on pages 151–52), cover, and store in the refrigerator for up to 5 days or in the freezer for many months.

This stock makes great turkey gravy, and the meat from the drumsticks can be shredded for turkey salad or Turkey Curry (page 235).

Duck Stock

Makes 2 to 3 quarts

2 duck carcasses (with the breasts, legs, and thighs removed)

2 tablespoons vinegar

2 to 3 quarts cold filtered water

2 large onions, ends cut off and coarsely chopped (skin may be left on)

2 carrots, peeled and coarsely chopped

2 celery sticks, coarsely chopped

1 *bouquet garni* made with parsley sprigs, thyme sprigs, and a bay leaf, tied together with
    kitchen string

2 cloves garlic, peeled and crushed (optional)

1 tablespoon whole black peppercorns, or green or white peppercorns, crushed

Place the duck carcasses in a stockpot. Add the vinegar and enough cold filtered water to cover the bones. Let stand for 30 to 60 minutes. Place over medium heat, uncovered, bring to a bare simmer, and carefully spoon off any scum that rises to the top. Add the onions, carrots, celery, *bouquet garni*, optional garlic, and peppercorns then lower the heat to low. Cook at a bare simmer with the lid off or slightly askew for 4 to 6 hours, occasionally skimming scum from the top as needed and checking to ensure that the bones remain covered with water and adding more water as needed.

Remove the carcasses with tongs and a slotted spoon. Strain the stock through a fine-mesh strainer into 2-quart Pyrex measuring containers or a large heatproof bowl (see tips for straining on page 149), and it's ready to use in your recipes. If not using right away, cool to room temperature, then refrigerate uncovered for several hours, until the fat rises to the top and congeals. If desired, skim off this fat (you can use it in your cooking; duck fat is highly prized for roasting potatoes) and transfer the stock to containers (see tips on choosing and filling your containers on pages 151–52), cover, and store in the refrigerator for up to 5 days or in the freezer for many months.

Clear Broth

In our family, we know that if you want clear broth, you don't let the broth come to a boil. To keep your broth from becoming cloudy, let it simmer it with the lid askew (this also can help prevent an accidental boil). My great-grandmother was known for her gorgeous clear chicken broth, and no one in the family even recognizes what cloudy chicken broth is.

—Laurel Lovelace, Elizabethton, Tennessee

Pheasant Broth

Barbara Gilmore, Grafton, Wisconsin

My absolute favorite food is pheasant broth. My husband is a hunter, and although I like the meat, I love the broth. To make my broth, I debone the breasts and thighs, reserving for other uses, and put the rest of the bones and the rest of the pheasant in a pot of water. I add just a little sea salt and white pepper, and simmer it for a few hours. When I'm feeling a cold coming on or am just under the weather, I take out a quart and heat it up. With my first sip I never fail to say, "*Aahh*, this is the best thing I've ever tasted." And by that evening I am usually beginning to feel better.

Makes 3 to 4 quarts

3 to 4 pheasants
¼ cup apple cider vinegar
½ teaspoon freshly ground white pepper
About 4 quarts cold filtered water
Sea salt

Remove the breasts and legs from the pheasants. Separate the legs from the thighs and remove the thighbones. (Reserve the thighs, legs, and breasts for other uses.)

Place the pheasant carcasses and leg bones in a stockpot. Add the vinegar, pepper, and enough cold filtered water to cover the bones. Let stand for 30 to 60 minutes. Place over medium heat, uncovered, bring to a bare simmer, and carefully spoon off any scum that rises to the top. Lower the heat to low. Cook at a bare simmer with the lid off or slightly askew for 4 to 6 hours, occasionally skimming scum from the top as needed and checking to ensure that the bones remain covered with water and adding more water as needed.

Remove the bones with tongs and a slotted spoon. Strain the broth through a fine-mesh strainer into 2-quart Pyrex measuring containers or a large heatproof bowl (see tips for straining on page 149), and it's ready to use in your recipes. If you are consuming immediately, season to taste with sea salt. If not using right away, cool to room temperature, then refrigerate uncovered for several hours, until the fat rises to the top and congeals. Skim off this fat (you can use it in your cooking) and transfer the broth to containers (see tips on choosing and filling your containers on pages 151–52), cover, and store in the refrigerator for up to 5 days or in the freezer for many months.

Classic Veal Stock

Makes 4 to 5 quarts

About 5 pounds veal knucklebones

1 whole calf's foot, or several pieces of calf's foot (optional)

½ cup vinegar

Cold filtered water

About 2 pounds meaty bones such as short ribs and shanks (preferably veal, but beef is fine)

3 onions, ends cut off and coarsely chopped (skin may be left on)

3 carrots, peeled and coarsely chopped

3 celery sticks, coarsely chopped

1 *bouquet garni* made with parsley sprigs, thyme sprigs, and a bay leaf, tied together with
    kitchen string

1 tablespoon whole black peppercorns, or green or white peppercorns, crushed

Preheat the oven to 350°F.

Place the knucklebones and optional calf's foot in a stockpot. Add the vinegar and enough cold filtered water to cover the bones. Let stand for 30 to 60 minutes. Meanwhile, place the meaty bones in a stainless steel roasting pan, place in the oven, and roast, turning them once or twice for about 30 minutes. When well browned add the bones to the pot. Pour the fat out of the roasting pan, add a little cold filtered water to the pan, set the pan over high heat, and bring to a boil, stirring with a wooden spoon to loosen up any browned bits, and add this liquid to the pot. Add additional water to cover the bones if necessary.

Place over medium heat, uncovered, bring to a simmer, and carefully spoon off any scum that rises to the top. Add the onions, carrots, celery, *bouquet garni*, and peppercorns, return to a simmer, then lower the heat to low. Cook at a bare simmer with the lid off or slightly askew for at least 6 hours and as long as 24 hours, occasionally skimming scum from the top as needed and checking to ensure that the bones remain covered with water and adding more water as needed.

Remove the bones and meat with tongs and a slotted spoon. Strain the stock through a fine-mesh strainer into 2-quart Pyrex measuring containers or a large heatproof bowl (see tips for straining on page 149), and it's ready to use in your recipes. If not using right away, cool to room temperature, then refrigerate uncovered for several hours, until the fat rises to the top and congeals. If desired, skim off this fat (you can use it in your cooking) and transfer the stock to containers (see tips on choosing and filling your containers on pages 151–52), cover, and store in the refrigerator for up to 5 days or in the freezer for many months.

Veal Double Stock

Double stock is highly valued in French cuisine for rich sauces and consommé.

Makes 4 to 5 quarts

About 5 pounds veal knucklebones

1 whole calf's foot, or several pieces of calf's foot (optional)

½ cup vinegar

About 4 quarts cold Classic Veal Stock (page 166)

About 2 pounds meaty bones such as short ribs and shanks (preferably veal, but beef is fine)

3 onions, ends cut off and coarsely chopped (skin may be left on)

3 carrots, peeled and coarsely chopped

3 celery sticks, coarsely chopped

1 *bouquet garni* made with parsley sprigs, thyme sprigs, and a bay leaf, tied together with kitchen string

1 tablespoon whole black peppercorns, or green or white peppercorns, crushed

Preheat the oven to 350°F.

Place the veal knucklebones and optional calf's foot in a stockpot. Add the vinegar and veal stock and let stand for 30 to 60 minutes.

Meanwhile, place the meaty bones in a roasting pan, place in the oven, and roast, turning them once or twice, for about 30 minutes, until well browned. Add these bones to the pot. Pour the fat out of the roasting pan, add a little cold filtered water to the pan, set the pan over high heat, and bring to a boil, stirring with a wooden spoon to loosen up any browned bits, and add this liquid to the pot. Add additional water to cover the bones if necessary.

Place over medium heat, uncovered, bring to a simmer, and carefully spoon off any scum that rises to the top. Add the onions, carrots, celery, *bouquet garni*, and peppercorns, return to a simmer, then lower the heat to low. Cook at a bare simmer with the lid off or slightly askew for about 6 hours, occasionally skimming scum from the top as needed and checking to ensure that the bones remain covered with water and adding more water as needed.

Remove the bones and meat with tongs and a slotted spoon. Strain the stock through a fine-mesh strainer into 2-quart Pyrex measuring containers or a large heatproof bowl (see tips for straining on page 149), and it's ready to use in your recipes. If not using right away, cool to room temperature, then refrigerate uncovered for several hours, until the fat rises to the top and congeals. If desired, skim off this fat (you can use it in your cooking) and transfer the stock to containers (see tips on choosing and filling your containers on pages 151–52), cover, and store in the refrigerator for up to 5 days or in the freezer for many months.

Classic Beef Stock

Good beef stock requires several sorts of bones: knucklebones and feet impart large quantities of gelatin to the broth; marrowbones impart flavor and the healthy fats of bone marrow; and meaty ribs and shanks add color and flavor. We have found that grass-fed beef bones work best—the cartilage melts more quickly, and the smell and flavor are delicious.

Makes 4 to 5 quarts

About 4 pounds beef marrow and knucklebones

1 calf's, beef, or pig's foot, preferably cut into pieces (optional, but the results will be much better if included)

½ cup vinegar

4 to 5 quarts cold filtered water

3 pounds meaty bones such as short ribs and beef shanks

1 small can or jar tomato paste (optional)

3 onions, ends cut off and coarsely chopped (skin may be left on)

3 carrots, peeled and coarsely chopped

3 celery sticks, coarsely chopped

1 *bouquet garni* made with parsley sprigs, thyme sprigs, and and a bay leaf, tied together with kitchen string

1 tablespoon whole black peppercorns, or green or white peppercorns, crushed

Preheat the oven to 350°F.

Place the beef marrow and knucklebones and optional foot in a stockpot. Add the vinegar and enough cold filtered water to cover the bones. Let stand for 30 to 60 minutes.

Meanwhile, place the meaty bones in a roasting pan. For a particularly aromatic stock, brush the bones with tomato paste. Place in the oven and roast, turning them once or twice, for about 30 minutes, until well browned. Add these bones to the pot. Pour the fat out of the roasting pan, add a little cold filtered water to the pan, set the pan over high heat, and bring to a boil, stirring with a wooden spoon to loosen up any browned bits, and add this liquid to the pot. Add additional water to cover the bones if necessary.

Place over medium heat, uncovered, bring to a simmer, and carefully spoon off any scum that rises to the top. Add the onions, carrots, celery, *bouquet garni*, and pepper-corns, return to a simmer, then lower the heat to low. Cook at a bare simmer with the lid off or slightly askew for about least 12 and as long as 24 hours, occasionally skimming scum from the top as needed and checking to ensure that the bones remain covered with water and adding more water as needed.

Remove the bones and meat with tongs and a slotted spoon. Strain the stock through a fine-mesh strainer into 2-quart Pyrex measuring containers or a large heatproof bowl (see tips for straining on page 149), and it's ready to use in your recipes. If not using right away, cool to room temperature, then refrigerate uncovered for several hours, until the fat rises to the top and congeals. If desired, skim off this fat (you can use it in your cooking) and transfer the stock to containers (see tips on choosing and filling your containers on pages 151–52), cover, and store in the refrigerator for up to 5 days or in the freezer for many months.

NOTE: The marrow may be removed from the marrowbones a couple of hours into the cooking and spread on whole grain sourdough bread. If left in the pan for the entire cooking time, the marrow will melt into the broth, resulting in a broth that is cloudy but highly nutritious.

VARIATION: LAMB STOCK

Use lamb bones, preferably including lamb neck bones and riblets. Ideally use all the bones left after butchering the lamb and be sure to add the feet if you have them. This makes for a delicious stock.

VARIATION: VENISON STOCK

Use venison meat and bones, including the feet of the deer and a section of the antlers if possible. Add 1 cup dried wild mushrooms if desired.

On the Wild Side

Our bone broths are frequently made with wild animals, including ruffed grouse, wild turkey, and white-tailed deer (though we use pastured chickens and free-range sheep as well). We focus on the joints of larger animals, so cartilage and connective tissue are simmered. The sheep we like to use are from coastal islands in Downeast, Maine, and they feed only on grasses and broad-leaved herbs during the summer and, when snow covers the islands, travel to the shoreline to consume various species of marine algae. They have never eaten grain.

Our bone broths are made with spring water and simmered for at least 12 hours to as many as 24 hours, and we almost always include wild-collected mushrooms, most frequently hen-of-the-woods or fall oyster mushrooms. In a gallon-sized pot, we add a handful of dried mushrooms (equal to 2 or 3 handfuls fresh) and cook them in the broth the entire time the animal carcasses are simmering, which releases into the broth immune-modulating polysaccharides (beta-glucans). These bolster the health value of the broth and add a wonderful flavor. The mushrooms have been sun-dried, so their levels of vitamin D (D_2) have been increased over dehydrator-dried versions. We live in a northern climate and consider this part of our overall vitamin D strategy (along with summer sun exposure, marine oils, pastured eggs, liver, and so on). I do not take supplements, so I use the bone broth as a way to get in nutrients that are beneficial for my joints (I train in Brazilian jiu-jitsu, a ground-fighting art that demands high flexibility and joint health). I have had fewer injuries (and no serious ones) to my joints since incorporating bone broths into my diet.

—Arthur Haines, Delta Institute of Natural History, Canton, Maine

Classic Fish Stock

Classic cooking texts advise against using oily fish such as salmon for making broth, probably because highly unsaturated fish oils become rancid during cooking. The cartilage in fish bones "melts" very quickly, so fish broth needs only a short cooking time.

Makes about 4 quarts

1 whole carcass of a large, non-oily fish such as sole, turbot, rockfish,
    or snapper, or 2 to 3 fish heads from non-oily fish
2 tablespoons butter
2 onions, peeled and coarsely chopped
1 carrot, peeled and coarsely chopped
1 cup mushroom stems, coarsely chopped
    (optional)
½ cup dry white wine or vermouth
About 4 quarts cold filtered water
1 *bouquet garni* made with parsley sprigs,
    thyme sprigs, and a bay leaf, tied together
    with kitchen string

Remove the gills from the fish head or heads, and wash the carcass or heads thoroughly with cold water.

Over medium-low heat melt the butter in a stockpot large enough to hold the fish carcass or heads. Add the onions, carrot, and optional mushroom stems, and cook, stirring occasionally, for about 30 minutes, until the vegetables are softened. Add the wine, increase the heat to medium, and bring to a boil. Add the fish carcass or heads, then add enough cold filtered water to cover the bones. Bring to a bare simmer and carefully skim off any scum that rises to the top. Add the *bouquet garni* and lower the heat to low. Cook at a bare simmer with the lid off or slightly askew for about 1 hour, occasionally skimming scum from the top as needed and checking to ensure that the bones remain covered with water and adding more water as needed.

Remove the carcass or heads with tongs and a slotted spoon. Strain the stock through a fine-mesh strainer into 2-quart Pyrex measuring containers or a large heatproof bowl (see tips for straining on page 149), and it's ready to use in your recipes. If not using right away, cool to room temperature, then refrigerate uncovered for several hours, until the fat rises to the top and congeals. Skim off this fat and transfer the stock to containers (see tips on choosing and filling your containers on pages 151–52), cover, and store in the refrigerator for up to 5 days or in the freezer for many months.

Asian Fish Stock

Use this stock to make Authentic Miso Soup (page 194).

Makes about 2 quarts

2 medium fish carcasses, including heads, of non-oily fish such as turbot, rockfish, or snapper

Shells (and heads if available) from ¾ pound fresh shrimp (reserve the shrimp for another use)

¼ cup rice vinegar

About 2 quarts cold filtered water

3 celery sticks, chopped

4 cloves garlic, peeled and chopped

1-inch piece fresh ginger, peeled and chopped

1 teaspoon whole black peppercorns

Remove the gills from the fish heads and wash the carcasses and heads thoroughly with cold water. Place the fish carcasses and heads and shrimp shells in a stockpot. Add the vinegar and enough cold filtered water to cover the bones. Place over medium heat, uncovered, bring to a bare simmer, and carefully skim off any scum that rises to the top. Add the celery, garlic, ginger, and peppercorns, return to a simmer, then lower the heat to low. Cook at a bare simmer with the lid off or slightly askew for about 1 hour, occasionally skimming scum from the top as needed and checking to ensure that the bones remain covered with water and adding more water as needed.

Remove the carcasses and shrimp shells with tongs and a slotted spoon. Strain the stock through a fine-mesh strainer into 2-quart Pyrex measuring containers or a large heatproof bowl (see tips for straining on page 149), and it's ready to use in your recipes. If not using right away, cool to room temperature, then refrigerate uncovered for several hours, until the fat rises to the top and congeals. Skim off this fat and transfer the stock to containers (see tips on choosing and filling your containers on pages 151–52), cover, and store in the refrigerator for up to 5 days or in the freezer for many months.

Russian Fish Broth

Adapted from The Art of Russian Cuisine, *by Anne Volokh and Mavis Manus*

This simple and delicious fish broth calls for small whole smelts; the smelts should be gutted, with the gills and scales removed. Use the broth to make Amber Fish Soup (page 207).

Makes about 2 quarts

1 onion, peeled and chopped

1 carrot, peeled and chopped

1 leek, white part only, washed and chopped

1 parsnip, peeled and chopped

1 teaspoon sea salt

2 quarts cold filtered water

1 pound fresh or frozen smelts

10 whole black peppercorns

2 to 3 bay leaves

Combine the onion, carrot, leek, parsnip, and salt in a stockpot and add the cold filtered water. Place over medium heat, uncovered, bring to a bare simmer, then lower the heat to low and cook at a bare simmer with the lid slightly askew for 30 minutes. Add the smelts, peppercorns, and bay leaves, return to a simmer, and simmer for 20 minutes.

Strain the broth through a fine-mesh strainer into a 2-quart measuring container or large heatproof bowl (see tips for straining on page 149), and it's ready to use in your recipes (the vegetables and fish can go onto the compost pile, or the fish can be given to your cat). If not using right away, cool to room temperature, then transfer the broth to containers (see tips on choosing and filling your containers on pages 151–52), cover, and store in the refrigerator for up to 5 days or in the freezer for many months.

Bonito Broth

Bonito broth, or *dashi*, is a Japanese fish stock made from the flakes of dried, fermented, smoked tuna, and is the fastest and easiest broth you can make. Bags of shaved bonito are available in Asian markets.

Makes about 1 quart

5 cups cold filtered water

5 ounces bonito flakes

1 tablespoon rice vinegar

1 (4- to 6-inch) piece kombu or kelp (optional)

Place all the ingredients in a large saucepan and let sit for 30 minutes. Bring to a bare simmer over medium heat, uncovered, and carefully spoon off any scum that rises to the top as best you can. Simmer for about 1 hour, then strain through a fine-mesh strainer (you may line the strainer with cheesecloth if it's available) into a 1-quart Pyrex measuring container or a medium heatproof bowl and cool. Transfer to containers (see tips on choosing and filling your containers on pages 151–52) and store in the refrigerator for up to 3 days or in the freezer for many months.

Shrimp Shell Broth

Use this broth in Shrimp Étouffée (page 248).

Makes about 6 cups

Shells and tails from about 2 pounds shrimp

1 medium onion, peeled and coarsely chopped

1 stick celery, chopped

2 cloves garlic, peeled and chopped

1 organic lemon, sliced

1 *bouquet garni* made with parsley sprigs, thyme sprigs, and a bay leaf, tied together with kitchen string

1 teaspoon whole black peppercorns

About 6 cups cups cold filtered water

Combine all the ingredients in a 2-quart saucepan. Place over medium heat, uncovered, bring to a bare simmer, and carefully skim any scum that rises to the top. Lower the heat and cook at a bare simmer with the lid off or slightly askew for 45 to 60 minutes, occasionally skimming scum from the top as needed.

Strain the broth through a fine-mesh strainer into a 2-quart Pyrex measuring container or a large heatproof bowl (see tips for straining on page 149), and it's ready to use in your recipes. If not using right away, cool to room temperature and transfer the broth to containers (see tips on choosing and filling your containers on pages 151–52), cover, and store in the refrigerator for up to 3 days or in the freezer for many months.

Shrimp Shell Stock

Shrimp shell stock can be used to make the most delectable shrimp bisque or shrimp sauce. The secret is plenty of shells and including the heads if you have them, so whenever you can, buy shrimp with the shells and heads on. Shells and heads can be saved up in the freezer until you have enough to make stock.

The collagen in shrimp is located in the flesh—in this case the flesh in the heads and the little remaining in the tails. Pigment and flavors come from the hard shells, and these are more easily extracted in oil rather than water, which is why the recipe calls for cooking the shells in butter before adding water. The resulting "stock" of this recipe is actually somewhat thick and completely opaque.

Makes about 1 quart

1 cup (2 sticks) softened butter
About 8 cups shrimp shells, tails, and heads
About 1 quart cold filtered water

Melt ½ cup (1 stick) of the butter in a large saucepan over medium heat. Add the shrimp shells, tails, and heads and sauté until they turn pink, about 20 minutes. Add enough cold filtered water to cover, bring to a bare simmer, then lower the heat to low and cook at a bare simmer with the lid off or slightly askew for about 1 hour, removing any scum that rises to the surface. Turn off the heat and let cool. Remove the shells and heads with a slotted spoon and place them in a blender. (Note: A blender works better than a food processor for grinding the shells.) Add the remaining ½ cup (1 stick) softened butter and blend until very smooth. Press the pureed shells through a fine-mesh strainer, or a chinois if you have one, into a large heatproof bowl, adding the cooking broth little by little until all the liquid is mixed with the pressed and strained shells. Discard the larger pieces that remain in the strainer.

The stock can now be thickened with tomato paste and blended with cultured cream and sherry to make shrimp bisque (page 208) or reduced to produce a delectable shrimp sauce (page 266). If not using right away, cool to room temperature, then transfer the stock to containers (see tips on choosing and filling your containers on pages 151–52), cover, and store in the refrigerator for up to 3 days or in the freezer for many months.

Continuous Slow Cooker Broth

Jenny McGruther, Nourished Kitchen *blog, Crested Butte, Colorado*

Makes about 1 quart per day

1 whole chicken (or the carcass and bones of a roasted chicken)
2 chicken feet and 1 chicken head, if available
2 bay leaves
1 tablespoon whole black peppercorns
¼ cup apple cider vinegar
Any vegetable scraps you have on hand
Cold filtered water

Place the whole chicken or the carcass of a roasted chicken and optional head and feet into your slow cooker; add the bay leaves, black peppercorns, vinegar, and any vegetable scraps you have on hand (if using carrots, peel them before adding). Add enough cold filtered water to cover the bones, cover, and cook on low for 1 week (this process is safe as long as there is plenty of liquid in the slow cooker), checking occasionally to ensure that the ingredients remain covered with water and adding more water as needed.

After 24 hours, you may begin using the broth. Simply dip a ladle or measuring cup

into the slow cooker to remove the amount of broth you need. Pour it through a fine-mesh strainer or a reusable coffee filter to remove any solids. Replace the broth you remove from the slow cooker with an equivalent amount of filtered water. If you're using a whole fresh chicken, you may also remove chicken meat from the slow cooker to use in stir-fries and other dishes, soups, or salads.

At the end of the week, strain off any remaining broth. Wash the insert of your slow cooker and start again.

Making Broth a Routine

My family has included broth as a staple in our diets for the past few years. At first making broth and stock seemed like a time-consuming, messy job. Now, however, I am in a routine where making broth is just a part of my life. Each time I cook a chicken, I put the carcass directly into my slow cooker, along with carrots, onions, celery, apple cider vinegar, and seasonings, and I flip the switch. A day later, I find that the broth comes out beautifully, with loads of gelatin "jiggle." I feel secure when I open my freezer and see jar after jar of different types of broth. It is the basis of all my cooking. I "stock-pile" bones in my freezer and fill my huge stockpot with bones, chicken feet, vinegar, and aromatic vegetables. This might sit on my stovetop for up to 48 hours at barely a simmer. My two children enjoy slurping up their broth with Japanese-style soupspoons. They both have an amazing ability to focus in school, rarely get ill, and have nice healthy teeth—all of which I credit to our homemade broth.

—Emily Merenghi, Portola Valley, California

Slow Cooker Beef Foot Broth

Amanda Rose, Hot Springs, California

The discovery—or rather, rediscovery—of just how much gelatin can be extracted from beef foot bones was made by Amanda Rose, who has posted the happy results on YouTube (www.youtube.com/watch?v=WGUCSaud1kI). Beef feet can be purchased at ethnic grocery stores; as an alternative, use a calf's foot, also available at ethnic markets. This technique will also work with two whole pig's feet. You will need a 6-quart slow cooker.

Makes about 12 quarts gelatinous broth

1 beef foot (about 3 pounds, available from ethnic markets)
2 tablespoons apple cider vinegar per batch
About 2 quarts cold filtered water

Place the beef foot in a 6-quart slow cooker and add the vinegar. Add cold filtered water to cover. Cover and cook on low for 24 hours, checking occasionally to ensure that the feet remain covered with water and adding more water as needed.

Ladle 1 quart broth through a fine-mesh strainer into a 1-quart measuring container or a medium heatproof bowl (see tips for straining on page 149), and it's ready to use in your recipes. If not using right away, cool to room temperature, then refrigerate uncovered for several hours, until the fat rises to the top and congeals. If desired, skim off this fat (you can use it in your cooking) and transfer the broth to a container (see tips on choosing and filling your containers on pages 151–52), cover, and store in the refrigerator for up to 5 days or in the freezer for many months.

Add another quart or so of cold filtered water and 2 tablespoons vinegar to the slow cooker, cover, and cook on low for another 24 hours; strain as above and repeat. You should be able to extract 1 quart of gelatin-rich stock 12 days in a row!

Mixed Bone Broth

This recipe calls for egg shells, which will increase the level of calcium in your broth.

Evelyn Luis, Los Angeles, California

Makes 4 to 5 quarts

About 4 pounds chicken bones

About 6 pounds pork bones

Raw egg shells (collected and saved in the freezer)

½ cup vinegar

4 to 5 quarts cold filtered water

¼ cup peeled chopped fresh ginger

Place the bones and egg shells in a slow cooker, add the vinegar, then add enough cold filtered water to cover the bones. Let stand for 30 to 60 minutes. Add the ginger, cover, and cook on low for 12 to 24 hours, checking occasionally to ensure that the bones remain covered with water and adding more water as needed. If your slow cooker won't maintain a simmer, leave the lid slightly ajar to prevent boiling.

Remove the bones and egg shells with tongs and a slotted spoon, then strain the broth through a fine-mesh strainer into 2-quart measuring containers or a large heatproof bowl (see tips for straining on page 149), and it's ready to use in your recipes. If not using right away, cool to room temperature, then refrigerate uncovered for several hours, until the fat rises to the top and congeals. If desired, skim off this fat (you can use it in your cooking) and transfer the broth to containers (see tips on choosing and filling your containers on pages 151–52), cover, and store in the refrigerator for up to 5 days or in the freezer for many months.

Herb Broth

Adapted from 2009 Herb Quarterly

Use either fresh herbs you have gathered yourself or dried herbs (the herbs used can be easily found online).

Makes about 6 quarts

3 to 4 poultry carcasses

2 chicken feet or 1 split pig's foot

¼ cup apple cider vinegar

About 6 quarts cold filtered water

2 onions, ends cut off and coarsely chopped (no need to remove the skin)

2 carrots, peeled and coarsely chopped

2 celery sticks, coarsely chopped

3 tablespoons nettle leaf

3 tablespoons seaweed flakes, such as kelp or wakame

2 tablespoons calendula flowers

5 astragalus root slices

5 long codonopsis root pieces

1 medium burdock root, chopped

1 large maitake mushroom or 20 shiitake mushrooms

Ground cayenne (optional)

Sea salt and freshly ground black pepper

Place the poultry carcasses and chicken feet in a stockpot. Add the vinegar and enough cold filtered water to cover the bones. Let stand for 30 to 60 minutes. Place over medium heat, uncovered, bring to a bare simmer, and carefully spoon off any scum that rises to the top. Add the onions, carrots, and celery, return to a bare simmer, then lower the heat to low. Cook at a bare simmer with the lid off or slightly askew for about 3 hours, occasionally skimming scum from the top as needed and checking to ensure that the bones remain covered with water and adding more water as needed. Add the nettle leaf, seaweed, calendula flowers, astragalus, codonopsis, burdock, and mushroom and cook for another 3 hours.

Strain the broth through a fine-mesh strainer into 2-quart Pyrex measuring containers or a large heatproof bowl (see tips for straining on page 149) and season with optional cayenne, and sea salt and black pepper. Heat to a simmer and serve in mugs, like tea.

If not using right away, cool to room temperature, then refrigerate uncovered for several hours, until the fat rises to the top and congeals. If desired, skim off this fat (you can use it in your cooking) and transfer the broth to containers (see tips on choosing and filling your containers on pages 151–52), cover, and store in the refrigerator for up to 5 days or in the freezer for many months.

Allspice Broth

Elly Morrison, PhD, Bellingham, Washington

Makes about 4 quarts

2 to 3 pounds beef bones, including marrow, knuckle, and shank bones

¼ cup apple cider vinegar

About 4 quarts cold filtered water

1 unpeeled onion, ends cut off, chopped

1 *bouquet garni* made with parsley sprigs, thyme sprigs, and a bay leaf, tied together with kitchen string

1 teaspoon whole black peppercorns, or green or white peppercorns, crushed

3 whole allspice berries

Place the bones in a stockpot. Add the vinegar and enough cold filtered water to cover the bones. Let stand for 30 to 60 minutes. Place over medium heat, uncovered, bring to a bare simmer, and carefully spoon off any scum that rises to the top. Add the onion, *bouquet garni*, peppercorns, and allspice, return to a bare simmer, then lower the heat to low. Cook at a bare simmer with the lid off or slightly askew for a minimum of 6 and up to 48 hours, occasionally skimming scum from the top as needed and checking to ensure that the bones remain covered with water and adding more water as needed.

Remove the bones with tongs and a slotted spoon. Strain the broth through a fine-mesh strainer into 2-quart Pyrex measuring containers or a large heatproof bowl (see tips for straining on page 149), and it's ready to use in your recipes. If not using right away, cool to room temperature, then refrigerate uncovered for several hours, until the fat rises to the top and congeals. If desired, skim off this fat (you can use it in your cooking) and transfer the broth to containers (see tips on choosing and filling your containers on pages 151–52), cover, and store in the refrigerator for up to 5 days or in the freezer for many months.

Easy Pressure Cooker Broth

Laura Livingston, Brooksville, Maine

Those living on a farm or who are lucky enough to be able to purchase directly from a farmer will appreciate this easy, inexpensive, and simple way to make stock. If you are saving bones from chicken or turkey dinners, keep them in a plastic bag stored in the freezer. After the broth has cooked, city folk can feed the soft bones to their dog or cat; those living on farms can give them to their chickens or pigs.

Makes 5 to 6 quarts

2 to 3 spent hens or roosters or bones from several roast chicken or turkey dinners

6-quart pressure cooker

¼ cup apple cider vinegar or lemon juice

About 4 quarts cold filtered water

Place the hen, rooster, chicken, or turkey bones in a pressure cooker and add the vinegar and enough water to cover. Cover and secure the lid. Raise the heat to high and bring the pot up to full pressure; this will take about 15 minutes. Lower the heat to maintainer the pressure and cook for 45 minutes. Turn off the burner and allow the pot to release pressure naturally, about 15 minutes.

Open the pressure cooker and remove the bones with tongs and a slotted spoon. Strain the broth through a fine-mesh strainer into 2-quart Pyrex measuring containers or a large heatproof bowl (see tips for straining on page 149), and it's ready to use in your recipes. If not using right away, cool to room temperature, then refrigerate uncovered for several hours, until the fat rises to the top and congeals. If desired, skim off this fat (you can use it in your cooking) and transfer the stock to containers (see tips on choosing and filling your containers on pages 151–52), cover, and store in the refrigerator for up to 5 days or in the freezer for many months.

‒◇‒

I'd like to share my way of making bone broth in a stainless steel pressure cooker: I cover the bones with water and ½ cup apple cider vinegar, cooking chicken bones for 1 hour and beef bones (beef ribs make the nicest broth) for 2 hours. It's important not to let the pressure cooker get dry! After the broth is finished and cooled, I take out the large hard bone pieces and discard them. I then take the broth and soft bone pieces and process them in a blender to make a gruel. Then I put the gruel through a strainer, transfer the gruel to freezer bags, and freeze it. This broth can be used in any recipes that call for water. I use it in bread, rice, and spaghetti sauce. For soups, I cook up organic potatoes with the skins and process them in a blender, then add the bone matrix along with mixed vegetables. This method keeps the bone gruel from settling to the bottom and makes an extremely nutrient-dense soup without the unpleasantness of bone fragments.

—Bonnie Engels, Big Rapids, Michigan

‒◇‒

Slow Cooker Chicken Broth

Rebecca Stults, Langley, Washington

Makes about 4 quarts

4 to 5 pounds leftover chicken bones, or 1 whole stewing chicken

2 to 6 chicken feet

2 to 3 tablespoons apple cider vinegar

About 4 quarts cold filtered water

2 to 3 celery sticks

1 large yellow or red onion, root end cut off and quartered, with skin left on

Sea salt

Place the bones and feet in a slow cooker, add the vinegar, then add enough cold filtered water to cover the bones. Let stand for 30 to 60 minutes. Add the celery and onion, cover, and cook on low for 1 to 2 days, checking occasionally to ensure that the feet remain covered with water and adding more water as needed. If your slow cooker won't maintain a simmer, leave the lid slightly ajar to prevent boiling.

Remove the bones and feet with tongs, then strain the broth through a fine-mesh strainer into 2-quart measuring containers or a large heatproof bowl (see tips for straining on page 149), and it's ready to use in your recipes. If not using right away, cool to room temperature, then refrigerate uncovered for several hours, until the fat rises to the top and congeals. If desired, skim off this fat (you can use it in your cooking) and transfer the broth to containers (see tips on choosing and filling your containers on pages 151–52), cover, and store in the refrigerator for up to 5 days or in the freezer for many months.

Use the broth as base for any soup, sauce, or gravy, or sip as you would tea or coffee. Season individual servings with salt.

<o>

Life-Saving

Just recently an acquaintance told me she thought my broth had saved her life. She had been sick for quite a while and was having difficulty keeping anything down. After eating some chicken noodle soup made with my broth she said her body felt like a sponge soaking up all the nutrients in the soup and comforting her both physically and emotionally. She wanted another batch the next day, as nothing else sounded appealing to her. I think "saved her life" was a bit of a stretch, but I certainly know how that feels.

—Rebecca Stults, Langley, Washington

<o>

Liquid Gold

Emma Watterson, Hayes, Virginia

The turmeric in this recipe gives not only flavor but also a beautiful yellow color to the broth; oregano adds a south-of-the-border taste.

Makes about 4 quarts

About 4 pounds chicken bones and pieces

2 to 4 chicken feet (optional)

¼ cup apple cider vinegar

About 4 quarts cold filtered water

1 large onion, ends cut off, quartered, with skin left on

1 head garlic, sliced in half (no need to peel it)

1 teaspoon ground turmeric

1 tablespoon dried oregano

Sea salt and freshly ground black pepper

Place the chicken bones and optional feet in a stockpot. Add the vinegar and enough cold filtered water to cover the bones. Let stand for 30 to 60 minutes. Place over medium heat, uncovered, bring to a bare simmer, and carefully spoon off any scum that rises to the top. Add the onion, garlic, turmeric, and oregano, return to a simmer, then lower the heat to low. Cook at a bare simmer with the lid off or slightly askew for 4 to 6 hours, occasionally skimming scum from the top as needed and checking to ensure that the bones remain covered with water and adding more water as needed.

Remove the bones and feet with tongs and a slotted spoon (when cooled, pick any meat off the bones and use in soups, casseroles, and other dishes). Strain the stock through a fine-mesh strainer into 2-quart Pyrex measuring containers or a large heat-proof bowl (see tips for straining on page 149), and it's ready to use in your recipes. If not using right away, cool to room temperature, then refrigerate uncovered for several hours, until the fat rises to the top and congeals. If desired, skim off this fat (you can use it in your cooking) and transfer the stock to containers (see tips on choosing and filling your containers on pages 151–52), cover, and store in the refrigerator for up to 5 days or in the freezer for many months. Season individual servings with salt and pepper.

Broth as a Staple

With three small children to care for, a healthy and nourishing bone broth is a staple in my refrigerator. Chicken is the most popular bone broth in my home. It's an easy routine to keep a supply on hand by cycling the chicken bones and carcasses from various recipes to a large bag in the freezer. Then, every two weeks or so, I place the contents of the "chicken bag" into a pot for broth. There's always plenty on hand for quick and easy soups, sauces, gravies, and whatever else is needed from this liquid gold.

—Emma Watterson, Hayes, Virginia

Slow Cooker Herbed Beef Shank Broth

Anita Reusch, Grosslangenfeld, Germany

This broth makes a great soup base, or it can be strained for making sauces or gravy. You can shred the meat from the beef shank to make Beef Noodle Soup (page 198).

Makes 4 to 5 quarts

4 to 5 pounds beef shank, cut into slices of about 1-inch
3 bay leaves
5 whole black peppercorns
1 sprig fresh thyme

1 sprig fresh rosemary

1 dried red chile

Greens from 1 leek, chopped

1 clove garlic

1 small piece fresh ginger

Pinch of ground turmeric

½ teaspoon black cumin seeds

2 teaspoons fresh or 1 teaspoon dried lovage

2 teaspoons fresh or 1 teaspoon dried summer savory

4 to 5 quarts cold filtered water

Preheat the oven to 450°F.

Place the beef shank in a roasting pan and roast, turning once or twice, until well browned, about 20 minutes. Transfer to a slow cooker and add the remaining ingredients along with enough cold filtered water to cover. Cover and cook on low for 3 to 4 hours or up to 12 hours, checking occasionally to ensure that the beef shank remains covered with water and adding more water as needed.

Remove the beef shank with tongs and a slotted spoon, then strain the broth through a fine-mesh strainer into 2-quart measuring containers or a large heatproof bowl (see tips for straining on page 149), and it's ready to use in your recipes. If not using right away, cool to room temperature, then refrigerate uncovered for several hours, until the fat rises to the top and congeals. If desired, skim off this fat (you can use it in your cooking) and transfer the broth to containers (see tips on choosing and filling your containers on pages 151–52), cover, and store in the refrigerator for up to 5 days or in the freezer for many months.

Oven-Baked Broth

Deanne Yoder, Molalla, Oregon

This ingenious recipe for long-simmered broth keeps the stovetop free and also provides a safe method for those who worry about leaving the stovetop on overnight or when they leave the house. You will need an old-fashioned turkey roasting pan with a cover for this recipe.

Makes about 5 quarts

About 5 pounds bones (chicken, beef, veal, turkey)

4 to 6 extra chicken feet, or ½ split pig's foot

About ¼ cup olive oil or melted butter

3 large onions, ends cut off, coarsely chopped
   (skin may be left on)

4 carrots, peeled and chopped

4 celery sticks, chopped

¼ cup apple cider vinegar

About 5 quarts cold filtered water

Preheat the oven to 450°F.

Place the bones and feet in a turkey roasting pan with a cover and toss with oil to coat. Brown with the cover off for about 20 minutes (be careful not to overbrown). Add the onions, carrots, celery, vinegar, and enough cold filtered water to cover the bones.

Reduce the oven temperature to 200 to 220°F, place the lid on the pan slightly askew, bring the broth to a bare simmer in the oven, and simmer for 1 hour. Remove the cover and skim off any scum that has risen to the top. Cover and simmer in the oven for about 24 hours.

Remove the pan from the oven and let cool about 30 minutes. Remove the bones and vegetables with tongs and a slotted spoon. Put an empty stockpot in the sink with a fine-mesh strainer in it. Pour the broth through the strainer into the pot (you may fill the sink with cold running water to hasten cooling). When the broth is cooled, transfer to containers and refrigerate uncovered for several hours, until the fat rises to the top and congeals. If desired, skim off this fat (you can use it in your cooking) and transfer the broth to containers (see tips on choosing and filling your containers on pages 151–52), cover, and store in the refrigerator for up to 5 days or in the freezer for many months.

Clarified Stock

For most recipes, clarification is unnecessary. However, if you want a perfectly clear stock, here's how to do it.

Makes 4 quarts

4 quarts defatted stock

4 to 6 egg whites, lightly beaten

Pour the stock into a large saucepan. Add the egg whites and bring to a boil, whisking with a wire whisk. Stop whisking when the stock is at a boil and let boil for 3 to 5 minutes. A white foam, gradually becoming a spongy crust, will form on the surface. Remove the pan from the heat and let cool. Lift off the crust and strain the stock through a fine-mesh strainer into a heatproof bowl.

My Broth Tips

Here are some tips I have come up with after several years of making broth:

Add half a turnip to the broth with the vegetables. The taste it adds to the finished broth is beautifully tangy.

Use a giant fishnet-style Chinese soup ladle, available at restaurant supply stores. It's the perfect straining scooper for the bones.

I measured my freezer to determine how many mason jars I could easily store in it. When I came up with eighteen, I bought the right size broth pot to make just that much.

After I strain, cool, and de-fat the broth, I put it back in the pot and cook it with the lid off until it reduces by at least one inch. What you are getting with this second simmer/reduction is a slightly thickened broth with a fine flavor ambrosia. You can watch the broth come to life in smell, color, and appearance.

I drink one coffee mug full of heated broth for breakfast every morning to replace coffee, tea, or juice—it's so warming and nourishing.

I keep two big defrosted mason jars of broth in my fridge at all times. The rest stays in the freezer. One to enjoy straight heated up and the other to easily turn into a soup by adding beans, tomato sauce, leftovers, and so on.

I'm a leftovers and bone collector. I save every bone we eat of chicken, pork, and beef, throw them in a freezer bag, and pop them into my next broth. It has become an obsession to go to good butchers and farms to get exotic parts like chicken necks, feet, and backs and gizzards or oxtail and marrowbones. Each new broth becomes an adventure in bones and organ meats.

Before adding bones, gizzards, livers, and chicken hearts to the broth, I deeply brown them on both sides for about 20 minutes at 350°F. This deep browning adds an incredible depth of color and flavor.

In winter and fall I make bone broth from pig's feet, chicken bones, and organs and beef bones; in the summer I switch to fish broth. The change is major, and each broth tastes all the more wonderful when you switch back.

—Mary Evans, Flushing, New York

CHAPTER 22

Soups

"A first-rate soup is more creative than a second-rate painting," said Abraham Maslow.

Louis P. DeGouy, author of *The Soup Book* (1949), described soup in even more elegant terms: "Good soup is one of the prime ingredients of good living. For soup can do more to lift the spirits and stimulate the appetite than any other one dish." We all need to get back into the kitchen and prepare nourishing, comforting soups.

Soups provide the most common—and delicious—way to use bone broths. In fact, soups are the perfect way to get good nutrition into your family: an easy-to-digest amalgamation of nourishing broth; good fats such as butter, coconut oil, and cream; lots of vegetables; and small amounts of meat or organ meat. Served with sourdough bread and butter along with cheese or pâté, they make a perfect meal. Soups can be made in large quantities and reheated on successive evenings or frozen for easy meals on busy days.

While recipes provide guidelines for making soup, you don't really need recipes if you know the basic techniques. Soups fall into three general categories: unblended soups, blended soups, and soups that make their own broth.

Unblended Soups

These soups are based on clear broth to which chopped vegetables, animal protein (finely chopped meat, organ meats, or even chopped or beaten eggs), and a carbohydrate food (rice, barley, noodles, etc.) are typically added. The technique can be as simple as simmering the ingredients in broth until warmed through and tender, then seasoning to taste with sea salt and pepper. Tomato paste, cream, or coconut milk may be added, along with flavorings like dried herbs, turmeric, ginger, and curry powder. For additional flavor and the nutrition of healthy fats, first sauté the vegetables in coconut oil, butter, ghee, or lard. Then add broth and any other ingredients you like. The first recipes in this chapter are recipes for unblended soups, and they can be modified according to the ingredients you have on hand.

Blended Soups

Blended soups are thick and creamy; the basic technique goes like this:

Gently sauté or sweat nonstarchy chopped root and root-like vegetables (onions, leeks, peeled carrots, peeled parsnips, turnips, peeled celery root, fennel, etc.) in butter, ghee, lard, duck fat, or coconut oil until very soft, being careful not to let them burn. Seasonings like garlic, ginger, dried herbs, and curry powder can be added toward the end of the sauté.

Add broth and starchy ingredients (potatoes, squash, sweet potatoes, soaked lentils, or soaked dried peas), bring to a simmer, and cook gently until the vegetables are softened. Add chopped tender vegetables such as broccoli, asparagus, peppers, and greens and simmer until tender.

Blend the soup using a handheld blender (the easiest method because the soup remains in the pot) or in a blender or food processor. Use a food mill if you need to separate out skins (such as pepper skins) or fibrous material to produce a really smooth soup.

Return the soup to the pot and thin with water if necessary. Season the soup with sea salt and pepper to taste. You can add cream, sour cream, or crème fraîche. Adding cultured cream to the bowl after serving will preserve the enzymes in the cream.

Once you know the technique for blended soups, you can use the recipes for ideas and make your soup with whatever inspires you, using the ingredients you have on hand.

Soups That Make Their Own Broth

Using the techniques of unblended soups, cook the ingredients in water but add oxtail, beef shank, chicken feet, and/or a beef, calf's, or pig's foot to the pot. When the meat is cooked and tender, remove the meaty bones and cut up any meat adhering to them. Return the meat to the soup, reheat, season to taste, and serve.

Unblended Soups

Simple Chicken Noodle Soup

Adrienne Hew, Kailua-Kona, Hawaii

When I lived in Yugoslavia in the 1980s, this soup was often served at the start of the midday meal.

Serves 4

6 cups homemade chicken stock
¼ cup broken vermicelli noodles
2 tablespoons finely chopped fresh parsley
Sea salt

Bring the stock to a boil in a medium saucepan. Add the vermicelli and cook according to the package directions, 3 to 4 minutes. Add the parsley, season with salt, ladle into bowls, and serve.

Easy Kid's Wonton Soup

Emma Watterson, Hayes, Virginia

Serves 4

1 quart homemade chicken broth
8 frozen wontons
Sea salt
1 bunch green onions, finely chopped
About 1 cup watercress, finely chopped
1 hard-boiled egg, chopped

Bring the broth to a boil, add the wontons, and cook according to the package directions. Season with salt. Ladle 2 wontons into each of 4 bowls and pour the soup over the wontons. Serve the bowls garnished with green onion, watercress, and hard-boiled egg.

Consommé

Beef and vegetables add to the flavor of already highly flavored beef broth to make this delicious consommé. The onions are roasted to add even more flavor and a deep color to the soup. Although this recipe takes some time, the results are worth the effort.

Makes about 4 quarts

2 medium onions, roughly chopped

2 pounds ground beef

5 quarts homemade beef or veal stock, or veal double stock

2 carrots, peeled and grated

2 celery sticks, finely chopped

2 medium tomatoes, seeded and finely chopped

1 *bouquet garni* made with parsley sprigs, thyme sprigs, and a bay leaf, tied together with
   kitchen string

½ teaspoon crushed peppercorns

2 whole cloves

Sea salt

Preheat the oven to 400°F.

Arrange the onions in a roasting pan and roast for 20 to 30 minutes, stirring a couple of times, until they are deeply browned or blackened.

Heat a large cast-iron pan over medium-high heat, add the ground beef, and cook, stirring often, until cooked through, about 10 minutes. Add 2 cups of the stock, bring to a boil, and boil until the broth is absorbed into the beef. Add a little cold filtered water and stir to release any bits that have stuck to the pan.

Pour the remaining 4½ quarts stock into a stockpot. Add the cooked ground beef, the roasted onions, the carrots, celery, tomatoes, *bouquet garni*, peppercorns, and cloves. Place over medium heat and bring to a bare simmer (do not let it boil). You should see a little steam over the surface of the stock, but no bubbling, or as few bubbles rising to the surface as possible. Cook at a bare simmer, stirring occasionally, for 2–3 hours.

Strain the stock through a fine-mesh strainer or chinois lined with cheesecloth or a fine towel. If you'd like additional clarity, follow the instructions on clarifying broth with egg whites on pages 187–88. Season with salt, ladle into bowls or mugs, and serve.

Simple Chicken Rice Soup

Denise Tucker, Austin, Texas

When my son is sick and doesn't have an appetite, the one thing I can always count on is chicken bone broth with basmati rice, chopped carrot, and celery. He has always been able to hold this down, and he heals much quicker than he otherwise would. He's now fifteen years old, and he still takes the bone broth, especially when he's sick, and of course I use it in my cooking as well.

Serves 4

1 quart homemade chicken broth

¼ cup brown basmati rice

1 carrot, peeled, cut lengthwise, and thinly sliced

1 stick celery, thinly sliced

Sea salt

Combine the broth and rice in a large saucepan over high heat and bring to a boil. Remove any scum that rises to the top with a spoon. Reduce the heat and simmer until the rice is tender, about 1 hour. Add the vegetables and simmer another 15 minutes or until they are tender. Season with salt, ladle into bowls, and serve.

Golden Chicken Rice Soup

Serves 6

2 quarts homemade chicken broth

¼ teaspoon ground turmeric

½ cup brown rice

About ¾ cup finely chopped chicken meat (optional)

2 carrots, peeled and grated

1 ripe tomato, seeded and chopped

1 cup baby spinach leaves, chopped

Sea salt and freshly ground black pepper

Pour the broth into a large saucepan. Add the turmeric, place over high heat, and bring to a boil. Add the rice, reduce the heat, and simmer for about 1 hour, until the rice is cooked through. Add the optional chicken and the carrots, tomato, and spinach and simmer until cooked through. Season with salt and pepper, ladle into bowls, and serve.

Authentic Miso Soup

Serves 4

1 quart homemade fish broth, strained through a fine-mesh strainer or clarified
1 small onion, peeled, quartered, and thinly sliced
¼ head green cabbage, cored and finely sliced
1 tablespoon naturally fermented miso paste

Pour the broth into a large saucepan, place over high heat, and bring to a simmer. Add the onion and cabbage and simmer until softened, about 5 minutes. Off heat, whisk in the miso until dissolved. Ladle into bowls and serve.

Rich Vegetable Soup

Serves 8

1 pound bacon, cut into small pieces
1 medium onion, peeled and finely chopped
2 carrots, peeled and grated
2 celery sticks, finely chopped
1 red bell pepper, cored, seeded, and finely
    chopped
Additional bacon fat or lard if needed
1 cup port wine
1 (28-ounce) can chopped tomatoes
2 quarts homemade beef, veal, or chicken
    broth
Sea salt and freshly ground black pepper
2 tablespoons finely chopped fresh parsley

In a stockpot, cook the bacon over medium heat, stirring often, until the fat is rendered, about 15 minutes. Add the onion, carrots, celery, and bell pepper and sauté until the vegetables are softened, about 5 minutes, adding more bacon fat or lard to the pan if needed. Add the wine, increase the heat to medium-high, and reduce by half, about 10 minutes. Add the tomatoes and broth and return to a simmer. Season with salt and pepper. Serve garnished with parsley.

Tortilla Soup

Serves 4

¼ cup lard

4 corn tortillas, cut in half and then into thin strips

½ cup peeled and chopped onion

1 medium Anaheim, poblano, or jalapeño chile, seeded, veins removed, and chopped

2 cloves garlic, minced

1 quart Double-Cooked Mexican Caldo (page 159)

¼ cup tomato paste

Sea salt

1 cup shredded cooked chicken

1 ripe avocado, peeled, cut in half, pit removed, and chopped

1 cup shredded Monterey Jack or mild cheddar cheese

Chopped fresh cilantro

1 lime, cut into 4 wedges

In a large saucepan, heat the lard over medium-high heat. Working in two batches, fry the tortilla strips in the lard until lightly browned and crisp. Remove the tortilla strips from the pan using tongs to a paper towel–lined plate. Reduce the heat to medium, add the onion to the fat in the pan, and cook for 2 minutes, stirring frequently, until beginning to soften. Add the chopped chile and cook for 2 to 3 minutes more, until the onion and chile have softened. Add the garlic and cook for 30 seconds more. Add the *caldo* and tomato paste and season with salt. Bring to a simmer and simmer for 15 minutes. Add the shredded chicken and cook until heated through.

To serve, divide half of the tortilla strips among 4 individual serving bowls and ladle in the soup. Top with avocado and cheese and garnish with the remaining tortilla strips and some cilantro. Serve with lime wedges.

My Sicilian Grandmother's Sunday Meatball Soup

Joette Calabrese, Colden, New York

Serves 8 to 10

MEATBALLS

1 pound ground beef

1 pound ground pork

2 cups day-old bread, broken into small chunks or processed into breadcrumbs

2 eggs

1 cup finely grated pecorino cheese

Several sprigs fresh mint, finely chopped

Sea salt and freshly ground black pepper to taste

SOUP

1 gallon stock made from chicken bones with chicken feet, or beef bones, or pork bones

5 to 8 potatoes, peeled and diced

2 large onions, peeled and diced

2 to 4 cloves garlic, peeled and chopped

3 cups cooked chickpeas

Sea salt and freshly ground black pepper

1 packed cup fresh basil leaves

About 3 cups Swiss chard

¼ cup sherry

Pecorino cheese

In a large bowl, mix the meatball ingredients well with your hands. Form into walnut-size balls; after forming each ball, dip your hands into a bowl of cold water to keep the meat from sticking and to help shape the balls.

In a large pot, combine the stock and potatoes; bring to a simmer over high heat, then reduce the heat to medium and simmer until almost cooked through, about 15 minutes. Gently add the meatballs one at a time, then add the onions, garlic, and chickpeas. Season with salt and pepper. Return to a simmer and cook until the meatballs are cooked through and all the vegetables are tender, about 15 minutes. Chop the basil and chard and add at the end. Simmer about 5 minutes until they are tender. Turn off the heat and add the sherry.

Ladle into bowls, grate long, thin slices of cheese into each bowl, and serve.

Stracciatella Soup

Heather Lionelle, Salida, Colorado

My favorite dinner for a hectic night is my grandmother-in-law's stracciatella soup. *Stracciatella* translates to "little torn strips" and is the Italian version of egg drop soup. With just six ingredients it comes together in a trice and is packed full of nutrition.

Serves 4

2 eggs

2 tablespoons grated Parmesan cheese

2 tablespoons finely chopped fresh parsley

Pinch of freshly grated nutmeg

Pinch of sea salt

1 quart homemade chicken stock

In a small bowl, beat the eggs until just blended. Mix in the cheese, parsley, nutmeg, and salt.

In a large saucepan, bring the stock to a boil. In a thin stream, slowly pour in the egg mixture, stirring constantly with a whisk; it will form tiny flakes in the stock. Simmer for 2 to 3 minutes, ladle into bowls, and serve.

Chinese Egg Drop Soup

Donna and Ashley Sherman, Bloomington, Illinois

Serves 8

2 quarts homemade chicken stock

2 to 4 turnips, peeled and shredded

2 celery sticks, sliced thinly on the diagonal

1 onion, peeled and sliced into rings

3 carrots, peeled and thinly sliced

1 cup chopped cooked chicken or turkey (optional)

5 green onions, chopped

4 eggs, beaten

Sea salt

In a large saucepan, bring the stock to a gentle boil over medium-high heat. Add the turnips, celery, onion, carrots, and chicken, bring to a simmer, then reduce the heat and simmer until the vegetable are tender and the chicken is heated through, about 5 minutes. Add the green onions, raise the heat, and slowly pour in the eggs while stirring the soup. Cook for 1 minute more and season with salt. Turn off the heat and cover until ready to serve.

Beef Noodle Soup

Anita Reusch, Grosslangenfeld, Germany

Serves 6 to 8

2 tablespoons coconut oil

1 clove garlic, peeled and crushed

1-inch piece fresh ginger, peeled and grated

1 bell pepper, cored, seeded, and chopped

1 leek, washed well, white and light green parts, chopped

1 cup thin rice noodles broken into 1-inch pieces

2 quarts Slow Cooker Herbed Beef Shank Broth (page 185)

1 to 2 cups shredded beef from the broth

½ teaspoon ground turmeric

¼ teaspoon ground cayenne

1 teaspoon dried summer savory

1 egg, beaten (optional)

Sea salt

Finely chopped fresh parsley

Melt the coconut oil in a large saucepan over medium heat. Add the garlic, ginger, bell pepper, and leek and sauté until softened, about 5 minutes. Add the noodles and cook, stirring, until lightly browned, about 5 minutes. Add the broth and shredded beef, increase the heat to high, bring to a simmer, then reduce the heat. Add the turmeric, cayenne, and savory and simmer until noodles are tender, about 10 minutes. Whisk in the optional egg and season with salt. Ladle into soup bowls and serve garnished with parsley.

Cream of Gizzard Soup

Kaayla T. Daniel, Albuquerque, NM

I grew up on a small farm in the Hudson Valley. We raised chickens for eggs and meat, grew fruit, and tended to eat a lot of what wasn't quite presentable enough to sell to the public. I helped my Grandpa "candle" the eggs each night and took home the double and triple yolkers and any with a crack or a touch of blood. I don't think I ever had a boneless, skinless chicken breast until I went to college, but I remember plenty of gizzards during my childhood. We cooked them for a good long time until they were tender yet still chewy and served them up with salt and butter. Sometimes, though, the gizzards would go into chicken and rice or noodle soup if more meat was needed. Sometimes we enjoyed the special treat of cream of gizzard soup.

Serves 4

½ pound gizzards

4 tablespoons butter

2 medium onions, peeled and diced

2 celery sticks, chopped

1 quart homemade chicken broth

1 bay leaf

4 medium potatoes, peeled and diced into ½-inch pieces

½ cup cream, preferably raw

Sea salt and freshly ground black pepper

Wash the gizzards to remove any grit. Look them over for bits of wrinkly yellow skin, which is the inside of the gizzard, and remove it (it peels off easily). Cut the gizzards into 3 or 4 pieces each.

In a large saucepan, melt the butter over medium heat. Add the onion and celery and sauté for about 15 minutes, until soft and sweet. Add the chicken broth, bay leaf, and gizzards and increase the heat to high. Bring to a boil, then reduce the heat and simmer until the gizzards are tender, which could take anywhere from 1 to 2 hours, depending on the toughness of the gizzards and your height above sea level. Remove the bay leaf, add the potatoes, and cook until they're tender. Just before serving, stir in the raw cream and add salt and pepper to taste.

Polish Penicillin (Gizzard and Heart Soup)

Laurel Lovelace, Elizabethton, Tennessee

I grew up on chicken gizzards and hearts. My mom made soup from them every Sunday, and we called it Polish penicillin. My Polish great-grandmother made this soup and I'm the fourth generation (at least) still making it. Gizzards and hearts are great when simmered long enough to make them tender.

Serves 6 to 8

1 pound chicken gizzards

½ pound chicken hearts

2 quarts homemade chicken broth

1 onion, peeled and finely chopped

1 stick celery, finely chopped

2 carrots, peeled, cut lengthwise, and thinly sliced

10 whole allspice berries, placed in a tea ball

Sea salt and freshly ground black pepper

Cooked noodles

Finely chopped fresh parsley

Wash the gizzards and hearts. Look over the gizzards for bits of wrinkly yellow skin, which is the inside of the gizzard, and remove it (it peels off easily). Remove any blood clots from the hearts by squeezing them. Cut the gizzards into 2 or 3 pieces, but leave the hearts whole.

Place the cleaned gizzards and hearts in a large saucepan and add the broth; add additional water if necessary to cover the gizzards and hearts by 2 to 3 inches. Bring to a boil over medium heat and carefully skim the scum that rises to the surface with a slotted spoon or small wire strainer.

Add the onion, celery, carrots, and allspice, return to a simmer, then reduce the heat and simmer with the lid askew for about 2 hours, until the gizzards are very tender. Season with salt and pepper. Serve over noodles prepared according to package directions and garnish with parsley.

Soup Memories

My two German grandmothers, both still alive and in good health in their mid-nineties, cook the way they learned from their own mothers and grandmothers, using lots of bone broth, gravies, sauces, and stews. When I would arrive at my grandma's house after a seven-hour car ride, she would be waiting for me with her homemade bone broth; that was a soothing and replenishing moment. For her broth she would boil the meat on the bone, including some bones with lots of marrow, for about 2 hours. She would also add *Suppengrün*, which means "soup greens"; it is a bundle of roots, bulbs, and herbs, usually a couple of carrots, leeks, celery sticks, and some parsley. This bundle is available in German grocery stores and markets. The *Suppengrün* veggies are added whole to the broth and later discarded or sometimes eaten alongside the finished soup.

This kind of clear bone-veggie broth, or consommé, is usually eaten with something in it, like thin pancakes cut into strips (you pour the broth over them right before serving), little *Grießklößchen* (dumplings made of semolina), or my favorite, *Markklößchen*, or marrow dumplings.

The next day she would make my grandpa's favorite dish, *Tafelspitz* with *Meerrettichsauce*, which consists of the cut-up cooked meat from the broth and a delicious sauce made of bone broth, fresh cream, flour, and grated horseradish, served with cooked potatoes.

When I was a child, my favorite recipe was German oxtail soup, made with oxtail broth and cream. Only now I understand why I was craving this dish while I was going through my early childhood growing phase.

—Tamara Hiller, Itacaré, Brazil

Bone Marrow Dumpling Soup

Tamara Hiller, Itacaré, Brazil

Serves 8

2 quarts homemade beef stock, made with 8-inch marrowbones (along with the other bones),
    reserving the bones with their marrow
2 eggs
1 teaspoon finely chopped fresh parsley
Pinch of freshly grated nutmeg
Sea salt and freshly ground black pepper
1 to 2 cups sourdough breadcrumbs

Scoop out the marrow from the cooked bones and mash it with a fork, or pass it through a strainer by mashing it with a spoon.

In a medium bowl, mix the marrow with the eggs, parsley, nutmeg, salt and pepper to taste, and enough breadcrumbs for the dumplings to hold together. Form one ball, about ¾ inch in diameter; this is your test dumpling.

In a large saucepan, bring the stock to a simmer. Drop the test dumpling into the stock and cook until cooked through, keeping track of how long it took and adjusting the seasonings and amount of breadcrumbs if necessary. For example, if the dumpling is too soft or falls apart, add more breadcrumbs and try again. Once you have the mixture right, drop the marrow dumplings into the broth using a teaspoon and simmer them until cooked through. Ladle into bowls and serve.

Tom Yum Soup

Sharon Watt, Bay of Plenty, New Zealand

Serves 4

About 6 cups homemade chicken broth
Juice and grated zest of 1 large organic lemon
1 fresh red chile, seeded and finely chopped, or ½ teaspoon dried red chile flakes
1 spring onion, thinly sliced
3 to 4 tablespoons fish sauce, to taste
7 to 10 ounces raw chicken or beef, thinly sliced
¼ cup finely chopped fresh cilantro

Pour the broth into a large saucepan. Add the lemon zest and juice, the chile, spring onion, and fish sauce, place over medium-high heat, and bring to a simmer. Reduce the heat and simmer for 5 minutes, then add the chicken and simmer for another minute, or until cooked through. Remove from the heat and add the cilantro. Let it sit to infuse for a minute or two, then ladle into bowls and serve.

Spicy Coconut Chicken and Shrimp Soup

Barbara Drury, Whitehorse, Canada

Serves 8

2 cups very thinly sliced green cabbage

Juice of 1 lemon or lime

2 quarts homemade chicken broth

¼ cup coconut oil

1 pound cremini mushrooms, sliced

1 clove garlic, finely minced

3 to 4 fresh jalapeño chiles, seeded and chopped

⅓ cup grated fresh ginger

½ cup Pesto Sauce (page 269)

2 cups frozen peeled small shrimp

2 cups cooked diced chicken

1 (13.5-ounce) can coconut milk

Leaves from 1 bunch fresh cilantro, chopped

Tamari sauce

Fish sauce

Sea salt and freshly ground black pepper

In a large bowl, toss the cabbage with the lemon juice; set aside.

In a large saucepan, bring the broth to a simmer over medium-high heat.

While the broth is heating up, melt the coconut oil in a large sauté pan over medium heat. Add the mushrooms and garlic and sauté, stirring frequently, until softened, about 10 minutes. Add the jalapeños and ginger, cook for 1 minute, and transfer the contents of the pan to the broth. Stir in the pesto and shrimp. Return the broth to a simmer, stir in the chicken, cabbage, coconut milk, and cilantro, and cook to heat through. Season with tamari, fish sauce, and salt and pepper, ladle into bowls, and serve.

Borscht

Lorraine Carlstrom, Nelson, Canada

Serves 6 to 8

3 tablespoons butter or ghee

1 medium onion, peeled and chopped

½ cup chopped celery

1 medium carrot, peeled and chopped

2 medium potatoes, scrubbed and chopped

4 cloves garlic, peeled and crushed

4 cups homemade chicken or turkey stock

2 cups blended fresh tomatoes or 1 (28-ounce) can crushed tomatoes

1 medium beet, peeled and grated

½ head green cabbage, cored and shredded or very thinly sliced

2 tablespoons apple cider vinegar or lemon juice

1 cup heavy cream

¼ cup chopped fresh dill

Sea salt and freshly ground black pepper

Sour cream

In a large saucepan, melt the butter over medium heat. Add the onion and sauté for about 5 minutes, until it starts to soften. Add the celery and carrot and cook, stirring, for about 5 minutes, until softened. Add the potatoes, garlic, stock, tomatoes, beet, and cabbage. Increase the heat to medium-high, bring to a boil, then reduce the heat and simmer for 10 minutes, or until the potatoes are softened. Add the vinegar, cream, and dill and season with salt and pepper; cook for another 5 minutes. Ladle into bowls and serve with a dollop of sour cream.

Chicken Noodle Soup

Sarah Nicholson, Vale, Australia

Serves 4

1 cup cooked rice noodles

About 2 cups shredded vegetables such as carrots, cabbage, and spring onions

About 1 cup diced vegetables such as broccoli or snow peas

1 quart homemade chicken broth, brought to a simmer

Naturally fermented soy sauce or sea salt

Divide the noodles and shredded and diced vegetables among 4 bowls. Pour the simmering broth on top. Have your diners season their bowls with soy sauce to taste.

Spicy Beef Soup with Kale

Barbara Drury, Whitehorse, Canada

Serves 8

2 quarts homemade beef broth

⅔ cup coconut oil, lard, or beef fat

1 large or 2 medium onions, peeled and sliced

1 pound cremini or wild mushrooms, sliced

2 cloves garlic, finely minced

3 jalapeño chiles, seeds removed and thinly sliced

1 pound beef steak (such as sirloin or inside round), thinly sliced

Sea salt and freshly ground black pepper

Tamari sauce

Fish sauce

4 large leaves fresh kale, stemmed and chopped

1 bunch green onions, chopped

In a large saucepan, heat the broth to a simmer.

Meanwhile, melt ⅓ cup of the coconut oil in a large skillet over medium heat. Add the onions, mushrooms, 1 clove of the garlic, and the jalapeños and sauté until softened and lightly browned, about 10 minutes. Tip the contents of the pan into the broth and wipe out the pan.

Melt the remaining ⅓ cup coconut oil in the pan over medium-high heat. Pat the beef slices dry with paper towels, add to the pan along with the remaining garlic clove, and stir-fry, stirring constantly to prevent the beef and garlic from sticking to the bottom of the pan. Cook until the meat is pink. Tip the contents of the pan into the simmering broth.

Season the broth with salt, pepper, tamari, and fish sauce and simmer for 10 to 15 minutes for flavors to blend. Add the kale and cook until the kale turns an intense shade of green. Ladle into bowls and garnish with the green onions.

Seafood Chowder

Lorraine Carlstrom, Nelson, Canada

Serves 4 to 6

3 tablespoons butter or ghee

1 onion, finely chopped

3 celery sticks, finely chopped

½ cup white wine (optional)

5 cups homemade fish stock

½ cup tomato paste

2 large carrots, peeled and chopped

3 to 4 medium potatoes, cut into ¼-inch cubes

3 cloves garlic, minced

1 teaspoon dried thyme

½ teaspoon dried oregano

1 teaspoon sea salt, or to taste

Freshly ground black pepper

½ cup freshly grated Parmesan cheese

½ pound halibut or cod, cut into chunks

½ pound scallops, cut into pieces

½ pound prawns, cut into pieces, or ½ pound whole small shrimp

Melt the butter in a large heavy saucepan over medium heat. Add the onion and celery and sauté until softened, about 5 minutes. Add the optional wine and bring to a simmer. Add the stock, tomato paste, carrots, potatoes, garlic, thyme, oregano, salt, and pepper to taste. Increase the heat to high, bring to a boil, then reduce the heat, cover, and simmer for 15 to 20 minutes, until the vegetables are just tender. Add the cheese, halibut, scallops, and prawns, return to a simmer, and simmer until the seafood is just cooked through, about 5 minutes. Ladle into bowls and serve.

Asian Seafood Soup

Pamela Lund, Stanton, California

Serves 4 to 6

2 bunches green onions

6 cups homemade fish broth

¼ cup naturally fermented soy sauce

¼ cup fish sauce

1 clove garlic, peeled and minced

2 red chiles or jalapeño chiles, seeded and thinly sliced

1 tablespoon peeled and minced fresh ginger

1 cup sweet potato starch noodles (*dangmyeon*; optional)

1 head Napa cabbage, roughly chopped

4 cups seafood of choice, such as clams, mussels, scallops, shrimp, or fish fillets cut into chunks

Slice the white parts of green onions lengthwise; chop the green stems and reserve for garnish.

In a large saucepan, combine the broth, soy sauce, and fish sauce. Place over medium-high heat and bring to a simmer. Add the whites from the green onions, the garlic, chiles, and ginger and return to a simmer. Reduce the heat and simmer for 15 minutes. Add the optional noodles and simmer for about 10 minutes, until al dente. Lift bunches of noodles up from the pan, cut them with kitchen scissors (the noodles are almost impossible to cut when uncooked), and plunge them back into the pan. Add the cabbage, then add the seafood and simmer for about 5 minutes, until the clams or mussels open (discard any shells that don't open) or the scallops, shrimp, or fish are cooked through. Ladle into bowls and serve topped with the greens from the green onions.

Amber Fish Soup

Adapted from The Art of Russian Cuisine, *by Anne Volokh and Mavis Manus*

Serves 6

2 quarts Russian Fish Broth (page 173)

⅛ teaspoon saffron threads

3 medium potatoes, peeled and cut into 1-inch cubes

2 pounds fresh or frozen and thawed salmon, cut into 6 pieces

Sea salt

6 thin slices peeled lemon

Pour the broth into a large saucepan, place over high heat, and bring to a boil. Place the saffron in a cup or small bowl and add a little of the broth to help it "bloom"; set aside. Add the potatoes and the salmon to the broth, partially cover, and simmer for another 8 to 10 minutes, until the fish and potatoes are cooked through. Season with salt and add the reserved saffron and liquid.

To serve, place a piece of fish in each of 6 heated soup bowls, top with a thin slice of lemon, and pour the broth over the fish.

Blended Soups

Shrimp Bisque Method I

Bisque—a creamy thick soup based on shrimp or lobster—is the jewel in the crown of good chefs. Two methods are given here: one begins with already thickened shrimp shell stock, and the other uses a small amount of flour for thickening. Both versions are delicious!

Serves 6 to 8

4 cups Shrimp Shell Stock (page 175)
1 small can or jar tomato paste
1 cup crème fraîche
½ cup sherry
Sea salt and freshly ground black pepper
Chopped chives, croutons, or cooked shrimp

Combine the stock, tomato paste, and crème fraîche in a blender and blend until smooth. Transfer to a large saucepan and bring to a simmer. Stir in the sherry, turn off the heat, and season with salt and pepper. Ladle into heated bowls and serve. The soup can be garnished with chopped chives, homemade croutons, or a few cooked shrimp.

Shrimp Bisque Method II

Pamela Lund, Stanton, California

Serves 6

6 tablespoons butter
Shells from 1 pound medium to large shrimp
Heads from 1 pound medium to large shrimp (optional)
2 medium onions, cut in half and sliced
1 large carrot, peeled and sliced

2 celery sticks, sliced

5 to 6 cups homemade fish or chicken broth

Juice of ½ lemon

2 tablespoons tomato paste

2 bay leaves

6 cloves garlic, peeled and coarsely chopped

¼ cup unbleached white flour or potato flour

3 tablespoons brandy, Marsala, or Madeira

Sea salt

⅔ cup heavy cream

Freshly ground black pepper

Melt 2 tablespoons of the butter in a large saucepan over medium heat. Add the shrimp shells and optional shrimp heads, and cook, stirring, until the shells start to brown, about 10 minutes. Add the onions, carrot, and celery and cook, stirring occasionally, until the onions begin to soften, about 5 minutes. Add the broth, lemon juice, tomato paste, bay leaves, and garlic. Increase the heat to high, bring to a boil, skim the top of any scum, then reduce the heat and simmer about 45 minutes. Let cool and strain into a bowl. Rinse out the pan.

Melt the remaining 4 tablespoons butter in the pan over medium-low heat and stir in the flour. Cook the mixture, stirring constantly, until it starts to brown, about 10 minutes. Add the brandy and about a third of the shrimp stock and whisk vigorously to mix in the flour. Slowly add the rest of the stock 1 cup at a time, whisking the whole time to ensure that all of the flour is thoroughly mixed in. Cover and simmer for another 5 minutes, then season with salt. Add the cream, mix it in well, and heat it through. Ladle into bowls and serve topped with a grinding of pepper.

Curry Soup

Donna and Ashley Sherman, Bloomington, Illinois

Serves 12

¼ cup coconut oil

2 onions, peeled and chopped

2 tablespoons peeled and grated fresh ginger

5 cloves garlic, minced

1½ teaspoons ground coriander

1½ teaspoons ground cumin

1 teaspoon ground turmeric

½ teaspoon ground allspice

3 quarts homemade chicken stock

1 medium butternut squash, baked, seeds removed and flesh scooped out

1½ pounds spinach or other greens, chopped

2 cups chopped chicken meat

Sea salt

Heat the coconut oil in a large saucepan over medium heat. Add the onions and ginger and sauté until softened, about 5 minutes. Add the garlic, coriander, cumin, turmeric, and allspice and sauté for 1 minute. Add the stock and butternut squash, increase the heat to high, bring to a boil, and blend well with a whisk or handheld blender. Add the greens, return to a simmer, and simmer for about 3 to 5 minutes, until the spinach is wilted. Add the chicken and cook to heat it through. Season with salt, ladle into bowls, and serve.

Carrot Soup

Laurent Langlais, Antony, France

Serves 6

1 quart homemade chicken broth

2 pounds carrots, peeled and sliced

1 large yellow onion, peeled and sliced

2 cloves garlic, peeled and coarsely chopped

2 (13.5-ounce) cans coconut milk

Pinch of ground cinnamon

Pinch of ground cumin

Sea salt and freshly ground black pepper

Pour the broth into a large saucepan. Add the carrots, onion, garlic, and coconut milk, place over high heat, and bring to a simmer. Reduce the heat and simmer uncovered for 1½ to 2 hours, until the soup has reduced by about one-third and the carrots are tender. Transfer to a blender in batches and puree. Return to the pan, reheat if necessary, add the cinnamon and cumin, and season with salt and pepper. Ladle into bowls and serve.

Cream of Mushroom Soup

Pamela Lund, Stanton, California

To maximize the flavor of this delicious soup, cool the soup after preparing it, pour it into an airtight container, refrigerate overnight, and reheat the following day.

Serves 10 to 12

1 pound fresh mushrooms, such as cremini, shiitake, baby bella, or portobello

8 tablespoons (1 stick) butter

1 medium yellow onion, peeled and diced

6 cups homemade chicken or beef stock

1 large leek or 2 small leeks, white and light green parts, sliced

1 cup white wine

¼ to ½ cup heavy cream, plus more for serving if you like

Sea salt and freshly ground black pepper

Chopped fresh chives (optional)

Clean the mushroom tops with a dampened paper towel. Pull off the stems and set aside. Cut the mushroom caps into ¼-inch slices.

Melt 1 tablespoon of the butter in a large saucepan over medium heat. Add the mushroom stems and onion and sauté until the onion is softened and translucent, about 5 minutes. Add the stock, increase the heat to high, and bring to a simmer. Reduce the heat and simmer, uncovered, for 20 to 30 minutes, until the mushrooms are very tender. Strain the mushroom stems and onions from the stock into a large heatproof bowl; discard the mushroom stems and onions and reserve the stock.

While the stock is simmering, in a second large saucepan, melt 3½ tablespoons of the remaining butter over low heat, add the leeks, and sauté until the leeks start to color, about 5 minutes. Add the sliced mushroom caps and the remaining 3½ tablespoons butter. Cook for 10 to 15 minutes, stirring occasionally, until the mushrooms are softened and browned. Add the wine and simmer a few minutes. Add the strained stock to the pan and simmer for 10 to 15 minutes to combine the flavors.

Blend the soup with a handheld blender for a few seconds to chop up the mushroom pieces. Add the cream, starting with ¼ cup and working up until you find the consistency and flavor you like. If the soup is too thin, simmer uncovered a bit to reduce it. Season with salt and pepper. Ladle into bowls and serve topped with chives and an extra swirl of cream if you like.

Ancho Chile and Cauliflower Soup

Nicole Gustavson, Leesburg, Virginia

This soup freezes very nicely in quart containers, with about 2 servings per container.

Serves 10

3 tablespoons coconut oil or butter

2 tablespoons ground ancho chile (see Sources, page 295)

2 tablespoons sea salt

4 large heads cauliflower, cut into florets

6 large cloves garlic, peeled

2 large onions, peeled and roughly chopped

3 quarts homemade chicken broth

Leaves from 1 bunch fresh cilantro

Freshly ground white or black pepper

About 1 cup heavy cream or crème fraîche

Freshly grated Parmesan cheese

Melt the coconut oil or butter in a stockpot over medium heat. Add the chile powder and salt and stir to incorporate it into the oil. Add cauliflower florets, garlic, onions, and broth, increase the heat to high, and bring to a simmer. Reduce the heat, cover, and simmer until the florets, garlic, and onions are very soft, about 10 to 15 minutes. Add the cilantro and simmer for 1 to 2 minutes. Blend with a handheld blender or in a standing blender until smooth. Season with pepper. If soup is too thick, thin with a little water.

Ladle into bowls, swirl a generous spoonful of cream into the individual bowls, and sprinkle with cheese.

Asparagus Soup

Lydia Palermo, Monument, Colorado

Serves 4 to 6

1 tablespoon butter

1 small onion or large shallot, peeled and diced

3 cloves garlic, peeled and smashed

2 cups homemade chicken stock

1 bunch asparagus, woody ends trimmed (save them for stock), cut into 1-inch pieces

Sea salt and freshly ground black pepper

1 cup crème fraîche or sour cream, at room temperature

Extra-virgin olive oil

Melt the butter in a large saucepan over medium heat. Add the onion and sauté until softened, about 3 minutes. Add the garlic and sauté until colored, about 2 minutes. Add the stock and blend with a handheld blender until smooth. Add the asparagus, bring to a simmer, and simmer for 5 minutes, or until the asparagus is softened. Blend again with the handheld blender until smooth. Season with salt and pepper. Remove from the heat and let cool for a few minutes. Stir in the crème fraîche, ladle into bowls, and finish with a small drizzle of oil.

Apple-Onion Cream Soup

Adapted from Anne Mendelson, Milk: The Surprising Story of Milk Through the Ages

Serves 6

4 to 6 thick slices of bacon

3 to 4 tart juicy apples, peeled, cored, quartered, and coarsely diced

4 tablespoons butter

4 large onions, peeled and coarsely diced

1 quart homemade beef broth

6 to 8 whole allspice berries, lightly bruised

1 cup heavy cream

Sea salt and freshly ground black pepper

Dash of fresh lemon juice (optional)

1 teaspoon caraway seeds, lightly bruised (optional)

Cook the bacon slowly in a heavy skillet over low heat to render out all the fat and crisp it. Remove the bacon from the skillet, drain it on paper towels, and crumble it. Increase the heat under the skillet to medium, add the apples, and cook, stirring occasionally, until cooked through, about 5 minutes. Scoop out a few spoonfuls of the apples for garnish and set aside.

Meanwhile, melt the butter in a large heavy saucepan over low heat. When it foams and sizzles, add the chopped onions and sauté very patiently, stirring frequently, for 15 to 20 minutes, until the onions are well softened and starting to brown. Scoop out a few spoonfuls for garnish and set aside with the reserved apples.

Add the cooked apples to the onions, pour in the broth, add the allspice, and raise the heat to high. Bring to a simmer, then reduce the heat and simmer until the ingredients are nearly dissolved, 10 to 15 minutes. Fish out and discard the allspice berries.

Puree the soup in batches in a blender or food processor, leaving some chunks for a slightly coarse texture. Return the soup to the pan, bring just to a boil, and stir in the cream. Return to a boil, turn off the heat, and season with salt and pepper. If the soup needs a little brightening, add a little lemon juice. If it is too thick, thin it with some hot water.

Ladle into bowls and serve garnished with the reserved bacon, apple, and onion and a scattering of optional caraway seeds.

Cold Weather Root Soup

Serves 8

4 tablespoons (½ stick) butter

3 medium onions, peeled and sliced

2 leeks, white and light green parts, halved lengthwise, washed well, and sliced

5 carrots, peeled and sliced

3 cloves garlic, peeled and smashed

1 bay leaf

2 small turnips, peeled, quartered lengthwise, and thinly sliced

3 parsnips, peeled, halved lengthwise, and sliced

2 medium potatoes, peeled, quartered lengthwise, and thinly sliced

6½ cups homemade chicken broth

¼ teaspoon freshly grated nutmeg

1 cup heavy cream

Sea salt and freshly ground black pepper

Pinch of ground cayenne

Freshly grated Parmesan or cheddar cheese

Melt the butter in a large saucepan over medium heat. Add the onions, leeks, carrots, garlic, and bay leaf, tossing to coat them in the butter. Cover the pan and cook, stirring occasionally, until the vegetables are wilted, about 15 minutes. Add the turnips, parsnips, potatoes, broth, and nutmeg. Increase the heat to high and bring to a boil. Reduce the heat and simmer, covered, until the vegetables are very tender, about 1 hour. Remove the bay leaf.

Use a handheld blender to puree the soup. Add the cream and return to a simmer. Season with salt and pepper and the cayenne. If soup is too thick, thin it with a little water. Ladle into bowls and serve with a sprinkling of cheese.

Moroccan-Style Butternut Squash Soup

Serves 4 to 6

1 large butternut squash

¼ cup extra virgin olive oil

2 medium onions, peeled and chopped

5 large cloves garlic, chopped

½ teaspoon ground cumin

1 teaspoon ground coriander

¼ teaspoon ground cinnamon

¼ teaspoon ground allspice

¼ teaspoon ground turmeric

Scant ¼ teaspoon ground cayenne

½ teaspoon paprika

1 medium tart apple, cored, peeled, and chopped

1 quart homemade chicken broth

Sea salt and freshly ground black pepper

Juice of 1 lemon, strained

5 or 6 green onions, thinly sliced

¼ cup chopped fresh cilantro

Preheat the oven to 400°F.

Cut the squash in half lengthwise, remove the seeds, and place facedown on an oiled baking pan. Bake until tender, about 1 hour. Remove from the oven and let the squash cool. Scoop out and discard the seeds. Scoop the flesh out of the skin and reserve it.

Heat the oil in a large saucepan over medium heat. Add the onions and sauté until softened, about 5 minutes. Stir in the garlic, cumin, coriander, cinnamon, allspice, turmeric, cayenne, paprika, and chopped apple and sauté for about 30 seconds, until aromatic. Add the reserved squash and the broth, increase the heat to high, and bring to a simmer. Reduce the heat and simmer for about 20 minutes, or until the apple is very soft.

Remove from the heat, let the soup cool slightly, and puree it in the pan with a hand-held blender. Season with salt and pepper and stir in the lemon juice. Ladle into bowls and top each serving with green onion and cilantro.

Soups That Make Their Own Broth

Caribbean-Style Cock Soup

Adrienne Hew, Kailua-Kona, Hawaii

Cock soup is a tradition in many countries. It was especially reserved for pregnant women in Jamaican households, to ensure the birth of healthy babies. In fact, when my uncle left Jamaica to pursue his fortune in England before sending for his growing family, my grandfather prepared this soup every day for my aunt. It is clear from the beautiful bone structure, straight teeth, clear skin, and overall vibrant health of her children that feeding cock soup to pregnant women is the best way to avoid costly visits to the orthopedist, orthodontist, dermatologist, and even your regular family doctor. Many modern Jamaicans, however, have forgotten this practice and opt for the MSG-filled dried version widely sold in grocery stores. As a result, younger generations suffer the same deformities and problems as children in industrialized countries.

Serves 6

1 whole cock or chicken

1 tablespoon apple cider vinegar

About 4 quarts cold filtered water

½ pound yucca, peeled and diced

1 pound potatoes, peeled and diced

1 unripe chayote, peeled and diced

1 small onion, peeled and diced

2 cloves garlic, peeled and smashed

2 carrots, peeled and diced

2 celery sticks, finely chopped

5 sprigs fresh thyme, or 1 teaspoon dried thyme

Sea salt

1 whole scotch bonnet chile

Place the cock in a stockpot and add the vinegar and enough cold filtered water to cover. Place over medium heat, cover, and bring to a simmer. Reduce the heat to low and simmer for 60 minutes, removing any scum that accumulates at the top of the stock. Add the yucca, potatoes, chayote, onion, garlic, carrots, celery, and thyme to the pot and cook for another 60 minutes. Lift out the cock and remove the meat from bones. Reserve the bones for enriching other batches of stock. Return about 1 cup of meat to the pot, reserving the rest for another dish. Season with salt and add the chile. Be careful not to puncture the chile or your soup will be too peppery to enjoy; by leaving it whole, you will get the aroma of the chile, which is much more pleasing. Ladle into bowls and serve. Freeze extra for an easy dinner on a busy night.

Miracle Cock Soup

Adrienne Hew, Kailua-Kona, Hawaii

Yes, it's a bold claim to suggest that something as simple as a bowl of soup might actually be able to cure the common cold, but I have used this remedy for more than twenty years with great success. In fact, I have been able to chase colds and flu away in as little as two hours using this concoction, followed by a nap under a warm blanket. A few years ago a friend of mine was telling me that chicken soup was not helping her son's cold and fever. I suggested she add the following ingredients to the soup and try again, then have him take a nap in warm bedclothes. Three hours later, she called me to say that his fever had broken and he was acting like his old self. As the name of this soup indicates, it might have other beneficial effects that manifest after the flu is banished!

Makes about 4 quarts

1 whole cock or chicken, preferably including head and feet

1 tablespoon apple cider vinegar

About 4 quarts cold filtered water

1-inch piece fresh ginger, peeled and cut into 5 pieces

3 cloves garlic, peeled and smashed

1 large onion, peeled and thinly sliced

2 carrots, peeled and sliced on an angle

2 celery sticks, thinly sliced

3 cups assorted diced vegetables, such as leafy cooking greens, green beans, turnips,
    potatoes, or any other vegetables lying at the bottom of your crisper drawer

Sea salt

3 ounces mung bean noodles

Place the cock in a stockpot and add the vinegar and enough cold filtered water to cover. Add the ginger and garlic, place over medium heat, cover, and bring to a simmer. Reduce the heat to low and simmer, covered, for 60 minutes, removing any scum from the top of the stock. Add the onion, carrots, celery, and assorted vegetables to the pot and cook for another 60 minutes. Lift out the cock and remove the meat from the bones. Reserve the bones for making additional stock. Return about 1 cup of meat to the pot, reserving the rest for other dishes. Season with salt. Add the noodles and cook for about 2 minutes, until cooked through. Ladle into bowls and serve.

Vietnamese Beef Pho

Nourishing pho is a popular snack food in Vietnam, usually prepared by corner shop mom-and-pop vendors.

Serves about 10

5 pounds meaty beef knucklebones

2 gallons cold filtered water

½ cup vinegar

2 pounds beef oxtail

1 daikon radish, peeled and sliced

2 onions, peeled and chopped

⅓ cup whole star anise pods

½ cinnamon stick

2 whole cloves

1 teaspoon whole black peppercorns

1 slice peeled fresh ginger

1 tablespoon white sugar

1 tablespoon sea salt, or to taste

1 tablespoon fish sauce

1½ pounds dried flat rice noodles

½ pound frozen beef sirloin, partially thawed and sliced paper thin

TOPPINGS

Sriracha or Tabasco sauce

Hoisin sauce

Thinly sliced onion

Chopped fresh cilantro

Mung bean sprouts

Chopped fresh Thai basil

Thinly sliced green onion

Lime quarters

Place the beef knucklebones in a very large (9-quart or more) pot. Fill the pot with the 2 gallons of cold filtered water and the vinegar. Bring to a simmer over medium-high heat, then reduce the heat to low, carefully spoon off any scum that rises to the top, and simmer for about 2 hours.

Skim the fat from the surface of the soup and add the oxtail, radish, and onions. Tie the star anise pods, cinnamon stick, cloves, peppercorns, and ginger in cheesecloth and add it to the soup. Stir in the sugar, salt, and fish sauce. Return to a simmer and simmer for at least 4 more hours (the longer the better). Taste and add more salt if needed. Strain the broth and discard the spices and bones. Reserve the meat from the beef knucklebones for another use. Return the soup to the pot and keep it at a simmer.

Meanwhile, soak the rice noodles in a bowl of warm water for about 20 minutes, then drain. Bring a separate large pot of lightly salted water to a boil, add the noodles, and cook until softened, about 5 minutes. Drain.

Place some noodles into soup bowls and top with a few raw beef slices. Ladle simmering broth over the beef and noodles in the bowls. Serve with the toppings alongside for diners to add as they wish.

Rich Beef and Vegetable Bone Broth Soup

Katherine Pirtle, Addison, Illinois

Makes about 4 quarts

1 oxtail, cut into pieces

1 beef knucklebone

Several beef marrowbones

Several meaty soup bones, such as ribs or shank

2 tablespoons vinegar

About 4 quarts cold filtered water

1 to 2 pounds beef stew meat, cut into small pieces

2 to 3 large onions, peeled and chopped

4 large carrots, peeled and sliced

4 large beets, peeled and sliced

4 ounces Swiss chard, chopped

1 large bunch fresh parsley, chopped

Other vegetables of your choice (whatever you have available), chopped

2 cups dry red wine

Sea salt

Place the oxtail, knucklebone, marrow-bones, and soup bones in a stockpot. Add the vinegar and enough cold filtered water to cover the bones. Let stand for 30 to 60 minutes. Place over medium heat, uncovered, bring to a bare simmer, and carefully spoon off any scum that rises to the top. Lower the heat to low and cook at a bare simmer with the lid off or slightly askew for 3 to 4 hours, until the meat from the soup bones and oxtail is cooked. Remove the bones, let them cool, take the meat off the bones, and refrigerate the meat to add to the soup later. Put the bones back in the pot and continue simmering for about another 24 hours, occasionally skimming scum from the top as needed and checking to ensure that the bones remain covered with water and adding more water as needed.

Remove the bones with tongs and a slotted spoon. Strain the stock through a fine-mesh strainer into 2-quart Pyrex measuring containers or a large heatproof bowl (see tips for straining on page 149). Cool to room temperature, then refrigerate uncovered for several hours, until the fat rises to the top and congeals. Skim off this fat (you can use it in your cooking) and return the broth to a stockpot. (If not using right away, transfer the stock to containers, cover, and store in the refrigerator for up to 5 days or in the freezer for many months.) Add the reserved meat from the bones, the stew meat, onions, carrots, beets, chard, parsley, other vegetables, and wine. Bring to a simmer and simmer for about 20 minutes. Season with salt, ladle into bowls, and serve.

Pea and Ham Hock Soup

Jill Freeman, Bay of Plenty, New Zealand

Serves 8 to 12

1 ham hock

About 3 quarts cold filtered water

4 cups green split peas, soaked overnight in water and a splash of apple cider vinegar

2 carrots, peeled and diced

2 onions, peeled and diced

Sea salt and freshly ground black pepper

Place the ham hock in a large saucepan and add cold filtered water to cover. Place over medium heat, uncovered, bring to a bare simmer, and carefully spoon off any scum that rises to the top. Add the split peas, carrots, and onions, then lower the heat to low and cook at a bare simmer with the lid off or slightly askew for about 6 hours, until the meat comes off the bone easily, adding more water if needed.

Remove the ham hock from the soup and strip the meat from it, making sure to remove the layer of fat from the underside of the skin.

Cut the meat and fat into bite-size pieces and place them back in the pan. If soup is too thick, thin with some water. Season with salt and pepper, ladle into bowls, and serve.

Oxtail Soup

Beverly Rubik, PhD, Oakland, California

Makes about 4 quarts

3 to 4 tablespoons lard

2 to 2½ pounds oxtail pieces

About 4 quarts cold filtered water

2 bay leaves

1 cup red wine (optional)

½ cup pearled barley (optional)

1 pound carrots, peeled and cut into 1-inch pieces

1 pound parsnips, peeled and cut into 1-inch pieces

1 large turnip, peeled and cut into 1-inch pieces

1 large onion, peeled and diced

3 to 6 cloves garlic, minced

1 pound brown mushrooms, sliced

Sea salt and freshly ground black pepper

1 to 2 tablespoons of dried herbs de Provence (or 1 to 2 tablespoons dried thyme)

1 bunch fresh parsley, finely chopped

Melt the lard in a stockpot over medium heat. Add the oxtail pieces and cook, stirring, until lightly browned, about 10 minutes. Add cold filtered water to cover the oxtail pieces, then add the bay leaves. Place over medium heat, uncovered, bring to a bare simmer, and carefully spoon off any scum that rises to the top. Add the optional wine and optional barley, then lower the heat to low and cook at a bare simmer with the lid off or slightly askew for 90 minutes. Add the carrots, parsnips, turnip, onion, garlic, mushrooms, and more water, if necessary, to cover them, and simmer for another 45 minutes, or until tender. Season with salt and pepper. Add the herbs de Provence and simmer for another 30 minutes, or until the meat is falling off the bone.

Remove oxtail pieces with tongs and a slotted spoon. Remove the meat from the bones, chop it finely, and return it to the pot. Stir in the parsley and season with salt and pepper. Ladle into bowls and serve.

Geoffrey's Soup

Geoffrey Morell, Brandywine, Maryland

Sally's husband, Geoffrey, makes this soup every couple of months and freezes it in 1-quart containers. That way they always have nourishing, gelatin-rich soup ready to thaw, heat up, and eat. The best meat to use is oxtail, but other meaty bones will also work. Vegetables can be anything you have on hand—this is a great way to clean out the vegetable drawers in your refrigerator. To prepare the vegetables, peel and slice hard vegetables such as carrots, parsnips, and turnips. For softer vegetables such as broccoli, asparagus, cabbage, lettuce, peppers, tomatoes, and lettuce, place in a food processor in batches and pulse until cut into small pieces.

Makes about 8 quarts

About 5 pounds oxtail, cut into sections, or about 5 pounds meaty bones

About 8 quarts cold filtered water

1 cup pearled barley

1 cup red lentils

About 8 cups chopped vegetables

2-inch piece fresh ginger, peeled and grated

About ½ teaspoon ground cayenne, or to taste

1 teaspoon paprika

4 tablespoons dried herbs such as oregano, thyme, and sage

Sea salt

Finely chopped fresh parsley

Sour cream or crème fraîche

Place the oxtail in a stockpot and add the cold filtered water. Place over medium heat, uncovered, bring to a bare simmer, and carefully spoon off any scum that rises to the top. Add the barley, lentils, vegetables, ginger, cayenne, paprika, and herbs, then lower the heat to low. Cook at a bare simmer with the lid off or slightly askew for 4 to 8 hours, occasionally skimming scum from the top as needed and checking to ensure that the bones remain covered with water and adding more water as needed.

Remove the oxtail with tongs and a slotted spoon. Cut away the meat and cartilage, finely chop it, and set aside.

Use a handheld blender to partially blend the soup, leaving some chunks. Return the meat to the soup and season with salt.

Ladle into bowls and serve with a sprinkling of parsley and sour cream on the side, along with toasted sourdough bread and plenty of butter.

Slovenian Sour Pork Soup

This sour pork soup is traditionally the final dish served at wedding receptions, usually after midnight.

Serves 6

1 split pig's foot

About 1 pound combination of pork meat and organ meats, such as lung, stomach or tripe, and heart, diced

About 10 cups cold filtered water

1 bay leaf

4 sprigs fresh thyme, plus fresh thyme leaves

1 teaspoon cumin seeds

2 cloves garlic, chopped

2 tablespoons lard

1 onion, peeled and chopped

2 tablespoons unbleached white flour

½ teaspoon paprika

Apple cider vinegar or dry white wine

Sea salt and freshly ground black pepper

Place the pig's foot and organ meats in a stockpot and add cold filtered water to cover. Place over medium heat, uncovered, bring to a bare simmer, and carefully spoon off any scum that rises to the top. Add the bay leaf, thyme sprigs, cumin seeds, and garlic, then lower the heat to low. Cover and cook at a bare simmer for about 2 hours, occasionally skimming scum from the top as needed and checking to ensure that the bones remain covered with water and adding more water as needed, until the meat is tender.

Melt the lard in a medium skillet over medium heat. Add the onion and sauté until softened but not browned, about 5 minutes. Add the flour and paprika and stir to make a smooth paste. Cook, stirring, for 1 minute.

Remove the skillet from the heat. Gradually add a ladleful of liquid from the soup, stirring to thin out the paste. Stir the mixture into the soup and bring to a boil, stirring continuously. Remove the pig's foot and bay leaf from the soup.

Season with vinegar, salt, and pepper, ladle into bowls, and garnish the bowls with thyme leaves.

White Bean Soup with Sausage and Pesto

Serves 4 to 6

1 cup cooked white beans
1 quart homemade beef or chicken broth
½ cup Pesto Sauce (page 269)
½ pound dry Italian sausage, quartered and thinly sliced
Sea salt
Grated Parmesan cheese

Combine the beans and broth in a large saucepan, place over high heat, and bring to a simmer. Whisk in the pesto and add the sausage and cook to heat through. Season with salt, ladle into bowls, and serve topped with cheese.

CHAPTER 23

Aspics

Almost completely absent from modern tables, aspic, a dish in which ingredients are set into a chilled gelatin-rich meat stock or consommé, was once a popular dish in America, and remains so in Europe, especially middle Europe. Aspics hark back to the Middle Ages, when cooks discovered that a thickened meat broth could be made into a jelly. The earliest detailed recipe for aspic dates from 1375.

By the eighteenth century, aspics were popular dishes in France—French chefs included a variety of aspics in their repertoires. The dish came into prominence in America in the early twentieth century with the popularization of gelatin, which made gelling much easier and more predictable. By the 1950s, meat aspic was a popular dinner staple throughout the United States, as were other gelatin-based dishes such as tomato aspic, often served at buffets. Cooks liked to show off their creative skills by preparing original and colorful gelatin desserts.

Carefully crafted aspics showing geometric patterns of salad vegetables, peas, shrimp, and other ingredients can be found in Scandinavian cookbooks from the 1950s to the 1970s.

Today aspics have fallen from grace. It is our hope that the recipes included here help bring back this forgotten culinary art. From the folk dish of pickled pig's feet to the more gentle veal in aspic, these dishes are both healthful and practical, as the jellied stock helps preserve the meat and, of course, provides all the benefits of gelatinous broth. And homemade broth-based aspics provide a truly refreshing way to consume nourishing broth in the hot summer months.

When dehydrated and powdered gelatin came on the scene, books on "gelatine cookery" became popular. Gelatin, rather than gelatin-rich broth, was used to create a range of dishes, from sweetened mousse and other gelatin desserts, often mixed with cream, to savory aspics made with meat, chicken, shrimp, salmon, tongue, and even kidneys. *Cox's Manual of Gelatine Cookery*, featuring Cox's gelatin powder, produced in Scotland, was popular in England in the early twentieth century. The quivering molded culinary creations one sees on *Downton Abbey* were no doubt inspired by Cox's gelatin cookbook.

Sweetened aspics, called gelatin salads, originally were also made with meat stock or consommé, an ingredient later supplanted by powdered gelatin or presweetened gelatin in the form of Jell-O. Sometimes cream is added to the stock, in which case the dish is called a *chaud-froid*.

Aspics require a very gelatinous stock, from which the fat is removed and which is usually clarified with egg whites or by pouring it carefully through a jelly straining bag or a coffee filter. A small amount of gelatin may be added to obtain a good gel—we recommend the Great Lakes brand (see Sources, page 295). The standard technique is to fill a mold or terrine with pieces of meat and sometimes vegetables or fruit, pour the stock over the ingredients, and chill. Aspics can also be made in individual ramekins. Aspics are typically served on cold plates so the gel will not melt when plated. To remove a jellied dish from a mold, briefly dip the mold into hot water and then invert it onto the chilled plate. Refrigerate immediately and keep refrigerated until serving time.

Beef Aspic with Port Wine

Serves 6 to 8

4 cups homemade rich beef stock or consommé, clarified (see pages 187–88)
½ cup port wine
½ to 4 teaspoons Great Lakes gelatin
Sea salt

Chill the stock to determine the thickness of the gel.

In a large saucepan, bring the stock to a simmer and add the wine. If the stock had a firm gel, use ½ teaspoon gelatin. If the stock had a medium gel, use 2 teaspoons gelatin. If the stock had little gel, use 4 tablespoons gelatin. Add the gelatin by placing it in a small bowl and whisking a small amount of hot stock into the gelatin. Then whisk the gelatin mixture into the hot stock to dissolve it. Season with salt. Grease a 1-quart mold or 8 individual ½-cup molds, pour the mixture into the mold or molds, and refrigerate several hours or until firm.

Serve as an appetizer, spooned into small bowls or cups, in individual molds, or cut into wedges and presented on pieces of lettuce, with a garnish of tomatoes.

Calf's Foot Jelly

Calves' feet can be found at ethnic grocery stores, particularly those with a kosher butcher.

Serves 12 to 15 as an appetizer or snack

2 calves' feet, preferably cut into 1-inch cross sections

Cold filtered water to cover the feet, about 2 quarts

2 large carrots, peeled and diced

1 large onion, peeled and diced

Sea salt and freshly ground black pepper

5 cloves garlic, minced

3 hard-boiled eggs, sliced

5 lemons, sliced into wedges

Thoroughly rinse the calves' feet. Place them in a stockpot and add cold filtered water to cover. Place over medium heat, uncovered, bring to a boil, and spoon off any scum that rises to the top. Drain the calves' feet and cover again with a change of cold water. Bring almost to a boil, then lower the heat to the lowest setting possible. Add the carrots and onion and cook for a minimum of 6 hours, or preferably overnight, until any meat, cartilage, tendons, and ligaments separate easily from the bones.

Strain the stock through a fine-mesh strainer into a large heatproof bowl (see tips for straining on page 149). Reserve the meat but discard the bones and vegetables. Return the strained stock to the pot, place over medium heat, bring to a simmer, and simmer until reduced by about one-third, leaving you with about 6 cups. Taste the stock and season with salt and pepper.

Chop the meat, cartilage, and softened tendons and ligaments into small pieces, taking care to remove any bone fragments and to use only those pieces that can be easily cut with the knife. Add the garlic.

Grease a rectangular glass or enameled 9-by-13-inch baking dish and place the sliced eggs neatly in the bottom of the dish. Evenly distribute the meat-garlic mixture over the eggs. Pour the broth on top. The depth of the broth should be no less than 1 inch; 1½ inches is ideal.

Place in the refrigerator and chill until it solidifies, about 3 hours. Cut into squares and serve on chilled plates. Garnish each serving with a lemon wedge, which may be squeezed over the aspic for additional flavor.

Jellied Pig's Feet

Serves 8 to 10 as an appetizer

3 pig's feet

1 veal knuckle

Cold filtered water to cover the the pig's feet, about 2 quarts

1 small onion, peeled and sliced

1 clove garlic, peeled and smashed

¼ teaspoon dried sage

1 bay leaf

1 whole clove

2 whole black peppercorns

2 tablespoons apple cider vinegar

Sea salt

Thoroughly rinse the pig's feet and veal knuckle. Place them in a stockpot and add cold filtered water to cover. Place over medium heat, uncovered, bring to a boil, and carefully spoon off any scum that rises to the top. Add the onion, garlic, sage, bay leaf, clove, and peppercorns, then lower the heat to low and cook at a bare simmer with the lid off or slightly askew for 3 to 4 hours, until the meat falls from the bones. Strain the stock through a fine-mesh strainer into or a large heatproof bowl (see tips for straining on page 149), remove the meat from the bones, and finely chop it.

Rinse the pan, return the broth to the pan, and add the reserved meat and the vinegar. Place over medium heat and cook, uncovered, until the liquid is reduced by half. Season with salt. Turn into a 9-by-13-inch rectangular dish and chill until firm, about 3 hours.

Pork in Aspic

Adopted from Janez Bogataj, The Food and Cooking of Slovenia

There are many names for this dish, beloved across Europe, especially in Poland, Slovenia, and Latvia. The Slovenian version is called *Žolce*.

Serves 12 to 14

4 pig's knuckles and feet

1 pig's ear (optional)

Cold filtered water, about 3–4 quarts

1 onion, peeled and sliced

3 cloves garlic, sliced

1 bay leaf

1 sprig fresh thyme

1 sprig fresh marjoram

1 teaspoon black peppercorns

Sea salt

Apple cider vinegar

Place the knuckles and feet and optional pig's ear in a stockpot and add cold filtered water to cover. Place over medium heat, uncovered, bring to a bare simmer, and carefully spoon off any scum that rises to the top. Add the onion, garlic, bay leaf, thyme, marjoram, peppercorns, and a pinch of salt. Lower the heat to low and cook at a bare simmer with the lid off for about 3 hours, until the meat is falling off the bones, occasionally skimming scum from the top as needed and checking to ensure that the bones remain covered with water and adding more water as needed.

Remove the knuckles, feet, and ear, if you used it, with tongs and a slotted spoon.

Remove the meat from the bones and finely chop it. Place the meat in a greased 9-by-13-inch rectangular pan and set aside.

Return the bones to the stock and boil, uncovered, until reduced by about half (about 1 hour), leaving enough broth to cover the chopped meat. Strain the stock through a fine-mesh strainer or chinois lined with cheesecloth into a heatproof bowl (see tips for straining on page 149) and set aside to cool. Season with salt and pour the stock over the meat. Cover and chill until the stock has set to a jelly, about 3 hours or overnight. Cut into thick slices and serve on chilled plates with cider vinegar and dark rye bread. Eat within 2 to 3 days.

Veal or Beef in Aspic

This aspic is a good way to use the meat from the bones when making stock or for leftover stew meat.

Serves 6

About 3 cups cooked veal or beef, pulled apart or chopped

1 bunch green onions, chopped

1 red bell pepper, cored, seeded, and finely chopped

Sea salt and freshly ground black pepper

About 1 quart homemade gelatinous beef or veal broth, clarified (see pages 187–88) and warmed
Lettuce leaves and tomato wedges

In a large bowl, combine the veal, green onions, and bell pepper. Season with salt and pepper. Place in a greased 6-cup ring mold or rectangular pan and pour the broth over the meat. Refrigerate until the broth is set, about 4 hours.

To serve, spoon out and serve on lettuce leaves, or dip the mold briefly into hot water and invert onto a chilled plate, slice, and serve. Garnish with tomato wedges.

Chicken Salad Aspic

Makes 6 cups

2 cups shredded chicken meat

4 green onions, ends cut off and finely chopped

1 small red bell pepper, cored, seeded, and cut into slivers

1 tablespoon fresh tarragon leaves

Sea salt

1 quart homemade gelatinous chicken stock, clarified (pages 187–88)

Lettuce leaves, sliced tomatoes, and lemon wedges

In a medium bowl, combine the chicken meat, green onions, bell pepper, and tarragon. Season with salt.

Pour 1 cup of the stock into a saucepan and heat it until liquid. Grease a 6-cup mold, pour the stock into the mold, and chill it until jelled, about 2 hours. Arrange the chicken meat mixture over the jelled stock. Heat the remaining stock until liquid and pour it over the chicken. Chill until jellied, about 2 hours.

To serve, dip the mold briefly into hot water and invert onto a chilled plate. Return to the refrigerator to chill for about 1 hour. Slice into wedges and serve on lettuce leaves with sliced tomatoes and lemon wedges.

Eggs in Aspic (Oeufs en Gelée)

This is a classic French dish, rarely prepared at home, but purchased ready-made in local shops. It often serves as a meal for children or as a first course at an elegant dinner. Special oval molds give this dish a distinctive look.

Serves 4

1½ cups homemade gelatinous chicken broth, clarified (see pages 187–88)

3 tablespoons port wine

Sea salt

Up to 2 tablespoons Great Lakes gelatin, as needed

2 bell peppers, cored, seeded, and cut into ½-inch diamonds

4 eggs, poached and chilled

Microgreens

In a medium bowl, combine the broth with the wine, salt to taste, and chill to determine the thickness of the gel. If it is only lightly gelled, measure 1½ teaspoons gelatin into a small bowl; if fairly firm, measure ¾ teaspoon. If very firm, no gelatin is needed. Pour the broth into a medium saucepan and bring to a simmer. Add about ½ cup of the simmering stock to the gelatin and whisk to dissolve. Whisk the gelatin mixture into the pan. Turn off the heat and let cool.

Grease four 4-ounce oval aspic molds. Spoon about 2 teaspoons of the cooled broth into each mold. Chill until almost set, 8 to 10 minutes. Arrange 6 pepper diamonds, skin side up, in each mold on top of the aspic; top with 1 tablespoon cooled broth. Chill until set. Transfer the poached eggs to paper towels and trim away any ragged edges. Put an egg inside each mold and cover the egg by ¼ inch with the remaining aspic. Chill until completely set, about 2 hours.

To serve, dip the molds briefly into hot water and invert onto individual chilled plates. Keep refrigerated until you are ready to serve. Serve with microgreens.

Tomato Aspic

Arabella Forge, Richmond, Australia

Serves 6 as an appetizer

1½ cups homemade gelatinous stock made with calves' feet, pigs' feet, or chicken feet

1 to 2 teaspoons Great Lakes gelatin

4 bay leaves

2 cups tomato juice (see Note)

½ teaspoon paprika

Juice of 1 large lemon

Generous dash of Tabasco sauce

Sliced cucumbers or cucumber salad

Chill the stock to determine the thickness of the gel. If it is only lightly gelled, measure 2 teaspoons gelatin into a small bowl; if it is very firm, measure 1 teaspoon. Pour the broth into a medium saucepan, add the bay leaves, and bring to a simmer. Add about ½ cup of the simmering stock to the gelatin and whisk to dissolve. Then whisk the gelatin mixture into the pan, bring to a boil, then reduce the heat and simmer for 10 minutes. Remove the bay leaves and let cool to room temperature.

In a large bowl, whisk the stock with the tomato juice, paprika, lemon juice, and Tabasco. Grease 6 individual half-cup molds, pour the stock into the molds, and refrigerate until set, about 4 hours. To serve, dip briefly into hot water and invert onto chilled individual plates. Keep refrigerated until you are ready to serve. Garnish with sliced cucumbers or cucumber salad and serve.

Note: You can make your own tomato juice. Puree 5 to 6 very ripe tomatoes in a food processor or blender and strain through a strainer for 2 cups tomato juice.

Raspberry and Mint Jelly

Arabella Forge, Richmond, Australia

Serves 6 to 8

2¼ cups gelatinous Simple Slow Cooker Pig's Foot Broth (page 157), clarified (pages 187–88)

2 cups packed raspberries

1½ tablespoons honey

Up to 4 teaspoons Great Lakes beef gelatin

1 teaspoon finely chopped fresh mint leaves

Fresh fruit (optional)

Chill the broth to determine the thickness of the gel.

Combine the raspberries and honey in a large saucepan. Place over medium heat and bring to a simmer; simmer for 10 minutes, mashing and stirring frequently, until most of the liquid is evaporated. Add the stock, turn the heat off, and whisk to combine well.

Measure the total volume in the saucepan. If the stock was liquidy before cooking, use 1 teaspoon gelatin per cup of total volume. If your stock was jellylike and wobbly, use ½ teaspoon gelatin per cup, and if it was nicely firm (could be tipped upside down without falling out of the container), don't add any gelatin.

Place the needed gelatin in a small bowl, return the stock to a simmer, and whisk in about 1 cup of the simmering liquid to dissolve the gelatin. Add the gelatin mixture back into the saucepan and whisk well. Remove from the heat and stir in the mint leaves. Pour the mixture into individual ½-cup jelly molds or 1 quart-size mold and refrigerate until set, about 3 hours.

To serve, dip the molds or mold briefly into hot water and invert onto individual chilled plates. Chill again and keep refrigerated until serving time. Serve decorated with fresh fruit if you like.

Apple and Grape Jelly

Arabella Forge, Richmond, Australia

Serves 6

2¼ cups gelatinous Simple Slow Cooker Pig's Foot Broth (page 157), clarified (pages 187–88)

3 medium to large apples, peeled and cut into quarters

1½ tablespoons honey

1 cinnamon stick

2 whole cloves

2 cardamom pods

Up to 2 teaspoons Great Lakes gelatin

¾ to 1 cup grapes, cut in half

Fresh fruit (optional)

Chill the broth to determine the thickness of the gel.

In a large saucepan, combine the stock, apples, honey, cinnamon, cloves, and cardamom, place over medium heat, and bring to a gentle simmer; cook for 20 minutes, stirring frequently and mashing the apples. Remove from the heat and strain the mixture through a fine-mesh strainer into a heatproof bowl, pressing the apples against the strainer to extract all the liquid.

Measure the total volume in the saucepan. If the stock was liquidy before cooking, use 1 teaspoon gelatin per cup of total volume. If your stock was jellylike and wobbly, add ½ teaspoon per cup; and if it was nicely firm (could be tipped upside down without falling out of the container), don't add any gelatin. Return the stock to the saucepan and bring to a simmer.

Place the gelatin in a small bowl and whisk in about 1 cup simmering liquid to dissolve the gelatin, then return the gelatin mixture back to the saucepan and whisk well.

Grease 6 individual jelly molds and place a handful of grapes at the bottom of each mold. Pour the mixture into the molds, refrigerate immediately, and chill until set, about 3 hours.

To serve, dip the molds briefly into hot water and invert onto chilled plates. Chill again and keep refrigerated until serving time. Decorate with fresh fruit if you like and serve.

Strawberry Aspic

Serves 10

4 cups strawberries, hulled

Juice of 1 lemon, strained

2 to 3 tablespoons honey

3 cups gelatinous Simple Slow Cooker Pig's Foot Broth (page 157)

2 teaspoons Great Lakes gelatin

Fresh fruit (optional)

Puree the strawberries in a food processor or blender. Strain through a strainer into a bowl, pressing on the solids to extract all the liquid. Whisk the lemon juice and honey into the puree.

Bring the broth to a boil in a medium saucepan. Put the gelatin into a bowl, spoon a little broth into the gelatin, and whisk until melted. Whisk the melted gelatin back into the broth and simmer for 3 to 4 minutes.

Whisk the broth into the strawberry puree. Grease 10 individual molds, pour the mixture into the molds, and chill until set, about 3 hours. To serve, dip the molds briefly into hot water and invert onto individual chilled plates. Chill again and keep refrigerated until serving time. Decorate with fresh fruit if you like and serve.

CHAPTER 24

Stews and Stir-Fries

A s we have forgotten how to make broth, we have also forgotten how to make delicious and satisfying stews. But having broth on hand makes stew-making a cinch. The recipes in this chapter range from easy to moderately difficult, and some handily make their own gelatinous stock as they cook. Remember that stews can be frozen and reheated; if you are going to the trouble to make stew, be sure to make enough to have leftovers.

Chicken or Turkey Curry

Serves 4

4 tablespoons ghee or butter

1 medium onion, peeled and diced

3 tablespoons curry powder

2 tablespoons unbleached white flour

2 cups homemade chicken broth

3 cups shredded cooked chicken or turkey meat

1 cup heavy cream

Sea salt

Basic Brown Rice (page 276)

Chopped fresh cilantro, raisins, and cashews

In a heatproof casserole, melt the ghee over medium heat. Add the onion and sauté until softened, about 5 minutes. Add the curry powder and flour, blending it in well with a wooden spoon. Cook, stirring, for about 5 minutes. Slowly add the chicken broth, whisking it in to remove any lumps. Bring to a simmer, then add the chicken, lower the heat, cover, and simmer for about 10 minutes. Add the cream, return to a simmer, and simmer for 10 minutes. Season with salt.

Serve with brown rice and bowls of chopped cilantro, raisins, and cashews for garnish.

Simple Chicken and Sausage Gumbo

Emma Watterson, Hayes, Virginia

Serves 8 to 10

6 to 8 cups homemade chicken broth

Cooked meat from 1 whole chicken, chopped into bite-size pieces

8 to 10 links chicken sausage, sliced

About 15 pieces okra, chopped into bite-size pieces

3 to 4 cloves garlic, minced

Cajun spices (such as black pepper, cayenne pepper, oregano, basil, thyme, and paprika)

Sea salt

Basic Brown Rice (page 276; optional)

Combine the broth, chicken, and sausage in a large saucepan. Place over medium heat and bring just to a boil. Add the okra, garlic, and Cajun spices to taste, return to a simmer, and simmer until the okra is tender, about 10 minutes (the okra will thicken the gumbo). Season with salt and serve over brown rice if you like.

Chicken Stew

Serves 6

1 whole chicken

⅔ cup unbleached white flour

¾ teaspoon sea salt

¾ teaspoon dried thyme

½ teaspoon freshly ground black pepper

1 teaspoon paprika

2 teaspoons dry mustard

6 to 8 tablespoons lard, or a combination of butter and olive oil

2 cups fresh sliced mushrooms

½ cup dry white wine

3 to 4 cups chicken stock

1 cup heavy cream or crème fraîche

Sea salt and freshly ground black pepper

Basic Brown Rice (page 276)

Cut the chicken into 10 pieces: 2 wings, 2 thighs, 2 drumsticks, and 4 pieces of breast (remove the breast from its bone, leaving the skin on, and cut each breast in half). Reserve the back and neck for making stock.

In a shallow bowl, combine the flour, salt, thyme, pepper, paprika, and mustard. Dredge the chicken pieces in the flour mixture to coat thoroughly. Set aside.

Melt the lard in a large skillet over medium-high heat. Add the chicken pieces a few at a time and cook on all sides until thoroughly browned. Transfer to a large saucepan or slow cooker. Add the mushrooms to the fat in the pan you cooked the chicken in, reduce the heat to medium, and cook, stirring, until softened, about 5 minutes. Remove the mushrooms with a slotted spoon to the saucepan or slow cooker. Deglaze the pan with the wine and add the stock. Bring to a boil and reduce slightly; add the stock to the saucepan or slow cooker. Simmer over low heat or on low power with the lid askew for about 2 hours, until the meat is very tender. Stir in the cream and season with salt and pepper. Serve over brown rice.

Chicken and Beet Stir-Fry

Celeste Longacre, Alstead, New Hampshire

Serves 2 to 4

1 pound chicken meat, cut into bite-size pieces

4 to 6 cloves garlic, peeled and smashed

½ cup naturally fermented soy sauce

2 cups homemade chicken broth

2 to 4 beets, peeled and chopped

2 carrots, peeled and chopped

2 to 3 tablespoons coconut oil or lard

1 large onion, peeled and chopped

2 tablespoons arrowroot dissolved in ½ cup filtered water

Basic Brown Rice (page 276)

Place the chicken in a medium bowl. Add the garlic and soy sauce, cover, and refrigerate overnight to marinate.

Pour the broth into a large saucepan, place over medium-high heat, and bring to a simmer. Add the beets and carrots, return to a simmer, then lower the heat and simmer for about 1 hour, until softened.

Melt the oil in a large cast-iron skillet over medium-low heat. Add the onion and cook for about 30 minutes, until softened and browned. Add the chicken, raise the heat to medium, and cook for about 10 minutes, until cooked through. Add the carrots and beets with the broth, raise the heat, and bring to a boil. Stir in the arrowroot slurry, bring to a simmer, and simmer for a minute or two, until thickened. Serve over brown rice.

Ham Steak Stir-Fry

Serves 2 to 3

1 (1-pound) ham steak with plenty of fat around the edges

¼ cup rice vinegar

1 bunch green onions, ends cut off and cut into 1-inch pieces

2 carrots, peeled and cut into 1-inch sticks

1 red bell pepper, cored, seeded, and cut into 1-inch pieces

1 cup broccoli cut into small florets

1-inch piece fresh ginger, peeled and grated

¼ to ½ teaspoon red chile flakes

1 cup homemade beef or chicken broth

2 tablespoons naturally fermented soy sauce

1 tablespoon arrowroot powder mixed with 1½ tablespoons water

½ cup cashews, chopped

Basic Brown Rice (page 276)

Trim the fat from the ham steak, cut it into small pieces, and reserve it. Cut the ham into 1-inch strips; place in a bowl, toss with the vinegar, cover, and marinate in the refrigerator for at least 3 hours but preferably all day.

Cook the reserved ham fat in a cast-iron skillet or wok over medium heat until the fat is rendered, about 30 minutes. Remove the cracklings with a slotted spoon and reserve for another use (they are delicious in salads).

Dry off the ham pieces with paper towels and add them to the fat in the pan over medium heat. Add the green onions, carrots, and bell pepper and sauté, stirring constantly, until browned and cooked through, about 7 to 8 minutes. Add the broccoli and cook for about 5 minutes more, until tender.

Add the ginger, red chile flakes, broth, and soy sauce, and bring to a boil. Stir in the arrowroot slurry, return to a boil, and boil for about 1 minute, until the sauce thickens. Turn off the heat and stir in the cashews. Serve over brown rice.

Pork Backbone Stew

Marlene Mayman, Shepherdstown, West Virginia

If you have trouble finding pork backbone, you can use bone-in pork shoulder ribs or pork spareribs.

Serves 6

6 pounds pork backbones, cut into 2-inch segments by your butcher or using a sturdy cleaver

1 cup red wine or apple cider vinegar

1 tablespoon sea salt

1½ teaspoons ground cayenne

1 teaspoon ground cumin

1 teaspoon cracked black pepper

3 cloves peeled and smashed garlic, or to taste

2 cups unbleached white flour

½ to 1 cup pork lard or coconut oil

2 quarts homemade chicken broth

8 ounces button, shiitake, or cremini mushrooms, quartered

1 cup coarsely chopped onion

1 bell pepper, cored, seeded, and chopped into large pieces

2 cups minced onion

1 cup cored, seeded, and minced bell pepper

1 cup minced celery

½ cup red wine

3 cups Basic Brown Rice (page 276)

Place the pork pieces in a large bowl, toss with the vinegar, cover, and refrigerate for at least 4 hours or overnight to marinate. Remove the meat from the bowl and pat dry with paper towels.

Combine the salt, cayenne, cumin, black pepper, and garlic in a small bowl and put the flour in a shallow bowl. Rub the backbone pieces with the spice mixture, then dredge in the flour, shaking off the excess. Reserve ½ cup of the flour.

Heat the lard in a large cast-iron skillet over medium-high heat until hot but not smoking. Cook the backbones in batches, until darkened and crusty on both sides, about 5 minutes per side. Drain on paper towels.

Pour the broth into a large saucepan and bring to a rolling boil. Add the backbones, reduce the heat, and simmer for 30 minutes. Add the mushrooms, coarsely chopped onion, and chopped bell pepper and cook for another 30 minutes, until the meat is cooked through and the vegetables are tender.

Meanwhile, pour off all but about ½ cup of fat from the skillet, leaving the pork cracklings. Turn heat to medium-high and heat to just before fat begins to smoke, being careful not to let it burn. Slowly stir in the reserved ½ cup flour with a long-handled metal whisk (so you can avoid splattering hot oil) and cook, whisking constantly, until a dark red-brown roux is formed, about 4 minutes. Immediately add the minced onion, minced bell pepper, and celery and cook, stirring, for about 2 minutes, until softened. Remove from the heat.

Bring the stew to a boil over medium-high heat. Add the vegetable-flour mixture by the spoonful to the stew, gently stirring after each addition until well blended. Lower the heat and simmer uncovered for 30 minutes. Add the wine and cook until the meat is falling off the bone, about another 30 minutes. If the stew gets too thick, add more broth or water. Serve over brown rice.

Slow Cooker Beef Tips

Donna and Ashley Sherman, Bloomington, Illinois

Serves 4 to 6

2 pounds boneless beef tips (or beef sirloin or round steak), cubed

2 tablespoons tallow or butter

2 cups homemade beef stock

2 cloves garlic, peeled and minced

2 teaspoons sea salt

½ teaspoon freshly ground black pepper

½ teaspoon dried thyme

2 tablespoons arrowroot powder mixed with ¼ cup filtered water

Mashed potatoes or Basic Brown Rice (page 276)

Dry the beef pieces well with paper towels. In a large skillet, melt the fat over medium-high heat and brown the beef pieces in batches on all sides. Transfer to a slow cooker. Whisk the remaining ingredients except potatoes or rice into the skillet until smooth and bring to a boil. Pour over the beef in the slow cooker. Cover and cook on low for 8 hours, or until beef is tender. Serve over mashed potatoes or brown rice.

Beef Barley Stew

Karen Blumhagen, Tofield, Canada

Serves 4 to 6

1½ pounds beef stew meat, cut into 1-inch cubes

4 to 5 tablespoons tallow or lard

1 medium onion, peeled and chopped

5½ cups homemade beef broth

1 cup pearled barley

1 teaspoon dried thyme

½ teaspoon dried marjoram

¼ teaspoon dried rosemary

¼ teaspoon freshly ground black pepper

4 medium carrots, peeled and sliced

2 tablespoons chopped fresh parsley

Pat the meat pieces dry with paper towels. Heat the tallow in a Dutch oven or flameproof casserole over medium-high heat. Add the meat in batches and cook, stirring, until well browned on all sides. Remove the beef from the pan to a plate. Add the onion to the fat in the pan and cook, stirring, until browned, about 5 minutes. Return the meat to the pot. Add the broth, barley, thyme, marjoram, rosemary, and pepper; bring to a boil and skim. Reduce the heat, cover, and simmer for 1 hour.

Add the carrots and bring to boil. Reduce the heat, cover, and simmer for 30 to 40 minutes, until the meat and carrots are tender. Add the parsley just before serving.

Asian-Style Beef Short Ribs with Carrots

Cassie Snyder, Calgary, Canada

Serves 4

About 3 pounds bone-in beef short ribs

Freshly ground black pepper

2 to 3 tablespoons beef tallow or lard

1 onion, peeled and chopped

3 cloves garlic, peeled and smashed

1-inch piece ginger, peeled and sliced

1 cup homemade beef broth

1 teaspoon anise seeds

¼ cup naturally fermented soy sauce

2 tablespoons mirin (Japanese sweet rice wine)

2 tablespoons rice vinegar

2 to 3 carrots, peeled and sliced

2 cups Basic Brown Rice (page 276)

Season the ribs with pepper. Melt the tallow in a large skillet that has a lid or an ovenproof casserole over medium-high heat. Add the ribs and brown them all over. Use tongs to transfer them to a plate. Reduce the heat to medium-low, add the onion, and sauté until translucent, about 5 minutes, then add the garlic and ginger and sauté for another minute or so, until softened.

Add the broth, anise seeds, soy sauce, mirin, and vinegar, raise the heat to medium-high, and bring to a boil. Return the short ribs to the pan, bring to a simmer, then reduce the heat to low, cover, and cook for at least 2 hours, turning the ribs occasionally. (Alternatively, place the pan in a preheated 225°F oven or transfer the ingredients to a slow cooker on low and leave it to cook all day, about 7 to 8 hours.)

About 20 minutes before you're ready to serve, remove the short ribs from the pan to a plate. Bring the sauce to a boil over medium-high heat add the carrots. Cook until the sauce is reduced to a very thick consistency and the carrots are cooked through but still al dente. Divide the rice among 4 bowls, place the short ribs on top, pour the sauce along with the carrots over them, and serve.

Spiced Beef and Lamb Chili

Kristen Harvey, Raleigh, North Carolina

Serves 6 to 8

3 to 4 tablespoons lard
1 pound ground beef
1 pound ground lamb
½ cup chopped onion
2 carrots, peeled and sliced
2 celery sticks, chopped
2 to 3 cloves garlic, chopped
1 (28-ounce) can chopped tomatoes with juice
1 cup homemade beef broth
2 to 3 tablespoons chili powder
1 teaspoon dried oregano
2 teaspoons ground cumin
½ teaspoon ground ginger
1 teaspoon sea salt, or to taste
Freshly ground black pepper to taste
1 teaspoon ground cinnamon
Grated Monterey Jack or mild cheddar cheese, salsa, and avocado slices

Melt the lard in a large saucepan over medium heat. Add the ground beef and lamb and cook, stirring, until browned with no pink spots, about 10 minutes. Drain off excess fat. Add the remaining ingredients except the garnishes, bring to a simmer, then reduce the heat and simmer until the vegetables are softened, about 30 minutes. Serve with grated cheese, salsa, and avocado.

Bob's Chili

Sharon Miller, Reno, Nevada

Serves 8 to 10

2 tablespoons olive oil or lard

1 small onion, peeled and diced

1 red bell pepper, cored, seeded, and diced

2 pounds ground beef

2 (15-ounce) cans stewed or diced tomatoes

2 (15-ounce) cans tomato sauce

2 cups cooked kidney beans (soak for 18 to 24 hours before cooking)

1 quart homemade chicken or beef broth

¼ cup chili powder, or to taste

Sea salt and freshly ground black pepper

Grated Monterey Jack or cheddar cheese and sour cream

Heat the oil in a large saucepan over medium heat. Add the onion and bell pepper and sauté until softened, about 5 minutes. Add the ground beef and cook, stirring occasionally to break up the meat, until browned with no pink spots, about 10 minutes. Add the tomatoes, tomato sauce, beans, broth, and chili powder and season with salt and pepper. Bring to a simmer, then reduce the heat to low, cover, and cook for about 1 hour. Serve with grated cheese and sour cream.

Lorraine's Chili

Lorraine Carlstrom, Nelson, Canada

Serves 8 to 10

4 tablespoons ghee or beef fat

3 pounds ground beef or bison

¼ cup dry red wine

2 to 3 cups homemade beef stock

2 onions, finely chopped

1 red or yellow bell pepper, cored, seeded, and chopped

2 medium carrots, peeled and grated

1 (28-ounce) can crushed tomatoes, or 2 cups blended fresh tomatoes

3 cloves garlic, peeled and smashed

1 tablespoon chili powder

1 tablespoon ground cumin

2 tablespoons dried oregano

2 tablespoons dried basil, or ¼ cup chopped fresh basil

2 tablespoons honey

1 tablespoon coarse sea salt

1 teaspoon freshly ground black pepper

4 cups cooked kidney beans (soak for 18 to 24 hours before cooking)

Sour cream, avocado slices, and chopped fresh cilantro

Melt the ghee in a large saucepan over medium heat. Add the ground beef and cook, stirring, until browned with no pink spots, about 10 minutes. Add the wine, stock, onions, bell pepper, carrots, crushed tomatoes, garlic, chili powder, cumin, oregano, basil, honey, salt, and pepper, bring to a boil, then reduce the heat to low, cover, and simmer for 1 hour. Add the beans and cook for 30 minutes more. Serve garnished with sour cream, avocado slices, and cilantro.

Flemish Beef Stew

Gwenny Rul, Woodlands, Texas

I am from Belgium, and my grandmother was a chef. She made a lot of delicious traditional dishes, but Flemish beef stew was one of my favorites, and I now make it regularly. The bread acts like a thickener (in addition to providing flavor), so it should be fairly soft. The mustard spread on the bread slices makes them a little heavier so they can sink down into the broth. If they don't sink down all the way, push them a little until they become soaked in the sauce.

Serves 6

2 pounds beef stew meat, cut into 1-inch pieces

2 teaspoons sea salt

½ teaspoon freshly ground black pepper

½ teaspoon freshly grated nutmeg

4 tablespoons butter or ghee

2 onions, peeled and diced

2 bay leaves

½ teaspoon dried thyme

½ teaspoon dried rosemary, crushed

2 tablespoons mustard

1 large or 2 small slices bread

About 3 cups homemade beef stock

1 cup dark beer (optional)

Pat the beef pieces dry with paper towels. Combine the salt, pepper, and nutmeg in a small bowl and coat the beef with the seasonings.

Melt 2 tablespoons of the butter in a large saucepan over medium-high heat. Add the meat in batches and brown it on all sides.

Meanwhile, melt the remaining 2 tablespoons butter in a large skillet over medium heat. Add the onions and sauté until softened, about 10 minutes. Add the onions to the beef, then add the bay leaves, thyme, and rosemary. Spread the mustard on the bread and put it on top of the meat.

Add the stock and optional beer so the meat is almost covered in liquid. Bring to a boil, then reduce the heat to low, cover, and simmer for 2 to 4 hours, until the meat is tender, stirring every 30 minutes or so and adding water if it starts to get dry. The bread will mix in with the stew and thicken the sauce.

Savory Beef Stew with Vegetables

Serves 6

2 pounds beef stew meat, cut into 2-inch chunks

1 small can or jar tomato paste

½ cup red wine

2 to 3 cups homemade beef stock

2 tablespoons balsamic vinegar

4 to 5 strips orange zest

1 tablespoon green peppercorns, crushed

6 small red potatoes, cut into quarters

4 carrots, peeled and sliced at an angle

½ pound mushrooms, cut into quarters

1 tablespoon arrowroot powder dissolved in 1½ tablespoons water, if needed

Sea salt and freshly ground black pepper

4 ounces snow peas, cut in half at an angle

Preheat the oven to 450°F.

Place the beef in an ovenproof casserole, and using a basting brush, paint it with the tomato paste. Place in the oven and roast, uncovered, turning at least once, until the tomato paste has browned, about 30 minutes in all.

Place the casserole on the stovetop and reduce the oven temperature to 250°F.

Add the wine to the casserole, turn the heat to medium-high, and bring to a boil. Add the stock and vinegar and bring to a boil again. Skim any scum that rises to the top, add the orange zest and peppercorns, and turn off the heat.

Place the stew in the oven with the lid slightly askew and bake for 2 hours. Add the potatoes, carrots, and mushrooms and cook for another hour, or until the meat and vegetables are very tender.

Return the pot to the stovetop and adjust the sauce: If the sauce needs thickening, stir in the arrowroot mixture, bring to a boil, and boil for 1 minute. If the sauce needs thinning, add a little water. Season with salt and pepper. Strew the snow peas over the top, cover, and simmer for about 5 minutes, until the snow peas are tender but still bright green.

Slow Cooker Lamb Shank Stew

This easy stew makes its own broth from the cartilage in the shanks.

Serves 6 to 8

2 lamb shanks
¼ cup red wine vinegar
About 4 cups cold filtered water
1 (28-ounce) can chopped tomatoes
2 onions, peeled, quartered, and thinly sliced
Several pieces orange peel
1 teaspoon whole black peppercorns
1 sprig fresh rosemary
Sea salt

Place the lamb shanks in a slow cooker, add the vinegar, then add enough cold filtered water to cover the bones. Strew the tomatoes, onions, orange peel, and peppercorns over the shanks and top with the rosemary. Turn the slow cooker to high, and when the liquid comes to a simmer, reduce the heat to low. Simmer for at least 5 hours or all day, until the lamb is very tender.

Remove the rosemary sprig. Remove the shanks from the slow cooker, take the meat off the bone, and place the meat in bowls. Season the sauce with salt and ladle it over the meat.

Slow Cooker Irish Stew

Sylvia Anders, Athelstone, Australia

Serves 4 to 6

2 to 3 pounds lamb neck, cut into chops, or shoulder chops

2 large onions, sliced

4 to 6 carrots, peeled and sliced

2 to 3 turnips, peeled and cut into chunks

2 pounds potatoes, sliced

2 cups homemade chicken, veal, or lamb stock

1 *bouquet garni* made with parsley sprigs, thyme sprigs, and 2 bay leaves, tied together with kitchen string

Sea salt and freshly ground black pepper to taste

Chopped fresh parsley

Place all the ingredients except the parsley in a slow cooker, cover, and cook on low for 8 to 10 hours, until the lamb is very tender.

To serve, lift the meat and vegetables out of the pot and place in a serving bowl.

Transfer the sauce to a saucepan, place over medium-high heat, bring to a boil, and boil until reduced by half. Taste and season with salt and pepper if needed and pour over the meat and vegetables. Garnish with parsley.

Shrimp Étouffée

The beautiful flavor of étoufée comes primarily from Shrimp Shell Broth, made in advance from shrimp shells (and heads, if available). Don't forget to freeze the shells from the shrimp used in this recipe for future batches of Shrimp Shell Broth and Étoufée.

Serves 6

½ cup clarified butter or ghee

½ cup unbleached white flour

1 medium onion, peeled and chopped

1 red bell pepper, cored, seeded, and chopped

2 celery sticks, chopped

3 cloves garlic, finely minced

½ teaspoon freshly ground black pepper

½ teaspoon freshly ground white pepper

½ teaspoon ground cayenne

1 teaspoon Cajun seasoning

Dash of Tabasco sauce

2 cups Shrimp Shell Broth (page 174), warmed

1 (14.5-ounce) can diced tomatoes

Sea salt

2 pounds small or medium shrimp, peeled and deveined

2 tablespoons butter

½ cup minced fresh parsley

1 bunch green onions, light and green parts, finely chopped

Basic Brown Rice (page 276)

Melt the clarified butter in a large cast-iron skillet over low heat. Make a roux by whisking the flour into the butter and cooking, whisking constantly, until the mixture turns a caramel color and gives off a nutty aroma, 15 to 20 minutes. Add the onion, bell pepper, celery, and garlic and cook for about 5 minutes, until the vegetables are softened. Add the black pepper, white pepper, cayenne, Cajun seasoning, and Tabasco.

Gradually add the warmed shrimp shell broth, whisking to remove any lumps, then stir in the tomatoes with their juice. Season with salt. Raise the heat to medium-high, bring the mixture to a boil, then reduce the heat to low and simmer for 10 to 15 minutes, until the mixture is thick and smooth. Add the shrimp and cook, stirring, for about 3 minutes, until the shrimp is just cooked through. Remove from the heat and stir in the butter and parsley. Transfer to a serving bowl and garnish with the green onions. Serve over brown rice.

Portuguese Fish Stew

Serves 6 to 8

6 tablespoons olive oil

4 onions, peeled, quartered, and thinly sliced

4 cloves garlic, minced

¼ cup dry sherry

2 quarts homemade fish stock

3 large tomatoes, chopped, or 1 (28-ounce) can diced tomatoes

3 medium potatoes, peeled and cubed

2 whole cloves

2 bay leaves

1 tablespoon minced fresh parsley

1 teaspoon fresh or ½ teaspoon dried tarragon

1 teaspoon fresh or ½ teaspoon dried marjoram

Sea salt and freshly ground black pepper

2 pounds fresh skin-on fish fillets, cut into ½-inch chunks

1 pound small shrimp, clams, mussels, or scallops

3 tablespoons butter

1 garlic clove, minced

12 to 16 slices sourdough bread, crusts removed

½ cup freshly grated Parmesan cheese

1 tablespoon chopped fresh parsley

Heat 3 tablespoons of the oil in a large flameproof casserole over medium heat. Add the onions and garlic and sauté until softened, about 10 minutes. Add the sherry and stock, increase the heat to medium-high, and bring to a boil, skimming any scum that rises to the top. Add the tomatoes, potatoes, cloves, bay leaves, minced parsley, tarragon, and marjoram and season with salt and pepper, return to a boil, then reduce the heat and simmer, uncovered, for about 30 minutes, until the potatoes are softened but still fairly firm. Add the fish chunks to the stew and simmer for 5 minutes, or until barely cooked through (keeping the skin on the fish chunks prevents them from disintegrating).

Just before serving, strew the shellfish (add clams or mussels with mouths facing up) over the top of the stew, cover, and cook for 3 to 4 minutes, until the shrimp or scallops are cooked through or the clams or mussels open (clams or mussels may take longer; discard any that do not open).

Meanwhile, melt the butter in the remaining 3 tablespoons oil over medium heat. Add the garlic and let it sizzle. Add the bread slices and fry on each side until golden.

Serve the stew in soup bowls and top each with 2 slices bread and some Parmesan cheese. Garnish with the chopped parsley.

CHAPTER 25

Sauces

In *The Devil's Dictionary* (1911) Ambrose Bierce defined *sauce* as follows: "SAUCE, n. The one infallible sign of civilization and enlightenment. A people with no sauces has one thousand vices; a people with one sauce has only nine hundred and ninety-nine. For every sauce invented and accepted a vice is renounced and forgiven."

"Sauces comprise the honor and glory of French cookery," wrote the self-styled Prince of Gastronomy Curnonsky. "They have contributed to its superiority, or pre-eminence, which is disputed by none. Sauces are the orchestration and accompaniment of a fine meal, and enable a good chef or cook to demonstrate his talent."

Americans generally think sauce is made with tomatoes or comes in a bottle, but sauce is traditionally made with stock, and the making of delicious broth-based sauce has a long history.

In typical fashion, the French have turned sauce making into a systematic art, one in which stock or broth serves as the central element. The basic stock-based sauce in French cuisine is the brown sauce, or *sauce espagnole*, made with beef or veal stock, butter browned in flour (brown roux), and tomato paste. Variations include the *bordelaise* (with red wine and shallots) and *diable* (white wine, shallots, and ground cayenne). The basic white sauce, or *velouté*, is made with light-colored stock (poultry or fish) and flour cooked gently in butter (a yellow roux) so that it does not brown. Variations include the *allemande* (with egg yolks and mushrooms) and *supreme* (with cream and butter).

French nouvelle cuisine uses alternatives to flour-thickened stocks, deemed old-school and too heavy, and favors lighter stocks thickened by reduction, that is, boiling off the liquid, allowing the gelatin to concentrate. These are sometimes enlivened with butter, heavy cream, or crème fraîche. Arrowroot or gelatin can also be used to thicken a reduction sauce.

The basic sauce in British and American cooking is gravy, made by cooking flour in pan drippings and then whisking in broth. While European chefs may turn their noses up at such an inelegant sauce, the principle is actually no different from the flour-based sauces of haute cuisine—flour is cooked in a fat (butter or pan drippings) and then stock is added.

There are other ways of thickening stock to make sauce. In medieval times, pureed liver or even sea urchin was used. Those on gluten-free diets have used coconut flour and almond flour. Some chefs have experimented with vegetable purees—onion pureed with stock or pan drippings works particularly well (see page 253).

The beauty of broth-based sauces is that they marry so well with the meat they are put on. The glycine in broth moderates the stimulating effects of the methionine in meat for a calm and balanced mental outlook (see chapter 17), and the gelatin in the sauce ensures complete digestion of the whole meal. Truly, the more sauce we eat—real sauce, made with broth—the fewer vices we will have.

Flour-Thickened Sauces

The basic principle involves cooking flour in fat—whether pan drippings or melted butter. Stock is then added slowly, using a whisk to prevent the formation of lumps. Additional ingredients, such as wine or brandy, tomato paste, or cream, can be mixed in.

For those on gluten-free diets, you can follow the directions for any flour-thickened sauce, omitting the flour, and proceeding with the recipe. At the end, thicken the sauce with 1 tablespoon arrowroot powder mixed with 1½ tablespoons water. Stir the slurry into the sauce and let it boil briefly. If the sauce needs more thickening, repeat with additional arrowroot mixed with water.

Gravy

For gravy, you need good drippings in the pan. To get there, before baking, brush whatever meat you are roasting—beef, leg of lamb, chicken, or turkey—with plenty of melted butter and put a sliced onion in the bottom of the pan. While the roast is cooking, the onion will brown in the butterfat and fat from the meat, adding a lovely dark color to the final gravy.

Serves 6 to 8

Pan drippings from a roast
¼ to ¾ cup unbleached white flour
2 to 4 cups homemade stock (see Note on page 254)
Sea salt

When your roast is done, remove it to a platter and keep hot in a warm oven. Place the roasting pan on the stovetop over medium heat. Stir the flour into the fat—start with a little and gradually add more until the fat is completely amalgamated with the flour. Cook, stirring constantly, until the flour browns (this step will prevent your gravy from tasting like raw flour).

Gently add stock as needed, whisking constantly. Strain the gravy into a saucepan to remove the onions. If the gravy is too thin, boil it down until it thickens; if it is too thick, thin it with a little water. Season with salt and serve. If not using the gravy right away, keep it covered and warm until ready to serve.

Note: The stock should match the meat you are cooking—chicken stock for roast chicken, beef or veal stock for roast beef, beef or lamb stock for leg of lamb.

Brown Sauce (Sauce Espagnole)

This basic sauce is delicious with beef, veal, or lamb.

Makes 1 quart

2 tablespoons clarified butter or ghee

1 cup diced onion

½ cup peeled and diced carrot

½ cup diced celery

2 tablespoons unbleached white flour

6 cups homemade beef or veal stock

¼ cup tomato paste

1 *bouquet garni* made with parsley sprigs, thyme sprigs, and a bay leaf, tied together with kitchen string

Melt the clarified butter in a heavy-bottomed saucepan over a medium heat until it becomes frothy. Add the onion, carrot, and celery and sauté for about 5 minutes, until lightly browned, being careful not to let the vegetables burn. Using a wooden spoon, stir the flour into the vegetables a little bit at a time until it is fully incorporated and forms a thick paste, or roux. Lower the heat and cook the roux for 5 minutes or so, stirring constantly, until it is light brown in color, again taking care not to let it burn.

Stirring with a wire whisk, slowly add the stock and then the tomato paste, whisking vigorously to remove any lumps. Increase the heat to medium-high, bring to a boil, then lower the heat to low, add the *bouquet garni*, and simmer for about 50 minutes, until it is reduced by about one-third, stirring frequently to make sure the sauce doesn't scorch at the bottom of the pan. Use a spoon to skim off any scum that rises to the surface.

Turn off the heat and remove the *bouquet garni*. For an extra-smooth consistency, pour the sauce through a fine-mesh strainer into a heatproof bowl. If not using the sauce right away, keep it covered and warm until ready to serve.

Sauce Bordelaise

As with Sauce Espagnole, Sauce Bordelaise is delicious with beef, veal, or lamb.

Makes about 5 cups

1 quart Brown Sauce (page 254)
1 cup red wine
2 tablespoons butter
2 tablespoons olive oil
1 pound mushrooms, sliced

Follow the directions for making the brown sauce; at the point when you add the stock, also add the wine.

While the brown sauce is reducing, melt the butter in the oil in a large skillet over medium heat. Add the mushrooms and cook, stirring, until well browned, about 10 minutes. When the sauce is finished, stir in the sautéed mushrooms and serve. If not using the sauce right away, keep it covered and warm until ready to serve.

Sauce Diable

This makes an excellent sauce for chicken or a dipping sauce for chicken, turkey, or pork.

Makes about 2 cups

1 cup dry white wine
3 shallots, peeled and chopped
Leaves from 1 sprig fresh chervil or parsley, chopped
1 tablespoon butter
2 tablespoons unbleached white flour
1½ cups homemade rich chicken stock
Generous pinch of ground cayenne
Sea salt

Combine the wine, shallots, and chervil in a small saucepan, place over medium heat, and bring to a simmer. Simmer until only about 3 tablespoons of liquid remain. Strain and reserve the liquid; discard the solids.

Melt the butter in a medium saucepan over medium heat. Using a wooden spoon, stir the flour into the butter until it is fully incorporated and forms a thick paste, or roux. Lower the heat and cook the roux for 3 minutes or so, stirring constantly, until it begins to color slightly. Raise the heat to medium and gradually add the stock, whisking all the while to incorporate it, then bring to a boil and cook until a very thick sauce is formed, about 10 minutes.

Add the reserved strained wine, season with the cayenne and salt, and bring to a boil. Remove from the heat and serve. If not using the sauce right away, keep it covered and warm until ready to serve.

Sauce Velouté

Considered a basic sauce in classic cuisine, Sauce Velouté has many variations, including Sauce Vin Blanc (white wine sauce); Sauce Supreme (cream sauce); and Sauce Allemande (German sauce, thickened with egg yolks and cream). Note: Do not season your *velouté*. Velouté is always used as a foundation for other sauces to which you then add seasonings.

Makes 1 quart

5 cups homemade white stock (veal, chicken, or fish)
4 tablespoons clarified butter
4 tablespoons unbleached white flour

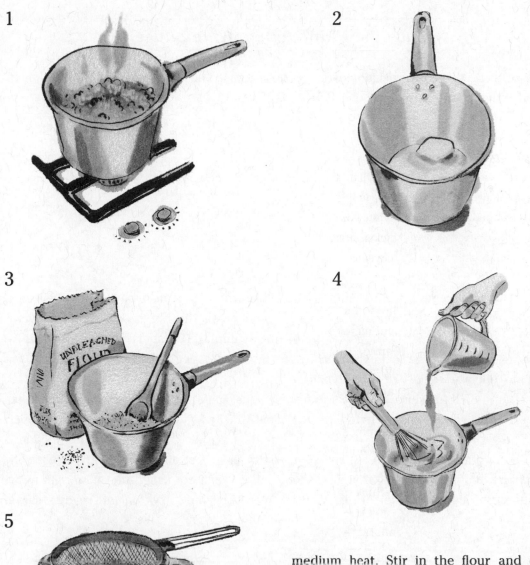

1

2

3

4

5

Heat the stock in a large saucepan over medium heat until simmering.

Meanwhile, in a small heavy-bottomed saucepan, melt the clarified butter over medium heat. Stir in the flour and cook, stirring, for about 5 minutes, until a lightly browned roux forms. Turn off the heat, let the roux cool slightly, then slowly whisk it into the simmering stock. Reduce the heat to low and simmer for 45 minutes to 1 hour, until it reaches the "napé" stage, meaning the sauce can thinly coat the back of a spoon. If the sauce needs thinning, add a little more hot stock. Strain through a fine-mesh strainer or a strainer lined with cheesecloth and serve. If not using the sauce right away, keep it covered and warm until ready to serve.

Sauce Vin Blanc (White Wine Sauce)

Sauce Vin Blanc is a variation of Sauce Velouté based on fish stock. This sauce goes well with just about any type of fish or seafood dish.

Makes 1 quart

½ cup dry white wine

1 quart Sauce Velouté (page 256) made with fish stock, simmering

½ cup heavy cream or crème fraîche

2 tablespoons butter

Sea salt and freshly ground white pepper

Fresh lemon juice

In a small saucepan over medium heat, bring the wine to a boil. Reduce by half and add to the Sauce Velouté. Boil the *velouté* gently until it reduces and reaches the "napé" stage, meaning the sauce can thinly coat the back of a spoon. If the sauce needs thinning, add a little more hot stock.

Before adding the cream to the sauce, it needs to be tempered, that is, brought up to a temperature similar to that of the sauce:

Place the cream in a bowl and whisk in a spoonful of the hot sauce. Repeat several times until the cream is warmed, then whisk the cream-sauce mixture into the sauce.

Just before serving, stir in the butter until melted and season with salt, pepper, and lemon juice. Strain through a fine-mesh strainer or a strainer lined with cheesecloth and serve. If not using the sauce right away, keep it covered and warm until ready to serve.

Sauce Supreme

Sauce Supreme is a very simple variation of Sauce Velouté based on chicken broth. This sauce is traditionally served with poached or steamed chicken or any delicately flavored poultry dish.

Makes 1 quart

1 quart Sauce Velouté (page 256) made with chicken broth

1 cup heavy cream or crème fraîche

2 tablespoons butter

Sea salt and freshly ground white pepper

Fresh lemon juice

Pour the Sauce Velouté into a large sauce-pan, place over medium heat, bring to a simmer, and simmer until reduced by one-quarter.

Before adding the cream to the sauce, the cream needs to be tempered, that is, brought up to a temperature similar to that of the sauce: Place the cream in a bowl and whisk in a spoonful of the hot sauce. Repeat several times until the cream is warmed, then whisk the cream-sauce mixture into the sauce.

Stir in the butter until melted and season with salt, white pepper, and lemon juice. Strain through a fine-mesh strainer or strainer lined with cheesecloth and serve. If not using the sauce right away, keep it covered and warm until ready to serve.

Sauce Allemande

Sauce Allemande is another simple sauce, this time based on Sauce Velouté made with veal stock. It's perfect sauce with veal scaloppine or veal chops.

Makes 1 quart

1 quart Sauce Velouté (page 256) made with veal stock
2 egg yolks
½ cup heavy cream or crème fraîche
Sea salt and freshly ground white pepper
Fresh lemon juice

Pour the Sauce Velouté into a large sauce-pan, place over medium heat, bring to a simmer, and simmer until reduced by one-quarter.

In a medium bowl, whisk the egg yolks with the cream. Before adding the cream–egg yolk mixture to the sauce, it needs to be tempered, that is, brought up to a temperature similar to that of the sauce: Whisk in a spoonful of the hot sauce. Repeat several times, until the cream–egg yolk mixture is warmed, then whisk the mixture into the sauce.

Season with salt, white pepper, and lemon juice. Strain through a fine-mesh strainer or strainer lined with cheesecloth and serve. If not using the sauce right away, keep it covered and warm until ready to serve.

Wow Wow Sauce

The French have many variations on the basic flour-thickened sauce. Here is an English variation; its surprising ingredients have amused many food commentators. Wow Wow Sauce is traditionally served with roast beef.

Makes about 2 cups

4 tablespoons butter

2 tablespoons unbleached white flour

1 cup homemade beef stock

1 tablespoon red wine vinegar

1 teaspoon prepared English mustard

1 tablespoon port wine

1 tablespoon finely chopped parsley

6 pickled walnuts (see Sources, page 296), or 3 gherkins, finely diced

Melt the butter in a medium saucepan over low heat. Stir in the flour and cook, stirring, for 2 to 3 minutes, until the flour is completely amalgamated into the butter and has turned slightly brown.

Slowly pour in the stock, whisking constantly to prevent lumps from forming. Add the vinegar, mustard, and port and simmer until the sauce reaches the consistency of heavy cream, then stir in the parsley and pickled walnuts or gherkins. Heat through for another minute or so and serve hot. If not using the sauce right away, keep it covered and warm until ready to serve.

Reduction Sauces

Reduction sauces are thickened by the process of boiling to reduce the liquid in a stock; as the water portion evaporates, the remaining gelatin thickens the sauce.

You can start with stock that has already been boiled down; this is called demi-glace or *fumet*. Thin with water to achieve the desired consistency.

When boiling down a large amount of stock, you may wish to avoid boiling away most of the liquid by thickening it with a little unflavored gelatin (we recommend Great Lakes brand). Mix 2 teaspoons with about ½ cup of boiling stock and stir until dissolved and whisk into the stock. This step may be repeated for further thickening. Note, though, that the more gelatin you add, the less flavorful the final sauce will be.

You can also thicken a reduction sauce with arrowroot powder. Mix 1 tablespoon arrowroot with 1½ tablespoons water and stir into the boiling or simmering reduction sauce. This may be repeated if further thickening is needed.

Red Wine Sauce

Red wine sauce is delicious with roast beef or beef tenderloin. This sauce simmers away for many hours as the thin beef stock reduces to a thick sauce. The amount of sauce you end up with depends on the gelatin level in the stock—very gelatinous stock will thicken faster as the liquid evaporates, leaving you with more sauce.

Makes 2 to 3 cups

2 quarts homemade beef or veal stock
2 cups red wine
1 tablespoon red currant jelly (optional)
Sea salt if needed

Combine the stock and wine in a large heavy-bottomed pan. Place over medium-high heat, bring to a simmer, then reduce the heat and simmer throughout the day, from 4 to 8 hours depending on the amount of gelatin in the stock, occasionally skimming any scum that rises to the surface. The sauce is ready when it coats a wooden spoon. Stir in the optional red currant jelly and season with salt if needed.

White Wine Sauce

As with the Red Wine Sauce (page 261), stock simmers for several hours until it reduces to a thick sauce.

Makes 1 to 2 cups

2 quarts thin homemade chicken broth or 1 quart rich chicken stock
1 cup white wine
Sea salt if needed

Combine the stock and wine in a large heavy-bottomed pan. Place over medium-high heat, bring to a simmer, then reduce the heat and simmer throughout the day, anywhere from 2 to 4 hours, depending on the amount of gelatin in the stock, occasionally skimming any scum that rises to the surface. The sauce is ready when it coats a wooden spoon. Season with salt if needed.

Mustard Cream Sauce

Makes 1½ cups

1 cup White Wine Sauce (above)
½ cup heavy cream or crème fraîche
2 tablespoons Dijon-style mustard

Heat the White Wine Sauce in a small saucepan until hot.

Mix the cream and mustard in a small heatproof bowl. Slowly add the hot White Wine Sauce, whisking constantly. Return the sauce to the pan, bring to a simmer, and simmer for about 10 minutes to reduce it further.

Sauce Lyonnaise

This reduction sauce is often served with leftover meats.

Makes 2 cups

1 tablespoon butter
½ cup finely chopped onion

½ cup white wine

2 cups homemade beef or veal stock

Melt the butter in a medium saucepan over medium heat. Add the onion and cook for about 5 minutes, until softened but not colored. Add the wine and cook until reduced by half, then stir in the stock. Bring to a simmer and cook until reduced by half, about 45 minutes. Strain and serve.

Miscellaneous Sauces

Gluten-Free Sauce Thickener

Kay Siefken, Bellingham, Washington

This ingenious recipe can be used by those who are avoiding all grains, flours, starches, and thickeners (including arrowroot powder). Add it to stock to create a sauce with whatever thickness you desire. Use drippings for a thick gravy-like sauce and stock for a thinner sauce.

Makes about 1½ cups

1 medium onion, chopped
1 cup pan drippings from a roast, or 1 cup homemade stock

Boil the onion in water until soft, about 30 minutes; strain through a strainer. Combine the onion and pan drippings in a blender and blend until smooth. Add a little at a time to sauces to thicken to desired consistency.

Chilaquile Sauce

Serve this Mexican-style sauce over scrambled eggs with tortilla chips, grated cheese, and chopped cilantro. Chopped avocado makes a nice garnish.

Judy Griffin, Sunnyvale, California

Makes about 2 cups

1 large onion, peeled and chopped
2 large tomatoes, chopped
1 to 2 jalapeño chiles, seeded and chopped (optional)
About 2 cups homemade chicken broth
Sea salt and freshly ground black pepper
1 bunch fresh cilantro, chopped

Combine the onion, tomatoes, and optional jalapeños in a large saucepan and add enough chicken broth to cover. Place over medium heat, bring to a simmer, then reduce the heat and simmer for about 30 minutes, until the ingredients are softened. Transfer to a blender, add salt and pepper to taste and the cilantro, and blend until well combined.

Curry Sauce

Makes 2 cups

4 tablespoons ghee

1 to 2 tablespoons curry powder

1 cup homemade chicken stock

1 cup heavy cream

Sea salt

Melt the ghee in a medium saucepan over medium heat. Stir in the curry powder. Add the stock and bring to a boil, whisking until smooth. Gradually stir in the cream, return to a boil, and gently boil until reduced by about half. Remove from heat, season with salt, and serve.

Parsley Butter Sauce

Makes about 1 cup

3 tablespoons minced shallot or green onion

2 tablespoons sherry vinegar

¼ cup dry white wine

1 cup homemade fish, chicken, or beef stock

½ cup heavy cream or crème fraîche

3 tablespoons butter, softened

1 tablespoon grainy mustard

Sea salt

2 tablespoons finely chopped fresh parsley

Combine the shallot, vinegar, wine, stock, and cream in a small saucepan. Place over medium heat, bring to a boil, and reduce by about half to thicken the sauce. Reduce the heat and whisk in the butter and mustard. Season with salt and stir in the parsley just before serving.

Enchilada Sauce

Making enchilada sauce is easy when you start with ground chiles.

Makes about 2 quarts

½ cup lard

6 ounces ground New Mexico chile (see Sources, page 295)

1 teaspoon ground cumin

1 quart homemade beef or chicken stock, heated

2 cloves garlic, peeled and smashed

2 (7-ounce) jars tomato paste

1 tablespoon red wine vinegar

¼ cup maple syrup

Sea salt

Melt the lard in a large heavy-bottomed pan. Stir in the ground chile and cumin to make a thick paste. Slowly add the stock, whisking constantly. Stir in the garlic, tomato paste, vinegar, and maple syrup, bring to a simmer, and simmer for about 30 minutes, until the sauce is reduced and thickened. Season with salt and serve.

Shrimp Sauce

Makes about 2 cups

2 cups Shrimp Shell Stock (page 175)

½ cup heavy cream or crème fraîche

2 tablespoons sherry

Sea salt

Combine the stock and cream in a medium saucepan. Place over medium heat, bring to a simmer, and simmer until the sauce thickens to the consistency of cream. Remove from the heat, stir in the sherry, and season with salt and serve.

Marbella Sauce

Three Stone Hearth Community Supported Kitchen, Berkeley, California

This sauce is a classic for chicken, with an intriguing combination of sweet, salty, and tart flavors. Use it to braise chicken parts, or heat up leftover roasted chicken in the sauce for a great change of pace. It's also good over rice and on fish or lamb.

Makes about 4 cups

¼ cup olive oil

1 cup pitted prunes, coarsely chopped

½ cup capers, rinsed and patted dry with paper towels

½ cup pitted green olives, cut in half

4 cloves garlic, peeled and pressed through a garlic press

¼ cup dried oregano

6 bay leaves

1 cup dry white wine

2 cups homemade chicken broth

¼ cup finely chopped Italian parsley

½ cup pitted prunes, finely minced

Sea salt and freshly ground black pepper

Heat the oil in a large sauté pan or skillet over medium heat. Add the prunes, capers, and olives and stir thoroughly. Stir in the garlic, oregano, and bay leaves. Add the wine, bring to a simmer, and simmer until the wine has mostly evaporated. Add the broth and bring to a simmer, then lower the heat, cover, and cook for 10 to 15 minutes, until the sauce reduces and thickens slightly. Remove from the heat and add the parsley and minced prunes. Season with salt and pepper and serve.

Puttanesca Sauce

Three Stone Hearth Community Supported Kitchen, Berkeley, California

This is a broth-based version of a classic Italian sauce. It is typically served on pasta but is also delicious over rice, polenta, summer squash, roasted eggplant, chicken, meatballs, or fish.

Makes about 1 quart

¼ cup olive oil

1 cup finely chopped onion

6 cloves garlic, minced

2 tablespoons minced anchovy fillets (about 8 fillets)

½ teaspoon red chile flakes, or to taste

2 tablespoons tomato paste

½ cup tomato puree

2 cups homemade beef broth

1 cup tightly packed pitted and halved Kalamata olives

2 tablespoons drained capers

½ cup minced fresh parsley

Sea salt

Heat the oil in a large sauté pan over medium heat. Add the onion and cook, stirring, until it is translucent, about 5 minutes. Add the garlic, anchovies, and chile flakes and cook, stirring, for 1 minute. Add the tomato paste, tomato puree, and broth. Bring to a simmer, then reduce the heat and cook, uncovered, for 30 minutes, stirring occasionally, until the sauce reduces and thickens slightly. Add the olives and capers and cook for another 10 minutes. Stir in the parsley and season with salt.

Coconut Tikka Masala Sauce

Three Stone Hearth Community Supported Kitchen, Berkeley, California

This is a dairy-free version of the classic sauce for chicken. It is also delicious over vegetables, rice, fish, eggs, and lamb meatballs. It may be frozen to turn another meal into something scrumptious!

Makes about 4 cups

2 tablespoons coconut oil

1 small onion, peeled and sliced

2 cloves garlic, peeled and smashed

2 tablespoons peeled and minced fresh ginger

4 teaspoons sweet paprika

1 tablespoon cumin seeds, toasted and ground

1½ teaspoons coriander seeds, toasted and ground

1 teaspoon ground cinnamon

1 teaspoon cardamom pods, toasted and ground

¼ to ½ teaspoon ground cayenne

½ teaspoon freshly ground black pepper

¼ cup tomato paste

2 cups homemade chicken broth

2 teaspoons coconut flour

1 (13.5-ounce) can coconut milk

Juice of 1 lemon, or to taste

Sea salt

Heat the oil in a small saucepan over medium heat. Add the onion, garlic, and ginger and sauté until the onion is translucent, about 5 minutes. Add the paprika, cumin seeds, coriander seeds, cinnamon, cardamom, cayenne, and black pepper. Add the tomato paste, then whisk in the broth and bring to a simmer. Simmer for 45 minutes until the sauce reduces and thickens slightly.

In a medium bowl, whisk the coconut flour into the coconut milk and set aside for a few minutes for the coconut milk to absorb the flour. Add the thickened coconut milk to the broth mixture and heat to warm it, then puree using a handheld blender. Add the lemon juice and season with salt.

Pesto Sauce

This sauce does not contain broth, but we include it because pesto blends beautifully into broth for a variety of soups, such as Spicy Coconut Chicken and Shrimp Soup (page 203) and White Bean Soup with Sausage and Pesto (page 224).

Makes about 1 cup

2 cups packed fresh basil leaves

2 to 4 cloves garlic, coarsely chopped

½ teaspoon sea salt

¼ cup toasted pine nuts

¼ cup freshly grated Parmesan cheese

¼ to ½ cup extra virgin olive oil

Place the basil leaves in a food processor and pulse until well chopped. Add the garlic, salt, pine nuts, and cheese and blend well. Add the oil in a thin stream through the hole in the lid and process to form a thick paste.

CHAPTER 26

Meat with Sauce

Having broth on hand allows you to make quick and easy reduction sauces for steak, gravy for roasts, and thickened sauces for stir-fries. With nourishing broth, there is no need to reach for MSG-laden bottled sauces to perk up your meat, poultry, and fish.

Pan-Roasted Chicken with Cream Sauce

Serves 4 to 6

1 whole chicken, cut into pieces

2 tablespoons butter, melted

2 tablespoons Dijon-style mustard

Sea salt and freshly ground black pepper

Several sprigs fresh tarragon or 1 teaspoon dried tarragon

½ cup dry white wine or vermouth

2 cups homemade chicken broth

½ cup heavy cream or crème fraîche

Preheat the oven to 400°F.

Cut up the chicken: Separate the legs and thighs, remove the bone from the breasts, and cut the breasts into 2 pieces. Reserve the back and neck for making stock.

Place the chicken pieces skin side up in a stainless steel roasting pan. In a small bowl, combine the melted butter and mustard and brush the skin of the chicken with the mixture. Sprinkle with salt and pepper. Strew the tarragon over the top. Bake for about 1 hour, until the chicken is cooked through and browned on the outside. Remove the chicken pieces to a platter and keep them warm. Place the baking pan over medium heat and deglaze the pan with the wine, stirring to remove any browned bits from the bottom of the pan. Add the broth, bring to a boil, and boil until reduced by about half. Gradually add the cream and boil to reduce it a little more, until a thick sauce consistency is reached. Season with salt. Strain the sauce into a heated bowl or gravy boat and serve with the chicken.

Baked Chicken with Gravy

Serves 4 to 6

1 whole chicken
4 tablespoons (½ stick) butter, melted
Sea salt and freshly ground black pepper
Several sprigs of fresh thyme
1 medium onion, peeled and thinly sliced
2 tablespoons unbleached white flour
2 to 3 cups homemade chicken broth
Sea salt

Preheat the oven to 350°F.

Place the chicken on a wire rack set over a stainless steel roasting pan. Brush the chicken with the melted butter and sprinkle with salt and pepper. Stuff the cavity with the thyme sprigs and scatter the sliced onion around the baking pan.

Bake for about 90 minutes, until the skin is nicely browned and the leg joint is loose.

Remove the chicken to a cutting board, cut it into pieces, place on a platter, and keep warm while you make the gravy.

To make the gravy, set the pan over medium heat on the stovetop. Stir the flour into the pan drippings and cook, stirring, for 3 to 4 minutes, or until the flour has browned. Slowly add the chicken broth, using a whisk to smooth out any lumps. If the gravy is too thick, add a little water or more stock; if it is too thin, boil it down until it thickens. Simmer for 5 to 10 minutes and season with salt.

Strain the gravy into a heated bowl or gravy boat and serve with the chicken.

Saucy Skillet Steaks

Donna and Ashley Sherman, Bloomington, Illinois

Serves 4

1 tablespoon lard or tallow

4 beef rib eye steaks, about ¾ inch thick

4 tablespoons (½ stick) butter

1 large onion, peeled and chopped

4 cloves garlic, minced

2 tablespoons Dijon-style mustard

Sea salt and freshly ground black pepper

1 cup homemade beef broth

¼ cup brandy or red wine (optional)

1 tablespoon minced fresh parsley

Preheat the oven to 250°F.

In a large skillet, melt the lard over medium-high heat. Add the steaks and cook for 1 to 2 minutes on each side to lightly brown them. Remove to a baking pan and keep warm in the oven.

Melt the butter into the fat in the pan, add the onion and garlic, and sauté until softened, about 5 minutes, stirring to loosen the browned bits from the bottom of the pan. Brush the steaks with the mustard, sprinkle with salt and pepper, and return them to the pan. Stir in the broth and optional brandy and cook for about 5 minutes on each side, until the meat reaches desired doneness (for medium-rare, a meat thermometer should read 145°F; for medium, 160°F; for well done, 170°F). Return the steaks to the baking pan, spoon the onion mixture over the steaks, and return to the oven to keep warm.

Meanwhile, boil down the broth in the skillet until thickened to sauce consistency. Remove the steaks from the oven, put them on plates, and spoon the sauce on top. Sprinkle with the parsley and serve.

Hamburger Stroganoff

Serves 2 to 3

2 to 3 tablespoons lard or bacon drippings

1 medium onion, peeled and chopped

5 or 6 medium mushrooms, stems removed, cut in half and sliced

1 pound ground beef

½ teaspoon paprika

¼ cup brandy

1 cup homemade beef broth

½ cup heavy cream, sour cream, or crème fraîche

Sea salt and freshly ground black pepper

Noodles, Basic Brown Rice (page 276), or pan-fried or toasted sourdough bread

In a large cast-iron skillet, melt the lard over medium heat. Add the onion and mushrooms and sauté until well browned, about 10 minutes. Push the mixture to one side and add the ground beef to the other side. Cook the beef until no longer pink and starting to brown, about 5 minutes. Stir in the paprika. Add the brandy and broth and bring to a boil, stirring to release any browned bits from the bottom of the pan. Add the cream, return to a boil, and boil until reduced by about half. Season with salt and pepper. Serve with noodles, brown rice, or fried sourdough bread.

Gluten-Free Meatballs and Gravy

Lori Clemmons, Cupertino, California

Serves 6 to 8

1 large head cauliflower

3 pounds ground beef

¼ pound liver, blended in a blender or food processor

2½ teaspoons sea salt

1 tablespoon dried thyme

3 cups homemade beef broth

1 large onion, peeled and finely chopped

Pulse the cauliflower in small batches in a food processor to about the size of short rice grains.

Combine the ground beef, liver, cauliflower, salt, and thyme in a large bowl and mix well. Form into 1-inch meatballs.

Pour the broth into a large skillet and add the onion. Bring to a simmer. Add the meatballs to the broth in batches and simmer for 20 minutes, or until cooked through. As the meatballs are done, remove them from the broth to a serving bowl and cover to keep warm. Puree the onions with the broth with a handheld blender to make a sauce for the meatballs. Serve the meatballs with the sauce.

Slow Cooker Roast

Larry Bowers, Ethridge, Tennessee

Serves 6 to 8

2 tablespoons apple cider vinegar

2 cloves garlic, peeled and smashed

½ teaspoon vanilla extract

2 to 3 tablespoons naturally fermented soy sauce

1 tablespoon low-sugar berry preserves

3 to 4 pounds bone-in fatty cut of beef, such as chuck or short ribs

3 to 4 cups homemade beef broth

1 to 2 onions, peeled and quartered

2 to 3 tablespoons beef tallow or lard

Combine the vinegar, garlic, vanilla, soy sauce, and preserves in a 6-quart slow cooker. Add the beef and enough broth to just cover the meat. Add the onions and dot the tallow on top. Cover and cook on low for 6 to 8 hours, until the meat is very tender. Remove the meat from the slow cooker, cool, then remove the meat from the bones and return the meat to the pot. Reheat and serve.

Leg of Lamb with Red Wine Reduction Sauce

Serves 6 to 8

1 leg of lamb, about 5 pounds

4 tablespoons (½ stick) butter, melted

¼ cup smooth Dijon-style mustard

Several sprigs fresh tarragon or rosemary

1 onion, peeled and sliced

4 cloves garlic, peeled

½ cup red wine

2 cups homemade beef broth

Preheat the oven to 400°F.

Set the leg of lamb on a wire rack over a roasting pan. In a small bowl, blend the melted butter with the mustard and paint the lamb with the mixture using a pastry brush. Top with the tarragon and strew the onion and garlic into the pan. Place in the oven and immediately turn the oven temperature down to 350°F. Cook the lamb for about 20 minutes to the pound, or until a meat thermometer indicates medium-rare (the lamb should be pink). Transfer the lamb to a heated platter, cover, and keep warm while you make the sauce.

Remove the rack from the pan and place the pan over a burner turned to medium-high heat. Add the wine to the pan and bring to a boil, scraping the bottom of the pan with a wooden spoon to release any browned bits. Add the broth and boil down until reduced by about one-third. Strain the sauce into a heated bowl or gravy boat, slice the lamb, and serve with the sauce.

CHAPTER 27

Grains and Legumes

Grains and legumes are, by nature, difficult to digest. Preparing them with broth makes digestion easier. Use of broth in grain and legume preparation is especially important for young children, the elderly, and those with impaired digestion.

Basic Brown Rice

Presoaking the rice and cooking it in gelatin-rich broth ensures that it will be very digestible, even by those generally very sensitive to grains.

Serves 6 to 8

2 cups long-grain brown rice

2 tablespoons vinegar, lemon juice, or yogurt

Warm filtered water

2 tablespoons butter

2 tablespoons olive oil

Seeds from 2 to 3 cardamom pods

4 cups homemade chicken broth (or a combination of broth and water)

Sea salt

Place the rice and vinegar in a quart-size jar and add enough warm filtered water to fill the jar with a little space remaining at the top. Cover tightly and leave at room temperature for about 7 hours. (If you are making rice in the evening, put it in to soak in the morning.) Drain the rice through a strainer, shaking to remove excess moisture.

Melt the butter in the oil in a flameproof casserole over medium heat. Add the rice to the casserole and heat until the grains start to turn whitish, stirring frequently. Stir in the cardamom pods and add the chicken broth. Increase the heat to high, bring to a boil, and boil vigorously until the liquid reduces to the level of the rice. Reduce the heat to low, cover tightly, and cook for about 2 hours, until the rice is thoroughly tender. Do not remove the lid for the first hour of cooking. Alternately, you can cover the casserole and bake the rice in the oven preheated to 275°F for 2 hours. Season with sea salt.

Mexican Rice

Heather Stein, Ste. Genevieve, Missouri

Serves 4

1 cup long-grain brown rice

2 tablespoons vinegar, lemon juice, or yogurt

Warm filtered water

2 cups homemade chicken stock

1 cup diced fresh tomatoes with liquid or ½ (14-ounce) can diced tomatoes

1 tablespoon minced onion

¼ teaspoon chili powder, or to taste

½ teaspoon salt

2 tablespoons butter

Place the rice and vinegar in a quart-size jar and add enough warm filtered water to fill the jar with a little space remaining at the top. Cover tightly and leave at room temperature for about 7 hours. (If you are making rice in the evening, put it in to soak in the morning.) Drain the rice through a strainer, shaking to remove excess moisture.

Combine the rice with the remaining ingredients in a medium saucepan with a tight-fitting lid. Bring to a boil over medium-high heat and skim any scum that forms at the top. Reduce the heat to low, cover, and simmer, for at least 60 minutes, until all the liquid is absorbed and the rice is tender.

Spanish Rice

Barbara Gilbert, Springfield, Ohio

Serves 6

1½ cups brown jasmine rice or basmati rice

1 tablespoon vinegar, lemon juice, or yogurt

1½ cups warm filtered water

2 tablespoons olive oil or lard

½ yellow onion, chopped

2 to 3 cloves garlic, minced

½ teaspoon sea salt

½ teaspoon freshly ground black pepper

1 cup chopped or diced fresh tomatoes

3 cups homemade chicken broth

1 teaspoon ground cumin

Place the rice and yogurt in a quart-size jar and add the warm water. Cover the container and set in a warm place. Cover tightly and leave at room temperature for about 7 hours. (If you are making rice in the evening, put it in to soak in the morning.) Drain the rice through a strainer, shaking to remove excess moisture.

Heat the oil in a 3½-quart or larger sauté pan with a lid over medium heat. Add the onion, garlic, drained rice, salt, and pepper and cook, stirring constantly, until the rice turns whitish, 5 to 10 minutes. Add the tomatoes and cook, stirring constantly, for 5 minutes. Add the broth and bring to a boil. Add the cumin, reduce the heat to low, cover, and cook for 45 minutes without lifting the lid. Turn off the heat and keep covered for an additional 15 to 25 minutes. Remove the lid, fluff the rice, and serve.

Mushroom Risotto

Lydia Palermo, Monument, Colorado

Serves 4

1 cup brown rice

Juice of ½ lemon

Warm filtered water

2 cups homemade chicken stock

1 teaspoon sea salt

1 cup white wine

2 tablespoons butter

2 cups sliced shiitake, chanterelle, or other mushrooms

1 cup freshly grated Parmesan cheese

½ teaspoon freshly grated nutmeg

1 tablespoon truffle oil or butter (optional)

Place the rice and lemon juice in a quart-size jar and add enough warm filtered water to fill the jar with a little space remaining at the top. Cover tightly and leave at room temperature about 7 hours. (If you are making rice in the evening, put it in to soak in the morning.) Drain the rice through a strainer, shaking to remove excess moisture.

Combine the stock, rice, and ½ teaspoon of the salt in a large saucepan. Place over medium-high heat and bring to a boil. Reduce the heat to low, cover, and cook for 45 minutes. Add wine, raise the heat, and and return to a boil. Cook, stirring, until the liquid is reduced to a thick sauce and the rice is fairly tender but still has a little bite to it.

Meanwhile, heat the butter in a large sauté pan over medium heat. Add the mushrooms and sauté until slightly caramelized, 10 to 15 minutes. Season the mushrooms with the remaining ½ teaspoon salt. Add the mushrooms to the rice and stir in the cheese, nutmeg, and optional truffle oil and serve.

Note: If the risotto is too thick, thin with a little stock, wine, or water. It should be more like a thick soup than a rice dish.

Slow Cooker New England Baked Beans

Serves 8

4 cups dry white navy beans

Warm and cold filtered water

½ pound bacon, cut into pieces

2 medium onions, peeled and chopped

2 teaspoons sea salt

2 tablespoons molasses

1 small can or jar tomato paste

1 teaspoon dry mustard

¼ teaspoon ground cayenne

1 tablespoon honey

About 1 quart homemade beef or chicken broth

4 kielbasa or bratwurst sausages, sliced

Sea salt

Pick over and wash the beans and soak them overnight in warm filtered water to cover. Drain and rinse the beans with fresh water.

Place the beans in a large saucepan and add enough cold filtered water to cover by 1 inch. Bring to a boil and skim off any scum that rises to the surface. Reduce the heat to low and simmer for about 4 hours, until the skins begin to split. Drain and put the beans into a slow cooker.

Stir in the bacon, onions, salt, molasses, tomato paste, mustard, cayenne, and honey.

Add enough broth to cover the beans. Cover and cook on low until the beans are tender, about 8 hours, adding water as needed to keep beans covered. Near the end of the cooking time, remove the cover to allow excess moisture to cook off, stirring the beans often to prevent sticking. Fifteen minutes before serving, stir in the sausage slices to warm through. Season with salt. Serve with sauerkraut, sourdough bread and butter, and a big salad.

Slow Cooker Sausage and Beans

This easy slow cooker dish makes its own stock.

Serves 8 to 10

4 cups white navy beans or heritage beans

Cold filtered water

1 beef marrowbone

1 piece split pig's foot

¼ cup lard

2 pounds sausage, cut into slices

Several sprigs fresh herbs, such as thyme or rosemary

Sea salt

Pick over and wash the beans and soak them overnight in cold filtered water to cover. Drain and rinse the beans with fresh water.

Place all the ingredients except the salt in a slow cooker and cook on low for about 12 hours or until the beans are very soft. Season with salt. Serve with sauerkraut, sourdough bread and butter, and a big salad.

Green Lentils

In France, lentils are traditionally served with leg of lamb.

Serves 4 to 6

2 cups green lentils
Juice of ½ lemon
Warm filtered water
4 slices smoked bacon, thinly sliced crosswise
1 tablespoon unsalted butter
1 small onion, finely chopped
1 small carrot, finely chopped
3 celery sticks, finely chopped
5½ cups homemade chicken broth or a combination of broth and water
1 *bouquet garni* made with parsley sprigs, thyme sprigs, and a bay leaf, tied together with
    kitchen string
Sea salt and freshly ground black pepper

Place the lentils in a quart-size jar with the lemon juice and enough warm water to fill the jar with a little room left at the top. Cover tightly and leave at room temperature for about 7 hours. (If you are making lentils in the evening, put it in to soak in the morning.) Drain through a strainer, rinse, and shake off excess water.

Cook the bacon in a 2-quart saucepan over medium-high heat until the fat has rendered, about 6 minutes. Add the butter, onion, carrot, and celery and cook until the vegetables are softened, about 15 minutes. Stir in the lentils and broth, bring to a boil, and skim any scum that rises to the surface. Reduce the heat to medium-low, add the *bouquet garni*, and simmer until lentils are tender, about 1 hour and 10 minutes. Discard the herbs, season with salt and pepper, and serve.

CHAPTER 28

Broth for Breakfast

Broth for breakfast? It might sound crazy, but broth for breakfast is a great way to start your morning, promoting increased energy, easy digestion, and a stable mood throughout the day.

Stellar Breakfast Miso Soup

Emily Marenghi, Portola Valley, California

Serves 2

2 cups homemade chicken broth

2 tablespoons naturally fermented red or white miso paste

2 poached eggs

2 green onions, ends cut off, thinly sliced

Bring broth to a boil in a medium saucepan. Lower the heat to a simmer and stir in the miso paste until dissolved. Divide between 2 bowls, gently set a poached egg on each, and scatter the green onions on top. Eat with a large spoon.

Eggs in Broth

Richard Hruby, Bloomington, Minnesota

Serves 1 to 2

1¼ cups homemade broth (any type)
3 or 4 eggs, separated
Sea salt and freshly ground black pepper

Bring the broth to a simmer in a medium saucepan. Lightly whip the egg whites and stir them into the simmering broth. Return to a light simmer, then pour the broth and whites over the uncooked yolks in bowls. Gently lift the whole yolks up with a wooden spoon to get the broth underneath them so that the white left on the yolk has a chance to cook. After a few minutes, break up the yolks and stir them in. Season with salt and pepper and serve.

Eggs in Broth with Sauerkraut

Rebecca L. Stults, Langley, Washington

Serves 1

1 cup homemade broth (any type)
2 eggs
Sea salt and freshly ground black pepper
2 tablespoons raw sauerkraut (optional)

Bring the broth just to a boil in a medium saucepan. Add the eggs and stir lightly so the whites congeal while the yolks remain soft. When the eggs are gently poached, remove from heat and pour the eggs and broth into a bowl. Season with salt and pepper. Cool slightly, then stir in the optional sauerkraut.

Breakfast Meat and Veggie Scramble

Susan Blake, Tacoma, Washington

My thirteen-year-old son and I have a meat and veggie scramble just about every morning for breakfast. It can be made with fresh meat and vegetables or leftovers and is easy and nutritious either way. Any combination of meat and vegetables will work, but we have a few favorites: (1) ground elk or beef, green beans, green cabbage, carrots, and onions; (2) pork and apple sausage slices, onions, mushrooms, cubed sweet potatoes, and zucchini; (3) shredded chicken, cooked lima beans, carrots, chard stems, and diced beets. My son has a sensitivity to eggs, so this makes a great nutritious substitute for an egg-based breakfast.

Serves 2

2 tablespoons lard, duck fat, suet, butter, or ghee, or a combination, plus more if needed

8 ounces meat (see headnote)

2 cups shredded or finely diced vegetables

Up to ½ cup homemade broth (any type)

Sea salt and freshly ground black pepper

Toppings: butter, grated raw cheese, sour cream, avocado, or raw sauerkraut

Melt the lard in a large cast-iron skillet over medium heat. Add the meat and cook it until browned, about 5 minutes. Remove the meat with a slotted spoon to a bowl. Add additional fat to the pan if necessary.

Add the vegetables to the fat in the pan and cook until tender. Start with onions, mushrooms, and more fibrous vegetables and add the more tender vegetables at the end. Add up to ½ cup bone broth, bring to a simmer, reduce the heat to low, and simmer for about 5 minutes. Season with salt and pepper. Add the meat to the vegetable mixture and cook until warmed through. Serve with your choice of toppings.

Breakfast Goulash

Megan Ulrichs, Bozeman, Montana

Serves 6

3 cups homemade chicken or beef broth

1½ cups polenta

3 to 4 tablespoons butter or ghee

1 pound sausage meat

6 to 8 eggs, poached or fried over easy

2 to 4 ounces raw cheddar or goat cheese

Sea salt and freshly ground black pepper

Pour the broth into a large saucepan and bring to a boil. Whisk in the polenta and cook, stirring often, for about 20 minutes.

Melt the butter in a large skillet. Crumble the sausage meat into the skillet and cook, stirring, until browned, about 10 minutes.

Stir the cooked eggs, sausage, cooking fat, and cheese into the polenta. Season with salt and pepper and serve.

Stock Eggs

Lydia Palermo, Monument, Colorado

Serves 1

2 cups homemade chicken stock

1 teaspoon sea salt

2 tablespoons apple cider vinegar

2 eggs

Bring the stock to a boil in a medium saucepan. Add the salt and 1 tablespoon of the vinegar. Reduce the heat to a low simmer and gently crack the eggs one at a time into the simmering water. Simmer for 3 minutes, or until cooked to your liking. Remove with a slotted spoon to a bowl. Cool for 2 minutes, top with the remaining 1 tablespoon vinegar, and serve.

Mighty Morphing Breakfast Soup

Lynn Kramer, Catskill, New York

This recipe combines grains with eggs and provides the best of both raw and cooked food.

Serves 2

2 tablespoons rolled oats

Squeeze of fresh lemon juice

Warm filtered water

1 cup homemade broth (any type)

¼ cup raw sauerkraut

¼ avocado, flesh scooped out and diced

2 eggs

Sea salt and freshly ground black pepper

Soak oats in a jar with the lemon juice and warm filtered water to cover at room temperature overnight. Drain and rinse.

Bring the broth to a boil in a small saucepan and add the soaked oats. Lower the heat and cook for 2 to 3 minutes, until softened.

Meanwhile, place the sauerkraut and avocado in a bowl. When the grain is cooked to your liking, separate the eggs. Put the whites in the pot and the yolks in the bowl. Gently cook the whites, stirring, until opaque, about 1 minute. Turn off the heat. Season with salt and pepper. Pour the oat–egg white mixture into the bowl with the raw ingredients and gently stir to break the yolks and blend them into the soup.

CHAPTER 29

Tonics

Any recipe prepared with broth will provide health benefits, but the recipes in this chapter are specifically targeted at supporting the immune system and good overall health.

Coconut Ginger Soup for Colds and Flu

Serves 4

1 quart homemade chicken stock

1 (13.5-ounce) can whole coconut milk

1-inch piece fresh ginger root, peeled and grated

Juice of 1 lemon or 2 limes, strained

¼ teaspoon red chile flakes

Sea salt

Combine the stock, coconut milk, ginger, lemon juice, and chile flakes in a large saucepan; place over medium-high heat and bring to a simmer. Remove from the heat, season with salt, and serve.

Pigskin Broth for Beautiful Skin

This is a wonderful tonic for the skin.

Makes 1 quart

About 2 cups rind from a ham or bacon, cut into pieces
2 tablespoons vinegar
1 quart cold filtered water

Place the rind in a small pot and add the vinegar and water. Place over medium heat, bring to a bare simmer, and carefully spoon off any scum that rises to the top. Lower the heat to low and cook at a bare simmer with the lid off for 4 to 6 hours, until the rind is almost disintegrated and the broth thickens. Occasionally skim scum from the top as needed and check to ensure that the ham remains covered with water, adding more water as needed.

Chicken Broth Pick-Me-Up

Serves 1

¼ teaspoon ground turmeric
¼ teaspoon sea salt
¼ teaspoon ground ginger
1 tablespoon molasses
1 tablespoon coconut oil
1 cup homemade chicken broth

Combine the turmeric, salt, ginger, molasses, and coconut oil in a mug. In a small saucepan, bring the broth to a boil and pour it into the mug. Stir to mix well and dissolve the seasonings and serve.

Hot and Sour Broth Tonic

Mary Evans, Flushing, New York

Serves 1

1 cup homemade beef broth, heated
1 teaspoon apple cider vinegar

1 teaspoon tomato paste

Dash of hot sauce

Mix all the ingredients in a mug, stirring to dissolve the tomato paste, and serve.

◄○►

Chicken Broth Cubes

Because I'm tight on storage space, when I make chicken stock I don't add vegetables until the day I'm using the stock; the result I seek is a concentrated thick gel that can be transferred to a shallow storage tray and placed in the refrigerator or freezer.

Once the carcass and bones have simmered for 24 hours, I remove the bones and boil the stock down to a thick gel, taking care not to let it stick to the bottom. To judge how well it has set, I test it by taking a soupspoon sample and letting it cool for a minute. If it's reasonably firm, then I know that it's ready to set and I pour it into the storage tray and place it in the fridge. After it has firmed up, I cut it into cubes and place the cubes in a zip-top bag. The cubes are easily removed and added to various dishes as needed.

My daughter, who was recovering from dehydration from intravenous drug care at a hospital in India, needed a quick remedy to overcome nausea and extreme weakness. I made a tonic by melting a cube or two of chicken stock in water with a teaspoon of chopped fresh ginger and served this to her several times a day. It proved beneficial and a welcome relief. We have relied on the cubes over several years as standard care for colds, flu, and respiratory disorders.

—Mary Pope, Glenroy, Australia

◄○►

◄○►

Encapsulated Broth

I'm not a great fan of drinking broth, and I travel a lot, so I encapsulate my broth. I make a very basic broth with various browned beef bones and a lot of garlic, using a minimum of water.

Once the broth is cooled and I have removed the fat and strained it, I put it in my biggest pot on the stove over low heat and cook it until it is greatly reduced, then I pour the reduced stock onto trays in a dehydrator and dehydrate it until very dry. Then I grind it up in my food processor, though you could use a mortar and pestle, and then pour the beef dust into empty gelatin capsules. Sometimes I will add ground dehydrated green vegetables if I have any. I take two of the capsules every morning so I am never without the health benefits of gelatinous broth!

—Jade Petersen, Peelwood, Australia

◄○►

CHAPTER 30

Broth on a Large Scale

Broth for Sale

We visited Jessica Prentice and Porsche Combash, two co-owners of Three Stone Hearth in Berkeley, California. This community kitchen prepares a wide variety of dishes, including broth-based soups and stews, pâté, breakfast cereals, lacto-fermented condiments and beverages, and broth-based gravies and sauces. They make thick, gelatinous chicken broth and beef broth and sell more than one hundred quarts of both types each week.

Broths (as well as soups and stews) are prepared in a 40-gallon rectangular stainless steel Cleveland tilt skillet. These are deemed easier to use and clean than the older steam-jacketed kettle, which was (and in many cases still is) standard restaurant equipment for making stocks and soups. The tilt skillet puts the broth at waist level so it is easy to stir and remove from the pan. New ones run about fifteen thousand dollars; they should be outfitted with a spigot on the front, which is another five hundred dollars to install.

At Three Stone Hearth, pastured chickens are roasted, then the meat is removed and used in soups and casseroles with the skin and

bones reserved for stock. The fat from roasting is also reserved; this is used to seal the top of the broth when it is put into jars.

One batch of broth calls for about 30 chicken carcasses and skin, plus an additional 25 pounds of chicken heads and feet. These are put in the tilt skillet and covered with reverse osmosis water. The only addition is 1 cup apple cider vinegar to help pull the minerals from the bones. Prentice and Combash believe that the mineral-free water also helps pull minerals from the bones. No vegetables are added to this basic stock, and the stock is not skimmed.

The water is brought to a boil and then reduced to a simmer. The broth simmers at a setting of 200°F for 24 hours with the lid closed. A very important step comes at the end, after the long simmering, when a masher (like a potato masher) is used to press down the now-softened bones. This releases more minerals into the broth, as well as nutrients from the marrow.

The broth is removed through the spigot and strained through a strainer into pitchers. It is then poured into 1-quart wide-mouth mason jars, which have been sterilized in an industrial dishwasher using very hot water. About 1 ounce melted chicken fat is added to the top of every jar. New lids are used with every batch; the lids are immersed in boiling water and placed on top of each jar with tongs. Jars are then sealed with the rings (which are reused, but recycled if they have any rust). One batch yields about 110 quarts of broth.

The jars are immediately placed in sinks to which a block of ice and cold water has been added. The temperature reduces to 72 to 73 degrees within 40 minutes. The jars are then refrigerated, which brings the temperature down to below 40 degrees within 2 hours.

The chicken broth sells for $13 per quart, plus a $1.50 deposit for the jar.

At Three Stone Hearth, they also make a "second boil" using the same bones; this stock is used for making soup. The bones are again covered with water; often more heads and feet are added. This time the simmer is only 6 hours. The result is a stock that has less gelatin but is more flavorful than the "first boil."

The final mashing step, described above, is considered very important.

The second-boil broth is cooled in 6-inch hotel pans and then put into plastic "cambos" (large rectangular containers) for the freezer. Yield is about 90 quarts. The remaining cooked-down bones and skin are composted.

Beef broth is likewise made in the tilt skillet. One batch calls for 110 pounds of gelatinous bones (such as knuckles) and marrowbones, sawed so that the marrow is exposed. An additional 10 pounds of trim meat is also used.

The meat is browned in the tilt skillet and then the bones are added, along with 1 cup apple cider vinegar. The bones are then covered with water, which is brought to a boil and then reduced to a simmer. At this point it is necessary to redistribute the bones (using tongs) so that water is covering all the bones, as the heat causes the tendons to shrink. No vegetables are added and the stock is not skimmed.

The stock is simmered at a 200°F setting with the lid closed for 24 hours. There is no mashing at the end as with chicken broth.

The broth is put into mason jars and chilled, using the same process as chicken broth. One ounce of melted beef fat is added to the top of each jar. Yield is about 100 quarts. The beef broth sells for $12 per jar, with a $1.50 deposit for the jar.

The bones get a second boil, which yields broth that is used in soups and stews. As with the chicken broth, the second boil will not be quite as gelatinous, but still makes a flavorful and deeply nutritious soup base.

Broth at a Hotel

We visited Executive Chef Marc Suennemann at the Sheraton Atlanta Hotel. His well-equipped kitchen has three rectangular tilt skillets and one steam-jacketed kettle.

The hotel uses the tilt skillets for a variety of dishes, such as soups and stews, but Chef Suennemann prefers to use the steam-jacketed kettle for stock. While Three Stone Hearth aims for maximum gelatin content and produces an opaque broth, Suennemann aims for a clear, light broth, avoiding what he calls "muddiness." He does not cover the broth when it is cooking, because this tends to make the broth muddy, he says. Also, in the tilt skillet, too much water evaporates, requiring more water to be added during cooking, thus diluting the broth. In the cylindrical kettle, the steam comes up around the edges and much of it curls back into the broth; there is less evaporation and less need to add additional water.

According to Suennemann, a light stock is best for clear reduction sauces, clear soups, and consommés; longer-cooked opaque sauces can be used for soups, gravies, and flour-based sauces.

For chicken broth, Chef Suennemann uses about 30 chickens. They are put into the steam kettle along with onion, carrots, celery, and herbs and simmered or gently boiled for only 45 minutes. The chickens are then taken out of the pot and the meat is removed from the carcasses. The carcasses are then returned to the kettle and simmered for another hour. Sometimes the carcasses are roasted before they are returned to the kettle; this results in a darker color to the broth. The second cooking is only 1 hour; then the broth is strained and cooled and used in soups or in small batches to create reduction sauces.

For beef broth, the staff roasts the bones and then simmers them along with vegetables and herbs in the steam kettle for 4 to 5 hours. The bones are then removed and the meat picked off. The bones are returned to the pot for another hour of cooking.

The stock is then strained and cooled. The congealed fat is reserved for roasting vegetables. This stock is used for consommé or reduction sauces and some of it is reserved and used as part of the liquid for the next batch of stock.

Broth in a Restaurant

We spoke to Nathanael Gregg, former chef de cuisine of Lincoln Restaurant in Washington, DC. He made chicken stock in a large stockpot. The recipe calls for 10 pounds of chicken backs and 5 pounds of chicken feet.

The pot is filled with water, which is brought to a boil and then simmered for one day at the lowest heat with the cover off.

The cooked bones are then strained off and 10 pounds of roasted bones are added to the stock, along with 1 pound each of carrots, onions, and celery; 4 heads of garlic; bay leaves; peppercorns; thyme sprigs; and some pieces of kombu. This is brought to a boil and then simmered for 6 hours, or until reduced by half.

The resulting stock forms the basis for all sauces in the restaurant and for gravy in chicken pot pie.

The broth is enhanced with additional flavor by adding 5 pounds of hard cheese rinds (tied up in cheesecloth) to the finished stock. This is brought to a boil and then simmered for 4 hours. This savory stock is used in a sauce for meatballs.

Sources

For an up-to-date list of products we endorse, please visit our website, www.nourishingbroth .com.

Homemade Bone Broth

Genuine bone broth, long-simmered and made with bones, is now available from dozens of producers, and it can be easily shipped frozen. For the most up-to-date list, purchase the **Find Real Foods** iTunes App, based on the Weston A. Price Foundation Shopping Guide.

The Shopping Guide is also available in print format, updated yearly, from the Weston A. Price Foundation at www.weston aprice.org; click on "Order Materials."

For local producers of broth who may not be listed in the Shopping Guide, contact the nearest local chapter of the Weston A. Price Foundation at www.westonaprice.org; click on "Find Local Chapter."

Broth-Making Classes

Classes on making bone broth are often given by the local chapters of the Weston A. Price Foundation: www.westonaprice.org; click on "Find Local Chapter."

Bovine Tracheal Cartilage Products

Most of the bovine tracheal cartilage products Dr. John Prudden used in his studies are no longer available. For current information about comparable products, contact Dr. Kaayla Daniel at Kaayla@DrKaaylaDaniel.com. We will also have information about suitable products on our website, www.nourishingbroth.com.

Chiles, Ground

For Ancho Chile and Cauliflower Soup and for Enchilada Sauce, visit loschileros.com. They sell various types of ground dried chile in 6-ounce packages.

Gelatin

Great Lakes Brand, www.greatlakesgelatin .com.

Slow Cooker

There are many brands available. A good quality brand that gets high marks is Cuisinart. For a discussion about lead in the enamel of slow cookers, see "The Skinny on Lead in Crock Pots," www.terminalverbosity .com/2009/11/09/the-skinny-on-lead-in-crock -pots-it-may-surprise-you/. Testing showed that lead was not present in a variety of slow cookers.

Stockpots, Enameled

Three good sources of enameled stockpots are Le Creuset, Cuisinart, and Martha Stewart, all available widely in stores and on the Internet.

Walnuts, Pickled

Visit www.jollygrub.com to find these nuts for the Wow Wow Sauce.

Acknowledgments

Nourishing Broth began as an idea that came to our literary agent Mary Evans. Without her brainchild and subsequent follow-up, there would be no book. Many thanks to literary agent Mitchell S. Waters of Curtis Brown Ltd, who encouraged Kaayla Daniel to accept this mission.

The research for this book began back in 1997 when the late Luise Light, DSci, editor of *New Age Journal,* connected Kaayla with the late John F. Prudden, MD, DSci. Although Dr. Prudden died in 1998, and he and Kaayla never completed the book they'd hoped to write together on the healing power of cartilage, we are honored to share his important findings in *Nourishing Broth.*

H. Ira Fritz, PhD, encouraged Kaayla to study proline and glycine as part of her PhD program at the Union Institute and University. Her paper on this topic led to the article "Why Broth Is Beautiful," first published in *Wise Traditions,* the journal of the Weston A. Price Foundation, in 2003. Mary G. Enig, PhD; Mitchell Ghen, PhD, DO; Barbara Dossey, RN, PhD; and Christina Jackson RN, PhD, also served on Kaayla's doctoral committee, and were careful readers as well.

We are deeply indebted to Sylvia Onusic, PhD, who pulled many of the late nineteenth- and early twentieth-century studies identified by Dr. Gotthoffer at the Library of Congress so we could read the full texts and evaluate Dr. Gotthoffer's conclusions. We now know for sure what we long suspected—Dr. Gotthoffer's research was impeccable and his 1945 book *Gelatin in Nutrition and Medicine* an extraordinary legacy. We would also like to thank intern Anika Poli for research assistance in the summer of 2013.

Over the past few years our task has been eased with the support of more friends and colleagues than we could ever name, including Esther Blum, RD; Jonny Bowden, PhD; David Brownstein, MD; Joette Calabrese, HMC, CCH, RSHom(Na); Natasha Campbell-McBride, MD; Monica Corrado; Thomas S. Cowan, MD; the late Robert Crayhon; Debra Lynn Dadd; Donna Gates; Chris Masterjohn, PhD; Jenny McGruther; the late Shari Lieberman, PhD; Dr. Joseph Mercola; Sarah Pope; Randy Roach; Julia Ross; Mark Schauss; Stephanie Seneff, PhD; Ron Schmid, ND; JJ Virgin; and Louisa Williams, DC, ND. Without all of them, this book would still be simmering on the back burner.

Particular thanks go to Jessica Prentice of Three Stone Hearth, for arranging the analyses of lead levels in broth; and to Kim Schuette, CN, of Biodynamic Wellness, for her analyses of mineral levels in broth and the comparison of amino acids in short-cooked and long-cooked broth.

We would especially like to acknowledge the many people who have shared their stories and recipes, and Kathy Kramer and Tim Boyd at the Weston A. Price Foundation's office, who helped us connect with these people. We especially appreciate Shantih Coro, RD, who helped set up numerous interviews with clients who were successfully healed with the help of broth. These stories are a healing gift to the world.

We both had the great pleasure of working with Karen Murgolo, VP and Editorial Director at Grand Central Life and Style, whose team edited this book with sensitivity, intelligence, and grace. We would particularly like to thank Kallie Shimek in managing editorial; Leda Scheintaub for copyediting (including a brilliant job on the recipes); Mary Woodin for illustrations; Brigid Pearson for art direction; and Sonya Safro for publicity. Pippa White and Morgan Hedden, editorial assistants to Karen Murgolo; and Brian McLendon, associate publisher in charge of marketing, both played invaluable roles.

Most of all we want to thank the home teams—Kaayla is deeply grateful to her two amazing children, Sunny and Kyrie Rose, who never complained about broth, bones, or a house littered with books and studies. Indeed, they continue to eat many bowls of soups and stews and cheerfully talk about it!

Sally appreciates the continuing support of her husband, Geoffrey, who also put up with the litter of papers and the time she spent on the book. He made many pots of soup during the process—good nourishing soup after a long day at the computer.

Particular thanks go to Sally's daughter Sarah Fallon, who discovered Gotthoffer's book *Gelatin in Nutrition and Medicine* in the UC Berkeley library in the mid-1990s. It was the book that provided the initial scientific validation of the traditional belief in broth as a nutritious, healing food.

Kaayla T. Daniel, PhD, CCN
Sally Fallon Morell
April 18, 2014

Notes

Introduction

3   **Nourishing broth dates back:** Richard Wrangham, *Catching Fire: How Cooking Made Us Human* (Basic, 2009), 124–125, 145; Janet Clarkson, *Soup* (Reaktion Books, 2010), 21–23; Thoms AV. The fire stones carry: ethnographic records and archaeological expectations for hot-rock cookery in western North America. *J Anthropological Archaeology.* 2008.27:443–460; Wu X, Zhang C, Goldberg P, et al. Early pottery at 20,000 years ago in Xianrendong cave, China. *Science.* 2012.336(6089):1696–1700; Shelach G. On the invention of pottery. *Science.* 2012.336(6089):1644–1645; Victoria R. Rumble, *Soup through the Ages: A Culinary History with Period Recipes* (McFarland, 2009), 6. The translations of *The Frogs* vary. Some say "soup" or "stew," others specify minestrone, pea, lentil. "Sudden urge" has also been translated as "burning desire."

4   **The Jewish philosopher:** Fred Rosner, *The Medical Legacy of Moses Maimonides* (Ktav, 1997), 27.

4   **According to Martin Yan:** Teresa M. Chen, *A Tradition of Soup: Flavors from China's Pearl River Delta*, foreword by Martin Yan (North Atlantic Books, 2009), xi.

4   **virtually all the feet:** Clifford Krauss, "Chinese Taste for Chicken Feet May Save US Exports," *New York Times*, September 15, 2009; Clifford Krauss, "Chewy Chicken Feet May Quash a Trade War," *New York Times*, September 15, 2009; "Chicken Feet to China: America's Next Great Export," *Bloomberg News*, December 10, 2012, http://www.nj.com/business/index.ssf/2012/12/chicken_feet_to_china_americas.html.

4   **Pat Willard notes old:** Pat Willard, *A Soothing Broth* (Broadway Books, 1998), 71, 124–125.

4   **Florence Nightingale emphasized:** Florence Nightingale, *Notes on Nursing* (Dover Books on Biology, 1969), 43.

4   **Broth would seem:** Rumble, *Soup through the Ages*, 123–124; Clarkson, *Soup*, 68–71; Betty Fussell, *Masters of American Cookery: M.F.K Fisher, James Andrew Beard, Raymond Craig Claiborne, Julia McWilliams Child* (University of Nebraska Press, 1983), 100.

5   **viable with Justus von Liebig:** http://en.wikipedia.org/wiki/Justus_von_Liebig; http://en.wikipedia.org/wiki/Meat_extract; http://en.wikipedia.org/wiki/Liebig_Extract_of_Meat_Company.

6   **military's need for portability:** http://en.wikipedia.org/wiki/Nicolas_Appert; Douglas Collins, *America's Favorite Food: The Story of Campbell Soup Company* (Harry N. Abrams, 1994), 18–20, 24; http://www.advertisement-gallery.com/food-ads/campbells-printanier-soup.jpg.php; Robert Reiss, "Creating Touch Points at Campbell Soup Company," *Forbes*, July 14, 2011, http://www.forbes.com/sites/robertreiss/2011/07/14/creating-touchpoints-at-campbell-soup-company/.

6   **John Lawson Johnston developed:** http://en.wikipedia.org/wiki/John_Lawson_Johnston; ww.bovril.co.uk/content/history/history.pdf.

7   **In 1679, Denis Papin:** Denis Papin, *A New Digester or Engine for Softening Bones: 1681,*

Containing the Description of Its Make and Use: Viz. Cookery (Dawsons Pall Mall, facsimile of 1681 edition, 1966).

8   **Charles Knox developed:** http://www.kraftbrands .com/knox/knox_history.html.

Chapter 1

13   **Collagen is the glue:** Amélie A. Walker, "Oldest Glue Discovered." *Archaeology*, May 21, 1998, http:// www.archaeology.org/online/news/glue.html.

13   **Types I to V are:** Kadler KE, Holmes DF. Collagen fibril formation [review article]. *Biochem J.* 1996.316:1–11; Peter Fratzl, *Collagen: Structure and Mechanics* (Springer, 2008); Di Lullo GA, Sweeney SM, Körkkö J, Ala-Kokko L, San Antonio JD. Mapping the ligand-binding sites and disease-associated mutations on the most abundant protein in the human, type I collagen. *J Biol Chem.* 2002.277(6):4223–4231.

13   **collagenous proteins are gigantic:** Rich A. The molecular structure of collagen. *J Mol Biol.* 1961.3(5):483–506; Rich A, Crick FHC. The structure of collagen. *Nature.* 1955.176:915–916; Fraser RDB, MacRae TP, Suzuki E. Chain conformation in the collagen molecule. *J Mol Biol.* 1979.129(3):463–481; Kadler, Holmes, Collagen fibril formation; Fratzl, *Collagen*.

14   **lower in cold-water fish:** Szpak P. Fish bone chemistry and ultrastructure: implications for taphonomy and stable isotope analysis. *J Archaeological Sci.* 2011.38(12):3358–3372.

16   **bovine gelatin sprays may:** Antoniewski MN, Barringer SA, et al. Effect of a gelatin coating on the shelf life of fresh meat. *J Food Sci.* 2007.72(6):E382–387.

16   **How Now Mad Cow:** "Questions and Answers about Bovine Spongiform Encephalopathy (BSE)," *Food Insight: Your Nutrition and Food Safety Resource*, April 24, 2012, http://www.foodinsight .org/Resources/Detail.aspx?topic=Questions _and_Answers_about_Bovine_Spongiform _Encephalopathy_BSE_; Gelatine Manufacturers of Europe (GME), "The Removal and Inactivation of Potential TSE Infectivity by the Different Gelatin Manufacturing Processes," June 2003, http://www.fda.gov/OHRMS/DOCKETS/ AC/03/briefing/3969B1_1d.pdf; Scientific Panel on Biological Hazards of the European Food Safety Authority (EFSA), "Quantitative Assessment of the Human BSE Risk Posed by Gelatine with Respect to Residual BSE Risk." January 18, 2006, http://www.efsa.europa.eu/ en/efsajournal/doc/312.pdf; US Food and Drug Administration, "The Sourcing and Processing of Gelatin to Reduce the Potential Risk Posed by Bovine Spongiform Encephalopathy (BSE) in FDA-Regulated Products for Human Use," http:// www.fda.gov/RegulatoryInformation/Guidances/ ucm125182.htm; European Commission: Health and Consumer Protection Directorate-General: The Scientific Steering Committee, "Updated Opinion on the Safety with Regard to TSE Risks of Gelatine Derived from Ruminant Bones or Hides," March 6–7, 2003, http://ec.europa.eu/ food/fs/sc/ssc/out321_en.pdf.

17   **FDA has also approved:** http://www.fda.gov/ ForConsumers/ConsumerUpdates/ucm049349 .htm.

Chapter 2

19   **most common type of cartilage:** Donald Resnick and Gen Niwayama, *General Diagnoses of Bone and Joint Disorders* (Saunders, 1988), 758; William J. Koopman, ed., *Arthritis and Allied Conditions: A Textbook of Rheumatology*, 13th ed. (Williams & Wilkins, 1997).

19   **A Change in Proportion:** Silberberg R, et al. Aging changes in ultrastructure and enzymatic activity of articular cartilage of guinea pigs. *J Gerontol.* 1970.25(3):184–198; Murakami H, Yoon TS, et al. Quantitative differences in intervertebral disc-matrix composition with age-related degeneration. *Med Biol Eng Comput.* 2010.48(5):469–474; Buckwalter JA, Rosenberg LC. Electron microscopic studies of cartilage proteoglycans. *Electron Microsc Rev.* 1988.1(1):87–112; Caplan AI. Cartilage. *Scientific American.* 1984.251:84–94; Soldani G, Romagnoli J. Experimental and clinical pharmacology of glycosaminoglycans (GAGS). *Drugs Exp Clin Res.* 1991.18(1):81–85; Rovetta G. Galactosaminoglycuronoglycan sulfate (matrix) in therapy of tibiofibular osteoarthritis of the knee. *Drugs Exp Clin Res.* 1991.17(1):53–57; Zheng H, Martin JA, et al. Impact of aging on rat bone marrow-derived stem cell chondrogenesis. *J Gerontol A Biol Sci Med Sci.* 2007.62(2):136–148; Roughley PJ, Alini M, Antoniou J. The role of

proteoglycans in aging, degeneration and repair of the intervertebral disc. *Biochem Soc Trans.* 2002.30(Pt 6):869–874; Rutjes AW, Jüni P, da Costa BR, Trelle S, Nüesch E, Reichenbach S. Viscosupplementation for osteoarthritis of the knee: a systematic review and meta-analysis. *Ann Intern Med.* 2012.157(3):180–191; Holmes MWA, Bayliss MT, Muir H. Hyaluronic acid in human articular cartilage: age related changes in content and size. *Biochem J.* 1988.250:435–441.

20 **Can We Regenerate Our Cartilage?:** All quotes from Dr. Prudden in this book came from telephone interviews with Kaayla T. Daniel on September 3, 8, 14, 19, 24, and 25 and October 3 and 8, 1997; Prudden JF. "Summary of Bovine Tracheal Cartilage (BTC) Research Programs," in *Foundation for Cartilage and Immunology Research: A Compilation of Scientific Research on Bovine Tracheal Cartilage*, Version 2.0 (Foundation for Cartilage and Immunology Research, August 9, 1996), 7.

21 **human body can revert:** Silberberg et al., Aging changes; Murakami et al., Quantitative differences; Buckwalter, Rosenberg, Electron microscopic studies; Caplan, Cartilage; Soldani, Romagnoli, Experimental and clinical pharmacology; Rovetta, Galactosaminoglycuronoglycan sulfate (matrix); Zheng et al., Impact of aging; Roughley et al., The role of proteoglycans; Rutjes et al., Viscosupplementation; Holmes et al., Hyaluronic acid.

Chapter 3

22 **mineral content found in bones:** "Overview of Calcium: Bone Formation and Remodeling," in *Dietary Reference Intakes for Calcium and Vitamin D*, edited by Institute of Medicine (US) Committee to Review Dietary Reference Intakes for Vitamin D and Calcium; Ross AC, Taylor CL, Yaktine AL, et al. (National Academies Press, 2011).

22 **in 1934 when researchers:** McCance RA, Sheldon W, Widdowson EM. Bones and vegetable broth. *Arch Dis Child.* 1934.52:251–258.

23 **Despite its low calcium content:** Anderson JJ, Roggenkamp KJ, Suchindran CM. Calcium intakes and femoral and lumbar bone density of elderly U.S. men and women: National Health and Nutrition Examination Survey 2005–2006 analysis. *J Clin Endocrinol Metab.* 2012.97(12):4531–4539; Shea B, Wells G, Cranney A, et al. Calcium supplementation on bone loss in postmenopausal women. *Cochrane Database Syst Rev.* 2004.1(1):CD004526; Bischoff-Ferrari HA, Dawson-Hughes B, et al. Calcium intake and hip fracture risk in men and women: a meta-analysis of prospective cohort studies and randomized controlled trials. *Am J Clin Nutr.* 2007.86(6):1780–1790; Cumming RG, Cummings SR, Nevitt MC, et al. Calcium intake and fracture risk: results from the study of osteoporotic fractures. *Am J Epidemiol.* 1997.145(10):926–934.

23 **larger reason broth supports bone:** Shuster S. Osteoporosis, a unitary hypothesis of collagen loss in skin and bone. *Medical Hypotheses.* 2005.65(3):426–432; Wegrzyn J, Roux JP, et al. The role of bone intrinsic properties measured by infrared spectroscopy in whole lumbar vertebra mechanics: organic rather than inorganic bone matrix? *Bone.* 2013.56(2):229–233; Saito M. [Biochemical markers of bone turnover. New aspect. Bone collagen metabolism: new biological markers for estimation of bone quality]. *Clin Calcium.* 2009.19(8):1110–1117 [Article in Japanese]; Leng H, Reyes MJ, et al. Effect of age on mechanical properties of the collagen phase in different orientations of human cortical bone. *Bone.* 2013.55(2):288–291; Turner CH, Wang T, Burr DB. Shear strength and fatigue properties of human cortical bone determined from pure shear tests. *Calcif Tissue Int.* 2001.69(6):373–378; George WT, Vashishth D. Susceptibility of aging human bone to mixed-mode fracture increases bone fragility. *Bone.* 2006.38(1):105–111; Arnold WV, Fertala A. Skeletal diseases caused by mutations that affect collagen structure and function. *Int J Biochem Cell Biol.* 2013.45(8):1556–1567.

23 **some people have bones thick:** Saito M, Marumo K. Bone quality in diabetes. *Front Endocrinol (Lausanne).* 2013.4:72.

24 **studied 120 osteoporosis patients:** Reinhard Schrieber and Herbert Gareis, *Gelatine Handbook: Theory and Industrial Practice* (Wiley-VCH, 2007), 307, with reference to Adam M. Welche Wirkung haben Gelatinepraraparte? *Therapiewoche.*1991.41:2456–2461.

24 **a study on 108 postmenopausal women:** Adam M, Spacek P, et al. [Postmenopausal osteoporosis: treatment with calcitonin and a diet rich in collagen proteins]. *Cas Lek Cesk.* 1996.135(3): 74–78 [Article in Czech].

24 **In 2000, Roland Moskowitz:** Moskowitz RW. Role of collagen hydrolysate in bone and joint disease. *Semin Arthritis Rheum.* 2000.30(2):87–99; Reginster J-Y, Burlet N. Osteoporosis: a still increasing prevalence. *Bone.* 2006.38:S4–S9.

25 **With osteoporosis a threat:** National Osteoporosis Foundation: available at http://www.nof.org.

Chapter 4

26 **a major role in human evolution:** "Ape-Man; Adventures in Human Evolution," BBC; 2003; http://bufvc.ac.uk/dvdfind/index.php/title/av34821; Aiello LC, Wheeler P. The expensive tissue hypothesis: the brain and digestive system in human and primate evolution. *Curr Anthropol.* 1995.36(2):199–221.

27 **amount and type of fat in bone marrow:** Loren Cordain, author of *The Paleo Diet*, reports "African ruminant marrow" to be nutrient dense with 488 calories, 51 grams of fat, and 7 grams of protein in just 3½ ounces or about 100 grams. Cordain L, Watkins BA, et al. Fatty acid analysis of wild ruminant tissues: evolutionary implications for reducing diet-related chronic disease. *Eur J Clin Nutr.* 2002.56(3):181–191; Diane Sanfilippo, author of *Practical Paleo*, offers figures for roasted beef marrow that are quite different: 132 calories and 9 grams of fat, of which 3.7 mg are saturated fat, 0.7 grams monounsaturated fat, and 0.2 grams polyunsaturated fat. Meanwhile, nutritiondata .self.com reports a 100-gram serving of caribou marrow to have 786 calories and 84 grams fat, which is not broken down into types of fat.

In terms of cholesterol, Sanfilippo reports 30.3 mg per 100 grams for the beef marrow, while nutritiondata.self.com reports zero cholesterol— nada!—for the caribou. Other Internet sources say 150 mg cholesterol per 100 grams, and so it goes. As for the fat, Loren Cordain thinks it's mostly monounsaturated, others believe it to be polyunsaturated, while others say almost entirely saturated.

Why such major discrepancies? Some of the data are undoubtedly for raw marrow. Sanfilippo's is for roasted, which would be markedly lower in fat and calories because of fat running off into the roasting pan. There may also be significant differences among African ruminants, caribou, and grass-fed beef, the three species tested.

Data on caribou bone marrow: http://nutritiondata.self.com/facts/ethnic -foods/8088/2; Roasted marrow bones recipe from *Practical Paleo*: http://nutritiondata .self.com/facts/recipe/2603988/2; Cholesterol in bone marrow: http://en.allexperts.com/q/ Heart-Cardiology-964/2008/3/cholestrol-bone -marrow.htm; C Wilson, K Meyerholtz, and S Hooser, "Bone Marrow Fat Analysis: To Support a Diagnosis of Starvation/Malnutrition," Purdue University, Spring 2007 Newsletter. https:// www.addl.purdue.edu/newsletters/2007/Spring/ BMFA.htm; Meyerholtz KA, Wilson CR, et al. Quantitative assessment of the percent fat in domestic animal bone marrow. *J Forensic Sci.* 2011.56(3):775–777.

27 **Different types of marrow:** Vilhjalmur Stefansson, *The Fat of the Land* (Macmillan, 1956), 27; Sally Fallon, "Bone Marrow," *Wise Traditions*, Summer 2007. http://www.westonaprice.org/food -features/bone-marrow.

27 **percentage of fat in bone marrow:** Wilson et al., "Bone Marrow Fat Analysis."

28 **Babies start out life:** Gurevitch O, Slavin S, Feldman AG. Conversion of red bone marrow into yellow: cause and mechanisms. *Med Hypotheses.* 2007.69(3):531–536; Malkiewicz A, Dziedzic M. Bone marrow reconversion: imaging of physiological changes in bone marrow. *Pol J Radiol.* 2012.77(4):45–50; Wilson et al., "Bone Marrow Fat Analysis."

28 **ability to perform hematopoiesis:** J Domen, A Wagers, and IL Weissman, "Bone Marrow (Hematopoietic) Stem Cells," National Institutes of Health, U.S. Department of Health and Human Services. http://stemcells.nih.gov/ staticresources/info/scireport/PDFs/D.%20 Chapter%202.pdf.

28 **Bovine marrow and spleen:** Dale Kiefer, "Anti Cancer Benefits of Shark Liver Oil," *Life Extension Magazine*, August 2005. http://www.lef.org/ magazine/mag2005/aug2005_report_shark_01.htm.

Pugliese PT, Jordan K, Cederberg H, Brohult J. Some biological actions of alkylglycerols from shark liver oil. *J Altern Complement Med.* 1998.4(1):87–99; Iannitti T, Palmieri B. An update on the therapeutic role of alkylglycerols. *Mar Drugs.* 2010.8(8):2267–2300; Kantah MK, Wakasugi H, et al. Intestinal immune-potentiation by a purified alkylglycerols compound. *Acta Biomed*. 2012.83(1):36–43.

28 **research on bone marrow stem cells:** "Stem Cell Information." National Institutes of Health. http://stemcells.nih.gov/info/basics/pages/basics6.aspx.

30 **Price learned marrow was highly prized:** Fallon, "Bone Marrow"; Weston A. Price, *Nutrition and Physical Degeneration*, 9th ed. (Price Pottenger Nutrition, 2009).

Chapter 5

31 **public health authorities enlisted:** Hemberger E. Gelatine as a food for the people. *Scientific American*. 1916(Suppl 2097):167; Totani G. Feeding experiments with a dietary in which tyrosine is reduced to a minimum. *Biochem*. 1916.10:390.

31 **Gotthoffer argued in his 1945 book:** Nathan R. Gotthoffer, *Gelatin in Nutrition and Medicine* (Grayslake, 1945), 3.

32 **exert "remarkable sparing powers,":** Gotthoffer, *Gelatin*, 7–9.

32 **Protein synthesis breaks:** Jackson AA. Amino acids: essential and non-essential? *Lancet*. 1983.1:1034–1037; Irwin MI, Hegsted DM. A conspectus of research on amino requirements of man. *J Nutr*. 1971.101:539–566; Jackson AA. The glycine story. *Eur J Clin Nutr*. 1991.45:59–65; Jackson AA. Salvage of urea nitrogen and protein requirements. *Proc Nutr Soc*. 1995.54:535–547; A. A. Jackson, "Critique of Protein-Energy Interactions in Vivo: Urea Kinetics," in *Protein-Energy Interactions: Proceedings of an I/D/E/C/G Workshop Held in Waterville Valley, NH, USA, October 21–25, 1991*, edited by NS Scrimshaw and B Schürch (Nestle Foundation, 1992); Gibson NR, Farook J, et al. Endogenous glycine and tyrosine production is maintained in adults consuming a marginal-protein diet. *Am J Clin Nutr*. 2002.75(3): 511–518; Persaud C, McDermott J, et al. The excretion of 5-oxyproline in urine as an index of glycine status during normal pregnancy. *Br J Obstet Gynaecol*. 1989.96:440–444; Irwin, Hegsted, A conspectus of research; Meakins TS, Jackson AA. Salvage of exogenous urea-nitrogen enhances nitrogen balance in normal men consuming marginally inadequate protein diets. *Clin Sci*. 1996.90:215–225; Segrest JP, Cunningham LW. Variations in human urinary o-hydroxylysyl glycoside levels and their relationship to collagen metabolism. *J Clin Invest*. 1970.49:1497–1509; Yu YM, Yang RD, et al. Quantitative aspects of glycine and alanine nitrogen metabolism in postabsorptive young men: effects of level of nitrogen and dispensable amino acid intake. *J Nutr*. 1985.115(3):399–410.

32 **has limiting amino acids:** Schwick HG, Heide K. Immunochemistry and immunology of collagen and gelatin: modified gelatins as plasma substitutes. *Bibl Haematol*. 1969.33:111–125.

33 **balance them out by eating parts:** C. Masterjohn, "Meat, Organs, Bones and Skin: Nutrition for Mental Health," *Wise Traditions*, Spring 2013, 35; Harper AE, Benevenga NJ, Wohlhueter RM. Effects of ingestion of disproportionate amounts of amino acids. *Physiolog Rev*. 1970.80(3):428–558. Meakins TS, Persaud C, Jackson AA. Dietary supplementation with L-methionine impairs the utilization of urea-nitrogen and increases 5-L-oxoprolinuria in normal women consuming a low protein diet. *J Nutr*. 1998.128:720–727; Sugiyama K, Kushima Y, Muramatsu K. Effect of dietary glycine on methionine metabolism in rats fed a high-methioine diet. *J Nutr Sci Vitaminol* (Tokyo). 1987.33(3):195–205; Roth JS, Allison JB. The effect of feeding excess glycine, L-arginine and DL-methionine to rats on a casein diet. *Proc Soc Exp Biol Med*. 1949.70(2):327–330.

Chapter 6

34 **individuals in normal health:** Jaksic T, Wagner DA, Young VR. Plasma proline kinetics and concentrations in young men in response to dietary proline deprivation. *Am J Clin Nutr*. 1990.52:307–312.

34 **the body cannot produce proline:** Richard S. Lord and Alexander Bralley, *Laboratory Evaluations for Integrative and Functional Medicine* (Metametrix Institute, 2008), 238.

34 **individuals will show low proline:** Lord and Bralley, *Laboratory Evaluations*, 238.

34 **suffer a proline shortfall:** Chris Masterjohn, "Meat, Organs, Bones and Skin: Nutrition for Mental Health," *Wise Traditions*, Spring 2013, 35–43.

35 **become proline deficient:** Bates CJ. Vitamin C deficiency in guinea pigs: changes in urinary excretion of proline, hydroxyproline and total amino nitrogen. *Int J Vit Nutr Res*. 1979.49:152–159; Lord and Bralley, *Laboratory*

Evaluations, 4–24; Richard S. Lord, IAACN Post-Graduate Seminars in Clinical Nutrition, Orlando, Florida, June 24, 2000; Nusgens B, Lapiere CM. The relationship between proline and hydroxyproline urinary excretion in human as an index of collagen catabolism. *Clinica Chimica Acta*. 1973.48:203–211; Kaddam IM, et al. Comparison of serum osteocalcin with total and bone specific alkaline phosphatase and urinary hydroxyproline creatinine ratio in patients with Paget's disease of bone. *Ann Clin Biochem*. 1994.31:327–330; Secrest JP, Cunningham LW. Variations in human urinary O-hydroxylysyl glycoside levels and their relationship to collagen metabolism. *J Clin Invest*. 1970.49:1497–1509; Walford M. Glutamine metabolism and function in relation to proline synthesis and the safety of glutamine and proline supplementation. *J Nutr*. 2008.138(10):2003S–2007S.

35 **Glycine is the other important:** Jackson AA. The glycine story. *Eur J Clin Nutr*. 1991.45:59–65; Jackson AA, et al. Urinary excretion of 5-oxoproline (pyroglutamic aciduria) as an index of glycine insufficiency in normal man. *Br J Nutr*. 1987.58:207–214; Wheeler MD, Ikejema K, et al. Glycine: a new anti-inflammatory immunonutrient. *Cell Mol Life Sci*. 1999.56(9–10):843–856.

35 **glycine contributes to gastric acid:** Richardson CT, et al. Studies on the mechanism of food-stimulated gastric acid secretion in normal human subjects. *J Clin Invest*. 1976.58:623–631; Wald A, Adibi SA. Stimulation of gastric acid secretion by glycine and related oligopeptides in humans. *Am J Physiol*. 1982.5:242, G86–G88.

35 **a vital role in wound healing:** Minuskin M, et al. Nitrogen retention, muscle creatine and orotic acid excretion in traumatized rats fed arginine and glycine enriched diets. *J Nutr*. 1981.3(7):1265–1274.

35 **copious amounts of glycine:** Ottenberg R. Painless jaundice. *JAMA*. 1935.104(9):1681–1687; Jackson AA, et al. Urinary excretion; Okoko T, Awhin EP. Glycine reduces cadmium-induced alterations in the viability and activation of macrophage U937 cells. *Food Chem Toxicol*. 2010.48(2):536–8.

36 **improve methylation:** Masterjohn, "Meat, organs, bones and skin," 35; Harper AE, Benevenga NJ, Wohlhueter RM. Effects of ingestion of disproportionate amounts of amino acids.

Physiolog Rev. 1970.80(3):428–558; Meakins TS, Persaud C, Jackson AA. Dietary supplementation with L-methionine impairs the utilization of urea-nitrogen and increases 5-L-oxoprolinuria in normal women consuming a low protein diet. *J Nutr*. 1998.128:720–727; Sugiyama K, Kushima Y, Muramatsu K. Effect of dietary glycine on methionine metabolism in rats fed a high-methioine diet. *J Nutr Sci Vitaminol* (Tokyo). 1987.33(3):195–205; Roth JS, Allison JB. The effect of feeding excess glycine, L-arginine and DL-methionine to rats on a casein diet. *Proc Soc Exp Biol Med*. 1949.70(2):327–330; Fukada S, Shimada Y, et al. Suppression of methionine-induced hyperhomocysteinemia by glycine and serine in rats. *Biosci Biotechnol Biochem*. 2006.70(10):2403–2409.

36 **diverse metabolic demands:** Jackson AA. Salvage of urea nitrogen and protein requirements. *Proc Nutr Soc*. 1995.54:535–547; Jackson et al. Urinary excretion; Gibson NR, Farook J, et al. Endogenous glycine and tyrosine production is maintained in adults consuming a marginal-protein diet. *Am J Clin Nutr*. 2002.75(3):511–518; Yu YM, Yang RD, Matthews DE, et al. Quantitative aspects of glycine and alanine nitrogen metabolism in postabsorptive young men: effect of level of nitrogen and dispensable amino acid intake. *J Nutr*. 1985.115:399–410.

36 **Glutamine becomes a conditionally:** Bertand J, Goichon A, et al. Regulation of intestinal protein metabolism by amino acids. *Amino Acids*. 2013.45(3):443–450; Newsholme P, Procopio J, et al. Glutamine and glutamate: their central role in cell metabolism and function. *Cell Biochem Funct*. 2003.21(1):1–9; Eagle H, Oyama VI, et al. The growth response of mammalian cells in tissue culture to l-glutamine and l-glutamic acid. *J Biol Chem*.1956.218:607–616; Wu G. Intestinal mucosal amino acid catabolism. *J Nutr*. 1998.128(8):1249–1252; Wang WW, Qiao SY, Li DE. Amino acids and gut function. *Amino Acids*. 2009.37(1):105–110; Lacey JM, Wilmore DW. Is glutamine a conditionally essential amino acid? *Nutr Rev*. 1990.48(8):297–309; Neu J, DeMarco V, Li N. Glutamine: clinical applications and mechanisms of action. *Curr Opin Clin Nutr Metab Care*. 2002.5(1):69–75; Windmueller HG, Spaeth AE. Uptake and metabolism of plasma

glutamine by the small intestine. *J Biol Chem.* 1974.249:5070–5079; Rhoads JM, Argenzio RA, et al. L-glutamine stimulates intestinal cell proliferation and activates mitogen-activated protein kinases. *Am J Physiol.* 1997.272:G943–G953; Labow B, Souba WW. Glutamine. *World J Surg.* 2000.24(12):1503–1513.

37 **Glutamine stimulates immune:** Newsholme EA. Why is L-glutamine metabolism important to cells of the immune system in health, post-injury, surgery, or infection? *J Nutr.* 2001.131: 2515–2522; Newsholme P, Curi R, et al. Glutamine metabolism by lymphocytes, macrophages, and neutrophils: its importance in health and disease. *J Nutr Biochem.* 1999.10(6):316–324; Newsholme EA. The possible role of glutamine in some cells of the immune system and the possible consequence for the whole animal. *Experientia.* 1996.52(5): 455–459; Bongers T, Griffiths RD, McArdle A. Exogenous glutamine: the clinical evidence. *Crit Care Med.* 2007.35(9 Suppl):S545–552; Kelly D, Wischmeyer PE. Role of L-glutamine in critical illness: new insights. *Curr Opin Clin Nutr Metab Care.* 2003.6(2):217–222; Wischmeyer PE. Clinical applications of L-glutamine: past, present, and future. *Nutr Clin Pract.* 2003.18(5):377–385; Kim H. Glutamine as an immunonutrient. *Yonsei Med J.* 2011.52(6):892–897; Tjader I, Berg A, Wernerman J. Exogenous glutamine: compensating a shortage? *Crit Care Med.* 2007.35(9 Suppl):S553–S556.

37 **Glutamine also supports liver health:** Wessner B, Strasser EM, et al. Effect of single and combined supply of glutamine, glycine, N-acetylcysteine, and R,S-alpha-lipoic acid on glutathione content of myelomonocytic cells. *Clin Nutr.* 2003.22(6):515–522; Jackson AA, Gibson NR, et al. Synthesis of erythrocyte glutathione in healthy adults consuming the safe amount of dietary protein. *Am J Clin Nutr.* 2004.80(1): 101–107; Jackson AA, Badaloo AV, Forrester T, Hibbert JM, Persaud C. Urinary excretion of 5-oxoproline (pyroglutamic aciduria) as an index of glycine insufficiency in normal man. *Br J Nutr.* 1987.58:207–214; Wang Y, Tao YX, et al. Protective effect of parenteral glutamine supplementation on hepatic function in very low birth weight babies. *Clin Nutr.* 2010.29(3):307–311; Naoyuki Taniguchi, *Glutathione Centennial: Molecular Perspectives*

and Clinical Implications (Academic Press, 1989); Hong RW, Rounds JD, et al. Glutamine preserves liver glutathione after lethal hepatic injury. *Ann Surg.* 1992.215(2):114–119; Kretzschmar M. Regulation of hepatic glutathione metabolism and its role in hepatotoxicity. *Exp Toxicol Pathol.* 1996.48(5):439–446; Yuan L, Kaplowitz N. Glutathione in liver diseases and hepatotoxicity. *Mol Aspects Med.* 2009.30(1–2):29–41.

37 **Soup is frequently prescribed:** N. Perricone, "The Perricone Weight Loss Program: Superstar Supplement #1—Glutamine," November 2005. http://www.lef.org/magazine/mag2005/nov2005 _cover_perricone_06.htm; Gamrin L, Essen P, et al. Protein-sparing effect in skeletal muscle of growth hormone treatment in critically ill patients. *Ann Surg.* 2000.231(4):577–586.

37 **Glutamine helps people who need:** Bonet A, Grau T. [Glutamine, an almost essential amino acid in the critically ill patient]. *Med Intensiva.* 2007.31(7):402–406 [Article in Spanish]; Andrews FJ, Griffiths RD. Glutamine: essential for immune nutrition in the critically ill. *Br J Nutr.* 2002.87(Suppl 1):S3–S8; Griffiths RD. The evidence for glutamine use in the critically ill. *Proc Nutr Soc.* 2001.60(3):403–410; Griffiths RD. Outcome of critically ill patients after supplementation with glutamine. *Nutrition.* 1997.13(7–8):752–754; Griffiths RD, Jones C, Palmer TE. Six-month outcome of critically ill patients given glutamine-supplemented parenteral nutrition. *Nutrition.* 1997.13(4):295–302; Sacks GS. Glutamine supplementation in catabolic patients. *Ann Pharmacother.* 1999.33(3):348–354; Jones C, Palmer TE, Griffiths RD. Randomized clinical outcome study of critically ill patients given glutamine-supplemented enteral nutrition. *Nutrition.* 1999.15(2):108–115; Kelly D, Wischmeyer PE. Role of L-glutamine in critical illness: new insights. *Curr Opin Clin Nutr Metab Care.* 2003.6(2):217–222; Wischmeyer PE. Clinical applications of L-glutamine: past, present, and future. *Nutr Clin Pract.* 2003.18(5):377–385; Beautheu S, Ouelaa W, et al. Glutamine supplementation, but not combined glutamine and arginine supplementation, improves gut barrier function during chemotherapy-induced intestinal mucositis in rats. *Clin Nutr.* 2013 Sep 25. pii: S0261-5614(13)00241-0; Novak F,

Heyland DK, et al. Glutamine supplementation in serious illness: a systematic review of the evidence. *Crit Care Med.* 2002.30(9):2022–2029; Houdijk AP, Rijnsburger ER, et al. Randomised trial of glutamine-enriched enteral nutrition on infectious morbidity in patients with multiple trauma. *Lancet.* 1998.352:772–776; O'Riordain MG, De Beaux A, Fearon KC. Effect of glutamine on immune function in the surgical patient. *Nutrition.* 1996.12:S82–S84; Sacks GS. Glutamine supplementation in catabolic patients. *Ann Pharmacother.* 1999.33(3):348–354; Ziegler TR, Young LS, et al. Clinical and metabolic efficacy of glutamine-supplemented parenteral nutrition after bone marrow transplantation: a randomized, double-blind, controlled study. *Ann Intern Med.* 1992.116:821–828; Ziegler RR. Glutamine supplementation in cancer patients receiving bone marrow transplantation and high dose chemotherapy. *J Nutr.* 2001.131(9 Suppl): 2578S–2584S, discussion 2590S.

37　**Glutamine can even counter some:** Hensley CT, Wasti AT, DeBarardinis RJ. Glutamine and cancer: cell biology, physiology, and clinical opportunities. *J Clin Invest.* 2013.123(9): 3678–3684; Shanware NP, Mullen AR, et al. Glutamine: pleiotropic roles in tumor growth and stress resistance. *Mol Med (Berl).* 2011.89(3):229–236; Kuhn KS, Muscaritoli M, et al. Glutamine as indispensable nutrient in oncology: experimental and clinical evidence. *Eur J Nutr.* 2010.49(4):197–210; Ziegler, Glutamine supplementation.

37　**For fitness buffs, glutamine stimulates:** Mason BC, Lavallee ME. Emerging supplements in sports. *Sports Health.* 2012.4(2):142–146; Clarkson P, Hubal M. Exercise-induced muscle damage in humans. *Am J Phys Med Rehabil.* 2002.81:52–69; Cruzat VF, Rogero MM, Tirapegui J. Effects of supplementation with free glutamine and the dipeptide alanyl-glutamine on parameters of muscle damage and inflammation in rats submitted to prolonged exercise. *J Cell Biochem Funct.* 2010.28:24–30; Kreider RB. Dietary supplements and the promotion of muscle growth with resistance exercise. *Sports Med.* 1999.27: 97–110; Phillips GC. Glutamine: the nonessential amino acid for performance enhancement. *Curr Sports Med Rep.* 2007.6(4):265–268.

37　**glutamine is a "brain food":** Albrecht J, Sidoryk-Wegrzynowicz M, et al. Roles of glutamine in neurotransmission. *Neuron Glia Biol.* 2010.6(4):263–276; Yamadera W, Inagawa K. Glycine ingestion improves subjective sleep quality in human volunteers, correlating with polysomnographic changes. *Sleep and Biological Rhythms.* 2007.5(2):126–131.

38　**fourth most prevalent amino acid:** Yu YM, Yang RD, et al. Quantitative aspects of glycine and alanine nitrogen metabolism in postabsorptive young men: effects of level of nitrogen and dispensable amino acid intake. *J Nutr.* 1985.115(3):399–410; Stellingwerff T, Anwander H, et al. Effect of two β-alanine dosing protocols on muscle carnosine synthesis and washout. *Amino Acids.* 2012.42(6):2461–2472; Stegen S, Bex T. et al. The beta-alanine dose for maintaining moderately elevated muscle carnosine levels. *Med Sci Sports Exerc.* 2014 Jan 1 [Epub ahead of print]; del Favero S, Roschel H, et al. Beta-alanine (Carnosyn™) supplementation in elderly subjects (60–80 years): effects on muscle carnosine content and physical capacity. *Amino Acids.* 2012.43(1):49–56; Smith AE, Stout JR, et al. Exercise-induced oxidative stress: the effects of β-alanine supplementation in women. *Amino Acids.* 2012.43(1):77–90; Stellingwerff T, Decombaz J, et al. Optimizing human in vivo dosing and delivery of β-alanine supplements for muscle carnosine synthesis. *Amino Acids.* 2012.43(1):57–65; Hipkiss AR. On the enigma of carnosine's anti-ageing actions. *Exp Gerontol.* 2009.44(4):237–242.

39　**Bones to Pick with the Lead in Bone Broth Study:** Monro, JA, Leon R, Puri BK. The risk of lead contamination in bone broth diets. *Med Hypotheses.* 2013 Jan 30. pii: S0306-9877(13)00013-3; Bradbury MW, Deane R. Permeability of the blood-brain barrier to lead. *Neurotoxicology.* 1993.14(2–3):131–136; Hou S, Yuan L, et al. A clinical study of the effects of lead poisoning on the intelligence and neurobehavioral abilities of children. *Theor Biol Med Model.* 2013.10(1):13; Kaayla T. Daniel, "Bone Broth and Lead Contamination: A Very Flawed Study in *Medical Hypotheses*," March 12, 2013. http://www.westonaprice.org/ blogs/kdaniel/2013/03/12/bone-broth-and-lead -contamination-a-very-flawed-study-in-medical -hypotheses/; Kaayla T. Daniel, "Chicken Soup with Lead? Looking into a Controversy," March 12, 2013. http://drkaayladaniel.com/boning-up-is-broth-contaminated-with-lead/; Kaayla T. Daniel, "Bones to Pick with the Lead in Bone Broth Study." http://www.thehealthyhomeeconomist.com/bones-to-pick-with-the-lead-in-bone-broth-study/; E-mail to Kaayla T. Daniel from the Breakspear Medical Group, July 2, 2013. The letter reads:

> Dear Dr. Daniel, am writing to apologise as you were previously informed that the chickens used in the study were raised on a farm (organic company called Highlander). I have since been told that they were, in fact, supplied by a local supermarket; With best wishes
> Vicky McLucas
> Medical Secretary
> Breakspear Medical Group Ltd

Results from National Food Lab, Livermore, CA. No lead detected in grass-fed beef broth, pastured chicken broth. On February 19, 2013, the broths were tested at the minimum detection level of 10 parts per billion. On March 5, 2013, a retest was performed at MDLs of 5 parts per billion. Both times no lead was detected in the reverse osmosis water at MDL of 1 part per billion. An online copy of the Analytical Report can be seen at: http://drkaayladaniel.com/boning-up-is-broth-contaminated-with-lead/.

40 **The Downside of Glutamine: The MSG Connection:** Rick Rockwell, "Side Effects of L-Glutamine," Livestrong.com. http://www.livestrong.com/article/70525-side-effects-lglutamine-supplement/; Kelly A, Stanley CA. Disorders of glutamate metabolism. *Ment Retard Dev Disabil Res Rev.* 2001.7:287–295; Russell Blaylock, *Excitotoxins: The Taste that Kills* (Health Press, 1996); Russell Blaylock, *Health and Nutrition Secrets*, rev. ed. (Health Press, 2006); "Names of Ingredients That Contain Processed Free Glutamic Acid (MSG)," March 2014. http://www.truthinlabeling.org/hiddensources.html; Joseph Mercola, "MSG: Is This Silent Killer Lurking in Your Kitchen Cabinets?" Mercola.com. April 21, 2009. http://articles.mercola.com/sites/articles/archive/2009/04/21/msg-is-this-silent-killer-lurking-in-your-kitchen-cabinets.aspx; Carol Hoernlein, "What Foods to Avoid," MST Truth. http://www.msgtruth.org/avoid

.htm; Natasha Campbell-McBride, *Gut and Psychology Syndrome: Natural Treatment for Autism, Dyspraxia, A.D.D., Dyslexia, A.D.H.D., Depression, Schizophrenia*, rev. ed. (Medinform, 2010); Kim Schuette, "Stock vs Broth: Are You Confused?" Biodynamic Wellness: http://www.biodynamicwellness.com/stock-vs-broth-confused/; Ghanizadeh A. Increased glutamate and homocysteine and decreased glutamine levels in autism: a review and strategies for future studies of amino acids in autism. *Dis Markers.* 2013.35(5):281–286; Kelly, Stanley, Disorders of glutamate metabolism; Ghanizadeh A. Targeting of glycine site on NMDA receptor as a possible new strategy for autism treatment. *Neurochem Res.* 2011.36(5):922–923; Blaylock, *Health and Nutrition Secrets*, 139–145; Alcaraz-Contreras, Garza-Ocanas L, et al. Effect of glycine on lead mobilization, lead-induced oxidative stress, and hepatic toxicity in rats. *J Toxicol.* 2011.430539.

Chapter 7

42 **In the 1930s, Dr. Francis Pottenger:** Pottenger F. Hydrophilic colloid diet. *Am J Digestive Diseases.* 1938.5(2)96–99; Iozzo RV. Matrix proteoglycans: from molecular design to cellular function. *Annu Rev Biochem.* 1998.67:609–652.

42 **Hyaluronic acid (HA) is a type of proteoglycan:** Toole BP. Hyaluronan is not just a goo! *J Clin Invest.* 2000.106(3):335–336; Fraser JRE, et al. Hyaluronan: its nature, distribution, functions and turnover. *J Intern Med.* 1997.242 (1): 27–33.

42 **Structured Like a Christmas Tree:** Iozzo, Matrix proteoglycans; Roughley PJ, Lee ER. Cartilage proteoglycans: structure and potential functions. *Microsc Res Tech.* 1994.28(5):385–397; Buckwalter JA, Rosenberg LC. Electron microscopic studies of cartilage proteoglycans. *Electron Microsc Rev.* 1988.1(1):87–112; Holmes MWA, Bayliss MT, Muir H. Hyaluronic acid in human articular cartilage: age related changes in content and size. *Biochem J.* 1988.250:435–441; Soldani G, Romagnoli J. Experimental and clinical pharmacology of glycosaminoglycans (GAGS). *Drugs Exp Clin Res.* 1991.18(1):81–85; Miller K, Clegg D. Glucosamine and chondroitin sulfate. *Rheum Dis Clin N Am.* 2011.37(1):103–118.

43 **Because HA lives three days or less:** Stern R. Hyaluronan catabolism: a new metabolic pathway.

Eur J Cell Biol. 2004.83(7):317–325; Yannariello-Brown J, Chapman SH, et al. Circulating hyaluronan levels in the rodent: effects of age and diet. *Am J Physiol.* 1995.268(4 Pt 1):C952–957; Rutjes AW, Jüni P, da Costa BR, Trelle S, Nüesch E, Reichenbach S. Viscosupplementation for osteoarthritis of the knee: a systematic review and meta-analysis. *Ann Intern Med.* 2012.157(3): 180–191; Holmes MWA, Bayliss MT, Muir H. Hyaluronic acid in human articular cartilage: age related changes in content and size. *Biochem J.* 1988.250:435–441.

43 **HA was once extracted:** "Find a Vitamin or Supplement: Hyaluronic Acid." WebMD. http:// www.webmd.com/vitamins-supplements/ ingredientmono-1062-HYALURONIC%20 ACID.aspx?activeIngredientId=1062&active IngredientName=HYALURONIC%20ACID; "Hyaluronan." Wikipedia. http://en.wikipedia.org/ wiki/Hyaluronan; "Hyaluronic acid—Hyasis." Novozymes. http://www.biopharma.novozymes.com/ en/products/hyaluronic-acid/Pages/default.aspx.

43 **often incorporated into skin lotions:** "Hyaluronan." Wikipedia; K. Kimata, "Report on the HA 2010 Conference," 8th International Conference on Hyaluronan Research, Kyoto, June 6–11, 2010. http://www .glycoforum.gr.jp/science/hyaluronan/HA36/ HA36E.html#1; "Hyaluronic Acid," Natural Medicines Comprehensive Database. http:// naturaldatabase.therapeuticresearch.com/nd/ Search.aspx?cs=&s=nd&pt=100&id=1062& AspxAutoDetectCookieSupport=1; Rutjes et al., Viscosupplementation; Goa KL, Benfield P. Hyaluronic acid: a review of its pharmacology and use as a surgical aid in ophthalmology, and its therapeutic potential in joint disease and wound healing. *Drugs.* 1994.47(3):536–566.

43 **modern medicine may soon promote HA:** Kwak TI, Jin MH, et al. Long-term effects of glans penis augmentation using injectable hyaluronic acid gel for premature ejaculation. *Int J Impot Res.* 2008.20(4):425–428; Kim JJ, Kwak TI, et al. Effects of glans penis augmentation using hyaluronic acid gel for premature ejaculation. *Int J Impot Res.* 2004.16(6):547–551.

43 **Glucosamine is a natural constituent:** Henrotin Y, Mobasheri A, Marty M. Is there any scientific evidence for the use of glucosamine in the management of human osteoarthritis? *Arthritis Res Ther.* 2012; 14(1): 201; Muller-Fassbender H, Bach GL, et al. Glucosamine sulfate compared to ibuprofen in osteoarthritis of the knee. *Osteoarthritis Cartilage.* 1994.2(1):61–69; Henrotin et al., Is there any scientific evidence; Bassleer C, Royati L, Franchimont stimulation of proteoglycan production by glucosamine sulfate in chondrocytes isolated from human osteoarthritic articular cartilage in vitro. *Osteoarthritis Cartilage.* 1998.6(6):427–434; Igarashi M, Kaga I, et al. Effects of glucosamine derivatives and uronic acids on the production of glycosaminoglycans by human synovial cells and chondrocytes. *Int J Mol Med.* 2011.27(6):821–827.

43 **In the gut, glucosamine helps:** Forstner JF. Intestinal mucins in health and disease. *Digestion.* 1978.17(3):234–263; Corfield AP, Carroll D, et al. Mucins in the gastrointestinal tract in health and disease. *Front Biosci.* 2001.6:D1321–D1357; Murch SH, MacDonald TT, Walker-Smith JA, Levin M, Lionetti P, Klein NJ. Disruption of sulphated glycosaminoglycans in intestinal inflammation. *Lancet.* 1993.341:711–714; Salvatore S, Heuschkel R, Tomlin S, et al. A pilot study of N-acetyl glucosamine, a nutritional substrate for glycosaminoglycan synthesis, in pediatric chronic inflammatory bowel disease. *Aliment Pharmacol Ther.* 2000.14:1567–1579; J. A. Walker-Smith and S. H. Murch, "Architecture and Matrix of the Small Intestine," in *Diseases of the Small Intestine in Childhood*, 4th ed. (Isis Medical Media, 1999), 11–27; Murch SH, MacDonald TT, et al. Disruption of sulphated glycosaminoglycans in intestinal inflammation. *Lancet.* 1993.341:711–714; Pender SLF, Lionetti P, et al. Proteolytic degradation of intestinal mucosal extracellular matrix after lamina propria T cell activation. *Gut.* 1996.39:284–290.

44 **Galactosamine, the other sugar:** Bond A, Cooke A, Hay FC. Glycosylation of IgG, immune complexes and IgG subclasses in the MRL-lpr/lpr mouse model of rheumatoid arthritis. *Eur J Immunol.* 1990.20(10):2229–2233; Kuroda Y, Nakata M, et al. Abnormal IgG galactosylation in MRL-lpr/lpr mice: pathogenic role in the development of arthritis. *Pathol Int.* 2001.51(12):909–915; Tertov VV, Orekhov AN, et al. Carbohydrate composition of protein and lipid components in sialic acid-rich and -poor

low density lipoproteins from subjects with and without coronary artery disease. *J Lipid Res.* 1993.34(3):365–375; Kamel M, Hanafi M, Bassiouni M. Inhibition of elastase enzyme release from human polymorphonuclear leukocytes by N-acetyl-galactosamine and N-acetyl-glucosamine. *Clin Exp Rheumatol.* 1991.9(1):17–21.

44 **Chondroitin is a large, gel-forming:** National Center for Complimentary and Alternative Medicine. The NIH Glucosamine/Chondroitin Arthritis Intervention Trial (GAIT). *J Pain Palliat Care Pharmacother.* 2008.22(1):39–43; Black C, Clar C, et al. The clinical effectiveness of glucosamine and chondroitin supplements in slowing or arresting progression of osteoarthritis of the knee: a systematic review and economic evaluation. *Health Tech Assess.* 2009.13(52). doi: 10.3313/hta13520; http://www.journalslibrary.nihr.ac.uk/__data/assets/pdf_file/0009/65268/FullReport-hta13520.pdf.

44 **Critics contend that chondroitin:** Joseph Pizzorno and Michael T. Murray, eds., *Textbook of Natural Medicine* (Elsevier Health Sciences, 2012), 1654; Guy Montague-Jones, "Martek Works on a Vegetarian Source of Chondroitin," March 31, 2010. NUTRA-Ingredients USA. http://www.nutraingredients-usa.com/Suppliers2/Martek-works-on-a-vegetarian-source-of-chondroitin.

45 **The Body's Many Sugars:** Emil Mondoa, *Sugars That Heal: The New Healing Science of Glyconutrients* (Ballantine 2001); Gardiner T. Biological activity of eight known dietary monosaccharides required for glycoprotein synthesis and cellular recognition processes: summary. *GlycoScience and Nutrition.* 2000.1(13):1–7; R. K. Murray, "Glycoproteins," in *Harper's Biochemistry*, 24th ed., edited by R. K. Murray, D. K. Granner, et al. (Appleton and Lange, 1996), 648–666; Schnaar RL, Freeze HH. A "glyconutrient sham" *Glycobiology.* 2008.18(9):652–657; Ray Sahelian, "Glyconutrients, an Honest Review," February 24, 2014. http://www.raysahelian.com/glyconutrients.html; Axford JS. 7th Jenner Glycobiology and Medicine Symposium. *Adv Exp Med Biol.* 2005.564:v–viii; Currier NL, Lejtenyi D, Miller SC. Effect over time of in-vivo administration of the polysaccharide arabinogalactan on immune and hemopoietic cell lineages in murine spleen and bone marrow. *Phytomedicine.* 2003.10:145–153; Hauer J, Anderer FA. Mechanism of stimulation of human natural killer cytotoxicity by arabinogalactan from Larix occidentalis. *Cancer Immunol Immunother.* 1993.36:237–244; Kaiser J. Science and commerce: who owns glycobiology? *Science.* 2007.318:734–737; Hurtley S, Service R, Szuromi P. Cinderella's coach is ready. *Science.* 2001.291(5512):2337. doi: 10.1126/science.291.5512.2337; Rudd PM, Elliott T, et al. Glycosylation and the immune system. *Science.* 2001.291(5512):2370–2376.

46 **Proteoglycans are valued for:** Pecora F, et al. In vivo contribution of amino acid sulfur to cartilage proteoglycan sulfation. *Biochem J.* 2006.398:509–514; Gandhi NS, Macera RL. The structure of glycosaminoglycans and their interactions with proteins. *Chem Biol Drug Des.* 2008.72(6):455–482.

46 **Sulfur deficiency is widespread:** S. Seneff, "Sulfur Deficiency," *Wise Traditions*, Summer 2011. http://www.westonaprice.org/vitamins-and-minerals/sulfur-deficiency; Black et al., The clinical effectiveness of glucosamine.

Chapter 8

49 **Why were the studies so variable:** Kaayla T. Daniel, "Why Broth Is beautiful," *Wise Traditions*, Spring 2003, 25–36; Nathan R. Gotthoffer, *Gelatin in Nutrition and Medicine* (Grayslake, 1945), 156–159.

50 **Dr. Prudden and Cartilage Research:** Quotations from Dr. Prudden throughout this book come from Kaayla T. Daniel's telephone interviews with him on September 3, 8, 14, 19, 24, and 25 and October 3 and 8, 1997.

54 **Nathan R. Gotthoffer, PhD:** http://en.wikipedia.org/wiki/Drackett; Nathan R. Gotthoffer and Charles T. Nugent, "Method of Manufacturing Soybean Protein." Publication # US 2172540A. Publication date July 5, 1955. Filing date September 16, 1953. http://www.google.com/patents/US2712540; *Cornell Alumni News*, "Alumni Notes," February 7, 1924, 240; *Cornell Alumni News*, "New Mailing Addresses," November 13, 1924, 112; *Cornell Alumni News*, "Alumni Notes," November 18, 1926; *Cornell Alumni News*, "News of the Alumni," January 1950, 242; *Cornell Alumni News*, "News from the Classes," May 1962, 45; *Cornell Alumni News*, "New Students Here This Year Include 340 Alumni Children,"

December 15, 1947, 206; *Cornell Alumni News*, "Alumni Deaths," July 1983, 48.

56 **John F. Prudden, MD, DSci:** John F. Prudden interviews with Kaayla T. Daniel during September and October 1997; Ford Burkhart, "John F. Prudden, 78, Surgeon and Researcher," *New York Times*, September 29, 1998; "Dr. John F Prudden Wins 'Linus Pauling Scientist of the Year' Award," *Townsend Letter for Doctors and Patients*, 1996, #150, 21; John F. Prudden, ed., *Foundation for Cartilage and Immunological Research: A Compilation of Scientific Research on Bovine Tracheal Cartilage: An Effective Agent in the Treatment of Cancer, Arthritis, Wound Healing, Skin Disorders and Other Conditions*, Version 2.0 (Foundation for Cartilage and Immunology Research, 1996); "Foundation for Cartilage and Immunology Research Press Release," Henry Kriegel & Associates, October 25, 1995.

Chapter 9

58 **More than 52.5 million Americans:** Centers for Disease Control and Prevention, "Arthritis: Frequently Asked Questions—General Public." http://www.cdc.gov/arthritis/basics/faqs.htm.

59 **Skeletal evidence proves that arthritic:** Dequeker J, Luyten FP. The history of osteoarthritis-osteoarthrosis. *Ann Rheum Dis.* 2008.67(1):5–10; Bridges PS. Prehistoric arthritis in the Americas. *Annu Rev Anthropol.* 1992.21:67–91; Buchanan WW, Kean WF, Kean R. History and current status of osteoarthritis in the population. *Inflammopharmacology.* 2003.11(4):301–316; Braunstein EM, White SJ, et al. Paleoradiologic evaluation of the Egyptian royal mummies. *Skeletal Radiol.* 1988.17(5):348–352; Rogers J, Watt J, Dieppe P. Arthritis in Saxon and mediaeval skeletons. *Br Med J (Clin Res Ed).* 1981.283(6307): 1668–1670; Thould AK, Thould BT. Arthritis in Roman Britain. *Br Med J (Clin Res Ed).* 1983.287(6409):1909–1911.

59 **the bones of healthy primitive people:** Weston A. Price. *Nutrition and Physical Degeneration*, 8th ed. (Price Pottenger Nutrition, 2009). www.westonaprice.org.

60 **"Imagine rubbing together:** Jason Theodosakis, Brenda Addly, and Barry Fox, *The Arthritis Cure* (St. Martin's, 1997), 23.

60 **No one knows what initial event triggers:** Caplan AI. Cartilage. *Scientific American.* 1984.251:84–94; F. A. Wollheim, "Pathogenesis of Osteoarthritis," in *Rheumatology*, vol. 2, 3rd ed., edited by M. C. Hochberg, A. J. Silman, et al. (Mosby, 2003); Felson DT, Lawrence RC, et al. Osteoarthritis: new insights, part 1: the disease and its risk factors. *Ann Intern Med*, 2000.133:635; K. D. Brandt, M. Doherty, et al., *Osteoarthritis* (Oxford University Press, 1998).

60 **University of Maryland Medical Center's health information website:** University of Maryland Medical Center. "Cartilage." https://umm.edu/health/medical/altmed/supplement/cartilage.

60 **Consumed every day, bone broth:** Reinhard Schrieber and Herbert Gareis, *Gelatine Handbook: Theory and Industrial Practice* (Wiley-VCH, 2007), 1.

61 **Broth also helps us recover from the athletic:** "Secondary Arthritis," *Arthritis Support.* Wikispaces.com. http://arthritis-support.wikispaces.com/Secondary+arthritis.

61 **According to the 2007 textbook:** Schrieber and Gareis, *Gelatine Handbook*, 94, 162, 238, 278, 301–309.

61 **In 1982, a report by B. Goetz:** Goetz B. Chondropathia patellae. *Aertzliche Praxis.* 1982.92:3130–3134.

61 **In 1989, Drs. Klaus Seeligmuller:** Seeligmuller K, Happel HK. Can a mixture of gelatin and l-cysteine stimulate proteoglycan synthesis? *Therapiewoche*, 1989.38:2456–2461.

62 **In 1991, Milan Adam:** Schrieber and Gareis, *Gelatine Handbook*, 304, 307.

62 **Since then, there have been at least nine:** Kaayla T. Daniel, telephone interview with Dr. Prudden. September 14, 1997.

62 **Over the years, sports physiologists:** Michael Teppner, ed., *Collagen Hydrolysate and Its Relationship to Joint Health: A Scientific Compendium* (Gelita Health Initiative, 2004); Schrieber and Gareis, *Gelatine Handbook*, 305.

63 **In 2008, Kristine L. Clark:** Clark KL, Sebastianell W, et al. 24-week study on the use of collagen hydrolysate as a dietary supplement in athletes with activity-related joint pain. *Curr Med Res Opin.* 2008.24(5):1485–1496.

63 **Collagen hydrolysate received its biggest boost:** Moskowitz RW. Role of collagen hydrolysate in

bone and joint disease. *Semin Arthritis Rheum.* 2000.30(2):87–99.

63 **In 2012, J. P. Van Vijven:** Van Vijven JP, Luijsterburg PA, et al. Symptomatic and chondroprotective treatment with collagen derivatives in osteoarthritis: a systematic review. *Osteoarthritis Cartilage.* 2012.20(8):809–821.

63 **Not long after, in 1997:** "Hard Knocks for Knox Nutrajoint: Company's Claim for Dietary Supplement Are Overblown," *Tufts University Health and Nutrition Letter,* 1997, 15, 6, 1.

63 **In a major article published in the summer 1974:** Prudden JF, Balassa L. The biological activity of bovine cartilage preparation: a clinical demonstration of their potent anti-inflammatory capacity. *Semin Arthritis Rheum.* 1974.3(4):187–321.

63 **"desperate over their pain:** Daniel, interview with Dr. Prudden, September 14, 1997.

64 **Thrilled by this success, Dr. Prudden:** Prudden, Balassa, The biological activity.

64 **"Growth factors are ideal:** Daniel, interview with Dr. Prudden, September 14, 1997.

64 **Dr. Rejholec concluded:** Rejholec V. Long term studies of antiosteoarthritic drugs: an assessment. *Sem Arth Rheum.* 1987.17(2 Suppl 1):35–53.

64 **was published by Alfred Jay Bollet:** Bollet AJ. Stimulation of protein—chondroitin sulfate synthesis by normal and osteoarthritic articular cartilage. *Arthritis Rheum.* 1968.11(5):663–673.

65 **during the same period, I. William Lane:** I. William Lane and Linda Comac, *Sharks Don't Get Cancer: How Shark Cartilage Could Save Your Life* (Avery, 1992).

65 **Anti-angiogenesis factors would be helpful:** Conversations with Drs. Folkman and Langer, reported by Dr. Prudden, October 3, 1997; Conversations with Drs. Folkman and Langer, reported in David Kirchhof and Elisabeth Kirchhof, *The Successful Use of Bovine Cartilage in the Treatment of Cancer* (Kriegel & Associates, 1995).

65 **Furthermore, Lane built:** Lane and Comac, *Sharks Don't Get Cancer*; I. William Lane and Linda Comac, *Sharks Still Don't Get Cancer* (Avery, 1996); "Dr. Serge Orloff." Zoomimfo. http://www.zoominfo.com/p/Serge -Orloff/370778399.

65 **Clearly Lane's marketing:** Sabo J, Enquist IF. Wound stimulating effect of homologous and heterologous cartilage. *Arch Surg.* 1965.91:523–525.

66 **Studies on chicken sternal cartilage:** Schauss A, Stenehjem J, et al. Effect of the novel low molecular weight hydrolyzed chicken sternal cartilage extract, BioCell Collagen, on improving osteoarthritis-related symptoms: a randomized, double-blind, placebo-controlled trial. *J Agric Food Chem.* 2012.60(16):4096–4101.

66 **Despite success with whole food:** Paul Coates, *Encyclopedia of Dietary Supplements* (CRC Press, 2005), 281.

66 **Chondroitin sulfate is a large:** J. L. Ong and Mark R. Appleford, *Introduction to Biomaterials: Basic Theory with Engineering Applications* (Cambridge University Press, 2013), 227.

66 **Glucosamine and chondroitin supplements:** Jason Theodosakis, Barry Fox, and Brenda D. Adderly, *The Arthritis Cure* (St. Martin's Press, 1997).

66 **Even so, glucosamine and chondroitin sulfate:** Sawitzke AD, Shi H, et al. Clinical efficacy and safety of glucosamine, chondroitin sulphate, their combination, celecoxib or placebo taken to treat osteoarthritis of the knee: 2-year results from GAIT. *Ann Rheum Dis.* 2010.69(8):1459–1464.

67 **The dangers of these over-the-counter drugs:** Gary S. Firestein, Ralph C. Budd, et al., *Kelley's Textbook of Rheumatology,* 9th ed. (Saunders, 2012), 883.

67 **Findings that glucosamine and chondroitin:** Sawitzke et al., Clinical efficacy and safety; Henrotin Y, Mobasheri A, Marty M. Is there any scientific evidence for the use of glucosamine in the management of human osteoarthritis? *Arthritis Res Ther.* 2012.14(1):201; Black C, Clar C, et al. The clinical effectiveness of glucosamine and chondroitin supplements in slowing or arresting progression of osteoarthritis of the knee: a systematic review and economic evaluation. *Health Tech Assess.* 2009.13(52). doi: 10.3313/ hta13520.

67 **The Glucosamine/Chondroitin Arthritis Intervention Trial:** Clegg DO, Reda DJ, et al. Glucosamine, chondroitin sulfate and the two in combination for painful knee osteoarthritis. *N Engl J Med.* 2006.354:795–808; Sawitzke et al., Clinical efficacy and safety.

67 **Although patient dropout complicates study:** Laba TL, Brien JA, et al. Patient preferences for adherence to treatment for osteoarthritis: the

Medication Decisions in Osteoarthritis Study (MEDOS). *BMC Musculoskelet Disord*. 2013.14:160.

68 **a year before his death, Dr. Prudden:** Daniel, interview with Dr. Prudden, September 24, 1997.

Chapter 10

69 **five-thousand-year-old mummy:** Hart FD. History of the treatment of rheumatoid arthritis. *British Med J*. 1976.1:763–765; Joshi VR. Rheumatology, past, present and future. *JAPI*. 2012.60; Aceves-Avila FJ, Medina F, Fraga A. The antiquity of rheumatoid arthritis: a reappraisal. *J Rheumatol*. 2001.28(4):751–757.

69 **ancient remedies:** Hart, History of the treatment; Joshi, Rheumatology; Aceves-Avila et al., The antiquity of rheumatoid arthritis; W. S. A. Copeman, *Short History of the Gout and the Rheumatic Diseases* (University of California, 1964), 144–146.

69 **three million people in the United States alone:** http://www.arthritis.org/files/images/newsroom/media-kits/Rheumatoid_Arthritis_Fact_Sheet.pdf; http://www.cdc.gov/arthritis/basics/rheumatoid.htm; Developer of new rheumatoid drug says 3 million have RA in the US. http://www.argentisrx.com/content/show.asp?mne=pipeline; Myasoedova E, Crowson CS, et al. Is the incidence of rheumatoid arthritis rising? Results from Olmsted County, Minnesota, 1955–2007. *Arth Rheum*. 2010.62(6):1576–1582.

71 **Dr. Prudden reported:** Prudden JF, Balassa L. The biological activity of bovine cartilage preparation: a clinical demonstration of their potent anti-inflammatory capacity. *Semin Arthritis Rheum*. 1974.3(4):187–321.

71 **Dr. Prudden used injections:** Conversations with Drs. Folkman and Langer, reported by Dr. Prudden, October 3, 1997; Conversations with Drs. Folkman and Langer, reported in David Kirchhof and Elisabeth Kirchhof, *The Successful Use of Bovine Cartilage in the Treatment of Cancer* (Kriegel & Associates, 1995).

71 **shark cartilage:** Chuan-Ying Y, Lei Z. Effects of shark cartilage polysaccharides on the secretion of IL-6 and IL-12 in rheumatoid arthritis. *Pharm Biol*. 2012.50(12):1567–1572.

71 **rats treated with glucosamine:** Haleagrahara N, Tudawe D, et al. Amelioration of collagen-induced arthritis in female dark agouti rats by glucosamine treatment. *ISRN Pharmacol*. 2013. 2013:562905.

72 **glucosamine and methionine:** Yamagishi Y, Igarashi M, et al. Evaluation of the effect of methionine and glucosamine on adjuvant arthritis in rats. *Exp Ther Med*. 2012.4(4):640–644.

72 **β-D-glucosamine:** Jawed H, Anjum S, et al. Anti-arthritic effect of GN1, a novel synthetic analog of glucosamine, in the collagen-induced arthritis model in rats. *Inflamm Res*. 2011.60(12)1113–1120.

72 **David E. Trentham, MD:** Trentham D, Dynesius-Trentham R, et al. Effects of oral administration of type ii collagen on rheumatoid arthritis. *Science*.1993.261(5129):1727–1730.

73 **Dr. Trentham and eleven other researchers:** Barnett ML, Kremer JM, et al. Treatment of rheumatoid arthritis with oral type II collagen: results of a multicenter, double-blind, placebo-controlled trial. *Arthritis Rheum*. 1998.41(2):290–297.

73 **Trentham and two colleagues:** Barnett ML, Combitchci D, Trentham DE. A pilot trial of oral type II collagen in the treatment of juvenile rheumatoid arthritis. *Arth Rheum*. 1996.39(4):623–628.

73 **Thomas McPherson Brown:** Thomas McPherson Brown and Henry Scammel, *The Road Back: Rheumatoid Arthritis, Its Cause and ITS Treatment* (Evans, 1988); Henry Scammel, *The New Arthritis Breakthrough: The Only Medical Therapy Clinically Proven to Produce Long-Term Improvement and Remission of RA, Lupus, Juvenile RS, and Other Inflammatory Forms of Arthritis* (Evans, 1998).

74 **"turn it right side up!":** Scammel, *The New Arthritis Breakthrough*.

74 **respect of many health experts:** Paulus, HE. Minocycline treatment of rheumatoid arthritis. *Ann Intern Med*. 1995.122:81–89; Tilley BC, Alarcon GS, et al. Minocycline in rheumatoid arthritis: a 48-week, double-blind, placebo-controlled trial. MIRA Trial Group. *Ann Intern Med*. 1995.15.122(2):81–89; Stone M, Fortin PR, et al. Should tetracycline treatment be used more extensively for rheumatoid arthritis? Metaanalysis demonstrates clinical benefit with reduction in disease activity. *J Rheumatol*. 2003.30(10): 2112–2122; Kim NM, Freeman CD. Minocycline for rheumatoid arthritis. *Ann Pharmacother*. 1995.29(2):186–187.

74 **theory of "molecular mimicry":** Zarnitsyna
VI, Evavold BD, et al. Estimating the diversity,
completeness, and cross-reactivity of the T
cell repertoire. *Front Immunol.* 2013.4:485;
Wucherpfennig KW, Stominger JL. Molecular
mimicry in T cell-mediated autoimmunity: viral
peptides activate human T cell clones specific for
myelin basic protein. *Cell.* 1995.890(5):695–705;
Wucherpfennig KW. Structural basis of molecular
mimicry. *J Autoimmun.* 2001.16(83):293–302.

74 **alternative practitioners:** David Brownstein,
Overcoming Arthritis (Medical Alternatives, 2001);
Joseph Mercola, "Rheumatoid Arthritis: Painful
Debilitating Disease More Devastating Than
Previously Recognized," August 16, 2010. http://
articles.mercola.com/sites/articles/archive/2010/08/
16/rheumatoid-arthritis-protocol.aspx.

74 **Thomas Cowan, MD:** Thomas S. Cowan, *The
Fourfold Path to Healing* (New Trends, 2004).

75 **fundamental causes of his disorder:** Cowan, *The
Fourfold Path to Healing.*

Chapter 11

76 **Scleroderma is an autoimmune disease:** "What
Is Scleroderma?" Scleroderma Foundation.
http://www.scleroderma.org/site/PageServer
?pagename=patients_whatis#.UyyXqlxD1Zg;
G. P. Rodnan, "Progressive System Sclerosis
(Scleroderma)," in *Arthritis and Allied Conditions*,
9th ed., edited by D. J. McCarty (Lea & Febiger,
1980), 762–810; Fleckman PH, Jeffrey JJ, Eisen
AZ. A sensitive microassay for prolyl hydroxylase
activity in normal and psoriatic skin. *J Invest
Dermatol.* 1973.60(1):46–52.

76 **injections of bovine tracheal cartilage:** Prudden
JF, Balassa L. The biological activity of bovine
cartilage preparation: a clinical demonstration
of their potent anti-inflammatory capacity
with supplementary notes on certain relevant
fundamental supportive studies. *Semin Arthritis
Rheum.* 1974.3(4):187–321.

77 **calcinosis cutis lesion:** Piombino L, Pallara T, et
al. A novel surgical approach to calcinosis cutis
using a collagen-elastin matrix. *J Wound Care.*
2013.22(1):22–23.

77 **Dr. Wuerthele-Caspe:** Wuerthele-Caspe
(Livingston) V. Scleroderma treated with
promin, with report of a case. *J Med Soc NJ.*
1947.44:52–53; Wuerthele-Caspe (Livingston) V,

Brodkin E, Mermod C. Etiology of scleroderma:
preliminary clinical report. *J Med Sci NJ.*
1947.44:256–259; Wuerthele-Caspe (Livingston)
V, Alexander-Jackson E, Anderson JA, et
al. Cultural properties and pathogenicity of
certain microorganisms obtained from various
proliferative and neoplastic diseases. *Am J Med
Sci.* 1950; 220:638–648.

77 **microbial cause and a possible cure for cancer:**
Virginia Livingston-Wheeler and Owen
Webster Wheeler, *The Microbiology of Cancer:
Compendium* (Livingston Wheeler Medical
Clinic, 1977), 18.

77 **found the bacteria in nine additional cases:**
Cantwell AR Jr, Wilson JR. Scleroderma with
ulceration secondary to atypical mycobacteria.
Arch Dermatol. 1966.94:663–664.

78 **Henry Scammell:** T. M. Brown and H. Scammell,
*The Road Back: Rheumatoid Arthritis—Its Cause
and Treatment* (Evans, 1988); H. Scammell, *The
New Arthritis Breakthough* (Evans, 1998); H.
Scammell, *Scleroderma: The Proven Therapy That
Can Save Your Life* (Evans, 1998).

78 **Alan R. Cantwell Jr., MD:** Cantwell, Wilson,
Scleroderma; Cantwell AR Jr, Craggs E, et al. Acid-
fast bacteria as a possible cause of scleroderma.
Dermatologica. 1968.136(3):141–150; Cantwell AR
Jr, Kelso DW. Acid-fast bacteria in scleroderma
and morphea. *Arch Dermatol.* 1971.104(1):21–25;
Cantwell AR Jr, Kelso DW, Rowe L. Hypodermitis
sclerodermiformis and unusual acid-fast bacteria.
Arch Dermatol. 1979.115(4):449–452; Cantwell
AR Jr. Histologic forms resembling "large bodies"
in scleroderma and "pseudoscleroderma." *Am J
Dermatopathol.* 1980.2(3):273–276; Cantwell AR,
Kelso DW. Histologic observations of pleomorphic
corynebacterium-like microorganisms in diabetic
scleredema adultorum. *Cutis.* 1980.26(6):575–583;
Cantwell AR Jr, Kelso DW. Autopsy findings of
nonacid-fast bacteria in scleroderma. *Dermatologica.*
1980.160(2):90–99; Cantwell AR Jr, Rowe L, Kelso
DW. Nodular scleroderma and pleomorphic acid-
fast bacteria. *Arch Dermatol.* 1980.116(11):1283–
1290; Cantwell AR Jr. Variably acid-fast bacteria
in a case of systemic sarcoidosis and hypodermitis
sclerodermiformis. *Dermatologica.* 1981.163(3):239–
248; Rowe L, Cantwell AR Jr. Hypodermitis
sclerodermiformis: successful treatment with
ultrasound. *Arch Dermatol.* 1982.118(5):312–314;

Cantwell AR Jr, Cove JK. Variably acid-fast bacteria in a necropsied case of systemic lupus erythematosus with acute myocardial infarction. *Cutis*. 1984.33(6):560–567; Cantwell AR Jr, Jones JE, Kelso DW. Pleomorphic, variably acid-fast bacteria in an adult patient with disabling pansclerotic morphea. *Arch Dermatol*. 1984.120(5):656–661; Cantwell AR Jr. Histologic observations of pleomorphic, variably acid-fast bacteria in scleroderma, morphea, and lichen sclerosus et atrophicus. *Int J Dermatol*. 1984.23(1):45–52.

78 **scientific community:** Amy Proal, "Bacteria and Cancer: An Interview with Dr. Alan Cantwell," Bacteriality: Exploring Chronic Disease. http://bacteriality.com/2007/09/11/cantwell/; Zarnitsyna VI, Evavold BD, et al. Estimating the diversity, completeness, and cross-reactivity of the T cell repertoire. *Front Immunol*. 2013.4:485; Wucherpfennig KW, Stominger JL. Molecular mimicry in T cell-mediated autoimmunity: viral peptides activate human T cell clones specific for myelin basic protein. *Cell* 1995.890(5):695–705; Wucherpfennig KW. Structural basis of molecular mimicry. *J Autoimmun*. 2001.16(83):293–302.

78 **publish his findings in the books:** Alan Cantwell, *AIDS and the Doctors of Death: An Inquiry into the Origin of the AIDS Epidemic* (Aries Rising Press, 1988); Alan Cantwell, *Queer Blood: The Secret AIDS Genocide* (Aries Rising Press, 1993); Alan Cantwell, *AIDS, the Mystery and the Solution* (Aries Rising Press, 1993); Alan Cantwell, *The Cancer Microbe* (Aries Rising Press, 1990); Alan Cantwell, *Four Women against Cancer* (Aries Rising, 2005).

79 **tuberculosis:** Nathan R. Gotthoffer, *Gelatin in Nutrition and Medicine* (Grayslake Gelatin, 1945), 77–80; Lack CH, Tanner F. The significance of pleomorphism in Mycobacterium tuberculosis var. hominis. *J Gen Microbiol*. 1953.8:18–26; Centers for Disease Control and Prevention (CDC), "Tuberculosis (TB)." www.cdc.com/tb.

79 **leprosy:** O. C. Gruner, *A Treatise on the Canon of Medicine of Avicenna* (Luzac; 1930), 407; Bar Sela A, Hoff HE, Faris E. Moses Maimonides' two treatises on the regimen of health. *Trans Am Phil Soc*. 1964.54(4). http://greenmedicine.ie/school/images/Library/Regimen%20of%20Health.pdf.

79 **Dr. Prudden put it:** Kaayla T. Daniel, interview with Dr. Prudden, October 3, 1997.

Chapter 12

80 **psoriasis:** National Psoriasis Foundation, "Psoriasis and Comorbid Conditions Issue Brief: Executive Summary." http://www.psoriasis.org/document.doc?id=793; Weger W. Current status and new developments in the treatment of psoriasis and psoriatic arthritis with biological agents. *Br J Pharmacol*. 2010.160(4):810–820.

80 **The problem begins:** Menter A, Gottlieb A, et al. Guidelines of care for the management of psoriasis and psoriatic arthritis: Section 1. Overview of psoriasis and guidelines of care for the treatment of psoriasis with biologics. *J Am Acad Dermatol*. 2008.58(5):826–850; Griffiths CE, Barker JN. Pathogenesis and clinical features of psoriasis. *Lancet*. 2007.370(9583):263–271; Krueger JG, Bowcock A. Psoriasis pathophysiology: current concepts of pathogenesis. *Ann Rheum Dis*. 2005.64(Suppl II):ii30–ii36.

80 **rich network of capillaries:** Telner P, Fekete Z. The capillary responses in psoriatic skin. *J Invest Derm*. 1969.20:225–230; Ross JB. The psoriatic capillary. *Br J Dermatol*. 2006.76(12).

81 **Dr. Prudden was called:** Prudden JF, Balassa L. The biological activity of bovine cartilage preparation: a clinical demonstration of their potent anti-inflammatory capacity with supplementary notes on certain relevant fundamental supportive studies. *Semin Arthritis Rheum*. 1974.3(4):187–321.

81 **Of all the remarkable cases:** Kaayla T. Daniel, interview with Dr. Prudden, October 3, 1997.

81 **psoriasis itself should be classified:** Prudden, Balassa, The biological activity; Daniel, interview with Dr. Prudden, October 3, 1997.

81 **Koebner theorized:** Kuta A, Neumann E. Koebner's phenomenon in a study concerning the primary epidermal pathogenesis of psoriasis. *Determatologica*. 1957.116(51).

82 **As Dr. Prudden put it:** Daniel, interview with Dr. Prudden, October 3, 1997.

83 **shark cartilage as a natural cure for cancer:** I. William Lane and Linda Comac, *Sharks Don't Get Cancer* (Avery, 1992); I. William Lane and Linda Comac, *Sharks Still Don't Get Cancer* (Avery, 1996); Folkman J. Angiogenesis in psoriasis: therapeutic implications. *J Invest Dermatol*. 1972.59(1):40–43.

83 **extracts of shark cartilage:** Dupont E, Savard PE, et al. Antiangiogenic properties of a novel shark

cartilage extract: potential role in the treatment of psoriasis. *J Cutan Med Surg.* 1998.2(3):146–152.

84 **Judah Folkman, MD:** Conversations with Drs. Folkman and Langer, reported by Dr. Prudden, October 3, 1997; Conversations with Drs. Folkman and Langer, reported in David Kirchhof and Elisabeth Kirchhof, *The Successful Use of Bovine Cartilage in the Treatment of Cancer* (Kriegel & Associates, 1995).

84 **anti-angiogenic factors survive the digestive process:** Sauder DN, Dekoven J, et al. Neovastat (AE-941), an inhibitor of angiogenesis: randomized phase I/II clinical trial results in patients with plaque psoriasis. *J Am Acad Dermatol.* 2002.47(4):535–541.

84 **side effects reported by clinicians:** University of Maryland Medical Center, "Cartilage." https://umm.edu/health/medical/altmed/supplement/cartilage.

84 **glucosamine:** McCarty MF. Glucosamine for psoriasis? *Med Hypotheses.*1997.48(5):437–441.

84 **literature review of chondroitin sulfate:** Vallieres M, du Souich P. Modulation of inflammation by chondroitin sulfate. *Osteoarthritis Cartilage.* 2010.18(Suppl 1):S1–S6; de Souich P, Garcia AG, et al. Immunomodulatory and anti-inflammatory effects of chondroitin sulphate. *J Cell Mol Med.* 2009.13(8A):1451–1463; Möller I, Pérez M, Monfort J, Benito P, Cuevas J, Perna C, et al. Effectiveness of chondroitin sulphate in patients with concomitant knee osteoarthritis and psoriasis: a randomized, double-blind, placebo-controlled study. *Osteoarthritis Cartilage.* 2010.8(Suppl. 1):532–540; Verges J, Montell E, Herrero M, Perna C, Cuevas J, Perez M, et al. Clinical and histo-pathological improvement of psoriasis with oral chondroitin sulfate: a serendipitous finding. *Dermatol Online J.* 2005.11:31.

84 **Gelatin served well:** Nathan R. Gotthoffer, *Gelatin in Nutrition and Medicine* (Grayslake, 1945), 149–151.

84 **pleomorphic bacteria:** Gilroy CB, Keat A, Taylor-Robinson D. The prevalence of Mycoplasma fermentans in patients with inflammatory arthritides. *Rheumatol.* 2001.40(12):1355–1358.

Chapter 13

86 **least eight studies:** Adelle Davis, *Let's Get Well* (Signet, 1972). Davis cites numerous studies on nutrition and wound healing from the 1930s to 1960s.

86 **Gelatin:** Nathan R. Gotthoffer, *Gelatin in Nutrition and Medicine* (Grayslake, 1945), 81–111.

87 **Chinese medicine:** Jing-Nuan Wu, *An Illustrated Chinese Materia Medica* (Oxford University Press, 2002), 284–285.

87 **Florence Nightingale:** Florence Nightingale, *Notes on Nursing* (Dover Books on Biology, 1969), 43.

87 **research on wound healing:** Prudden JF, Wolarsky ER, Balassa L. The acceleration of healing. *Surg Gynecol Obst.* 1969.128(6): 1321–1326.

87 **Dr. John F. Prudden:** Kaayla T. Daniel, telephone interview with Dr. Prudden, September 3, 1997.

88 **fast and positive result:** Daniel, interview with Dr. Prudden, September 3, 1997; Lattes R, Martin JR, et al. Effect of cartilage and other tissue suspensions on reparative processes of cortisone-treated animals. *Am J Pathol.* 1956.32(5):979–991.

89 **As he told the story:** Daniel, interview with Dr. Prudden, September 3, 1997.

89 **ascertain the rate of gain:** Prudden et al., Acceleration of healing.

89 **cartilage in the form of pellets:** Houck JC, Jacob RA, et al. Inhibition of inflammation and acceleration of tissue repair by cartilage powder. *Surgery.* 1962.51:632–638.

89 **cartilage therapy:** Prudden et al., Acceleration of healing.

89 **two sets of experiments:** Prudden JF, Allen J. The clinical acceleration of healing with a cartilage preparation: a controlled study. *JAMA.* 1965.192:352–356.

90 **The second was a better-controlled study:** Prudden, Allen, The clinical acceleration of healing.

90 **Dr. Lattes's finding:** Lattes et al., Effect of cartilage.

90 **His study:** Prudden JF, Wolarsky E. The reversal by cartilage of the steroid-induced inhibition of wound healing. *Surg Gynecol Obstet.* 1967.125(1):109–113.

90 **speed wound healing:** Prudden JF, Migel P, et al. The discovery of a potent pure chemical wound-healing accelerator. *Am J Surg.* 1970.119(5): 560–564.

91 **Whatever the type of cartilage chosen:** Sabo J, Enquist IF. Wound stimulating effect of homologous and heterologous cartilage. *Arch Surg.* 1965.91:523–525; Prudden et al., The discovery.

91 **Dr. J. Madden:** J. Madden, "Wound Healing," in *Sabiston's Textbook of Surgery* (Saunders, 1987).

91 **Dr. Prudden's comments in 1997:** Kaayla T. Daniel, telephone interview with Dr. Prudden, October 7, 1997.

91 **Back in 1965, an editorial:** Editorial: Healing with cartilage. *JAMA*.1965.192(5):151–152.

Chapter 14

92 **chicken soup's healing effect:** Saketkhoo K, Januszkiewicz A, Sackner MA. Effects of drinking hot water, cold water and chicken soup on nasal mucus velocity and nasal airflow resistance. *Chest*. 1978.74(4):408–410.

92 **chicken soup's healing power:** Rennard BO, Ertl RE, et al. Chicken soup inhibits neutrophil chemotaxis in vitro. *Chest*. 2000.118(4): 1150–1157; "Chicken Soup for a Cold: Research Hints That Chicken Soup Remedy May Have Scientific Validity in Reducing Cold Symptoms," Department of Public Relations, University of Nebraska Medical Center. October 21, 2008. http://www.unmc.edu/publicrelations/ chickensoup_newsrelease.htm; Bender BS. Barbara, what's a nice girl like you doing writing an article like this? The scientific basis of folk remedies for colds and flu. *Chest*. 2000.118(4)887–888; Duma RJ, Markowitz SM, Tipple MA. The chicken soup controversy [letter]. *Chest*. 1975.68:604; Green LF. The chicken soup controversy [letter]. *Chest*. 1975.68:605; Chutkow JG. The chicken soup controversy [letter]. *Chest*. 1975.68:606; Lawrence DS. The chicken soup controversy [letter]. *Chest*. 1975.68:606; Lavine JB. Chicken soup or Jewish medicine. *Chest*. 2001.119(4):1295; Hopkins AB. Chicken soup cure may not be a myth. *Nurse Pract*. 2003.28(6):16.

93 **greater neutrophil-inhibiting effect:** Rennard et al., Chicken soup.

93 **Tara Parker-Pope:** Tara Parker-Pope, "The Science of Chicken Soup," *New York Times*, October 12, 1007.

93 **effect on immunity is short term:** Babizhayev MA, Deyev AI. Management of the virulent influenza virus infection by oral formulation of nonhydrolized carnosine and isopeptide of carnosine attenuating proinflammatory cytokine-induced nitric oxide production. *Am J Ther*. 2012.19(1):e25–e47; Babizhayev MA, Deyev AI, Yegorov YE. Non-hydrolyzed in digestive tract and blood natural L-carnosine peptide

("bioactivated Jewish penicillin") as a panacea of tomorrow for various flu ailments: signaling activity attenuating nitric oxide (NO) production, cytostasis, and NO-dependent inhibition of influenza virus replication in macrophages in the human body infected with the virulent swine influenza A (H1N1) virus. *J Basic Clin Physiol Pharmacol*. 2013.24(1):1–26.

93 **Glutamine:** Levintow L, Eagle H Piez KA. The role of glutamine in protein biosynthesis in tissue culture. *J Biol Chem*. 1957.227:929–941; Eagle H, Oyama VI, et al. The growth response of mammalian cells in tissue culture to l-glutamine and l-glutamic acid. *J Biol Chem*. 1956.218:606–616; Salzman NP, Eagle H, Sebring ED. The utilization of glutamine, glutamic acid and ammonia for the biosynthesis of nucleic acid bases in mammalian cell cultures. *J Biol Chem*. 1958.230(2):1001–1012; Eagle H, Piez K. The population dependent requirement by cultured mammalian cells for metabolites which they can synthesize. *J Exp Med*. 1962.116:29–43; Eagle H, Washington CL, Levy M. End product control of amino acid synthesis by cultured human cells. *J Biol Chem*. 1965.240(10):3944–3950.

93 **John Alverdy, MD:** Soeters PB. Glutamine the link between depletion and diminished gut function? *J Am Coll Nutr*. 1996.15(3): 195–196; Burke DJ, Alverdy JC, et al. Glutamine-supplemented total parenteral nutrition improves gut immune function. *Arch Surg*. 1989.124(12): 1396–1399; Alverdy JA, Aoys E, et al. The effect of glutamine-enriched TPN on gut immune cellularity. *J Surg Res*. 1992.51(1):34–38.

93 **linked glutamine depletion to immunosuppression:** Castell LM, Newsholme EA. The relation between glutamine and the immunodepression observed in exercise. *Amino Acids*. 2001.20(1):49–61; Bailey DM, Castell LM, et al. Continuous and intermittent exposure to the hypoxia of altitude: implications for glutamine metabolism and exercise performance. *Br J Sports Med*. 2000.34 (3):210–212; Castell LM, Newsholme EA. The effects of oral glutamine supplementation on athletes after prolonged exhaustive exercise. *Nutr*. 1997.13(7–8):738–742; Newsholme EA, Calder PC. The proposed role of glutamine in some cells of the immune system and speculative consequences for the whole animal. *Nutr*. 1997.(7–8):728–730;

Castell LM, Poortmans JR, Newsholme EA. Does glutamine have a role in reducing infections in athletes? *Eur J Appl Physiol Occup Physiol.* 1996.73(5):488–490; Newsholme EA. Biochemical mechanisms to explain immunosuppression in well-trained and overtrained athletes. *Int J Sports Med.* 1994.15(Suppl 3):S142–S147; Parry-Billings M, Budgett R, et al. Plasma amino acid concentrations in the overtraining syndrome: possible effects on the immune system. *Med Sci Sports Exerc.* 1992.24(12):1353–1358; Parry-Billings M, Baigrie RJ, et al. Effects of major and minor surgery on plasma glutamine and cytokine levels. *Arch Surg.* 1992.127(10):1237–1240; Parry-Billings M, Evans J, et al. Does glutamine contribute to immunosuppression after major burns? *Lancet.* 1990.336(8714):523–525; Parry-Billings M, Blomstrand E, et al. A communicational link between skeletal muscle, brain and cells of the immune system. *Int J Sports Med.* 1990.11(Suppl 2): S122–S128; Newsholme EA. Psychoimmunology and cellular nutrition: an alternative hypothesis. *Biol Psychiatry.* 1990.27(1):1–3; Parry-Billings M, Evans J, et al. Does glutamine contribute to immunosuppression after major burns? *Lancet.* 1990.336(8714):523–525.

94 **said Dr. Prudden:** Daniel, telephone interview with Dr. Prudden, September 19, 1997.

94 **Cartilage doesn't kill viruses directly:** John F. Prudden, "Summary of Catrix Research Programs," in *A Compilation of Scientific Research on Bovine Tracheal Cartilage: An Effective Agent in the Treatment of Cancer, Arthritis, Wound Healing, Skin Disorders and Other Conditions,* Version 2.0 (Foundation for Cartilage and Immunology Research, 1996), 5.

94 **Arthur G. Johnson, PhD:** Arthur G. Johnson, "Immunological Research Project," in *A Compilation of Scientific Research on Bovine Tracheal Cartilage: An Effective Agent in the Treatment of Cancer, Arthritis, Wound Healing, Skin Disorders and Other Conditions,* Version 2.0 (Foundation for Cartilage and Immunology Research: August 9, 1996).

94 **killer T-cells:** Durie BGM, Soehnlen B, Prudden JF. Anti-tumor activity of bovine cartilage extract (Catrix-S) in the human tumor stem cell assay *J Biol Response Mod.* 1984.4:490–595; Rosen J, Sherman WT, Prudden JF, Thorbecke

GJ. Immunoregulatory effects of catrix. *J Biol Response Mod.* 1988.7:498–512.

95 **natural killer (NK) cells:** Durie et al., Anti-tumor activity.

95 **respiratory and digestive viruses:** Rosen et al., Immunoregulatory effects.

95 **The same has been found:** Houck JC. The inhibition of inflammation and the acceleration of tisue repair by cartilage powder. *Surg.* 1962.51:632; Nathan R. Gotthoffer, *Gelatin in Nutrition and Medicine* (Grayslake, 1945).

96 **G. Gautieri:** Gotthoffer, *Gelatin,* 60–61.

96 **In 1932, researchers:** Gotthoffer, *Gelatin,* 152.

96 **Florence Nightingale:** Florence Nightingale, *Notes on Nursing* (Dover Books on Biology, 1969), 43.

Chapter 15

98 **Tens of millions of Americans:** "National Digestive Diseases Information Clearinghouse." National Institutes of Health (NIH) U.S. Department of Health and Human Services publication (94-1447). http://digestive.niddk.nih.gov/statistics/statistics.aspx.

98 **In the nineteenth century:** Pat Willard, *A Soothing Broth* (Broadway Books, 1998), 71, 124; Florence Nightingale, *Notes on Nursing* (Dover Books on Biology, 1969), 43.

98 **Broth and gelatin:** Nathan R. Gotthoffer, *Gelatin in Nutrition and Medicine* (Grayslake, 1945), 70–75.

99 **Nathan Gotthoffer:** Gotthoffer, *Gelatin,* 25–37.

99 **Mary G. Enig, PhD:** Authors' conversations with Mary G. Enig, PhD.

99 **"It is said to be retained:** Hogan quoted in Gotthoffer, *Gelatin,* 26.

99 **Gelatin was valued:** Gotthoffer, *Gelatin,* 7–9.

99 **Gelatin was also widely recognized:** Gotthoffer, *Gelatin,* 62–69, 76–80.

100 **Doctors also valued gelatin:** Gotthoffer, *Gelatin,* 66.

100 **Christian Archibald Herter, MD:** Christian Archibald Herter, *On Infantilism from Chronic Intestinal Infection: Characterized by the Overgrowth and Persistence of Flora of the Nursling Period, a Study of the Clinical Course, Bacteriology, Chemistry and the Therapeutics of of Arrested Development in Infancy* (Ulan Press, 2012, reprint of book first published in 1908).

100 **broth was a staple:** Reinhard Schrieber and Herbert Gareis, *Gelatine Handbook: Theory and Industrial Practice* (Wiley, 2007), 233; "Bland

Diet," *Medline Plus: A Service of the US National Library of Medicine.* http://www.nlm.nih.gov/medlineplus/ency/patientinstructions/000068.htm; "Bland Diet for Peptic Ulcer Patients, History." Raw Food Explained.com. http://www.rawfoodexplained.com/there-are-no-cures/bland-diet-for-peptic-ulcer-patients.html; Haubrich WS. Sippy of the Sippy diet Regimen. *Gastroenterology.* 2005.128(4):832. http://www.gastrojournal.org/article/S0016–5085(05)00358–6/abstract; Gluck SM. Modification of the Sippy diet. *JAMA.* 1984.251(16):2083–2084; William Ira Bennet, "Body and Mind; Overactive Machinery," *New York Times,* May 7, 1989.

100 **Francis Pottenger Jr., MD:** Pottenger FM. Hydrophilic colloidal diet. *Am J Digest Dis.* 1938.5(2):96–99.

101 **To condense his main points:** "Summary: Hydrophilic Colloidal Diet by F.M. Pottenger," SpringerLink. http://link.springer.com/article/10.1007%2FBF03010602#page-1.

101 **Soymilk, tofu, and other soy foods:** Kaayla T. Daniel, *The Whole Soy Story: The Dark Side of America's Favorite Health Food* (New Trends, 2005).

102 **Gut Associated Lymphoid Tissue (GALT):** Scaldaferri F, Pizzoferrato M, et al. The gut barrier: new acquisitions and therapeutic approaches. *J Clin Gastroenterol.* 2012.46(Suppl):S12–S17.

103 **gastric acid secretion:** Richardson CT, et al. Studies on the mechanism of food-stimulated gastric acid secretion in normal human subjects. *J Clin Invest.* 1976.58:623–631.

104 **Glycine is one of those that do:** Wald A, Adibi SA. Stimulation of gastric acid secretion by glycine and related oligopeptides in humans. *Am J Physiol.* 1982.5(242):G86–G88.

104 **Herbert G. Windmueller:** Windmueller HG, Spaeth AE. Uptake and metabolism of plasma glutamine by the small intestine. *J Biol Chem.* 1974.249:5070–5079; Windmueller HG, Spaeth AE. Respiratory fuels and nitrogen metabolism in vivo in small intestine of fed rats: quantitative importance of glutamine, glutamate and aspartate. *J Biol Chem.* 1980.255(1):107–112; Windmueller HG, Spaeth AE. Intestinal metabolism of glutamine and glutamate from the lumen as compared to glutamine from blood. *Arch Biochem Biophys.* 1975.171(2):662–672;

Eisenberg S, Windmueller HG, Levy RI. Metabolic fate of rat and human lipoprotein apoproteins in the rat. *J Lipid Res.* 1973.14(4):446–458; Dewitt Stetten, *NIH: An Account of Research in Its Laboratories and Clinics* (Academic Press, 1984; Forgotten Books, 2013).

104 **Glutamine also nourishes the GALT:** Li J, King BK, et al. Glycyl-l-glutamine-enriched total parenteral nutrition maintains small intestine gut-associated lymphoid tissue and upper respiratory tract immunity. *JPEN J Parenter Enteral Nutr.* 1998.22(1):31–36; Newsholme P. Why is l-glutamine metabolism important to cells of the immune system in health, postinjury, surgery or infection? *J Nutr.* 2001.131:2515S–2522; Newsholme P, Curi R, et al. Glutamine metabolism by lymphocytes, macrophages and neutrophils: its importance in health and disease. *J Nutr Biochem.* 1999.10(6):316–324; Newsholme EA, Carrie AL. Quantitative aspects of glucose and glutamine metabolism by intestinal cells. *Gut.* 1994.35(1 Suppl):S13–S17; Sevastiadou S, Malamitsi-Puchner A, et al. The impact of oral glutamine supplementation on the intestinal permeability and incidence of necrotizing enterocolitis/septicemia in premature neonates. *J Matern Fetal Neonatal Med.* 2011.24(10):1294–1300.

104 **Glutamine furthermore stems the loss of electrolytes:** Li Y, Guo M, Li J. Effect of growth hormone, glutamine, and enteral nutrition on intestinal adaptation in patients with short bowel syndrome. *Turk J Gastroenterol.* 2013.24(5):463–468; Byrne TA, Morrissey TB, et al. Growth hormone, glutamine, and a modified diet enhance nutrient absorption in patients with severe short bowel syndrome. *JPEN J Parenter Enteral Nutr.* 1995.19(4):296–302; Braga-Neto MB, Warren CA, et al. Alanyl-glutamine and glutamine supplementation improves 5-fluorouracil-induced intestinal epithelium damage in vitro. *Dig Dis Sci.* 2008.53(10):2687–2696; Carneiro-Filho BA, Oria RB, et al. Alanyl-glutamine hastens morphologic recovery from 5-fluorouracil-induced mucositis in mice. *Nutrition.* 2004.20(10):934–941; Steinmetz OK, Meakins JL. Care of the gut in the surgical intensive care unit: fact or fashion? *Can J Surg.* 1991.34(3):207–215; Ding LA, Li JS. Effects of glutamine on intestinal permeability and bacterial translocation in TPN-rats with endotoxemia.

World J Gastroenterol. 2003.9(6):1327–1332; Buchman AL. Glutamine for the gut: mystical properties or an ordinary amino acid? *Curr Gastroenterol Rep.* 1999.1(5):417–423.

105 **John F. Prudden, MD, DSci:** Prudden JF, Balass L. The biological activity of bovine cartilage preparation: a clinical demonstration of their potent anti-inflammatory capacity. *Semin Arthritis Rheum.* 1974.3(4):187–321.

106 **Dr. Prudden said:** Kaayla T. Daniel, telephone interview with Dr. Prudden, September 25, 1997.

Chapter 16

108 **More than fifteen hundred Americans:** "Cancer Facts and Figures, 2013," American Cancer Society. http://www.cancer.org/research/cancerfactsstatistics/cancerfactsfigures2013/index.

108 **Susan Sontag:** *Illness as Metaphor* (Farrar, Straus & Giroux, 1977).

108 **Brian G. M. Durie, MD:** Durie BG, Soehnlen B, Prudden JF. Antitumor activity of bovine cartilage extract (Catrix-S) in the human tumor stem cell assay. *J Biol Response Mod.* 1985.4(6):590–595.

108 **Dr. Prudden thought it was:** John F. Prudden, "Summary of Catrix Research Programs," in *Foundation for Cartilage and Immunology Research: A Compilation of Scientific Research on Bovine Tracheal Cartilage: An Effective Agent in the Treatment of Cancer, Arthritis, Wound Healing, Skin Disorders and Other Conditions,* Version 2.0 (Foundation for Cartilage and Immunology Research, 1996), 5.

109 **Dr. Johnson also found:** Arthur G. Johnson, "Immunological Research Project," in *Foundation for Cartilage and Immunology Research: A Compilation of Scientific Research on Bovine Tracheal Cartilage: An Effective Agent in the Treatment of Cancer, Arthritis, Wound Healing, Skin Disorders and Other Conditions,* Version 2.0 (Foundation for Cartilage and Immunology Research, 1996).

110 **Bruce Ames, PhD:** Jane Brody, "Scientist at Work: Bruce N. Ames; Strong Views on Origins of Cancer," *New York Times,* July 5, 1994.

110 **Peyton Rous, MD:** G. Klein, "Award Ceremony Speech, The Nobel Prize in Physiology or Medicine, 1966. Peyton Rous, Charles B. Huggins," in *Nobel Lectures, Physiology or Medicine 1963–1970* (Elsevier, 1972). http://

www.nobelprize.org/nobel_prizes/medicine/laureates/1966/press.html.

110 **virus theory of cancer:** Ralph Moss, *The Cancer Answer* (Equinox, 1996), 274.

110 **Theories of pleomorphic bacteria:** Barry Lynes, *The Cancer Cure That Worked! Fifty Years of Suppression* (Marcus Books, 1987), 17–24; Thomas A. Dorman, "On a Competitive Balance within the Endobiont," Live Blood Analysis Diploma Course. http://www.professorenderlein.com/CompBalance.html; Nenah Sylver, *Rife Frequency Handbook* (Desert Gate, 2011); Louisa Williams, *Curing CASPERS: A Naturopathic Doctor's Guide to Treating Chronic, Autoimmune Stealth Pathogens Evolved from Resistant Bacteria Syndrome,* ebook 2013. http://www.radicalmedicine.com/product/curing-caspers/; Christopher Bird, *The Persecution and Trial of Gaston Naessens: The True Story of the Efforts to Suppress an Alternative Treatment for Cancer, AIDS, and Other Immunologically Based Diseases* (Kramer, 1991); Antoine Bechamp, *The Blood and Its Third Element* (Review, 2002); Ethel D. Hume, *Bechamp or Pasteur?: A Lost Chapter in the History of Biology* (CreateSpace, 2011); Alan Cantwell Jr., *The Cancer Microbe* (Aries Rising, 1990); Alan Cantwell Jr., *Four Women against Cancer* (Aries Rising, 2005); Gerald Domingue, *Cell Wall-Deficient Bacteria: Basic Principles and Clinical Significance* (Addison-Wesley, 1982); Philip Hadley, "Microbic Dissociation," Santa Monica Ca Institute of Science; Shakman SH. 2012. Originally published in *J Infect Disease.* 1927.240(1); Lida Mattman, *Cell Wall Defective Forms: Stealth Pathogens,* 3rd ed. (CRC Press, 2001); Louisa Williams, *Radical Medicine* (Healing Arts Press, 2011).

110 **Dr. Livingston:** Cantwell, *The Cancer Microbe;* Cantwell, *Four Women against Cancer;* Virginia Livingston-Wheeler, *The Conquest of Cancer: Vaccines and Diet* (CreateSpace, 2013); Edmond G. Addeo, *The Woman Who Cured Cancer: The True Story of Cancer Pioneer Dr. Virginia Livingston-Wheeler* (CreateSpace, 2012).

111 **Instead, the medical establishment:** Kaayla T. Daniel, telephone interviews with Dr. Prudden, October 3 and 8, 1997.

111 **Dr. Prudden repeatedly demonstrated:** John F. Prudden, "Summary of Catrix Research

Programs," in *Foundation for Cartilage and Immunology Research: A Compilation of Scientific Research on Bovine Tracheal Cartilage: An Effective Agent in the Treatment of Cancer, Arthritis, Wound Healing, Skin Disorders and Other Conditions*, Version 2.0 (Foundation for Cartilage and Immunology Research, 1996), 5.

112 **Dr. Prudden suggested:** Daniel, interview with Dr. Prudden, October 8, 1997.

112 **Dr. Prudden published:** Prudden JF. Treatment of human cancer with agents prepared from bovine cartilage. *J Biol Response Mod.* 1985.4(6):551–584.

114 **As of 1997, Dr. Prudden reported:** Daniel, interviews with Dr. Prudden, October 3 and 8, 1997.

115 **anti-angiogenesis protein:** Raza Forough, ed., *New Frontiers in Angiogenesis* (Springer, 2006), 1.

115 **Normal cartilage has no blood vessels:** Clarkin C, Olsen BR. On bone-forming cells and blood vessels in bone development. *Cell Metab.* 2010.12(4):314–316.

115 **interest in anti-angiogenesis:** Folkman J. Tumor angiogenesis: therapeutic implications. *N Engl J Med.* 1971.258(21):1182–1186; Folkman J. Tumor angiogenesis: a possible control point in tumor growth. *Ann Intern Med.* 1975.82(1):96–100; Folkman J. The vascularization of tumors. *Scientific American.* 1976.234:5973; Folkman J. How is blood vessel growth regulated in normal and neoplastic tissue? *Cancer Res.* 1986.46(2):467–473; Langer R, Brem H, et al. Isolation of a cartilage factor that inhibits tumor neovascularization. *Science.* 1976.193(4247): 70–72; Langer R, Conn H, et al. Control of tumor growth in animals by infusion of an angiogenesis inhibitor. *Proc Natl Acad Sci USA.* 1980.77(7):4331–4335; Robert Langer, as quoted by Henry Kriegel, "Dr John Prudden and Bovine Tracheal Cartilage Research," *Alternative and Complementary Therapies*, April/May 1995, 188.

115 **protein molecules that give cartilage:** Mathews J. Sharks still intrigue cancer researchers. *J Natl Cancer Inst.* 1992.84(13):1000–1002.

115 **One of Dr. Prudden's dreams:** Daniel, interview with Dr. Prudden, October 8, 1997.

115 **I. William Lane's book:** Conversations with Drs. Folkman and Langer, reported by Dr. Prudden, October 3, 1997; Conversations with Drs. Folkman and Langer, as reported in David Kirchhof and Elisabeth Kirchhof, *The Successful Use of Bovine Cartilage in the Treatment of Cancer* (Kriegel & Associates, 1995), 14–15.

115 **unwarranted claim:** I. William Lane and Linda Comac, *Sharks Don't Get Cancer* (Avery, 1992), 45; Conversation between Dr. Langer and Dr. Prudden, as reported by Dr. Prudden to Kaayla T. Daniel in telephone interview, October 3, 1997.

115 **therapeutic effect:** Daniel, interview with Dr. Prudden, October 3, 1997.

116 **Dr. Prudden pointed to the fact:** Daniel, interview with Dr. Prudden, October 3, 1997.

116 **Dr. Prudden was intrigued:** Daniel, interview with Dr. Prudden, October 3, 1997.

116 **Robert Atkins, MD:** Atkins R. Don't put the cartilage before the horse. *Dr. Robert Atkins's Health Revelations.* 1996.4(3):6–7.

116 **Alan Gaby, MD:** Alan Gaby, Editorial. *Townsend Letter for Doctors*, April 1994.

117 **non-cartilage components of broth:** Inamura Y, Koide T, et al. In vivo anti-tumor activities of gelatin. *Exp Oncol.* 2009.31(3):144–148; Castro GA, Maria DA, et al. In vitro impact of a whey protein isolate (WPI) and collagen hydrolysates (CHs) on B16F10 melanoma cells proliferation. *J Dermatol Sci.* 2009.56(1):51–57.

117 **glucosamine inhibition:** Ju Y, Yu A, et al. Glucosamine, a naturally occurring amino monosaccharide, inhibits A549 and H446 cell proliferation by blocking G1/S transition. *Mol Med Rep.* 2013.8(3):794–798.

118 **glucosamine and chondroitin:** Kantor ED, Lampe JW, et al. Use of glucosamine and chondroitin supplements and risk of colorectal cancer. *Cancer Causes Control.* 2013.24(6):1137–1146.

118 **It began trials:** Romano, C, Lipton A, et al. A phase II study of Catrix-S in solid tumors. *J Biol Response Mod.* 1985.4(6):585–589.

118 **The failure:** Kaayla T. Daniel, interview with Dr. Prudden, October 8, 1997.

118 **The dark side of glutamine:** Aidan Goggins, "Glutamine and Cancer: What You Need to Know," *Huffpost Lifestyle United Kingdom*, February 22, 2013; Vander Heiden MG, Cantley, LC, Thompson CB. Understanding the Warburg Effect: the metabolic requirements of cell proliferation. *Science.* 2009.324(5930): 1029–1033; Wise DR, Thompson CB. Glutamine addiction: a new therapeutic target in cancer.

Trends Biochem Sci. 2010.35(8):427–433; Dang CV. Glutaminolysis: supplying carbon or nitrogen or both for cancer cells? *Cell Cycle.* 2010.9(19):3884–3886; DeBerardinis RJ, Cheng T. Q's next: the diverse functions of glutamine in metabolism, cell biology and cancer. *Oncogene.* 2009.29(3):313–324; Shanware N, Mullen AR, et al. Glutamine and cancer. *J Mol Med (Berl).* 2011.89(3):229–236; Huang W, et al. A proposed role for glutamine in cancer cell growth through acid resistance. *Cell Res.* 2013.23(5):724–727; Kuhn KS, et al. Glutamine as indispensable nutrient in oncology: experimental and clinical evidence. *Eur J Nutr.* 2010.49(4):197–210; Kuhn KS, Muscaritoli M, et al. Glutamine as indispensable nutrient in oncology: experimental and clinical evidence. *Eur J Nutr.* 2010.49(4): 197–210; Hensley CT, Wasti AT, DeBerardinis RJ. Glutamine and cancer: cell biology, physiology, and clinical opportunities. *J Clin Invest.* 2013.123(9):3678–3684; Shanware NP, Mullen AR, et al. Glutamine: pleiotropic roles in tumor growth and stress resistance. *Mol Med (Berl).* 2011.89(3):229–236; Souba WW. Glutamine and cancer. *Ann Surg.* 1993.218(6):715–728; Beautheu S, Ouelaa W, et al. Glutamine supplementation, but not combined glutamine and arginine supplementation, improves gut barrier function during chemotherapy-induced intestinal mucositis in rats. *Clin Nutr.* 2013 Sep 25. pii: S0261-5614(13)00241-0; Yoshida S, Kaibara A, et al. Glutamine supplementation in cancer patients. *Nutrition.* 2001.17(9):766–768; Ziegler RR. Glutamine supplementation in cancer patients receiving bone marrow transplantation and high dose chemotherapy. *J Nutr.* 2001.131(9 Suppl): 2578S–2584S, discussion 2590S.

118 **As Dr. Prudden found:** Daniel, interview with Dr. Prudden, October 8, 1997.

119 **Dr. Prudden felt it may:** Daniel, interview with Dr. Prudden, October 8, 1997.

119 **Dr. Prudden felt massive research was needed:** Daniel, interview with Dr. Prudden, October 8, 1997.

Chapter 17

120 **diagnosable mental disorder:** http://www.nimh .nih.gov/health/publications/the-numbers-count -mental-disorders-in-america/index.shtml; Kessler RC, Chiu WT, Demler O, Walters EE. Prevalence, severity, and comorbidity of twelve-month DSM-IV disorders in the National Comorbidity Survey Replication (NCS-R). *Archives of General Psychiatry*, 2005.62(6):617–627.

120 **Chris Masterjohn, PhD:** Chris Masterjohn, "Meat, Organs, Bones and Skin: Nutrition for Mental Health," *Wise Traditions*, Spring 2013, 35.

121 **Moses Maimonides:** Fred Rosner, *Medicine in the Bible and the Talmud: Selections from Classical Jewish Sources* (Ktav, 1995), 136–139; Rosner F. Medical writings of Moses Maimonides. *N Y State J Med.* 1987.87(12):656–661; J. O. Leibowitz and S. Marcus, *Moses Maimonides on the Causes of Symptoms* (University of California Press, 1974), 113–114.

121 **Rebecca Schwartz, ND, LAc:** Rebecca Schwartz, "Medicine in a Bowl," Blog at Dr. Rebecca Schwartz.com. http://drrebeccashwartz .com/2012/01/04/medicine-in-a-bowl/.

121 **One exception is a 2003 study:** Zain AM, Syedsahiliamalulail S. Effect of taking chicken essence on stress and cognition of human volunteers. *Malays J Nutr.* 2003.9(1):19–29.

122 **Nathan Gotthoffer, PhD:** Nathan R. Gotthoffer, *Gelatin in Nutrition and Medicine* (Grayslake, 1945), 129–131.

123 **Francis Pottenger Jr., MD:** Pottenger FM. Hydrophilic colloidal diet. *Am J Digest Dis.* 1938.5(2):96–99.

123 **glycine's role in glucose manufacture:** Alvarado-Basquex N, Zamudio P, et al. Effect of glycine in streptozotocin-induced diabetic rats. *Comp Biochem Physiol C Toxicol Pharmacol.* 2003.134(4):521–527; Alvarado-Vásquez N, Lascurain R, et al. Oral glycine administration attenuates diabetic complications in streptozotocin-induced diabetic rats. *Life Sci.* 2006.79(3):225–232; Bahmani F, Bathaie SZ, et al. Glycine therapy inhibits the progression of cataract in streptozotocin-induced diabetic rats. *Mol Vis.* 2012.18:439–448; Lezcano Meza D, Teran Ortiz L, et al. Effect of glycine on the immune response of the experimentally diabetic rats. *Rev Alerg Mex.* 2006.53(6):212–216; Ramakrishnan S, Sulochana KN, Punitham R. Free lysine, glycine, alanine, glutamic acid and aspartic acid reduce the glycation of human lens proteins by galactose. *Indian J Biochem Biophys.* 1997.34:518–523; Gannon MC, Nuttal JA, Nuttal FQ. The metabolic

response to ingested glycine, *Am J Clin Nutr.* 2002.76(6):1302–1307.

123 **Glycine also improves sleep quality:** Luppi PH, Clement O, et al. New aspects in the pathophysiology of rapid eye movement sleep behavior disorder: the potential role of glutamate, gamma-aminobutyric acid, and glycine. *Sleep Med.* 2013.14(8):714–718; Bannai M, Kawai N, et al. The effects of glycine on subjective daytime performance in partially sleep-restricted healthy volunteers. *Front Neurol.* 2012.3:61; Yamadera W, Inagawa K. Glycine ingestion improves subjective sleep quality in human volunteers, correlating with polysomnographic changes. *Sleep and Biological Rhythms.* 2007.5(2):126–131; Inagawa K, Hiraoka T, Kohda T, Yamadera W, Takahashi M. Subjective effects of glycine ingestion before bedtime on sleep quality. *Sleep and Biological Rhythms.* 2006.4(1):75–77.

123 **Both glycine and glutamine:** Cocchi R. Antidepressive properties of I-glutamine: preliminary report. *Acta Psychiatr Belg.* 1976.76(4):658–666; Young LS, Bye R, et al. Patients receiving glutamine-supplemented intravenous feedings report an improvement in mood. *JPEN J Parenter Enteral Nutr.* 1993.17(5):422–427; Jukic T, Rojc B, et al. The use of a food supplementation with D-phenylalanine, L-glutamine and L-5-hydroxytriptophan in the alleviation of alcohol withdrawal symptoms. *Coll Antropol.* 2011.35(4):1225–1230; Cross DR, Kellermann G, et al. A randomized targeted amino acid therapy with behaviourally at-risk adopted children. *Child Care Health Dev.* 2011.37(5):671–678; R. Cocchi, "Glutamine as the Key Amino Acid in Promoting Cell-Mediated Immunity: 20 Years of Clinical Experience," Paper presented at the 6th International Congress on Amino Acids, Bonn 1999. http:// www.stress-cocchi.net; Newsholm EA, Calder C. The proposed role of glutamine in some cells of the immune system and speculative consequences for the whole animal. *Nutrition.* 1997.13:728–730.

123 **glycine as a neurotransmitter:** Levy U, Javitt DC, et al. Efficacy of high-dose glycine in the treatment of enduring negative symptoms of schizophrenia. *Arch Gen Psychiatry.* 1999.56:29–36.

124 **Renato Cocchi, MD, PhD:** Cocchi, Antidepressive properties of I-glutamine; Cocchi, "Glutamine as the Key Amino Acid."

124 **glutamate, which is excitatory:** Russell Blaylock, *Excitotoxins: The Taste That Kills* (Health Press, 1996); Russell Blaylock, *Health and Nutrition Secrets*, rev. ed. (Health Press, 2006); Kelly A, Stanley CA. Disorders of glutamate metabolism. *Ment Retard Dev Disabil Res Rev.* 2001.7:287–295.

124 **Glutamine supplements:** Young et al., Patients receiving glutamine-supplemented intravenous feedings.

Chapter 18

125 **High-protein diets:** Kaayla T. Daniel, *The Whole Soy Story: The Dark Side of America's Favorite Health Food* (New Trends, 2005).

125 **Randy Roach:** Randy Roach, *Muscle, Smoke and Mirrors*, vol. 1 (AuthorHouse, 2008); Randy Roach, *Muscle, Smoke and Mirrors*, vol. 2 (Author House, 2011); Randy Roach, "Splendid Specimens: The History of Nutrition in Bodybuilding," *Wise Traditions*, Fall 2004. http://www.westonaprice .org/mens-health/splendid-specimens.

126 **Bovril ads:** Bovril, Wikipedia. http://en.wikipedia .org/wiki/Bovril; Google Images, Vintage Bovril advertisements.

126 **Walter Meredith Boothby, MD:** Boothby WM, Adams M, Power MH, et al. Myasthenia gravis: second report on the effect of treatment with gycine. *Mayo Clin Proc.* 1932.1:1200–1201; Manwaring WH. Editorial comment: GLYCIN and muscular fatigue. *Cal West Med.* 1939.51(1):9; Keesey JC. A history of treatments for myasthenia gravis. *Semin Neurol.* 2004.24(1):5–16.

126 **Dr. Boothby's finding was confirmed:** Nathan R. Gotthoffer, *Gelatin in Nutrition and Medicine* (Grayslake, 1945), 45–46.

126 **Professor Lazar Remen:** Freedman S. Anti-Semitism and the history of myasthenia gravis. *IMAJ.* April 2010.12:195–197; Ohry, A. Dir Lazar Remen (1907–74): a forgotten pioneer in the treatment of myasthenia gravis. *J Med Biography.* 2009.17(2):73.

127 **Regidius M. Kaczmarek:** Kaczmarek RM. Effect of gelatin on the work output of male athletes and non athletes and girl subjects. *Research Quarterly. American Association for Health, Physical Education and Recreation.* 1940.11(4):110–119.

127 **Russell Morse Wilder, MD:** Randall G. Sprague, "Russell Morse Wilder Sr (1885–1959)." http://

diabetes.diabetesjournals.org/content/9/5/419.full
.pdf+html.

127 **glycine-endurance controversy:** Wilder quoted in Gotthoffer, *Gelatin*, 57.

127 **One such effort:** Gotthoffer, *Gelatin*, 52–53.

127 **Nathan Gotthoffer, PhD:** Gotthoffer, *Gelatin*, 48.

128 **results of bodybuilders:** Roach, *Muscle, Smoke and Mirrors*, Vol. 1.

129 **Milk contains glutamine, glycine, and proline:** Emilia H, Manso H, et al. Glutamine and glutamate supplementation raise milk glutamine concentrations in lactating gilts, *J Animal Sci Biotechnol*. 2012.3(1):2.

129 **In 1985, researchers concluded:** Minuskin M, et al. Nitrogen retention, muscle creatine and orotic acid excretion in traumatized rats fed arginine and glycine enriched diets. *J Nutr*. 1981.3(7):1265–1274.

129 **Another popular supplement among athletes:** Mason BC, Lavallee ME. Emerging supplements in sports. *Sports Health*. 2012.4(2):142–146; Clarkson P, Hubal M. Exercise-induced muscle damage in humans. *Am J Phys Med Rehabil*. 2002.81:52–69; Cruzat VF, Rogero MM, Tirapegui J. Effects of supplementation with free glutamine and the dipeptide alanyl-glutamine on parameters of muscle damage and inflammation in rats submitted to prolonged exercise. *J Cell Biochem Funct*. 2010.28:24–30; Kreider RB. Dietary supplements and the promotion of muscle growth with resistance exercise. *Sports Med*. 1999.27: 97–110; Phillips GC. Glutamine: the nonessential amino acid for performance enhancement. *Curr Sports Med Rep*. 2007.6(4):265–268.

129 **glutamine supplements:** Reinhard Schrieber and Herbert Gareis, *Gelatine Handbook: Theory and Industrial Practice* (Wiley, 2007), 230.

130 **glutamine supports the immune system:** Newsholme EA. Why is L-glutamine metabolism important to cells of the immune system in health, post-injury, surgery, or infection. *J Nutr*. 2001.131:2515–2522; Newsholme P, Curi R, et al. Glutamine metabolism by lymphocytes, macrophages, and neutrophils: its importance in health and disease. *J Nutr Biochem*. 1999.10(6):316–324; Newsholme EA. The possible role of glutamine in some cells of the immune system and the possible consequence for the whole animal. *Experientia*. 1996.52(5):455–459; Bongers T, Griffiths RD, McArdle A. Exogenous

glutamine: the clinical evidence. *Crit Care Med*. 2007.35(9 Suppl):S545–S552; Kelly D, Wischmeyer PE. Role of L-glutamine in critical illness: new insights. *Curr Opin Clin Nutr Metab Care*. 2003.6(2):217–222; Wischmeyer PE. Clinical applications of L-glutamine: past, present, and future. *Nutr Clin Pract*. 2003.18(5):377–385; Kim H. Glutamine as an immunonutrient. *Yonsei Med J*. 2011.52(6):892–897; Tiader I, Berg A, Wernerman J. Exogenous glutamine—compensating a shortage? *Crit Care Med*. 2007.35(9 Suppl):S553–S556.

130 **neurotransmitter GABA:** Powers M. GABA supplementation and growth hormone response. *Med Sport Sci*. 2012.59:36–46; Cavagnini F, Invitti C, et al. Effect of acute and repeated administration of gamma aminobutyric acid (GABA) on growth hormone and prolactin secretion in man. *Acta Endocrinol (Copenh)*. 1980.93(2):149–154; Cavagnini F, Benetti G, et al. Effect of gamma-aminobutyric acid on growth hormone and prolactin secretion in man: influence of pimozide and domperidone. *J Clin Endocrinol Metab*. 1980.51(4):789–792.

130 **collagen hydrolysate:** Schrieber and Gareis, *Gelatine Handbook*, 305; Michael Teppner, ed., *Collagen Hydrolysate and Its Relationship to Joint Health: A Scientific Compendium* (Gelita Health Initiative, 2004); Clark KL, Sebastianell W, et al. 24-week study on the use of collagen hydrolysate as a dietary supplement in athletes with activity-related joint pain. *Curr Med Res Opin*. 2008.24(5):1485–1496.

131 **The usual treatment:** Gary S. Firestein, Ralph C. Budd, et al., *Kelley's Textbook of Rheumatology*, 9th ed. (Saunders, 2012), 883.

131 **William Campbell Douglass II, MD:** William Campbell Douglass II, "Super-charge Your Muscle without Strenuous Exercise," *The Douglass Report: Real Health News from Medicine's Most Notorious Myth-Buster*. October 13, 2013.

Chapter 19

132 **Linus Pauling, PhD:** Linus Pauling, *How to Live Longer and Feel Better* (Avon, 1987), 143.

133 **Currently 65 percent of Americans:** Centers for Disease Control, "Health, United States, 2012, table 63." http://www.cdc.gov/nchs/data/hus/hus12 .pdf#063; "U.S. Weight Loss Market Forecast to

Hit $66 Billion in 2013: Growth to Improve Due to Pent-up Demand," *Finds Marketdata Enterprises* (PRWEB), December 31, 2012. http://www.prweb.com/releases/2012/12/prweb10278281.htm.

133 **This surprising finding:** Flegal KM, Kit BK, et al. Association of all-cause mortality with overweight and obesity using standard boyd mass index categories: a systematic review and meta-analysis. *JAMA*. 2013.309(1):71–82; Flegal KM, Graubard BI, et al. Excess deaths associated with underweight, overweight and obesity. *JAMA*. 2005.293(15):1861–1867; Vitousek KM, Gray, JA, Grubbs KM. Caloric restriction for longevity, 1: Paradigm, protocols and physiological findings in animal research. *Eur Eat Disorders Rev*. 2004.12:279–299.

134 **David Weeks, MD:** David Weeks and Jamie James, *Secrets of the Superyoung* (Villard, 1998).

135 **Dr. Prudden's least known research:** Prudden JF, Balassa L. The biological activity of bovine cartilage preparation: a clinical demonstration of their potent anti-inflammatory capacity with supplementary notes on certain relevant fundamental supportive studies. *Semin Arthritis Rheum*. 1974.3(4):187–321; Elson ML. The anti-inflammatory effect of bovine cartilage preparation on Retin-A irritation. *J Dermatol Treatment*, 1993.4:45–46.

136 **Cartilage cream and suppositories:** Prudden, Balassa, The biological activity.

136 **Dr. Prudden performed no studies:** Kaayla T. Daniel, telephone interviews with Dr. Prudden, September 14 and 19, 1997.

136 **Moses Maimonides:** Fred Rosner, *Medicine in the Bible and the Talmud: Selections from Classical Jewish Sources* (Ktav, 1995), 137–139.

136 **famous cookbook published in Naples:** Ken Albala, *Food in Early Modern Europe* (Greenwood, 2003), 32.

136 **velvet deer antler:** Gilbey A, Perezgonzalez JD. Health benefits of deer and elk velvet antler supplements: a systematic review of randomised controlled studies. *N Z Med J*. 2012.125(1367): 80–86; Li C, Suttie JM. Histological studies of pedicle skin formation and its transformation to antler velvet in red deer (Cervus elaphus). *Anat Rec*. 2000.260(1):62–71; Price JS, Fauceux C, Allen S. Deer antlers as a model of mammalian regeneration. *Curr Top Dev Biol*. 2005.67: 1–48; Price JS, Allen S, et al. Deer antlers: a zoological curiosity or the key to understanding organ regeneration in mammals? *J Anat*.

2005.207(5):603–618; Wu F, Li H, et al. Deer antler base as a traditional Chinese medicine: a review of its traditional uses, chemistry and pharmacology. *J Ethnopharmacol*. 2013.145(2):403–415; Park HJ, Lee DH, et al. Proteome analysis of red deer antlers. *Proteomics*. 2004.4(11):3642–3653.

138 **Broth for Cellulite:** Avram MM. Cellulite: a review of its physiology and treatment. *J Cosmet Laser Ther*. 2004.6(4):181–185; L. Kravitz and B. S. Achenbach, "Cellulite: A Review of Its Anatomy, Physiology and Treatment." http://www.unm.edu/~lkravitz/Article%20folder/cellulite2.html; Rosenbaum M, Prieto V, et al. An exploratory investigation of the morphology and biochemistry of cellulite. *Plastic Reconstructive Surgery*. 1998.101:1934–1939; Katherine Harman, "Is Cellulite Forever?" *Scientific American*, May 4, 2009. http://www.scientificamerican.com/article/is-cellulite-forever/; Hexsel D, Siega C, et al. A comparative study of the anatomy of adipose tissue in areas with and without raised lesions of cellulite using magnetic resonance imaging. *Dermatol Surg*. 2013.39(12):1877–1886; Pierard GE, Nizet JL, and Pierard-Franchimont C. Cellulite: from standing fat herniation to hypodermal stretch marks. *American J Dermatopathology*. 2000.22(1):34–37; Rawlings AV. Cellulite and its treatment. *Int J Cosmet Sci*. 2006.28(3):175–190; Pierard-Franchimont C, Pierard GE, et al. A randomized placeobo-controlled trial of topical retinol in the treatment of cellulite. *Am J Clin Dermatol*. 2000.1(6):369–374; Lionel Bisson, *The Cellulite Cure* (Meso Press, 2006), 3–4; Rossi AB, Vergnanini AL. Cellulite: a review. *J Eur Acad Dematolo Veneroel*. 2000.14(4):251–262; Wanner M, Avram M. An evidence-based assessment of treatments for cellulite. *J Drugs in Dermat*. 2008.7(4):341–345.

Chapter 20

144 **become entangled:** Harold McGee, *On Food and Cooking: The Science and Lore of the Kitchen*, rev. upd. ed. (Scribner, 2004), 603.

144 **Meat contains only:** McGee, *On Food and Cooking*, 598.

146 **more cross-linked collagen:** McGee, *On Food and Cooking*, 598.

148 **The cold start:** McGee, *On Food and Cooking*, 600.

Index

Note: Page numbers in *italics* indicate recipes.

About the Authors

SALLY FALLON MORELL is the leading voice for a return to the nourishing traditional foods of our ancestors, including genuine bone broths, sourdough breads and soaked grains, lacto-fermented foods, and meat, eggs, butter, and dairy products from grass-fed animals. Many of these ideas were first introduced to the public in her best-selling cookbook, *Nourishing Traditions*, with well over one-half million sold.

Fallon Morell is the founding president of the influential nutrition education nonprofit the Weston A. Price Foundation, where she also serves as the editor of the Foundation's quarterly journal, *Wise Traditions*. In addition, she is the founder of A Campaign for Real Milk, which advocates for nationwide availability of clean, whole raw milk from pastured cows.

In addition to numerous articles on nutrition and health, Fallon Morell is coauthor of *Eat Fat Lose Fat* (with Mary G. Enig, PhD) and *The Nourishing Traditions Book of Baby & Child Care* (with Thomas S. Cowan, MD). She is an acclaimed speaker at conferences and seminars worldwide. Her publishing company, NewTrends Publishing (www .newtrendspublishing.com), publishes important books on diet and health.

When not engaged in writing and editing, Fallon Morell works with her husband, Geoffrey Morell, at their mixed-species, pasture-based dairy farm, P A Bowen Farmstead (pabowen farmstead.com).

KAAYLA T. DANIEL, PhD, CCN, is Vice President of the Weston A. Price Foundation and serves on the board of directors of the Farm-to-Consumer Legal Defense Fund. She is known as The Naughty Nutritionist™ because of her ability to outrageously and humorously debunk nutritional myths.

Dr. Daniel earned her PhD in Nutritional Sciences from the Union Institute and University in Cincinnati and is certified as a clinical nutritionist (CCN) by the International and American Association of Clinical Nutritionists in Dallas. In 2005, she received the Weston A. Price Foundation's Integrity in Science Award.

Her book *The Whole Soy Story: The Dark Side of America's Favorite Health Food* (2005) has received endorsements from leading health experts, including Drs. Russell Blaylock, David Brownstein, Larry Dossey,

Nicholas Gonzalez, Joseph Mercola, Kilmer McCully, Doris J. Rapp, JJ Virgin, and Jonathan Wright.

Dr. Daniel has been a guest on *The Dr. Oz Show*, PBS's *Healing Quest*, NPR's *People's Pharmacy*, ABC's *View from the Bay*, and Discovery Channel's *Medical Hotseat*; and she has shared the stage with Dr. Mark Hyman, JJ Virgin, Gary Taubes, Charles Poliquin, Dr. Joseph Mercola, Joel Salatin, David Wolfe, and other prominent health experts at professional conferences, including Wise Traditions, the National Association of Nutritional Professionals (NANP), BoulderFest, and Bio-Signature.

Subscribe to Dr. Kaayla's *Naughty Edge* newsletter at her website www.drkaayladaniel.com and join her on Facebook at www.facebook.com/DrKaaylaDaniel.